Corporate Reputation

Brand and Communication

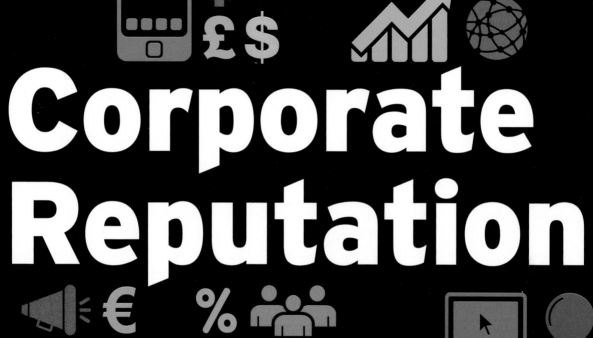

Corporate Reputation

Brand and Communication

Stuart Roper
Chris Fill

PEARSON

Harlow, England • London • New York • Boston • San Francisco • Toronto • Sydney • Auckland • Singapore • Hong Kong
Tokyo • Seoul • Taipei • New Delhi • Cape Town • São Paulo • Mexico City • Madrid • Amsterdam • Munich • Paris • Milan

Pearson Education Limited
Edinburgh Gate
Harlow
Essex CM20 2JE
England

and Associated Companies throughout the world

Visit us on the World Wide Web at:
www.pearson.com/uk

First published 2012

© Pearson Education Limited 2012

ISBN 978-0-273-72759-0

British Library Cataloguing-in-Publication Data
A catalogue record for this book is available from the British Library

Library of Congress Cataloging-in-Publication Data
A catalog record for this book is available from the Library of Congress

10 9 8 7 6 5 4 3 2 1
15 14 13 12

Typeset in 10/12pt Minion by 35
Printed and bound by Rotolito Lombarda, Italy

Brief contents

Guided tour xiv
Preface xvi
Acknowledgements xxi
Publisher's acknowledgements xxii

Part 1 Corporate reputation 2

Chapter 1 The rise of corporate reputation 4
Chapter 2 The scope of corporate reputation 27
Chapter 3 The significance of corporate culture 52
Chapter 4 Measuring corporate reputation 75
Minicases for Part 1 101

Part 2 Corporate branding 104

Chapter 5 The branding-reputation dilemma 106
Chapter 6 The rise of corporate brands 134
Chapter 7 Measuring corporate brands 159
Chapter 8 The future for brands 183
Minicases for Part 2 204

Part 3 Corporate communication 208

Chapter 9 The dimensions of corporate communication 210
Chapter 10 Contexts for corporate communication 237
Chapter 11 Symbols, tools and the media 265
Chapter 12 Methods of corporate communication 290
Minicases for Part 3 319

Index 325

For further insight and information please see the Pearson companion website that supports this book (**www.pearsoned.co.uk/roperfill**) and also **www.fillassociates.co.uk**

To my daughter Kate, and for Charlotte, with much love.
Stuart Roper

To Karen and our boys: with all my love and fondest thoughts
as always. Brilliant times.
Chris Fill

Contents

Guided tour xiv

Preface xvi

   Reasons to read about corporate reputation xvi

   Overview of the book xvii

   Structure xviii

   Design features and presentation xix

   Support materials xx

Acknowledgements xxi

Publisher's acknowledgements xxii

Part 1 Corporate reputation 2

Chapter 1 The rise of corporate reputation 4

Aims and learning objectives 4

Introduction 5

Definitions of reputation 5

Why does reputation matter? 9

Levels of reputation - average or aggregate? 11

• Viewpoint 1.1 Flying in the face of reputation - Ryanair 12

Reputational association 14

• Viewpoint 1.2 Negative associations for Burberry 15

Reputation may vary - it's good to be bad? 16

• Viewpoint 1.3 Pulp Juice bars getting fitter 17

The strategic use of reputation 17

Reputations are falling 18

• Viewpoint 1.4 Banking on a reputational crisis 18

The difficulty of controlling reputation in the 21st century 20

• Viewpoint 1.5 Congested reputation on a charge 22

Corporate reputation as 'Gestalt' 23

Chapter summary 23

Discussion questions 24

References 25

Chapter 2 The scope of corporate reputation 27

Aims and learning objectives 27

Introduction 28

Connecting employees with the company 29

• Viewpoint 2.1 Full cream employment at Cadbury 30

Corporate identity and its relationship with corporate image and corporate reputation 31

• Viewpoint 2.2 Identity personified at Body Shop 32

The building blocks of corporate reputation 34
Influences on corporate reputation 37
• Viewpoint 2.3 Two universities go into one 40
Criteria that influence corporate reputation 42
• Viewpoint 2.4 Moving culture with MTV 44
• Viewpoint 2.5 Declining reputation at Woolworths 46
Chapter summary 48
Discussion questions 49
References 50

Chapter 3 The significance of corporate culture 52

Aims and learning objectives 52
Introduction 53
Who is responsible for corporate reputation? 53
• Viewpoint 3.1 Dyson - culturally determined and innovative 54
Is reputation management embedded in the culture of the organisation? 55
What is corporate culture? 56
The types of organisational culture 59
• Viewpoint 3.2 Offside at the Football Association 61
The difficulty of changing cultures 63
• Viewpoint 3.3 Is the culture nicked at the Met? 64
Culture and values of the brand 65
• Viewpoint 3.4 Everyone satisfied at John Lewis! 67
The employer as brand 68
• Viewpoint 3.5 To find a great place to work . . . Google it! 69
Quality of management and people management 70
Chapter summary 71
Discussion questions 73
References 73

Chapter 4 Measuring corporate reputation 75

Aims and learning objectives 75
What price your reputation? 76
The reputational audit 76
The broad indicators of corporate reputation 77
• Viewpoint 4.1 BA's terminal reputation 79
The financial value of reputation 80
The development of measures of corporate reputation 81
Specific tools of reputation measurement 82
• Viewpoint 4.2 Reputational heritage assists Adidas 84
• Viewpoint 4.3 Reputational highs at Richer Sounds 86
Measuring tangible and intangible facets of corporate reputation 89
Harris-Fombrun Reputation Quotient 90
Reputation Institute's RepTrak 91
The Corporate Character Scale 93
• Viewpoint 4.4 Médecins Sans Frontières (Doctors Without Borders) 95
Best Companies to Work For 96
• Viewpoint 4.5 A delight to work at P3 97
Chapter summary 98
Discussion questions 99
References 99

Minicases for Part 1 101

Minicase 1.1 Ericsson – from product supplier to solution provider: how corporate reputation can facilitate business transformation 101

Minicase 1.2 Harley-Davidson – balancing corporate image and corporate reputation 102

Part 2 Corporate branding 104

Chapter 5 The branding-reputation dilemma 106

Aims and learning objectives 106
Branding background 107
Definitions of a brand 108
Characteristics of brands 110
Types of branding 111
Moving towards corporate branding 111
The importance of trust to a brand 113
• Viewpoint 5.1 Encyclopaedic brand adaptation 114
The link between branding and reputation 116
Brands, reputation and corporate social responsibility 119
• Viewpoint 5.2 FC Barcelona/Aston Villa FC 120
• Viewpoint 5.3 Starbucks' rise with CSR 123
• Viewpoint 5.4 CSR – old and new perspectives and dilemmas 124
The triple bottom line 125
• Viewpoint 5.5 Triple hit for The Co-operative Bank 126
Investigating the co-creation of brands 128
The emotional power of brands 128
Chapter summary 129
Discussion questions 130
References 131

Chapter 6 The rise of corporate brands 134

Aims and learning objectives 134
Introduction 135
• Viewpoint 6.1 Unilever develops its profile 135
Defining corporate brands 136
Values, culture and personality 138
Brand promise 139
• Viewpoint 6.2 Disney across the eras 140
The halo of the corporate brand 140
The growth of the service industry and corporate branding 141
Differences between product brands and corporate brands 142
• Viewpoint 6.3 Mixing ingredient brands 145
The rise of corporate brands 146
• Viewpoint 6.4 Building the corporate brand: Abu Dhabi and Manchester City FC 147
Strategic problems: gaps in the corporate brand 149
Success and failure of corporate branding 151
• Viewpoint 6.5 Innovating Chester Zoo 153
Chapter summary 154
Discussion questions 155
References 156

Chapter 7 **Measuring corporate brands** 159

Aims and learning objectives 159
What are brands worth and how are they measured? 160
• Viewpoint 7.1 What value Amnesty International? 160
Brand equity 162
• Viewpoint 7.2 Thrills and spills as Merlin entertains 164
Measuring corporate brands 166
Difficulties with measuring brands 171
Brand personality 171
Third sector corporate brands 173
• Viewpoint 7.3 Finding a match with Anthony Nolan 174
• Viewpoint 7.4 A new identity to reinvigorate the NCT 177
Measuring third-sector organisations 178
Chapter summary 180
Discussion questions 181
References 182

Chapter 8 **The future for brands** 183

Aims and learning objectives 183
Brands with a comprehensive reputation 184
• Viewpoint 8.1 Every little helps Tesco's reputation 185
Brands that do good 186
• Viewpoint 8.2 Unorthodox yet Innocent 187
New types of corporate brand 189
• Viewpoint 8.3 Face-to-face through Facebook 189
New types of brand – celebrity brands 190
• Viewpoint 8.4 Basket case or just an excellent reputation? 190
Authenticity and the brand 192
New types of brand – country brands 193
Brand communities 195
• Viewpoint 8.5 What's the personality: Gates or Jobs? 195
The anti-branding movement 197
Do we need to love brands? 198
The future of branding 199
Chapter summary 200
Discussion questions 202
References 202

Minicases for Part 2 204

Minicase 2.1 David Beckham – the individual as a corporate brand 204
Minicase 2.2 Warburtons – a brand built on family values 205

Part 3 Corporate communication 208

Chapter 9 **The dimensions of corporate communication** 210

Aims and learning objectives 210
Introduction 211
• Viewpoint 9.1 More than a Shell of corporate communication 211
Establishing the scope of corporate communication 213

Reasons to use corporate communication 214
• Viewpoint 9.2 Using photographs to impel strategic change 215
Dimensions of corporate communication 216
• Viewpoint 9.3 Rebranding the Royal & Sun Alliance 218
The roles and tasks of corporate communication 219
• Viewpoint 9.4 RWE uses corporate communication in a merger 221
• Viewpoint 9.5 MDA communicate change 224
Corporate communication activities 226
Integrated corporate communication 227
• Viewpoint 9.6 Integrating Microsoft's communication 232
Chapter summary 232
Discussion questions 234
References 234

Chapter 10 Contexts for corporate communication 237

Aims and learning objectives 237
Introduction 238
The influence of culture on corporate communication 238
• Viewpoint 10.1 Global growth through corporate culture 239
• Viewpoint 10.2 Are these oily corporate values? 241
Communication climate 242
• Viewpoint 10.3 Philips – simply making sense out of tradition 243
Communicating corporate objectives: vision and mission 244
Criteria for effective corporate communication 246
The corporate identity mix 250
Messages and organisational positioning 252
• Viewpoint 10.4 Far from being saucy, the HP story 253
Communicating corporate responsibility 255
• Viewpoint 10.5 M&S take full responsibility 256
Chapter summary 261
Discussion questions 262
References 262

Chapter 11 Symbols, tools and the media 265

Aims and learning objectives 265
Introduction 266
Message framing 266
• Viewpoint 11.1 Obesity – you've been framed 267
The use of symbols in developing corporate reputation 267
• Viewpoint 11.2 British Airways in a tailspin 268
Rebranding for strategic change 270
The tools for corporate communication 271
• Viewpoint 11.3 The flexibility of corporate advertising 274
• Viewpoint 11.4 Oily support for corporate sponsorships 280
Cause-related marketing 282
• Viewpoint 11.5 Cause it's the right thing to do 282
Media for corporate communication 283
• Viewpoint 11.6 Using media to differentiate and grow 284
Chapter summary 285
Discussion questions 287
References 287

Chapter 12 Methods of corporate communication 290

Aims and learning objectives 290
Introduction 291
Investor relations 291
• Viewpoint 12.1 In-house and personal investor relations at SingTel 293
Public affairs 295
• Viewpoint 12.2 Try Google for lobbying 296
Internal communications 298
• Viewpoint 12.3 Microsoft look through yet more windows 301
Managing customers – media relations 302
• Viewpoint 12.4 Authoritative Greenpeace 302
Issues management 305
• Viewpoint 12.5 Putting the squeeze on blackcurrant juice 305
Defensive or crisis communications 307
• Viewpoint 12.6 Communicating the withdrawal of Vioxx 311
Measuring corporate communication 313
Chapter summary 314
Discussion questions 315
References 316

Minicases for Part 3 319

Minicase 3.1 Marks & Spencer – 'Plan A' sustainability strategy 319
Minicase 3.2 Primark – defending a reputation with social media 321

Index 325

Supporting resources

Visit **www.pearsoned.co.uk/roperfill** to find valuable online resources:

Companion Website for students
- Annotated links to relevant sites on the Web
- Video podcasts
- A glossary of key terms

For instructors
- Customisable PowerPoint slides which are downloadable and available to use for teaching
- Complete downloadable Instructors' Manual

Also: The Companion Website provides the following features:

- Online help and support to assist with website usage and troubleshooting

For more information please contact your local Pearson Education sales representative or visit **www.pearsoned.co.uk/roperfill**

Guided tour

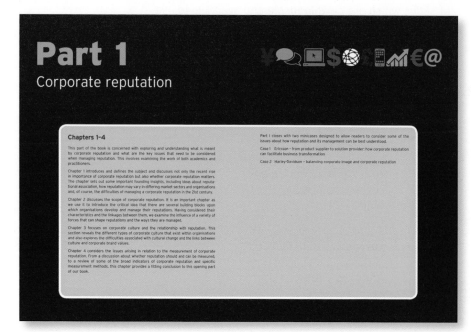

Part 1

Corporate reputation

Chapters 1-4

This part of the book is concerned with exploring and understanding what is meant by corporate reputation and what are the key issues that need to be considered when managing reputation. This involves examining the work of both academics and practitioners.

Chapter 1 introduces and defines the subject and discusses not only the recent rise in importance of corporate reputation but also whether corporate reputation matters. The chapter sets out some important founding insights, including ideas about reputational association, how reputation may vary in differing market sectors and organisations and, of course, the difficulties of managing a corporate reputation in the 21st century.

Chapter 2 discusses the scope of corporate reputation. It is an important chapter as we use it to introduce the critical idea that there are several building blocks upon which organisations develop and manage their reputations. Having considered their characteristics and the linkages between them, we examine the influence of a variety of forces that can shape reputations and the ways they are managed.

Chapter 3 focuses on corporate culture and the relationship with reputation. This section reveals the different types of corporate culture that exist within organisations and also explores the difficulties associated with cultural change and the links between culture and corporate brand values.

Chapter 4 considers the issues arising in relation to the measurement of corporate reputation. From a discussion about whether reputation should and can be measured, to a review of some of the broad indicators of corporate reputation and specific measurement methods, this chapter provides a fitting conclusion to this opening part of our book.

Part I closes with two minicases designed to allow readers to consider some of the issues about how reputation and its management can be best understood.

Case 1   Ericsson - from product supplier to solution provider: how corporate reputation can facilitate business transformation.

Case 2   Harley-Davidson - balancing corporate image and corporate reputation

◀ **Part openers** summarise the key points in each chapter. They also provide a summary of the engaging case studies you can find in each part.

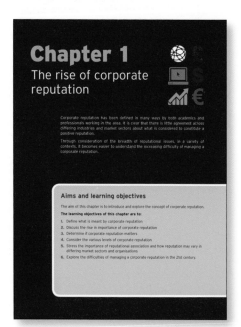

Chapter 1

The rise of corporate reputation

Corporate reputation has been defined in many ways by both academics and professionals working in the area. It is clear that there is little agreement across differing industries and market sectors about what is considered to constitute a positive reputation.

Through consideration of the breadth of reputational issues, in a variety of contexts, it becomes easier to understand the increasing difficulty of managing a corporate reputation.

Aims and learning objectives

The aim of this chapter is to introduce and explore the concept of corporate reputation.

The learning objectives of this chapter are to:

1. Define what is meant by corporate reputation
2. Discuss the rise in importance of corporate reputation
3. Determine if corporate reputation matters
4. Consider the various levels of corporate reputation
5. Stress the importance of reputational association and how reputation may vary in differing market sectors and organisations
6. Explore the difficulties of managing a corporate reputation in the 21st century.

◀ **Aims and learning objectives** enable you to focus on what you should have achieved by the end of the chapter.

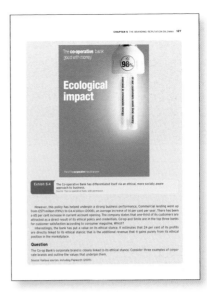

Snappy **Viewpoints** boxes improve your understanding by providing different perspectives. Each one ends with a question.

Great colour **photography** from real high-profile marketing campaigns is used throughout the book.

Summaries clinch the important concepts that have just been presented, to reinforce learning and review the chapter objectives.

Every chapter ends with **Discussion questions** that test your understanding and help you to track your progress.

Each chapter is supported by a list of **References** directing your independent study to a variety of sources.

Each part concludes with two **Minicases** which encourage stimulating debate and class discussion.

Each Minicase is accompanied by **Questions** which will help you apply what you have read.

Preface

This book has been written for people who want to know more about corporate reputation. If that applies to you then thank you for choosing to read our book. The book is intended to support a range of people. These include university and college students who are studying corporate reputation, branding and public relations. Some people may be studying for professional qualifications, such as those offered by the Chartered Institute of Marketing. Indeed, this book has been written to closely support students studying the Postgraduate Professional Diploma module, Managing Corporate Reputation.

Some readers may not fall into these categories and may have other reasons to learn more about corporate reputation – for example, students reading for dissertations, commercial and business people preparing reports and presentations, public service professionals seeking explanations and, of course, those who are just inquisitive. Whoever you are, and whatever your motivation, we hope you find this text accessible and that you find the answers to your questions.

Reasons to read about corporate reputation

Corporate reputation is a complex subject and draws on a variety of disciplines. It is increasingly recognised as an important organisational activity, an essential aspect of contemporary management.

This book has been written with a view to disentangling some of the complexity. It has been written largely, but not entirely, from an academic perspective, and not from a technical or practitioner's point of view. The aim, therefore, is to provide an insight into why corporate reputation, branding and communication work in particular ways, and of course, why they do not work in other ways. The aim is for you to enjoy the subject, to be stimulated to want to know more and to engage further with the strategic world of corporate reputation.

All organisations, large and small, commercial, government, charities, educational and other not-for-profit enterprises, need to develop and sustain a positive reputation amongst their stakeholders. This may be in order to get materials and services to undertake their business activities, to attract, recruit and retain the best employees, to secure favourable financial arrangements, to collaborate and co-ordinate with others, and to secure suitable distribution for their goods and services. In addition, there are consumers to appeal to, people just like you, who are free to choose among the many hundreds and thousands of companies to buy from.

Media is all-pervasive and companies are a good source of news. Bad news is good news as far as the media is concerned and they are more than happy to provide stories that question the reputations of companies. The public expect more from their companies nowadays. They are expected to be good citizens and often to give something back to the economies that they operate in.

We are living in a service economy and it is difficult to judge a service without actually using it. The greater risk attached to the purchase decision means that it is often the strength of the brand and its reputation that is a key factor in making a choice. In a similar vein, product parity (the fact that many products and services seem almost identical in terms of features and quality) means that the brand and the trust we have in it are the deciding factors for consumers.

Reputations are fragile. They may take a considerable time to build but can be destroyed very quickly. As a result they are not something that should be left to chance but should be actively managed in the same way that a brand is managed. This management means that everything the company does should be considered in terms of the reputational effect that the action will have. Certainly managing corporate reputation does not just mean having a crisis management plan in place.

There is considerable discussion amongst experts about the value of brands. This book deals with this issue but the discussion highlights the fact that it is the brand name, and its reputation, that is the most valuable asset that the company has. The intangible asset of the brand name is often worth far more than all the tangible resources that the firm owns. In this case it would seem foolish not to dedicate some resource to protecting and managing the corporate reputation.

In addition, it must be noted that it is not just commercial organisations that need to be aware of reputation. Some of the best brands out there, certainly in the service sector, are non-profit third-sector concerns. Branding and corporate reputation is just as important for the third sector as it is for private companies and we deal with this issue in our book.

This book introduces you to the critical world of corporate reputation and allows you to appreciate some of the issues associated with the way reputation can be developed and sustained, and the activities that have an impact on corporate personality, identity, branding and corporate communications.

Overview of the book

This book is presented as 12 chapters. This enables the book to be used as a core part of a one-semester or one-term programme. Corporate reputation embraces a number of key topics: corporate personality, identity, branding, image and communication. We present these as building blocks and build discussion and insight around these topics throughout the book.

The three parts to the book – reputation, branding and communication – should be regarded as an integrated whole. The topics are interlinked and each chapter is used to consider the characteristics and key issues and encourages readers to actively consider some of the ideas and challenges faced by those charged with managing corporate reputation. This is facilitated by a questioning style of writing, one in which we ask the reader to pause and consider a particular issue before we elaborate and explore possible responses.

The book draws on a variety of academic materials and applies these to practice. These academic materials are explained and evaluated before various examples are used to demonstrate theory in practice. In each chapter there are five or six examples of organisations demonstrating good, and sometimes not so good, practice. These are to be found under the heading of 'Viewpoints'. Each Viewpoint contains a question which readers can use to explore or develop the ideas illustrated in the example.

This book brings together different ideas relating to corporate reputation, unlike other books that focus on one particular topic, such as corporate communication or branding, without considering the whole. The approach taken here thus invites readers to consider reputation as a core business activity and not as a peripheral or optional add-on.

This book also seeks to stimulate thought and consideration about a wide range of inter-related issues. To help achieve these aims, a number of theories and models are advanced. Some of these theories reflect management practice, while others are offered as suggestions for moving the subject forward. Many of the theories are abstractions of actual practice, some are based on empirical research and others are pure conceptualisation. All seek to enrich the subject, but not all need carry the same weight of contribution. Readers should form their own opinions based upon their reading, experience and judgment.

This book uses core academic materials to explore how organisations develop, use and abuse corporate reputation in practice. It is therefore a blend of theory and practice. The book uses examples to illustrate how organisations use corporate reputation and related topics.

Structure

There are three main parts to this book and each has four chapters.

Part 1 is about corporate reputation and there are four chapters:

Chapter 1   The rise of corporate reputation

Chapter 2   The scope of corporate reputation

Chapter 3   The significance of corporate culture

Chapter 4   Measuring corporate reputation

The book opens with an exploration of what corporate reputation means before discussing its recent rise in importance. Embedded in this is a consideration of whether corporate reputation is important, and we achieve this partly by looking at different levels and types of reputation adopted by different sectors and markets. The first chapter closes with a view of the difficulties of managing corporate reputation.

Having grounded some ideas about what reputation might be and what it might not be, the second chapter introduces the building blocks of corporate reputation and, in doing so, sets out the scope of the subject and the broad structure of the book. These blocks are corporate personality, corporate identity/branding, corporate image and corporate communication.

The third chapter is used to examine corporate culture, a major part of the corporate personality. In addition to considering the characteristics of corporate culture, and ideas about strong and weak cultures, the chapter makes important linkages with cultural change and brand values. The final chapter in this opening part considers ways in which corporate reputation can be measured as well as ways in which the corporate personality, or character, can be measured.

Part 2 is concerned with corporate brands and comprises the following four chapters:

Chapter 5   The branding–reputation dilemma

Chapter 6   The rise of corporate brands

Chapter 7   Measuring corporate brands

Chapter 8   The future for brands

Chapter 5 opens with an examination of what a corporate brand means and makes critical links with corporate reputation. This underpins the subsequent discussion about corporate social responsibility and more contemporary ideas about co-creation and the emotional power of corporate brands.

The sixth chapter considers the rise of corporate brands and their significance to organisations and stakeholders. One of the important points we make is to flag the differences between product and corporate brands. This serves to provide clarity and enable a consideration of the advantages and disadvantages of corporate branding.

Apart from reviewing the issues and techniques associated with measuring corporate brands, Chapter 7 explores branding in the third sector. This is an important topic, and one which is not covered in any depth in other texts. The second part closes with a chapter that reviews some of the important issues and developments that might affect corporate brands in the future. Some thought-provoking ideas about brand authenticity, anti-branding movements and the development of celebrity and country brands seek to help readers consider some of the wider issues associated with this critical yet fascinating topic.

Part 3 focuses on corporate communication, and the titles of the four chapters are as follows:

Chapter 9   The dimensions of corporate communication

Chapter 10   Contexts for corporate communication

Chapter 11   Symbols, tools and the media

Chapter 12   Methods of corporate communication

Corporate communication is the means by which organisations communicate with their various stakeholder audiences. However, there are a number of issues and influences that can affect the efficacy of corporate communication programmes. Part 3 opens with an exploration of the nature and role of corporate communication before examining the reasons why organisations use corporate communication and the tasks and activities that need to be accomplished.

Chapter 10 builds on ideas introduced in Chapter 3 about corporate culture. It is used to explore issues concerning the different situations and cultural influences that inform the communications used by organisations. A key part of this chapter concerns ideas about the corporate identity mix and the way in which organisations choose to position themselves.

The following chapter is used to reflect on the use of symbolism as part of the identity mix, and on its impact on corporate reputation. The chapter considers some of the core characteristics of the primary tools used as a part of a corporate communication strategy. The chapter closes with an examination of the characteristics of the main media used as part of a corporate communication programme.

The closing chapter provides an insight into the different methods organisations can use to communicate with particular stakeholder audiences. The text covers investor relations to reach financial stakeholders, public affairs to influence regulators, internal communications or employee relations to reach internal members of staff, and media relations to influence customers. The final sections consider issues of management, crisis communications and ways in which the effectiveness of corporate communication can be measured.

Design features and presentation

In addition to the three-part structure of the book, there are a number of features that are intended to help readers.

Chapter objectives

Each chapter opens with a brief commentary on the broad issues that should be addressed and this is followed by both the aims of what is to be covered and a list of (learning) objectives. These help to signal the primary topics that are covered in the chapter and so guide the learning experience.

Navigation

Important key text is extracted and presented as 'quotes' in the margin. This helps readers to locate relevant material quickly and highlights key issues. In addition, to assist readers through the various chapters, the title of the left-hand page identifies the page number as well as the part number and title. To complement this, the right-hand page flags the page number and the chapter title.

Visual supports

This book is produced in four colours and throughout the text there are numerous colour and black-and-white exhibits, figures (diagrams) and tables of information. These serve to highlight, illustrate and bring life to the written word.

The pictures used serve either to illustrate particular points by demonstrating theory in practice or to complement individual examples. The examples are normally highlighted in the text as Viewpoints. These are easily distinguishable through the colour contrasts and serve to demonstrate how a particular aspect of corporate reputation has been used by an organisation in a particular context. We hope you enjoy these Viewpoints of various aspects of corporate reputation, branding and communication.

Summaries and minicases

At the end of each chapter there is a summary and a series of review and discussion questions. Readers are encouraged to test their own understanding of the content of each chapter by considering some or all of the discussion questions. In this sense the questions support self-study but tutors might wish to use some of these as part of a seminar or workshop programme.

In addition, each part of the book opens with a synopsis of its content. Each part closes with several minicases and supportive questions, designed to help readers apply some of the subject matter explored therein. These short cases can be used in class for discussion purposes and to explore some of the salient issues that have been raised. Students working alone can use the minicases to test their own understanding and to consolidate their understanding.

Support materials

Students and lecturers who adopt this text have a range of support materials and facilities to help them.

Readers are invited to visit the companion website for the book at www.pearsoned.co.uk/roperfill. Here they have access to further materials, including video podcasts, an online glossary and annotated weblinks. For lecturers and tutors there is a password-protected section of the companion website; from here they can access an Instructors' Manual and customisable PowerPoint slides for teaching.

Acknowledgements

This book could not have been written without the support of a wide range of brilliant people. Contributions include those who provided information and permissions, those who wrote minicases, answered questions and those who tolerated the length of time we took to complete the manuscript, those who sent through photographs, answered phone calls and emails and those who simply liaised with others. Finally, there are those who have read and reviewed drafts, made constructive comments and provided moral support and encouragement.

The list of individuals and organisations involved with this book is extensive. Our thanks are offered to all of you. We have tried to list everyone but if anyone has been omitted then we offer our sincere apologies.

Chris Raddats	University of Liverpool – author of two case studies
Jonathan Shrager	For valuable assistance with several Viewpoints and two of the case studies
Brian Jones	Leeds Metropolitan University
John Temperley	Leeds Metropolitan University
Nigel Markwick	littlebig fish
Debra Weatherley	FindPhoto
John Dixon	InterComm

Above all, perhaps, are the various individuals at Pearson and their associates who have taken our manuscript, managed it and published it in this form. In particular, we would like to thank our editor, Rachel Gear. As usual she has been supremely professional, yet enthusiastic, supportive and patient. In much the same way, Emma Violet continues to provide the materials and resources that help us to get things done. In addition we would like to thank Philippa Fiszzon for transforming the manuscript into the final product. Thank you all.

Stuart Roper and Chris Fill
2011

Publisher's acknowledgements

We are grateful to the following for permission to reproduce copyright material:

Figures

Figure 1.1 adapted from 'Reputation: realizing the value from the corporate image', *Harvard Business School Press* (Fombrun, C.J., 1996), copyright © 1996 by the President and Fellows of Harvard College. All Rights Reserved; Figure 3.1 from *The Corporate Culture Survival Guide: Sense and Nonsense About Culture Change*, Jossey Bass (Schein, E.H., 1999), copyright © 1999. Reproduced with permission of John Wiley & Sons, Inc.; Figure 3.2 from 'What holds the modern company together?', *Harvard Business Review* (Goffee, R. & Jones, G., 1996), copyright © 1996 by the President and Fellows of Harvard College. All Rights Reserved; Figure 4.1 from 'Reputation: realizing the value from the corporate image', *Harvard Business School Press*, p. 207 (Fombrun, C.J., 1996), copyright © 1996 by the President and Fellows of Harvard College. All Rights Reserved; Figure 4.2 'The RepTrak System' from *Essentials of Corporate Communication*, Routledge (van Riel & Fombrun, 2007) copyright © Reputation Institute. All rights reserved; Figure 5.3 from *Corporate Reputation and Competitiveness*, Routledge (Davies, G., Chun, R., da Silva, R. & Roper, S., 2003) p. 76. Reproduced by permission of Taylor & Francis Books (UK); Figure 6.2 from 'The Corporate Brand: Dealing with Multiple Stakeholders', *Journal of Marketing Management*, Vol 23 (1–2), pp. 75–90 (Roper, S. & Davies, G., 2007), copyright © Westburn Publishers Ltd. Reprinted by permission of Taylor & Francis Ltd, www.tandfonline.com on behalf of Westburn Publishers Ltd; Figure 7.4 from BrandAsset Valuator, www.brandassetconsulting.com, Reproduced with permission from BrandAsset Valuator Consulting; Figure 10.2 from *Managing Public Relations*, Holt, Rineholt & Winston, NY (Grunig, J. & Hunt, T., 1984). Reproduced with permission from James E. Grunig; Figure 11.2 adapted from 'A new framework for evaluating sponsorship opportunities', *International Journal of Advertising*, Vol 25 (4), pp. 471–487 (Poon, D.T.Y. & Prendergast, G., 2006), copyright © WARC; Figure 12.1 from 'Rethinking internal communication: a stakeholder approach', *Corporate Communications: an International Journal*, Vol 12 (2), pp. 177–198 (Welch, M. & Jackson, P.R., 2007), Copyright © 2007, Emerald Group Publishing Limited.

Tables

Table 1.1 adapted from 'The reputation quotient: a multi-stakeholder measure of corporate reputation', *The Journal of Brand Management, Palgrave Macmillan*, Vol 7 (4), pp. 241–255 (Fombrun, C.J., Gardberg, N.A. & Sever, J.M., 2000). Reproduced with permission of Palgrave Macmillan; Table 1.2 from 'Britain's Most Admired 2000 and 2009', *Management Today* (Brown, M. & Turner, P., 2008). Reproduced with permission from Haymarket Direct; Table 4.4 from 'Best Companies to Work For, 2010' http://www.bestcompanies.co.uk/ copyright © Best Companies Limited; Table 5.3 from 'Defining a "brand": Beyond the Literature with Experts' Interpretations', *Journal of Marketing Management*, Vol 14 (5), pp. 417–443 (de Chernatony, L. & Riley, F.D'O., 1998), copyright © Westburn Publishers, reprinted by permission of Taylor & Francis Ltd, www.tandfonline.com on behalf of Westburn

Publishers; Table 5.4 from 'Top 10 Superbrands', copyright © Superbrands (UK) Ltd; Table 6.1 from 'Corporate marketing: integrating corporate identity, corporate branding, corporate communications, corporate image and corporate reputation', *European Journal of Marketing*, Vol 40 (7/8), pp. 730–741 (Balmer, J.M.T. & Greyser, S.A., 2006), copyright © 2006, Emerald Group Publishing Limited; Tables 7.1 'Interbrand's Top Global Brands 2010', and Table 7.2 'Ten Measures of Brand Strength', www.interbrand.com, copyright © Interbrand; Table 7.3 from 'BrandZ Top 100 Most Powerful Brands', copyright © Millward Brown Optimor; Table 10.1 Petrobras Mission Statement. Reproduced with permission; Table 12.1 from 'Rethinking internal communication: a stakeholder approach', *Corporate Communications: an International Journal*, Vol 12 (2), pp. 177–198 (Welch, M. & Jackson, P.R., 2007), copyright © 2007, Emerald Group Publishing Limited.

Text

Quote on page 140 from the Microsoft strapline. Microsoft is a registered trademark of Microsoft Corporation in the United States and/or other countries. Corporate Reputation is an independent publication and is not affiliated with, nor has it been authorized, sponsored, or otherwise approved by Microsoft Corporation; Extract on page 197 from www.corporatewatch.org. Reproduced with permission; Extract on page 291 from "What is investor relations?", www.irs.org.uk, The Investor Relations Society (2009). Reproduced with permission.

Photographs

(Key: b-bottom; c-centre; l-left; r-right; t-top)

Adidas: 85; **Alamy Images:** Kevin Allen 80, Patrick Batchelder 196, bildbroker.de 145, Ashley Cooper 64, Photogenix 277, SiliconValleyStock 254; **Amnesty International:** © Marie-Anne Ventoura 161; **Anthony Nolan. www.anthonynolan.org:** 174t, 174b; **Bigpicturesphoto.com:** 15; **Courtesy of Chester Zoo:** Design and concept by dan pearlman www.danpearlman.com 153; **The Co-operative bank:** 127; **Courtesy of Dyson:** 54; **Courtesy of Philips Consumer Electronics:** 243; **Courtesy of Procter & Gamble UK:** 8; **© 2011 Encyclopædia Britannica, Inc:** 115b, © 2007 William J. Bowe, reproduced by permission 115t; **Getty Images:** 303, Jonathan S. Blair / National Geographic 107, Richard Heathcote 148, JOSEP LAGO / AFP 120, NBAE 191, Mark Thompson / The FA 62; **Photo courtesy Google UK:** 297; **© Inter IKEA Systems BV 2011:** 240; **Image courtesy of The Advertising Archives:** 274; **Innocent Ltd:** 188, 283; **Magen David Adom UK:** 224; **Marks and Spencer plc (company):** 58, 256; **Médecins Sans Frontières:** 95; **Merlin Entertainment UK:** 165; **Mirrorpix:** 47t; **MTV:** © MTV Networks Europe. All Rights Reserved 45; **Courtesy of NCT:** 177; **nisyndication.com:** The Times 313; **Pearson Education Ltd:** Naki Kouyioumtzis 92, Photodisc 221; **Photolibrary.com:** 19; **Press Association Images:** 269, David Davies 47b; **richersounds.com:** 87; **Courtesy of SAS:** 215; **Shell Brands International AG:** 212; **SingTel:** 293; **Sky.com:** 10; **Tesco Stores Ltd:** 185; **The Body Shop:** 33; **TMS Reprints:** Dana Summers / The Permissions Group, Inc. 14; **Used by permission of Unilever PLC:** This logo is a Registered Trade Mark of Unilever PLC. 136; **University of Manchester:** 41.

In some instances we have been unable to trace the owners of copyright material, and we would appreciate any information that would enable us to do so.

Part 1
Corporate reputation

Chapters 1-4

This part of the book is concerned with exploring and understanding what is meant by corporate reputation and what are the key issues that need to be considered when managing reputation. This involves examining the work of both academics and practitioners.

Chapter 1 introduces and defines the subject and discusses not only the recent rise in importance of corporate reputation but also whether corporate reputation matters. The chapter sets out some important founding insights, including ideas about reputational association, how reputation may vary in differing market sectors and organisations and, of course, the difficulties of managing a corporate reputation in the 21st century.

Chapter 2 discusses the scope of corporate reputation. It is an important chapter as we use it to introduce the critical idea that there are several building blocks upon which organisations develop and manage their reputations. Having considered their characteristics and the linkages between them, we examine the influence of a variety of forces that can shape reputations and the ways they are managed.

Chapter 3 focuses on corporate culture and the relationship with reputation. This section reveals the different types of corporate culture that exist within organisations and also explores the difficulties associated with cultural change and the links between culture and corporate brand values.

Chapter 4 considers the issues arising in relation to the measurement of corporate reputation. From a discussion about whether reputation should and can be measured, to a review of some of the broad indicators of corporate reputation and specific measurement methods, this chapter provides a fitting conclusion to this opening part of our book.

Part I closes with two minicases designed to allow readers to consider some of the issues about how reputation and its management can be best understood.

Case 1   Ericsson – from product supplier to solution provider: how corporate reputation can facilitate business transformation

Case 2   Harley-Davidson – balancing corporate image and corporate reputation

Chapter 1
The rise of corporate reputation

Corporate reputation has been defined in many ways by both academics and professionals working in the area. It is clear that there is little agreement across differing industries and market sectors about what is considered to constitute a positive reputation.

Through consideration of the breadth of reputational issues, in a variety of contexts, it becomes easier to understand the increasing difficulty of managing a corporate reputation.

Aims and learning objectives

The aim of this chapter is to introduce and explore the concept of corporate reputation.

The learning objectives of this chapter are to:

1. Define what is meant by corporate reputation
2. Discuss the rise in importance of corporate reputation
3. Determine if corporate reputation matters
4. Consider the various levels of corporate reputation
5. Stress the importance of reputational association and how reputation may vary in differing market sectors and organisations
6. Explore the difficulties of managing a corporate reputation in the 21st century.

Introduction

We are living in an age of 24-hour mass media. This media has to provide interesting stories in order to justify its existence. An area of interest for it is business and the brands that exist in the marketplace. Such brands, the executives who run them and their interaction and place within society are now a constant focus of attention. Such a development has significantly enhanced the importance of reputation management for brands worldwide. Every single move, decision taken and isolated event that involves a company is scrutinised, documented and publicised globally, compounding the task of reputation managers. Just ask BP or Toyota.

> Every single move, decision taken and isolated event that involves a company is scrutinised.

In such an intense climate of surveillance, it could be argued that it is virtually impossible for major companies to completely avoid negative commentary at some stage. Such commentary, however, must not be permitted to damage the brand and its equity in the long term, again underlining the necessity for reputation management.

Brand management as a strategic practice is well established and has been exercised by great corporations such as Unilever and Procter and Gamble since the 1920s. Reputation management is considerably newer. Indeed, it is possible to have a strong brand but a relatively poor corporate reputation. This book aims to synthesise the important areas of corporate branding, corporate reputation and corporate communications.

Definitions of reputation

Charles Fombrun, a prominent writer on the topic of reputation, graphically manifests corporate reputation within the form of a matrix, predicating that it comprises a quartet of elements (social image, financial image, product image and recruitment image). These factors may also be readily mapped onto Kotler *et al.*'s (2005, p. 556) definition of brand equity, which proclaims that 'brand equity is the value of a brand, based on the extent to which it has high brand loyalty, name awareness, perceived quality, strong brand associations', given that all the factors outlined by Kotler *et al.* that encompass brand equity seemingly stem from corporate reputation.

> Corporate reputation comprises social image, financial image, product image and recruitment image.

The dictionary definition of reputation is 'the opinions that are generally held about someone or something' or 'the estimation in which a person is held, repute, known or reported character, general credit, fame, renown'. A reputation is therefore a combination of the views and impressions of many different people, not unanimously held, but in general. The reputation of a product will largely be formed by the views of its consumers and customers, but the reputation of an organisation is built on the impressions held by a number of different classes of people in addition to the consumers of the end product or service; in Fombrun's (1996) words, 'the overall estimation in which a company is held by its constituents'.

> Reputation is the overall estimation in which a company is held by its constituents.

Fombrun (1996) defines reputation as 'the net perception of a company's ability to meet the expectations of all its stakeholders'. de Chernatony & Harris (2000) agree that the opinion of all stakeholders must be considered and that reputation is a representative evaluation of a brand's identity. Bromley (2000) defines reputation as an index of a company's worth or value. Bromley (2001) also emphasises the importance of differing opinions and describes reputation as a distribution of opinions about a person or organisation. As with the term branding, some authors struggle to define reputation precisely, and Schweizer

> Reputation is an index of a company's worth or value.

& Wijnberg (1999) state that reputation has been classified as an intangible component of a firm's pool of resources.

Reputation is not separate from employee or customer satisfaction, financial performance or other indicators. It is a sum of all of these things (Griffin, 2008). Creating a favourable reputation should not be just an isolated objective of the organisation, it should be the very means by which an organisation develops (van Riel & Fombrun, 2007), grows and flourishes.

The word corporate comes from the Latin 'corpus' meaning 'body' or 'the whole' (van Riel & Fombrun, 2007, p. 22) and therefore corporate reputation is concerned with the overall estimation in which the organisation is held by its constituents (Fombrun, 1996).

Corporate reputation is concerned with the overall estimation in which an organisation is held.

In Fombrun's diagram of the relationship between image and reputation, reputation comprises social image, financial image, product image and recruitment image. Reputations are 'aggregate perceptions by stakeholders of an organisation's ability to fulfil their expectations' (van Riel & Fombrun, 2007, p. 43).

Academic perspectives on corporate reputation

Academically, corporate reputation is not a stand-alone discipline but one that draws from many different perspectives. These include strategic management, organisational theory, economics, marketing, communications, accounting and finance (Fombrun & van Riel, 1997; Balmer, 1998). Investment in reputation, in the same way as branding, allows a company to charge a premium for its products.

Reputation is not a stand-alone discipline.

Again, as with branding, a service brand will rely more on its reputation than a product brand, as there is much less tangible evidence available upon which to judge it. In service companies there are particular problems related to reputation. The UK and other western economies are service economies. The intangible nature of services together with the IHIP factors (intangibility, heterogeneity, inseparability and perishability) really mean that all a service company has to protect is its reputation. The service firm does not have the assets of a petrochemical company, for example. It is people-based and these people can enhance or damage its reputation. Therefore, shouldn't such organisations really do the most to protect their reputations?

All a service company has to protect is its reputation.

Branding is at the centre of reputation management for marketers. Bennett & Gabriel (2001) state the importance of the historical nature of reputation formation. As with branding, it is consistency over time that is crucial. Argenti (1998) writes from the perspective of corporate communication and says that a reputation is created from the bottom up, as each of us applies our own personal combination of economic and social, selfish and altruistic criteria in judging an organisation and its future prospects.

Branding is at the centre of reputation management.

A well-respected reputation will communicate the firm's mission, the quality and professionalism of its leadership, the talent of its employees and its role within the marketing environment (Dowling, 1994). Economists and strategists are interested in reputation due to the competitive benefits that can be accrued from a positive reputation. Organisational theorists see reputation as the thing that helps employees make sense of a company. It is very much linked with the culture and identity of the organisation. From the sociological perspective, corporate reputations are the aggregated assessments of a company's prestige and are rooted in the social system surrounding firms and their industries. Therefore, the performance of a firm will be judged relative to other firms in the same industry and the expectations and norms of that industry.

Accountants are interested in reputation due to the gap that is growing between the actual worth of a company and its market valuation. It is recognised that the tangible assets of an organisation may be worth considerably less than the intangible assets, i.e. the company's

Table 1.1	Definitions of corporate reputation
Discipline	**Definition**
Economics	Reputations are traits or signals that describe a company's probable behaviour in a particular situation.
Strategy	Reputations are intangible assets that are difficult for rivals to imitate, acquire or substitute and so create mobility barriers that provide their owners with a sustained competitive advantage.
Accounting	Reputation is one of many types of intangible assets that are difficult to measure but that create value for companies.
Marketing	Reputation describes the corporate associations that individuals establish with the company name.
Communication	Reputations are corporate traits that develop from relationships companies establish with their multiple constituents.
Organisational theory	Reputations are cognitive representations of companies that develop as stakeholders make sense of corporate activities.
Sociology	Reputational rankings are social constructions emanating from the relationships firms establish with stakeholders in their shared institutional environment.

Source: Fombrun *et al.* (2000). Palgrave Macmillan, with permission.

brand and reputation. It is now possible to include intangible assets on a balance sheet, but only a small percentage of brand owners practise this. It could be argued that accountancy methods are outdated in the emphasis they provide on the factual.

A reputation, therefore, is a snapshot that reconciles the multiple images of an organisation held by all of its constituencies. It signals the overall attractiveness of the company to employees, consumers, investors and communities (Blackstad & Cooper, 1995).

Reputation reconciles the multiple images of an organisation.

Fombrun *et al.* (2000) sum up the multi-dimensional nature of corporate reputation by providing the definitions from the different disciplines (see Table 1.1).

The following definition by Fombrun (1996) provides a good summary of the various interpretations of reputation:

A corporate reputation is a collective representation of a firm's past actions and results that describes the firm's ability to deliver valued outcomes to multiple stakeholders. It gauges a firm's relative standing both internally with employees and externally with its stakeholders, in both its competitive and institutional environments.

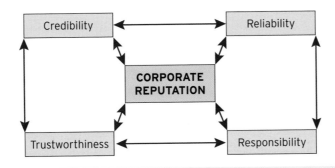

Figure 1.1	What makes a good reputation?

Source: Fombrun (1996). Harvard Business School Publishing, with permission.

Figure 1.1 (on p. 7) summarises the reinforcing network of factors that helps organisations build strong and favourable reputations. Therefore, investment in reputation, in the same way as branding, allows a company to charge a premium for its products and services. There is also likely to be an assumption amongst the audience that a company with a respected reputation will produce products and services that are of a higher quality than the competition (see Exhibit 1.1), such that reputation mitigates against uncertainty (Dowling, 1994; Yoon *et al.*, 1993; Berens & van Riel, 2001).

To round off this section on how corporate reputation might be considered, we introduce the work of Dowling (1994). His interpretation is helpful because he considers reputation in the context of both corporate identity and corporate image. This is depicted at Figure 1.2. These interconnections are important because they encompass an inward and not just an outward or external perspective of reputation. This approach will be revisited in Chapter 2.

Exhibit 1.1	A selection of trusted brands from P&G.
	Source: Courtesy of Procter & Gamble UK.

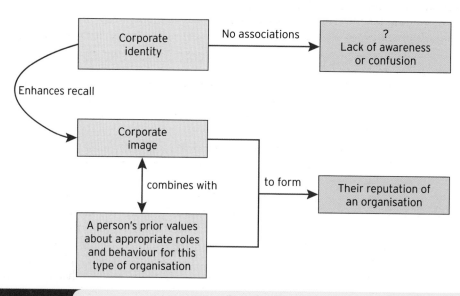

Figure 1.2	Dowling's perspective of corporate reputation.
	Source: Dowling (1994).

Why does reputation matter?

Of course, using the terminology of strategy, reputation provides us with a competitive advantage, a means of differentiation from the competition. The company's stock is more valuable and more people are willing to invest in it. The company's value as a long-term investment is often, in itself, a marker of its reputation. This provides much needed revenue that can be ploughed back into expensive areas of business management such as research and development and corporate communication, thus again reinforcing and enhancing the corporate reputation.

> Reputation provides a competitive advantage.

Customers are more likely to move up the loyalty ladder and become advocates of the company rather than merely customers. At the other end of the ladder, companies that develop poor reputations may encounter 'terrorists', those who actively seek to interfere with the smooth running of the firm. Companies with good reputations can restrict and reduce friction with regulators such as government officials and offset the worst effects of legislation (Gaines-Ross, 2008). Weber Shandwick's 'safeguarding reputation' research goes so far as to claim that 63 per cent of a company's market value is attributable to its reputation.

Milton Friedman, in his seminal article for the *New York Times Magazine* in 1970, famously declared that 'the business of business is business'. Companies have found that adopting this at face value will damage their reputation in the 21st century. And it is not just one's own organisation that must consider its reputation; its suppliers may also damage the brand. For example, an undercover reporter claimed to have been paid only £133 for a 43-hour week working at TNS Knitwear, a Manchester factory that supplies over 20,000 items a week to retailer Primark. This works out at £3.09 per hour, well below the legal minimum wage of £5.73 (*Manchester Evening News*, 2009). Although Primark takes considerable care on its website to defend its ethical principles, such news stories are damaging to the brand's reputation. See the Primark case study (Minicase 3.2) on page 321.

Consider the fall in reputation of once great companies. Woolworths no longer exists as a high-street presence, having closed down completely in January 2009. *In Search of Excellence* by Tom Peters and Robert Waterman is one of the best selling business books of all time. Millions bought the book originally published in 1982 that described the secrets of the most successful US companies. Within a few short years, however, *Businessweek* (1984) reported that of 43 so-called 'excellent' companies one-third were having financial difficulties within 5 years of Peters and Waterman's surveys. Recovering reputation is considered much more difficult than building and maintaining it and therefore the active management of corporate reputation should be considered a priority by management. A quick glance at the results of *Management Today*'s most admired British companies from 2000 compared with the latest results from 2010 provides an indication of the precarious nature of such league tables (Table 1.2).

> Consider the fall in reputation of once great companies.

> Recovering reputation is much more difficult than building and maintaining it.

Only three companies make it into both lists, Unilever, Shell and Tesco. BP was in the 2009 list but its problems with the Deepwater Horizon disaster ensured that it has also now dropped out.

The demands on companies are unquestionably greater than they were. We are surrounded and dominated by 24-hour media that has a huge capacity to fill. Journalists are constantly looking for stories, and perceived poor behaviour by the business community is always popular fare. The modern corporation cannot be invisible in the way it used to be. Organisations cannot hide their wrong-doings by merely shifting them to a remote developing-world destination or getting a supplier to do their dirty work for them. The fact is that we are under scrutiny all the time from the media and others. The information revolution is here and has changed things irrevocably. Often uncensored and unlicensed individuals are communicating if not on behalf of the organisation then with a clear link to its brand name.

Table 1.2	Britain's most admired – 2000 and 2010	
Position	2000	2010
1	GlaxoSmithKline	Unilever
2	BP	Serco
3	Shell	Shell
4	Cadbury Schweppes	Sky
5	Tesco	Whitbread
6	Excel	Berkeley Group
7	Astra Zeneca	Rolls-Royce
8	Sage (software)	Tesco
9	Unilever	BG Group
10	GKN	Diageo

Source: *Management Today*. Haymarket Business Publications Ltd, with permission.

Exhibit 1.2 Sky – a major player in the media revolution.
Source: Sky.com, with permission.

The brand is multi-dimensional and is no longer in control of its own communications in the way it once was. Large organisations such as Boots and Tesco have been embarrassed by employees posting insulting comments about customers on Facebook. Tesco staff complained that customers were 'rude, smelly and stupid'. Virgin Atlantic staff also used the site to describe the airline's customers as 'chavs' and to question the safety record of the company. The company eventually sacked 13 employees following an investigation (Brand Republic, 2009).

A GfK report (Griffin, 2008) suggests that consumers feel that the ethical stance of companies is getting worse. This is despite the escalation of terms such as 'reputation management' and 'corporate social responsibility' which have come to the fore within organisations and within the general business lexicon in the last decade. Much of the talk about reputation has been focused on negative reputational stories – in such a situation it brings the management of reputation even more to the fore. If an organisation is able to maintain its reputation in such an environment then clearly it will be in a strong position.

The rise of the anti-globalisation movement over the last 20 years has helped to seriously erode trust in companies. The public now often expect companies to get things wrong and have developed a cynical view of the business community. At the worst this can result in the boycotting of companies by customers. Griffin delineates crisis management, a traditional reputation worry for which companies lay down plans and often have written procedures, and 'issues management', which involves dealing with the many different stories that circulate about a company during the course of its business. These are not crises but have the potential to further undermine an organisation and add to any reservoir of bad will that might exist. Issues such as redundancies or treatment of the work force, including working conditions of supplier companies, perhaps in the developing world, will fall under this heading.

> The public have developed a cynical view of the business community.

Levels of reputation – average or aggregate?

Reputation, of course, exists in context. There is the reputation of a product or service class within which the organisation is operating to consider. Then there is the industry reputation. Mini-cabs as an industry, for example, suffer from a poor reputation. Unreliable, dirty, poorly maintained and expensive are often criticisms levelled at the industry by consumers. Any new mini-cab business is therefore likely to find itself tarred with the same brush, and this can be both a problem and an opportunity.

There are multiple levels and categories of reputation to consider, therefore. Consider 'junk mail' as an interchangeable term for direct mail, and junk food likewise for fast food. Here are two legitimate industries conducting business among a public that have been made sceptical by the constant use of such negative terminology. What of the reputation of the users of particular products? Burberry's reputation took a blow when it became associated with 'chavs' in the UK, even though such consumers were often wearing counterfeit products (see Viewpoint 1.2, p. 15). Corporate reputation, however, refers to the organisation as a whole.

We also have impressions of the reputation of particular countries (Passow *et al.*, 2005). To many, Germany has a reputation for engineering prowess, hence the premium prices attracted for its automotive brands; Japan and its reputation for efficient production and zero defects set a new standard in car production that forced the rest of the world to raise its own standards; how has the United States' foreign policy affected that nation's reputation over the last decade? These views may be stereotypes but, once formed, it seems we are happy to endorse these countries and the industries that come from them as having strong reputations in their own field.

Bromley (2000) talks of three levels of information processing that help form impressions of a company:

- Information processing at a primary level – based upon personal experience
- Information processing at a secondary level – based upon what friends or colleagues say about an organisation or product
- Information processing at a tertiary level – based upon mass media information including paid advertising and unpaid-for publicity.

The primary effects are, of course, the strongest, but there are relatively few of these compared with the information provided by the other two sources. Think of how many organisations you have formed an opinion about based upon information received from the media rather than from your personal dealings with them.

The concepts of trust and reputation are clearly related.

As demonstrated in Figure 1.1, the concepts of trust and reputation are clearly related. Schweizer & Wijnberg (1999) agree that in most relevant studies the definition of reputation in some way includes the concept of credibility. Similarly to Bromley's (2000) explanation, they tell us that trust will play differing roles in reputation building depending upon the method of transmission of information. Individuals can acquire information about an organisation via direct interaction; they can receive the information secondhand from a more knowledgeable third party; or they can use other information in their possession to make a judgment on the reputation of the firm in question. Therefore the beliefs that individuals have in the flow of information towards them is closely related to trust, whereas it is the *overall* stock of information held about the company that forms the reputation. This would lead to the belief that a person may be willing to overlook less than satisfactory interactions as long as there is already a positive feeling towards the brand and its reputation.

It is the overall stock of information held about a company that forms its reputation.

This relates to the 'averaging' principle of reputation (Bennett & Gabriel, 2001). That is, customers tend to average out the information received about a company rather than 'aggregate' it, i.e. add one piece of bad information to another to form a cumulative score. They balance their impression of reputation, and this provides another benefit of building a positive reputation. A poor experience on one occasion will tend to be overlooked by a customer in favour of the generally good impression they have of the organisation.

The reputation of an organisation is therefore viewed from different levels. There is the 'individual' level and the 'corporate' level. At the former level the firm's audience uses the reputations and trustworthiness of the individuals within the firm in order to ascribe the same character to the organisation as a whole. The individual employees can therefore be the brand and the reputation of their firm and this is particularly the case in people-based service industries (see Viewpoint 1.1 on Ryanair).

Viewpoint 1.1 | **Flying in the face of reputation – Ryanair**

Ryanair is the low-cost airline that has reinvented the entire notion of air travel. In an industry previously based upon customer service, chief executive Michael O'Leary has boasted of how little attention is paid to customer service at his organisation. The company believed that its USP, in the form of budget flights (price budget strategy), signified that they could neglect the idea of amenable/amicable staff, expected levels of customer service or a recognisable complaints procedure.

Their aggressive, unapologetic chief executive shoots down ideas of relationship marketing and customer service; he says he doesn't care if customers are unhappy and claims that branding and marketing are a waste of time. He is, however, a master at getting free publicity for his organisation. Ryanair likes to position itself as the downtrodden, small start-up business, whereas it is the most profitable airline in the world.

From a reputational perspective, Ryanair does not fare too well in the traditional measures of successful airlines, but its low-cost, low-fare reputation elevates it in the minds of the hordes of travelling consumers. O'Leary boasts that all unnecessary costs are pared to the bone in order to provide the lowest possible fares. The customer may love the prices but there is growing discontent about the service, together with seemingly unavoidable extra charges (e.g. a charge for checking in online whilst simultaneously scrapping check-in desks at airports). Brown (2006) calls Ryanair 'the brand we love to hate'.

There is no doubt that this strategy has been successful and has differentiated the brand in a crowded marketplace. Thankfully Ryanair has a good safety record but the issues that surround the company due to its abrasive approach would be intensified should the airline suffer an accident. It is uncertain as to whether the current reputational deficiencies in the traditional areas for airline companies could withstand such an unfortunate event.

Less dramatically it is to be wondered if there is a tipping point at which some of the negative imagery surrounding the brand begins to impact upon its success. How easily would it now be able to alter its brand essence?

Question

Can it be good to have a negative reputation?

At a second level, there is a relationship between 'corporate' and 'collective' reputations. The reputation of an individual firm can be determined by an audience in the light of the overall reputation of the industry within which it operates. A mini-cab operator may thus find that his company has a poor reputation not due to an individual weakness but due to the generally unfortunate reputation of the competition. Conrad & Pooler (1998) agree, stating that reputation is a cognitive feature of an industry that crystallises an organisation's perceived ranking within the field of its rivals.

The challenge for a company may be to set the standards by which the whole industry is judged. Are there unique qualities about one firm that allow this to happen? Bromley (2001) discusses 'reputational space' which examines the total amount of interest and involvement in an organisation by stakeholders. The results of such an exercise could provide a share-of-space study, i.e. how large is the reputation of one organisation in comparison to competitors in the same field? Ewing *et al.* (1999) emphasise the growing importance of size in judging the reputation of business-to-business services. They state that it is increasingly difficult for smaller firms to gain business due to the perceived risk involved in the eyes of the client with an unfamiliar, untried firm. Although they find that a positive reputation does not eliminate risk, it is important in narrowing the choice set of a potential client.

Finally, there is the level of 'corporate and system' reputation. System trust is similar to social trust, the general standards of behaviour that are implicit in the business conducted by the firms within that industry sector. There may be certain standards of behaviour that are considered *de rigueur* within the industry that it is expected will be followed. Arthur Andersen was severely criticised for its part in the Enron scandal. Other members of the accountancy profession were quick to distance themselves from much of the behaviour exhibited by Andersen's staff, e.g. the shredding of crucial documents (see Exhibit 1.3). Reputation transfer has taken place here (Schweizer & Wijnberg, 1999). This is particularly important in an age of mergers in which we are living. Two companies may pool their collective reputations, which invariably can have serious implications for reputation management, particularly if they come from differing systems.

Reputation needs to be the responsibility of all: just as marketing is too important to leave in the hands of the marketing department, reputation is too important to leave to the public relations department. The management of reputation must therefore be embedded in the culture of the organisation. However, the organisation must speak with one voice when it comes to presenting co-ordinated integrated corporate communication. Inconsistent and contradictory corporate messages, however they are delivered, can damage a company's reputation.

> Reputation needs to be the responsibility of all; it is too important to leave to the public relations department.

We have mentioned the relevance of industry reputations. Of course, such notions are open to question, as demonstrated by Ryanair (Viewpoint 1.1).

Reputational association

A reputation may be affected by those with whom we associate.

The purpose of this chapter is to stimulate thought about reputation and corporate reputation in the wider sense. To this end it is helpful to consider how a reputation may be affected by those with whom we associate. Let us consider how the type of reputation will vary according to the industry we are in and the target audience we wish to attract.

To some extent the management of our reputation may be out of our hands. The people we associate with, the supplier companies that a brand deals with, or the customer or user groups of a brand can also enhance or damage the corporate reputation. For example, there was great consternation when Ben & Jerry's was taken over by Unilever. As a consequence it dropped from fifth to 30th place in the *Wall Street Journal*'s list of socially responsible firms (Simmons, 2006). The founders of the company have subsequently been openly critical of the Unilever brand and its reluctance to follow the clear ethical stance upon which the firm was founded.

Reputational association is therefore important (see, for example, the problems of negative associations for Burberry, Viewpoint 1.2). Even at the height of his extraordinary powers, World Heavyweight boxing champion Mike Tyson earned nothing outside the ring in terms of endorsements. Conviction for rape and a variety of unsavoury newsworthy incidents meant that no organisation wished to risk damaging their brand name, by associating it with Iron Mike. Similarly, the huge endorsements of the late Michael Jackson by Pepsi during the early 1980s disappeared rapidly following the child abuse allegations that dogged him over the last 15 years of his life. One's reputation, no matter how good, is fragile. An individual's reputation will be affected by those that they associate with, as well as their own actions and activities.

One's reputation, no matter how good, is fragile.

Viewpoint 1.2 Negative associations for Burberry

Burberry represents an excellent illustration of the problems of negative association, with an assortment of negative meanings associated with the brand due to the profile of its consumers. Burberry's history showcases a fascinating tale of a brand that was adopted by groups that represented the antithesis of their original clientele base, and which in the process found its reputation under threat.

Burberry, renowned for its classic tartan print, has been throughout the 20th century the quintessential British clothing brand. Its position as a bastion of Britishness was underscored by the fact that it was commissioned by the War Office to adapt the British Army officer's coat to suit the conditions of contemporary warfare, resulting in the 'trench coat'. Sported by the typical 'London gent' (whose noble background led to the clothing being associated with aristocratic leisure pursuits), its reputation as a classic/vintage

Exhibit 1.4 Burberry – fighting back against an association with 'chav' culture.
Source: © Bigpicturesphoto.com.

manufacturer remained intact until the 1990s, at which point it was assumed by the British football casual cult, leading to its synonymy with 'chav' culture (defined in the dictionary as 'A common person who is likely to be violent, use abusive language towards others and binge-drink on a regular basis. He/she is predisposed towards wearing "Burberry" clothing') and football hooligans, many of whom could be seen sporting a Burberry check baseball cap.

Association with customers so far removed from the original target market of the brand helped to undermine the long-established associations of quality painstakingly built by the brand throughout its long history. Such was the damage to the brand by this negative reputational association, that Burberry stopped production of its £50-a-time baseball cap. The fact that many of its undesirable consumers were wearing counterfeit versions of the original demonstrates another problem for the modern brand.

Burberry has fought back from this position. More recently the brand has successfully been relaunched with advertisements in high-end magazines such as *Vogue*, *Tatler* and *Harper's Bazaar*. Furthermore, a new creative designer has reworked the original aristocratic style, with much more subtle/understated usages of the vulgar/kitsch 'chav' version of the tartan print. The current website imagery also evidences the reversion to its fundamental classic style.

Question

Is it possible to avoid such negative reputational associations? How might this be achieved?

Reputation may vary – it's good to be bad?

The demographic profile of the target audience can have a significant impact upon the type of reputation that is seen as desirable. Infamy and ill repute can actually serve to multiply record sales and concert attendance and accompanying paraphernalia amongst particular musical genres, notably 'gangster rap'. Often narcissistic and introspective, with lyricists using the medium to brag about material possessions, and supported by the presentation of an overtly menacing persona, the aggressive style actively increases the reputation of artists by alienating more mainstream segments of society, including politicians. Gangster rappers' (even the title is implicitly negative) espousal of gun crime and the peddling of narcotics, not to mention the misogynistic undertones of many of their lyrics, do them no harm amongst their key target audiences.

Even more extreme are the examples of those rappers who suffered the ultimate cost, losing their lives as a direct result of leading the gangster lifestyle they actively championed in their music. Tupac Shakur and Notorious B.I.G. are the best examples: their homicides have rendered these two rap juggernauts even more iconic with their spirit surviving through their material, and with their mothers taking charge of their sons' estates by releasing a number of lucrative posthumous albums.

As with Shakur and B.I.G., in Elvis Presley and Frank Sinatra, both deceased, we have a pair of musicians who have become institutions. The wholesome content of their music and their righteous and pure stage images contrast with the way they conducted their private lives away from the media and the public gaze. Sinatra had known links to the Mafia, was a prolific drinker and a voracious womaniser. Presley lived a life replete with boundless and perennial excess, eventually dying of a prescription drug overdose. It appears that troubled musicians are exonerated for their renegade activities, eulogised after death and thus acquire a positive reputation. The death of such stars only appears to enhance their iconic status.

Associations can be forced upon an organisation, however. It is important to note that we live in an era of large-scale mergers, acquisitions and alliances. The joining together of two corporate brands has reputational issues, potentially positive and negative for both organisations. In respect of positive reputational associations, a 'halo effect' can be attained whereby the positive associations of one brand are reflected on its partner (see Viewpoint 1.3).

Viewpoint 1.3 | Pulp Juice Bars getting fitter

Pulp Juice Bars sought to squeeze the utmost out of the growing fresh juice market, forming a partnership with gymnasium chain Fitness First throughout Australia. Pulp Health has also established partnerships with Virgin Active and is currently seeking to expand its products to Richard Branson's brand of gyms in Britain and South Africa. It is seemingly an ideal match, 'a marriage of convenience'. The two companies subsume both the components of health (exercise, diet) and thus perfectly complement each other in what is known as the 'halo effect'.

The addition of juice bars (essentially just another amenity like a sauna/steam room) can only serve to enhance the appeal of the gym to prospective members whilst endorsing the juice brand on a wider scale. It also reciprocally reinforces both the gym's and juice company's commitment to health via the positive/vibrant associations. Hence, given the nature of the partnership, the risk to the primary brand is minimal, whilst the gain to the secondary brand is potentially enormous, in particular if it manages to establish a partnership with more than one of the most commonly recognised chains of gyms. The chairman of Pulp juices encapsulated these ideas by affirming, 'We are preaching to the converted in that health market, but that's why it's a perfect opportunity.'

Question

Provide three examples of organisations that have enhanced their own reputation via positive associations with unrelated companies.

The strategic use of reputation

Although companies use the language of reputation and talk of the management of reputation and its strategic importance, just how strategic is it? Does it really permeate the core of the business to all levels of employees and all the dealings and standards of behaviour that the company and its employees exhibit? To what extent has reputation permeated the company beyond the PR department and its element of press relations? A company may have drawn up crisis management plans but are the employees of the company ensuring in their day-to-day operations that they are protecting the reputation of the business, or indeed enhancing it?

> Are the employees of the company protecting the reputation of the business?

Surveys suggest that CEOs consider corporate reputation to be vital. Gaines-Ross (2008) reports an Economist Intelligence Unit study stating that executives considered reputation risk to surpass all other risks to their business. However, there may be social response bias here. No chief executive is going to say no when asked if their corporate reputation and its management are important to him/her. Do they, and more importantly, do the company, act on a day-to-day basis in a manner that protects and enhances its corporate reputation?

It is possible to have a poor reputation but still be a commercially successful company. The example of Ryanair in Viewpoint 1.1 and Primark (Minicase 3.2) suggest that providing low-price goods to customers will provide insulation from the effects of a negative reputation. However, perhaps in these

> It is possible to have a poor reputation but still be a commercially successful company.

instances there is a need to beware of the inherent danger of opinion polls (Griffin, 2008). It is interesting that certain polls often name celebrities as the most interesting as well as the most boring, as the best dressed and the worst dressed. As a nation we are over-polled and asked to give our opinion on everything from which companies are deemed to be the least ethical to which performers we like best in TV talent shows. Such opinions are often given without a great deal of thought and often contradict actual behaviour. Behavioural loyalty is far more valued by the firm than attitudinal loyalty, and it may be that customer choice is something that should also be considered within the reputation mix.

However, despite these difficulties and contradictions, reputation should not and cannot be ignored. It may be that whilst the organisation holds a key competitive advantage, such as lowest cost (in the case of Ryanair), it is able to circumnavigate reputational issues or ensure that its reputation is based thoroughly on its source of advantage. However, if there is a weakening of that advantage, then a poor reputation may become a real problem as customers who were looking for an excuse to move elsewhere take the opportunity. Market conditions may well have had a significant impact upon company success but if this changes then reputational issues may impact very quickly.

Reputations are falling

There is a good deal of evidence that the public are correct in their assumption that ethical practice is in decline. The fixation with financial results, and particularly the necessity to maintain and improve these in the short term, is surely a problem for companies that are trying to manage and improve their reputation. Are staff rewarded on the reputation rankings of the company or are they rewarded, and in some cases awarded huge bonuses, on the short-term financial success of the same (Griffin, 2008)?

Are staff rewarded on the reputation rankings of the company?

People will evaluate the importance of objectives to their organisation and themselves by the reward, and often the penalties on offer, for achieving or failing to meet these objectives. An organisation that rewards employees purely on financial results rather than perhaps also including some form of reputational incentive could be setting itself up for a reputational crisis. Has business managed to turn things on its head here? Has short-termism led us to the state where damaging reputations for the sake of short-term profitability has become the norm? The example of the banking industry surely demonstrates this (see Viewpoint 1.4).

Viewpoint 1.4   **Banking on a reputational crisis**

The banking crisis was caused by a liquidity shortfall in the United States. Its effects resulted in the governments of many countries implementing austerity measures. The collapse of house prices in the US was the starting point. Of course, the boom in prices had been unsustainable as banks aiming for continued growth put their faith in the sub-prime market. This basically involved offering mortgages to those on low incomes at initial, very favourable or deferred rates of interest. Once the initial or introductory period had expired, however, borrowers often found it difficult to refinance their loans on anywhere near as favourable terms. Defaulting on loans and subsequent repossession of properties worth less than the mortgage owed on them stoked the lack of confidence in the markets.

Low interest rates in general generated a consumer sales boom around the western world. Buying consumer goods on credit had become a way of life. As with the sub-prime market, the desire for profit from the banks and financial services industry led to a lack of checks to ensure those borrowing money were in a position to repay it. As the housing markets suffered, draining money from the financial institutions, so did the increase in defaulting on many other types of loan. The almost total lack of regulation on investment banks led to greater and greater risk-taking. As the funding of these organisations suffered, their ability to lend to others declined, spiralling into the general lack of confidence known as the credit crunch. Major investment bank Lehman Brothers collapsed in September 2008 causing panic in the financial markets. Governments were forced to bail out banks and financial institutions in order to preserve the market system.

In the UK, companies such as Royal Bank of Scotland and HBOS that had been declaring multi-billion-pound profits the previous year came within hours of total collapse, that is customers being unable to withdraw money from cash machines. Had this happened, civil disorder would have surely followed. Fuelled by a system of bonuses that led investment bankers to abandon caution in favour of high-risk speculation, and to bring many western economies to the brink, there has been little sign of humility from those responsible.

Exhibit 1.5 Banking crisis – the meltdown.
Source: Photolibrary.com.

Despite RBS declaring the biggest loss in corporate history (£24 billion in 2008) its management still deemed it appropriate to pay out £1 billion in bonuses to its staff that year. Despite being 84 per cent owned by UK taxpayers, the bonuses keep coming, RBS paying out £1.3 billion in 2010. Chief executive Sir Fred Goodwin, having received many millions of pounds in bonuses himself as he presided over this corporate disaster, retired early on a pension of £700,000 a year.

Whilst the bankers immediately returned to a system that created the problem in the first place, it was left to the public sector to pay for their greed by being first in line for the swingeing cuts imposed in the 2010 budget statement and public spending review.

Question

To what extent has the banking crisis damaged the reputation of business?

The reputation of international capitalism needs to be rebuilt.

Following the banking crisis there can be little doubt that the reputation of international capitalism needs to be rebuilt. For the last 20 years the popular view is that capitalism has triumphed over other economic models, most notably socialism. Why then has the very foundation upon which the capitalist world depends needed to be bailed out by the taxpayer in recent years? It would appear that the western capitalist system has been saved by socialism. It is surely a poor strategy that talks about the survival of the fittest but then itself refuses to be judged in the same way when its own self-inflicted hour of need arrives. We have expected too little from companies in terms of their reputational attributes or their brand values. Despite

We have expected too little from companies in terms of their reputational attributes.

having to be rescued and now being owned by the taxpayer, RBS still felt it must pay out huge sums in bonuses in 2009/2010. This rather begs the question when do its senior managers feel that it is *not* appropriate to pay a bonus?

It is clear that national governments also are at fault here. They have allowed a deregulated system to take over whereby institutions that are absolutely crucial to the way of life that we all know in effect regulate themselves. They have been judged by their peers and the market on the amount of profit made and their share price. It is a clear sign of change in the order of the world that companies worry more about the actions of pressure groups, often small and concentrating on single issues (e.g. animal welfare), than they do about regulation and control by national governments. It is within this extremely difficult situation that we discuss corporate reputation in this book.

The difficulty of controlling reputation in the 21st century

Our reputations are now at risk, due to the rapidly changing technological environment.

An individual's personal reputation has always been important. Friends and family often ask for advice before purchasing particular products or services. They rely on the fact that we have their best interests at heart in the advice given. However, our personal reputations are now at risk, due in part to the rapidly changing technological environment.

Many individuals have been victims of identity theft and have had their credit rating destroyed in a matter of weeks. People leave traces of their activities and behaviour in many different places. A manager considering someone for a job may type their name into Google to see what emerges. Being directed to a report in a local newspaper detailing their arrest on a charge of being drunk and disorderly 3 years ago, is unlikely to enhance their prospects. The internet now provides an archive of information available to people worldwide giving details of what might once have been a local and ephemeral issue.

Open privacy settings may allow an employer to access less than savoury photos of their staff on Facebook. Indeed, people leave their profiles wide open on social networking sites, encouraging others (including their managers) to draw a conclusion about their reputation that they may find unflattering. Otherwise innocent information and photographs, when taken out of context, can look damning. So, if individuals are not able to bury bad news, how difficult is it for companies to do the same?

Information posted on the internet presents a particular problem for companies. The vast majority of information on the net is not peer-reviewed. Essentially anyone can post anything that they please and our reputation can be called into question through this uncensored media. Individuals are able to create a website with the specific intention of posting negative commentary about any organisation they choose.

Individuals can gain worldwide publicity for their personal views that are completely disproportionate to their relevance and importance. If just a handful of others join a cause then a powerful viral campaign can be launched, calling into question the reputation of a company. All this can be achieved by the expenditure of only a small amount of time and even less money. Griffin (2008) questions whether these unelected and quite probably unrepresentative groups should be empowered by pandering to them or engaging them in dialogue. This highlights the difficulty of both protecting and managing reputation.

Is it easier for private companies, those without public shareholders, to have a strong reputation? Unencumbered by the demands of financial analysts, people whose own reputation is now at rock bottom, they are able to concentrate on the long-term reputational issues. The particular difficulties of the herd instinct of journalists and particularly financial advisers means that there is a multiplying effect of news, either good or bad. Good stories generate more good stories and vice versa. Once certain journalists get their teeth into your company it can be difficult to escape.

Some readers may recall the difficulties encountered by Sainsbury's several years ago when particular journalists were entering their stores daily with a shopping list to test their stock-out position. The store had got themselves a reputation

> We now have to build and protect our reputations amongst a sceptical public.

for poor inventory management, the heart of successful retailing, and this was exaggerated by hostile press stories. Newspaper journalists would visit a Sainsbury's store with a shopping list of popular goods and publish the failures of Sainsbury's to supply the goods on the list. Notably, when Justin King took over as chief executive he determined that the re-establishment of this basic competence would be the starting point of their reputational fightback.

Individuals are much more aware of their rights and are also more litigious than they used to be. They are increasingly fearful and worried about their safety and are encouraged in this by government and health and safety legislation. Any individual can demand to see information by reference to the Freedom of Information Act and may also cite the Human Rights Act in order to challenge a particular organisation.

Most people carry around mobile phones and can record video footage of scenes they come across. If these are of a particularly important newsworthy event they may appear on national or even international television news channels and websites. There are therefore a whole army of cameramen and women capable of recording something that may impact upon a corporate reputation.

Outrage was the reaction of the British public when the UK Members of Parliament expenses scandal broke in the *Daily Telegraph* and monopolised the news for much of 2009. Clear evidence of MPs manipulating their expenses to maximise their earnings and a series of ridiculous personal claims for items such as duck houses and moat cleaning brought the reputation of parliament to a new low. The decline in respect for the great institutions of state demonstrates the difficult landscape in which we now have to build and protect our reputations amongst a sceptical public – see Viewpoint 1.5.

Viewpoint 1.5	Congested reputation on a charge

The Greater Manchester congestion charge scheme was proposed in 2008 as part of a bid to the government's Transport Innovation Fund. The deal was that Greater Manchester would receive £3 billion from the fund to pay for improvements to public transport, notably an extension to the city's Metrolink tram system. In exchange, a vehicle congestion charge was to be levied based upon two zones, an outer ring bounded by the M60 motorway that surrounds the city and an inner zone around the city centre. The charge would have been operational at peak times in the morning and evening and would have cost a commuter travelling to work during office hours £6 per day by the time the scheme was due to become operational. A working person using their car to go to work would have been approximately £1,200 per year worse off under the scheme.

An extensive marketing campaign costing £34 million was launched supporting the introduction of the charge. Despite this huge spend and without a similarly funded campaign to oppose the plan, the referendum of Greater Manchester citizens comprehensively rejected the proposed charge by a vote of 79 per cent against and 21 per cent in favour in December 2008.

It was felt that it was reputational issues that led to the comprehensive rejection of the plans. Many who voted no to a scheme that would have ensured significant extra spending on public transport in exchange for a peak-time congestion charge for motorists did so even though they themselves were frequent users of public transport.

The reputation of the existing transport system is low, with frequent complaints to the *Manchester Evening News* about overcrowding, delays, fare increases and safety concerns, and this meant that the public did not trust the present providers of public transport to improve matters. The message from the public seemed to be that if the existing provider cannot be trusted to get the current system right, why should they be trusted to spend billions of pounds of public money expanding the system?

Secondly, the rejection of the scheme was a reflection of the poor reputation of politicians, both local and national, who lined up to support the introduction of the road tolls. Infamously, senior councillors from the 10 local authorities affected by the scheme attended a meeting in Bury to support it. Despite the venue being around the corner from the tram station, all the politicians arrived by car! The already heavily taxed motorist was not prepared to believe that the new congestion charge would not be introduced until improvements to public transport had been completed, as promised by politicians who themselves appeared to be above using public transport.

Question

What are the key reputational issues that face an operator of public transport?

Germany is said to be a country with high levels of trust (Ind, 1997) due to its Protestant ethic and the development of intermediate organisations between the family and the state. Denmark is similar. The UK should also be in a similar situation given its make-up. However, trust in companies here is low. Could this be linked to the Anglo-American shareholder-value, free-market approach that has developed over the last 30 years, encouraged by politicians? The general public in the western world are unimpressed. The public feel that companies will revert to their old ways as soon as the economic crisis has passed. According to the annual Edelman Trust Barometer, 2010, banks, unsurprisingly, are particularly disliked, while chief executives are also eyed with great suspicion. 'Trust in business has improved, but the patient has a long road to go for a full recovery,' said Richard Edelman, the chief executive at the PR firm.

The increase in trust in business belies its fragility. There is concern that short-term actions have been taken only as a result of the crisis and that government will need to remain a watchdog. Companies will have to prove the sceptics wrong and show they can achieve both profit and purpose. Worryingly for companies, chief executives are also held in low regard. In the US, just a quarter of the public trust chief executives; in the UK it is a third (BBC News website, 2010).

In the US, just a quarter of the public trust chief executives; in the UK it is a third.

Corporate reputation as 'Gestalt'

Corporate reputation comprises numerous, intelligible constituent parts and these will be discussed as this book progresses. It is important to realise, however, that reputation is a sum of the parts of the business or brand. Indeed the idea of reputation as 'Gestalt' is to consider that the reputation is greater than the mere sum of all the parts of the organisation. Thus, enterprises should ideally focus on procuring a comprehensively positive reputation, one which might be referred to as the 'total reputation', diligently cultivated via nurturing their intrinsic and extrinsic brand values, identity and image.

> Reputation is a sum of the parts of the business or brand.

Indeed, the individual components precipitate a synergistic effect and so no single facet can be optimised without careful consideration of the entire set-up. The ideal situation would be to attain the 'total reputation' since a chequered reputation impacts negatively upon all facets of a brand.

Chapter summary

In order to consolidate your understanding of the rise of corporate reputation, below are the key points summarised against each of the learning objectives.

1. Define what is meant by corporate reputation

Fombrun (1996) describes reputation as 'the overall estimation in which a company is held by its constituents' and states that it is 'the net perception of a company's ability to meet the expectations of all its stakeholders'. Reputation takes into account the overall opinion of a large variety of stakeholders, not just customers.

Academically, corporate reputation is not a stand-alone discipline but one that draws from many different perspectives. These include strategic management, organisational theory, economics, marketing, communications, accounting and finance (Fombrun & van Riel, 1997; Balmer, 1998).

2. Discuss the rise in importance of corporate reputation

Three-quarters of us now work in the service industry and the reputation of the company is often the key way that a customer can judge an intangible offering. Many studies show that those companies with the strongest corporate reputations outperform their rivals financially together with having increased levels of customer satisfaction.

There is a greater desire to measure reputation nowadays. Fortune 500 in the US, Management Today in the UK together with employee-based studies such as the *Sunday Times*' Best Companies to Work For guide ensure that corporate reputation is high up the news agenda.

3. Determine if corporate reputation matters

A good reputation provides the organisation with a competitive advantage. In general a company with a strong reputation will have a higher share price and more loyal customers. We have also moved away from the 'business is business' attitude and expect companies to behave in an ethically sound manner.

Certain companies that were considered great not too long ago have now disappeared completely or may be suffering financial difficulties. It is important to actually manage the corporate reputation to ensure that this decline is avoided.

4. Consider the various levels of corporate reputation

There are multiple levels of reputation to consider. The product class, the industry and the country are examples of areas that will have their own reputation and this will impact upon the corporate reputation of the individual firm. Bromley (2000) describes three levels of information processing that help to form impressions of a company. The primary level is based upon our personal experience. At a secondary level we consider reputation based upon what friends or colleagues say about an organisation or product. Finally, at a tertiary level we consider reputation based upon mass media information including paid advertising and unpaid-for publicity.

A benefit of building a positive reputation is the 'averaging' principle of reputation whereby a poor experience on one occasion will tend to be overlooked by the customer in favour of the generally good impression they have of the organisation. If our company is not as well known, consumers may 'aggregate' its reputation by allowing a piece of bad information to outweigh any positive messages they have previously received.

5. Stress the importance of reputational association and how reputation may vary in differing market sectors and organisations

Our corporate reputation is not created or maintained in isolation. In today's environment it is important for all elements of our supply chain to equally maintain the reputational criteria we set for our own company. Similarly we may find ourselves encountering difficulty through our customer's behaviour or via counterfeit products.

Of course it may be an advantage in certain industries to have a more edgy and non-mainstream reputation. Modern business involves mergers, takeovers and acquisitions and the joining together of two brands creates reputational issues, potentially positive and negative for both organisations. In respect of positive reputational associations, a 'halo effect' can be attained whereby the positive associations of one brand are reflected on its partner.

6. Explore the difficulties of managing a corporate reputation in the 21st century

We live in the age of 24-hour media where businesses are legitimate news stories. The internet and social media mean that a small number of people can have a disproportionately negative effect upon the reputation of an organisation. The general public are also far more cynical about the motives of businesses, and the banking crisis has rocked the very foundations upon which western capitalism is based.

Under such difficult circumstances the organisation must focus upon cultivating its overall corporate reputation in order that a synergistic effect is created.

Discussion questions

1. Outline the reasons that corporate reputation has become an important area for both practitioners and academics.
2. Provide a definition of corporate reputation.
3. Summarise how corporate reputation is assessed from the perspectives of the academic disciplines of accounting, economics, marketing, sociology, communication, organisational theory and strategy.
4. Weber Shandwick claims that as much as 63 per cent of a company's market value is attributable to its reputation. Is this a realistic claim?
5. Why has trust in companies declined over recent years? How can the management of corporate reputation improve this situation?

6. Explain the concepts of average and aggregate reputation.

7. Ryanair does not care very much about customer service yet is a very successful airline. What does this say for the management discipline of corporate reputation management?

8. In what circumstances might it be good to have a bad reputation?

9. Critics argue that reputation management should be built into the reward structures of the organisation. Provide examples of how this may be achieved.

10. Why is it more difficult to control corporate reputation in the 21st century than it has been previously?

References

Argenti, P.A. (1998). *Corporate Communication*, 2nd edition. London: McGraw Hill.

Balmer, J.M.T. (1998). Corporate identity and the advent of corporate marketing. *Journal of Marketing Management* 14(8), 963–996.

BBC Website (2010). 'Davos 2010: Business struggles to regain public trust'. Online: http://news.bbc.co.uk/1/hi/business/8481238.stm. Accessed: 10 September 2010.

Bennett, R. & Gabriel, H. (2001). Corporate reputation, trait covariation and the averaging principle: the case of the UK pensions mis-selling scandal. *European Journal of Marketing* 35(3/4), 387–413.

Berens, G. & van Riel, C.B.M. (2001). Does corporate brand value affect product evaluations? *Proceedings of the 5th International Conference on Corporate Reputation, Identity and Competitiveness*, Paris.

Blackstad, M. & Cooper, A. (1995). *The Communicating Organism*. London: IPD Publications.

Brand Republic (2009). 'Tesco investigates malicious staff comments on Facebook'. Online: http://www.brandrepublic.com/News/874256/Tesco-investigates-malicious-staff-comments-Facebook/. Accessed: 1 July 2010.

Bromley, D.B. (2000). Psychological aspects of corporate identity, image and reputation. *Corporate Reputation Review* 3(3), 240–252.

Bromley, D.B. (2001). Relationships between personal and corporate reputation. *European Journal of Marketing* 35(3/4), 316–334.

Brown (2006). Ryanair – The brand we love to hate. In: Schroeder, J.E., Salzer-Mörling, M. & Askegaard, S., eds, *Brand Culture*. London: Routledge.

Businessweek (1984). Oops: Who's excellent now? 5 November 1984.

de Chernatony, L. & Harris, F. (2000). Developing corporate brands through considering internal and external stakeholders. *Corporate Reputation Review* 3(3), 268–274.

Conrad, C. & Pooler, S. (1998). *Strategic Organizational Communication*, 4th edition. Fort Worth: Harcourt Brace.

Dowling, G.R. (1994). *Corporate Reputations*. London: Kogan Page.

Ewing, M.T., Caruana, A., & Loy, E.R. (1999). Corporate reputation and perceived risk in professional engineering services. *Corporate Communications* 4(3), 121–128.

Fombrun, C.J. (1996). *Reputation: Realizing the Value from the Corporate Image*. Boston: Harvard Business School Press.

Fombrun, C.J., Gardberg, N.A. & Sever, J.M. (2000). The reputation quotient: a multi-stakeholder measure of corporate reputation. *The Journal of Brand Management* 7(4), 241–255.

Fombrun, C.J. & van Riel, C.B.M. (1997). The reputational landscape. *Corporate Reputation Review* 1, 1/2, 5–13.

Fombrun, C.J. & van Riel, C.B.M. (2004). *Fame and Fortune: How Successful Companies Build Winning Reputations*. New Jersey: FT-Prentice Hall.

Friedman, M. (1970). 'The Social Responsibility of Business is to Increase its Profits'. *The New York Times Magazine*, 13 September.

Gaines-Ross, L. (2008). *Corporate Reputation: 12 Steps to Safeguarding and Recovering Reputation*. New Jersey: Wiley.

Griffin, A. (2008). *New Strategies for Reputation Management: Gaining Control of Issues, Crises and Corporate Social Responsibility*. London: Chartered Institute of Public Relations.

Ind, N. (1997). *The Corporate Brand*. Basingstoke: Macmillan Business.

Kotler, P., Wong, V., Saunders, J. & Armstrong, G. (2005). *Principles of Marketing*, 4th European edition. London: Pearson Education.

Manchester Evening News (2009). 'Shut down this Primark sweatshop'. 12 January 2009.

Passow, T., Fehlmann, R. & Grahlow, H. (2005). Country reputation – from measurement to management: the case of Liechtenstein. *Corporate Reputation Review* 7(4), 309–326.

Peters, T. & Waterman, R.H. (1982). *In Search of Excellence: Lessons from America's Best Run Companies*.

van Riel, C.B.M. & Fombrun, C. (2007). *Essentials of Corporate Communication*. Abingdon: Routledge.

Schweizer, T.S. & Wijnberg, N.M. (1999). Transferring reputation to the corporation in different cultures: individuals, collectives, systems and the strategic management of corporate reputation. *Corporate Reputation Review* 2(3), 249–266.

Simmons, J. (2006). *The Invisible Grail: How Brands can use Words to Engage with Audiences*. London: Marshall Cavendish Business.

Yoon, E., Guffey, H.J. & Kijewski, V. (1993). The effects of information and company reputation on intentions to buy a business service. *Journal of Business Research* 27(3), 215–228.

Chapter 2
The scope of corporate reputation

Reputation is not only a multi-dimensional concept, but it is also complex, involving a range of stakeholders. Reputation can be considered from an internal perspective, involving the important role that employees have to play in building a corporate reputation. There is also an external perspective, represented by customers, suppliers, the public, the media and other stakeholders. It is important therefore to understand the way in which these internal and external perspectives are linked.

Aims and learning objectives

The aim of this chapter is to examine the scope of corporate reputation and to introduce the building blocks that underpin the corporate reputation management process.

The learning objectives of this chapter are to:

1. Outline the difference between shareholders and stakeholders
2. Consider the relationship between corporate identity, corporate image and corporate reputation
3. Understand the building blocks of corporate reputation
4. Discuss the various forces that impact upon an organisation
5. Identify the criteria that influence our view of the corporate reputation of an organisation.

Introduction

As defined in Chapter 1, corporate reputation embraces the overall whole and not the narrow interests of any one group. This chapter discusses the relationship of corporate identity and corporate image with corporate reputation. In order to do this, it is important to ensure that we are familiar with the differences between shareholders and stakeholders.

Whilst it is fairly straightforward to define shareholders as individuals who own shares of a company's stock, thus having a vested interest in its economic performance, the categorisation of stakeholders is more ambiguous. The dictionary definition claims that it is 'a person with an interest or concern in something, especially a business' (www.oxforddictionaries.com), but this is capable of multiple interpretations. Indeed, this unrestricted classification can relate to virtually all members of society, including the shareholders themselves, employees, customers, local government, national government, media, trade unions, financial institutions, investors, suppliers, regulators as well as local communities and the general public (see Figure 2.1 for an example of a pharmaceutical company's stakeholders).

> **The corporate brand deals with the requirements of multiple stakeholders.**

Hatch & Shultz (2003) point out that the key to corporate branding, as opposed to product branding, is that rather than simply focusing on customers the corporate brand needs to deal with the requirements of multiple stakeholders. As far as reputation management is concerned, the two most important stakeholders in a commercial enterprise are likely to be the employees and the customers (Roper & Davies, 2007).

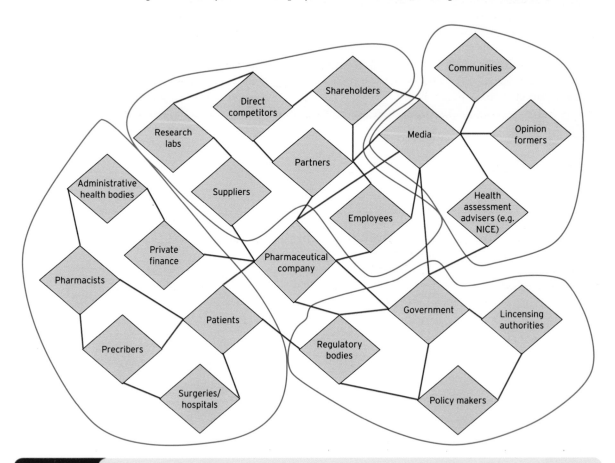

| **Figure 2.1** | A pharmaceutical company's clustered and networked stakeholders. The links shown are only indicative of the complex network of connections. (With acknowledgement to John Dixon.) |

The importance of employees is emphasised within the corporate branding literature (Ind, 1997; Wilson, 1997, 2001; de Chernatony, 2001; Harris & de Chernatony, 2001; Hatch & Schultz, 2001, 2003; Balmer & Gray, 2003). Employees, through their attitudes and behaviours, can make or break a corporate brand. They interact with customers and any negative attitudes will soon impact upon a customer's experience of the brand. Employees therefore need to become empathic with the corporate culture. Indeed, salient corporate brands tend to be those where staff clearly understand and share the vision, mission and values of the company. In addition, both Hart & Murphy (1998) and Ind (1997, 1998) state that strong corporate brands are able to recruit and retain the best people.

de Chernatony & Segal-Horn (2003) discuss the importance of values to service brands, and confirm that values are a key part of an organisation's reputation. Shared values between stakeholders will help to unify and strengthen a corporate brand. Ind (1997, 1998), de Chernatony & Harris (2000) and Pringle & Gordon (2001) all consider the importance of alignment between an employee's values and behaviour and the expectations of customers. If this is the case then the causes of satisfaction with the brand should be the same amongst differing stakeholder groups.

> **Values are a key part of an organisation's reputation.**

A strong corporate brand requires a clear corporate mission and philosophy. A brand's personality and identity need to be clearly understood and each stakeholder's perspective of these perceptions needs to be measured (Balmer, 1998). The emergence of gaps between differing stakeholders' perspectives of a corporate brand (Aaker, 1996; de Chernatony, 1999; Bickerton, 2000; Harris & de Chernatony, 2001) is considered a threat that must be guarded against.

Employees must be convinced about the quality of the service provided and have a strong level of job satisfaction. Whereas, consumers exchange economic resources for goods and services, employees exchange human resources for jobs and money, and should be content in order to be enthusiastic about expending their energy and providing quality.

Indeed, as stressed by Smith (2003) in his presentation of the Shareholder vs. Stakeholder debate, a stakeholder-centric policy is more beneficial to an organisation in the long term. It is, of course, true that stakeholder theory is more aligned to the direct concerns of consumers, who are likely to be more concerned by a company's customer service guidelines than its share prices.

Connecting employees with the company

It is clear that employees are a key stakeholder in the success of a corporate brand. However, there is a difficulty in determining the nature and strength of the connection between an employee and their company. In the past, the relationship between an employee and employer was often guided or structured around the association of the workplace and the social life of staff. In the days of the large industrial employers, such as the steelworks and mining industries, companies often ensured that staff were provided with access to their own sports facilities and social clubs, which sometimes included bands and even choirs. In these circumstances, the relationship between employees and the organisation was often strong and employees understood the organisation's values.

Since the decline and disappearance of such large-scale employers, however, work life and social life have increasingly become separate entities. The implications of such a development are inauspicious from a corporate perspective. The resulting weaker affiliation that employees generally feel towards their companies suggests they might not understand or live up to the values of the organisation. de Chernatony (2001) discusses the importance of the connection between employees and their organisation and concludes that employees are critically important in promoting and furthering a company's brand values. The connection between company and employee is clearly demonstrated by the Cadbury example outlined in Viewpoint 2.1.

> **Employees are critically important in promoting and furthering a company's brand values.**

Viewpoint 2.1 | Full cream employment at Cadbury

Cadbury was perhaps the original philanthropic business. It ensured the provision of housing, schooling and other social activities for those (and their immediate families) who worked for the corporation. In the 19th century, a higher standard of living was experienced by Cadbury workers than by the majority of the working class.

Many philanthropic companies invested in the surrounding areas in which their factories were situated. By 1900, George Cadbury had financed the construction of an estate that included 313 cottages and houses set on 330 acres (1.3 km²) of land. His objective in building the estate was, in his own words, to 'ameliorate the condition of the working-class and labouring population . . . by the provision of improved dwellings, with gardens and open space to be enjoyed therewith'. The designs of Bournville village close to Birmingham became a blueprint for many other model village estates around Britain. His legacy is an aesthetically delightful village with an enduring spirit, still deemed by its current residents as one of the nicest habitats in the UK. Loyal and diligent labourers were respected, enjoyed good working conditions and were well remunerated. Cadbury also pioneered pension schemes, joint works committees and a full staff medical service.

It is also interesting that Bournville has largely remained a 'dry zone' since its inception, on the wishes of Mr Cadbury who was a Quaker and thus adhered to the alcohol-free policy of the sect. Rowheath Pavilion is the only recognised licensed members' bar in the area. These work-based societies were invariably under-pinned by an evangelical rationale such as the politico-religious fervour embodied by the Quakers. Cadbury thought that his staff required life training together with reliable employment. It entailed a conventional existence centred around an ethos of hard work, abstinence and devotion to God.

The Cadburys also encouraged health and fitness in their workforce, integrating park and recreation areas into the Bournville village plans, and promoting all forms of outdoor sports. As the village developed, more land was purchased and football and hockey pitches created, together with a running track. Rowheath Pavilion was planned by George Cadbury and inaugurated in July 1924, functioning as the clubhouse and changing rooms for the acres of sports playing fields. The addition of bowling greens, a fishing lake and an outdoor swimming lido provided an indication of the importance the Cadbury family placed upon healthy recreation for their workforce and how central the company was to the lives of their staff.

Balls and dinners were held in the pavilion, and the whole area was specifically for the benefit of the Cadbury workers and their families. Sports facilities were free of charge to Cadbury workers. Amongst many other developments was the quaint cricket pitch adjacent to the factory site. A picture of the cricket ground appeared on boxes of Milk Tray chocolates during the 1950s and 1960s.

When one also considers the schools and medical facilities provided, it is not difficult to imagine the bond that existed between the workers and their employer. All of this was established long before there was talk of corporate branding and reputation management.

Question

What can the 21st century company do to facilitate stronger bonds between the organisation and its employees?

These philanthropic enterprises had an integral involvement in the lives of their workers. Indeed, many of these large-scale factory and mining companies created a social infrastructure that not only incorporated sport and music, but also provided better health and financial protection for their employees than other companies in the first half of the 20th century.

The employers' central position in the life of their communities was gradually eroded, along with the mines and heavy industry. Over the second half of the last century, work became far more functional, to the point where it is currently viewed purely as a form of employment, with other facets of social activity beyond its remit. Other issues concerning employees, such as life/health insurance/pension schemes, have also become a relatively distant aspect of a corporation's sphere of activity. Final-salary pension schemes, for example, are being closed at a rapid rate. The paternalistic employers of previous eras acquired a positive reputation, inspiring confidence, security and loyalty from their employees, who consequently viewed their jobs as a lifetime commitment. Today, employers are much less paternalistic, not so involved with their employees' lives outside of working hours, and as a result find it hard to develop the buy-in associated with a positive reputation.

In the modern business world we are accustomed to much higher rates of staff turnover. Ideas about a job for life have disappeared and there is a feeling of reduced loyalty from both employee and employer. However, whilst clearly a contributing factor, lower levels of employee loyalty cannot be the only reason for lower levels of employer compassion. Perhaps the change from manual labour to one based more on technology has helped lower the levels of employee interaction and camaraderie.

> In the modern business world, there is a feeling of reduced loyalty from both employee and employer.

The result appears to be a less united workforce, which can only decrease loyalty towards an organisation. It is true that certain companies, e.g. the traditional John Lewis or the more contemporary Google, still exhibit some of the paternalistic features mentioned earlier in an attempt to increase and maintain employee loyalty and we will examine some of the modern-day success stories.

Paternalistic employers, such as Cadbury, had what is now referred to as a clear corporate identity. Having a clearly defined corporate identity is the first step towards having a strong reputation. However, these terms – corporate identity, image and reputation – are often used interchangeably. This is misleading, as each has a clear, distinct building block and a clear role to play in the development and maintenance of corporate reputation. The next part of this chapter introduces and explores the relationship between them.

Corporate identity and its relationship with corporate image and corporate reputation

van Riel & Fombrun (2007, p. 61) consider identity and identification in the context of questions such as 'Who are we?', 'What do we stand for?', 'What is our core purpose?', and 'What does it mean to be involved in this company?' An important question for organisations is this: Is the public perception of an organisation similar to the story the organisation tells about itself? If there is a misbalance then there will be a negative effect on corporate reputation. Having a positive reputation will pro-

> Who are we, what do we stand for, what is our core purpose, and what does it mean to be involved in this company?

tect the organisation from the occasional glitch, but a consistent difference or gap between the two messages (internal identity and external image) will create lasting damage.

The first task when establishing a corporate brand, therefore, is to build the identity of the organisation. It is essential that the internal identity be based upon solid values and a discernible value system, if a strong corporate brand is to be constructed. The employees of an organisation must be clear about what this identity is and what it stands for. If a brand cannot convince its own employees about its direction and reason for being, its distinctiveness and its purpose, then how is it possibly going to convince outsiders?

Brand management at this stage needs to be based on an understanding of how a company is perceived by its stakeholders. Once this is known, the organisation can set about improving weak areas or concentrate on improving misconceptions, and perhaps narrowing the gap between the internal and external views. A consistent expression of this identity is needed, and providing and maintaining this is one of the functions of corporate communication. However, it is important not to get bogged down in the visual interpretation of corporate identity. The logos, livery and letterheads are the visual manifestation of corporate identity. More important is what this signifies. There is, of course a strong link between identity and corporate culture.

Chapter 1 detailed the differing academic perspectives on corporate reputation. Similarly, corporate identity has some quite different interpretations depending upon the academic background of the researcher.

The corporate personality is central to the corporate identity of any organisation.

van Riel & Fombrun (2007) state that the corporate identity mix comprises communication, behaviour and symbolism. Such a mix is the way in which an organisation manifests its personality. The corporate personality is central to the corporate identity of any organisation. Corporate image is the way that stakeholders and those external to the company interpret this personality.

Balmer & Greyser (2003, p. 37) states that 'identity management is concerned with the conception, development and communication of an organization's mission, philosophy and ethos'. Identity comes from within the organisation and this will be very much linked to the prevailing culture of the firm.

Identity is linked to the prevailing culture of the firm.

An organisation's corporate communication must reinforce this identity internally to the employees as well as externally to stakeholders. Many managers think that communications are just to be aimed at the external audiences, mainly customers. This is not correct. The development of a corporate brand must first be based on communications with employees.

Albert & Whetten (1985) stated that in order to determine the identity of an organisation, the viewpoints of members of the organisation should be taken and defined against three criteria:

- **Centrality** – what characteristics are widely shared among members throughout the organisation?
- **Continuity** – what characteristics of the organisation are most used by members to link the past to its present and future?
- **Uniqueness** – what characteristics of the organisation appear most unique to members in terms of their ability to differentiate the organisation from other similar organisations?

The corporate identity of The Body Shop has been a clear factor in its success (see Viewpoint 2.2). This identity is based upon its guiding philosophy for principled business. This is clearly understood by its employees and is therefore passed on to the external stakeholders of the company.

Viewpoint 2.2   **Identity personified at Body Shop**

Anita Roddick was the founder of The Body Shop, a British cosmetics company producing and retailing beauty products that helped to shape ethical consumerism. The company was one of the first to prohibit the use of ingredients tested on animals and one of the first to promote fair trade with developing countries. Roddick was also involved in activism and campaigning for environmental and social issues, including involvement with Greenpeace and *The Big Issue* and, of course, as her brand proclaimed, being against animal testing. Her pioneering activism within the corporate scene had moulded her (and her company) into a cult figure with a devoted customer-base.

Body Shop's identity is closely related to nature and natural things. Their corporate messages talk of 'beauty' and that there is only one way to secure beauty and this is 'nature's way'. The emphasis of the product offering is therefore on sourcing completely natural products in a sustainable manner. Roddick talked of 'changing the way business is carried out' and it is quite certain that her approach has impacted both consumers' and businesses' perspectives when considering their own identities and value systems.

The genius of bringing sustainable products to a mass market led Body Shop to grow exponentially to become a huge concern with 2,400 stores in over 60 countries. The company often helped to promote itself, not through traditional advertising/marketing messages but through supporting social and environmental campaigns such as that criticising the stereotypical media images of women, e.g. unrealistically skinny supermodels.

Throughout her life Roddick was a fierce critic of the global cosmetics industry, criticising both its attitudes towards and imagery of women and its insensitivity to the environment. Supporting programmes such

There are 3 billion women who don't look like supermodels and only 8 who do.

THE BODY SHOP

KNOW YOUR MIND LOVE YOUR BODY

Exhibit 2.1 The Body Shop – associated with social campaigns such as that criticising the media's stereotyping of women.
Source: The Body Shop, with permission.

as Trade not Aid, which campaigns for fair labour rates and working conditions and equal pay, Body Shop has shown that it is by no means anti-capitalist; it demonstrates that international business can be conducted in a fair and open manner. Over the years such a strong internal identity has led to customers becoming proponents of the brand (when a brand becomes so popular, primarily owing to the cause it espouses, customers inevitably become supporters/ambassadors as opposed to mere customers).

Controversially The Body Shop was acquired by cosmetics giant L'Oréal in 2006 for a price of £652.3 million. L'Oréal did not have the reputation for social justice that was claimed by Anita Roddick and indeed has been continually dogged by accusations of testing its cosmetics on animals. This would be in direct contradiction to one of The Body Shop's founding principles; the charge is denied by L'Oréal. Roddick herself claimed that she would be able to influence the corporate giant from within as a result of the takeover; however, she died in 2007.

Question

Outline the principles that The Body Shop's corporate identity was built upon. Has its identity changed since the takeover by L'Oréal?

Table 2.1	Five identities: the AC²ID Test
Identity	**Explanation**
Actual	This refers to the current attributes of the corporation. This is shaped by ownership issues, the prevailing management style, activities, the markets it works within and the set of values held by management and staff
Communicated	This identity is revealed through 'controllable' corporate communications paid for by the corporation and through 'non-controllable' communications such as word-of-mouth and media comment
Conceived	This refers to the opinions held by different stakeholders of the organisation's corporate image, corporate reputation and corporate branding
Ideal	The ideal identity refers to the optimum positioning of the organisation in its markets within a given time-frame. Strategic planning and research will indicate what is realistically achievable. The ideal identity may fluctuate due to macro-environmental changes, e.g. the diminished reputation of the oil industry after Deepwater Horizon (see this book's website www.pearsoned.co.uk/roperfill)
Desired	The desired identity reflects the vision for the organisation. Perhaps this is more ideological or aspirational than the ideal identity, which is based on more solid research

Source: Based on Balmer & Greyser (2002).

If there are gaps between the corporate identity and the corporate image, they should be addressed. This demands an initial audit to discover the current identity, and this should entail a consideration of the corporate character. The work of Balmer & Wilson (1998) explains that the effective management of corporate identity will result in a favourable corporate image and that, over time, this will result in a positive corporate reputation.

> The effective management of corporate identity will result in a favourable corporate image, which will result in a positive corporate reputation.

Balmer & Greyser (2002, p. 73) introduce what they call their AC²ID Test and talk of it 'encapsulating a mosaic of five different identities'. These are set out in Table 2.1.

When an organisation grows larger or operates on multiple sites, there is a distinct possibility of multiple sub-identities forming, adding to the difficulties of managing the corporate brand. The AC²ID Test demonstrates this notion of the existence of multiple identities.

Where corporate identity is concerned, management need to consider both the visual and verbal identity of the brand. Simmons (2006) refers to a brand's 'tone of voice', that is, what it says to its stakeholders and how it says it. A strong identity leads to a unity of purpose between the leaders of organisations and their employees (van Riel & Fombrun, 2007).

> A strong identity leads to a unity of purpose between the leaders of organisations and their employees.

The building blocks of corporate reputation

Corporate reputation as an academic area is relatively new. Research from the 1950s and 1960s looked at reputation from an external perspective, that of the customer. During the 1970s the views of staff, the internal perspective, received more attention, although both perspectives tended to be labelled as 'image' (Kennedy, 1977). Abratt (1989) points out the lack of an agreed glossary for the subject. The lack of clarity over an agreed lexicon has also resulted in a number of different models being produced over the years that link image and reputation

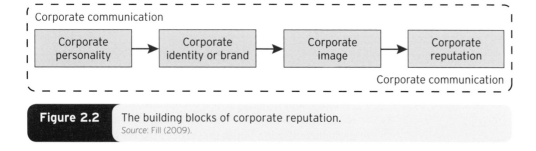

Figure 2.2 The building blocks of corporate reputation.
Source: Fill (2009).

(i.e. Kennedy, 1977; Abratt, 1989; Fombrun, 1996; Gray & Balmer, 1998; Hatch & Schultz, 1997; Whetten, 1997; Balmer, 1998; Davies & Miles, 1998).

The key focus of these models is the image of an organisation from a customer perspective. However, in the study of reputation it is vital that the perspective of employees is also taken into account. We have detailed the importance of the workforce, as it is important to consider the internal, employee view as well as the external view. This is because the attitude of the employee will ultimately have an impact on the external perspective of a brand. Associations can be made between the two perspectives and any gaps between the two can be identified.

> The attitude of the employee will ultimately have an impact on the external perspective of a brand.

As mentioned earlier, the terms identity, image, personality and communication should be considered as building blocks of corporate reputation. It is therefore important to understand clearly what these terms mean and how they are used in this book. Figure 2.2 sets out a visual interpretation of the building blocks. Each of these blocks is discussed throughout the book but here it is useful to set out what each means and embraces.

Corporate personality, sometimes regarded as the corporate character, refers to the core nature of an organisation, the way the organisation is. There are many facets that make up the corporate personality, but two key ones can be identified: the dominant corporate culture and the process through which strategy is developed (Markwick & Fill, 1997). These facets are inter-related.

> Corporate personality refers to the core nature of an organisation.

Organisational culture shapes the way the organisation behaves, both internally and externally. The strategy process refers to the different ways in which strategy is developed in organisations. Generally these can be regarded as emergent, incremental and planned processes. However, the most important aspect concerns the vision, mission and values. Are these understood? Are they enacted? How are they communicated? How do these shape the behaviour of employees and do they complement the actions of the organisations? Corporate personality refers to the totality of the characteristics that constitute an organisation and to what an organisation actually is.

Corporate identity is about how an organisation wants to be perceived, how it presents itself to both internal and external stakeholders. Identity is a means by which an organisation differentiates and positions itself with regard to other organisations and the achievement of its performance goals. According to Olins (1989), management of corporate identity can communicate three key ideas to its audiences: what the organisation is, what it does and how it does it. To achieve these, identity can be considered to be a configuration of three elements: symbolism, planned and unplanned communications, and the behaviour of management and employees. These are explored in later chapters.

> Corporate identity is how an organisation presents itself to both internal and external stakeholders.

Bernstein (1984) makes an important point when he observes that all organisations have an identity, whether they like it or not. Some organisations choose deliberately to manage their identities, just as individuals choose to frequent particular shops or restaurants, drive certain cars or wear specific fabrics or colours. Other organisations take less care over their identities and the way in which they transmit their identity cues, and as a result confuse and mislead members of their networks and underperform in the markets in which they operate. Corporate identity is the way an organisation presents itself to all of its stakeholders.

Corporate image is the perception that different audiences have of an organisation.

Corporate image is the perception that different audiences have of an organisation and results from the audience's interpretation and meaning that is ascribed to the cues presented by an organisation. As Bernstein (1984) says, 'the image does not exist in the organisation but in those that perceive the organisation'.

The images that stakeholders hold of an organisation are a result of a combination of different elements, but are essentially a distillation of the values, beliefs and attitudes that an individual or organisation has of that organisation. The images held by members of a marketing channel, a regulatory body or employees, for example, may vary according to their individual experiences, and will almost certainly be different from those that management thinks exist. This means that an organisation does not have a single image, but may have multiple images.

Corporate image is what internal and external stakeholders perceive the organisation to be.

Corporate reputation is a collective term referring to all stakeholders' views.

Corporate reputation is a collective term referring to all stakeholders' views of corporate reputation, including identity and image (see Fombrun, 1996; Hatch & Schultz, 1997; Balmer, 1998; Davies & Miles, 1998).

van Riel & Fombrun (2007) claim that in order to build a favourable reputation, four attributes need to be developed: credibility, trustworthiness, reliability and responsibility. Whilst the choice of these four particular criteria can be challenged, it is important to appreciate that corporate reputation refers to the views of all stakeholders, internal and external, and not just customers.

Corporate communication enables linkages between the building blocks.

Corporate communication enables linkages between the building blocks. It provides for a corporate reputation process to be developed and sustained. According to van Riel & Fombrun (2007), corporate communication consists of three main forms or clusters: management communications, marketing communications and organisational communications. These are set out in Table 2.2 and are explored in Chapters 9–12.

Gaps can occur at many points in the reputation management process. For example, there may be differences between what employees think the brand is (identity) and what the external stakeholders, such as customers, think it is (image). There may be a gap between the brand promise and the behaviour of employees, or between management communication and image.

Table 2.2	Forms of corporate communication
Form of corporate communication	**Explanation**
Management	Communications by employees who have a responsibility for the deployment of resources. These communications may be directed to internal or external audiences
Marketing	Communications designed to engage customer-orientated audiences with regard to the promotion of an organisation's products and services
Organisational	Communications aimed at a range of stakeholders, not just customers, that are designed to build identification, commitment and relationships with an organisation, and are not sales-orientated

Source: Based on van Riel & Fombrun (2007).

As an example, the image and identity of the Harley-Davidson brand are closely intertwined, giving it an overall strength and reputation that are the envy of many other organisations. This brand showcases the co-creation of value in the development of a formidable brand equity, which signifies that consumers themselves are simultaneously constructing and developing the corporation's reputation. For greater detail on Harley-Davidson see Minicase 1.2 (p. 102).

Managing corporate reputation is therefore partly about identifying and minimising the gaps that can emerge between the different building blocks and the corporate communication utilised by an organisation.

Influences on corporate reputation

Having explored the building blocks of corporate reputation it is important to consider the range of forces that can influence these blocks and the development of corporate reputation. Some of these forces can be controlled, namely the internal forces, and some are largely beyond an organisation's control, the external forces. However, there is a third force, referred to as relational forces, which we consider in more depth.

External forces

External forces are largely uncontrollable, and can be considered in terms of the PESTLE framework (see Table 2.3). The point is that when considering corporate reputation or preparing a reputational audit, this framework should be used to apply the different forces in a reputation context. That is, what is the likely impact of each force, on each of the building blocks of reputation? So, what might the influence on organisational communication be if there was a change in the legislation regarding the use of sponsorship? What might be the impact on the

Table 2.3	Examples of external influences on the building blocks of corporate reputation
PESTLE forces	**Examples**
Politics	Political (and social) pressure on banks regarding their contribution to the recession, and their attitude towards bonuses, has changed their image and reputation as held by consumers and other stakeholders.
Economic	Pharmaceutical companies seek to preserve their drug brands as public spending on health and related issues has been cut.
Social	Changes to the way many societies regard smoking contributed to the world's largest tobacco company, Philip Morris, rebranding as The Altria Group in 2003.
Technology	The development of social media and social networking has changed the way organisations relate to their stakeholders and the way stakeholders perceive and understand organisations. This change impacts identity, image and reputation.
Legal	Recent changes to the law relating to corporate hospitality (and bribery) might influence the way an organisation formulates its identity mix and organisational communication, which in turn could impact on relationships and corporate brand strength.
Ecological	The Japanese earthquake and tsunami disaster has led to a shortage of car parts, causing certain Japanese car manufacturers to limit production in their western manufacturing and assembly plants. The media use this as a news story which influences the perception and image consumers and other European parts suppliers have of these brands. The impact could also influence recruitment, deterring some people from choosing to work with these organisations.

behaviour of employees and the way they represent a brand after a merger and a change to a more authoritarian style of management communication?

Internal forces

One of the key characteristics of the internal forces and influences is that these can be controlled. Internal forces such as the corporate strategy, culture and use of resources, including financial, management and employee expertise, are more controllable and can be adapted to different contexts.

The impact of these forces is often noticeable in terms of the gaps that can arise. For example, gaps between the behaviour of employees and a brand promise will affect reputation. A gap may appear between an organisation's core message and its personality as vested in the mission values statements. Indeed, a change in corporate strategy might affect the organisation's image. For example, the financial link between Innocent and Coca-Cola was at first considered dubious and damaging to the ethical and environmental positioning first adopted by Innocent. A throwaway sentence or remark can also inflict severe brand and reputational damage. Equally a chance remark or a planned speech might limit any potential brand damage.

In April 2011, Sony experienced a network security breach which resulted in the loss of personal data and credit card details relating to 77 million PlayStation 3 customers. It could be argued that this was an external, and hence uncontrollable, force. However, security and protection are management activities and hence a controllable element. Furthermore, as Colvile (2011) suggests, this was not the first time this had happened to Sony. Both Sony's Blu-Ray DVD system and its PlayStation 3 games console, had both been 'severely compromised' in the previous few months. These early warnings appear to not have been acted upon. This indicates that had suitable protection been in place following these events, their reputation might not have had to take the battering it received across the globe.

Relational forces

To some extent an organisation may be able to avoid reputational issues hitting the bottom line depending upon the relational forces acting upon it. These forces concern the way an organisation competes, interacts and conducts itself within relationships. Relational forces also encompass the associations the company is perceived to make through partnerships and its behaviour with other organisations.

The oil companies may have poor reputations in the eyes of customers but are fortunate enough to work within monopolistic or oligopolistic markets and where there is an almost insatiable demand for their products. The same could be said of the UK banks. They have made huge profits, have run their businesses in the most short-sighted manner possible, necessitating their bail-out by the British taxpayer yet are still with us (see Viewpoint 1.4, p. 18). They are protected from new entrants into their home marketplace by law. If this law were to be relaxed, what would happen to their large market shares? Certainly in the UK Tesco is lobbying to be allowed to offer a full retail banking service. It is possible to be a very profitable company with a relatively poor reputation, depending upon the market situation within which the firm operates.

Porter's (1985) Five Forces Model encapsulates the various competitive pressures that an individual organisation may be subjected to.

The five forces are:

- The threat of new entrants to the market
- The bargaining power (strength) of suppliers

- The bargaining power (strength) of buyers (customers)
- The threat of substitute products or services
- The nature and strength of competition (competitive rivalry)

The oil industry does not contain many global players, thereby protecting individual companies from overly harsh pressure on their profitability, whilst the threat of new entrants to the high street banks is severely limited by law, a distinct advantage for the existing players. In industries with a greater degree of competitive rivalry, a corporate reputation may be more vulnerable to negative publicity, with a more immediate knock-on effect upon its profitability. The alternative offers of soft drinks in the marketplace are often used as an example of the threat of substitutes.

In the service industry substitutes can be a particular problem, as it is easy to copy a service that a rival firm has successfully promoted. Common forms of insurance, such as motor or home policies, have become much more competitive as new players have entered the marketplace, e.g. the major supermarkets. Price comparison sites such as confused.com have added further pressure. Without a strong brand and/or reputation, a company risks being judged purely on price, in effect becoming a commodity. The bargaining power of suppliers or buyers is relative to the strength of the companies within the industry itself.

> **It is easy to copy a service.**
>
> **Without a strong brand and/or reputation, a company risks being judged purely on price.**

In order to obtain products at the most favourable terms for themselves, extremely strong brands such as Tesco are able to exert financial power when dealing with suppliers. To over-exert such power may, however, damage the reputation of the organisation. Tesco itself has been accused of demonstrating an overly aggressive stance to its suppliers (*The Times*, 2010).

Another relational force can be the place of the organisation or brand within the life of the consumer and this may lessen reputational damage. One's decision to support sports teams or musicians is likely to be based upon deeper emotional bonds; for example, we may support a football team because of our allegiance to our birthplace and/or loyalty to our family. Our allegiance to banks, insurance companies or supermarkets is more likely to be based upon more functional criteria, such as their ability to provide an attractive marketing mix. The unswerving nature of our loyalty to football clubs can lessen reputational difficulties in many circumstances as we are far more likely to forgive, or at least tolerate, their faults or failures. Consumption in this case can often be irrational (Abosag *et al.*, 2012). However, our loyalty to commercial organisations is more likely to lead to a more precarious reputational position for the firm whereby we judge the firm on a more rational and practical level.

It may not be possible to avoid reputational damage over a period of time and large firms are constantly in the public eye and, therefore, at risk. Coming back from such damage is what counts. Gaines-Ross (2008) outlines a 12-step guide to restoring the corporate reputation. This is broken down into four main stages: rescue (minimising the damage), rewind (identifying what went wrong), restore (rebuilding reputation) and recover (sustaining reputation for the long term). This is certainly something that will need to be implemented by BP following its considerable difficulties and reputational damage caused by the Gulf of Mexico oil spill from its Deepwater Horizon platform. For more detail see this book's supporting website (www.pearsoned.co.uk/roperfill).

> **It may not be possible to avoid reputational damage over a period of time.**

Mergers and acquisitions

There are particular problems that relate to fusing separate corporate identities into one following a merger or acquisition. Since the early 1990s there have been a substantial number of large-scale mergers and acquisitions whereby companies may expand quickly by taking over or merging with rivals. Harnessing the competitive strengths of two companies can provide a much more powerful player in the marketplace. Cutting costs by having one research and development or marketing department rather than two and boosting revenues are often reasons behind such mergers and acquisitions.

The power of a newly merged company can be used to force down supplier prices. For example, recent major mergers and acquisitions include Glaxo Wellcome and SmithKline Beecham in 2000 in the pharmaceutical industry; Comcast Corporation and AT&T in 2006 in telecommunications; and Inbev Inc. and Anheuser-Busch Companies Inc in 2008 in the brewing industry. Many such mergers and acquisitions are driven by the fear of global competition, and perhaps also by the egos of the chief executives wanting to become even bigger players in their industries, not to mention the plethora of bankers, lawyers and consultants who stand to earn large fees from such activity.

There is a large element of a defensive strategy about mergers and acquisitions. A company may feel that without the critical mass generated by such partnerships, it will be acquired by a larger rival itself. However, having spent in many cases decades building and nurturing their individual corporate identities, significant issues need to be overcome when two companies become one. Two firms may have been attracted by product- or market-based synergies but they can run into huge difficulties when trying to merge corporate identities and cultures. Such difficulties can outweigh any economies of scale achieved.

Cartwright & Schoenberg (2006) discuss the lessons learned regarding corporate and social identity issues during 30 years of research into mergers and acquisitions. Empirical data over several decades show that the failure rates of acquisitions has remained at a fairly constant, high, level. Kitching (1974) revealed failure rates of 46–50 per cent, based on managers' self-report. Rostand (1994) and Schoenberg (2006) reported equally poor failure rates of 44–45 per cent, using similar methodology.

Research studies into the returns received by shareholders also demonstrate that acquisitions continue to produce negative average returns (Gregory, 1997; Agrawal & Jaffe, 2000). Difficulties encountered in managing the two sets of employees and the inherent difficulties of managing a new corporate identity are prominent in explaining such poor results.

Clearly the difficulty of merging two long-established corporate identities necessitates serious consideration of how to ensure the two groups of employees are not alienated by the decision to merge. An example of this from the university sector is provided in Viewpoint 2.3.

Viewpoint 2.3   Two universities go into one

Universities are institutions that have strong cultures. Staff members often feel a close connection to each other and to their institution. There is a great deal of 'emotional labour' involved in academic work and academic staff can be very sensitive about their work, their institution and their place within that institution.

Two institutions with strong academic reputations merged in 2004, the Victoria University of Manchester and UMIST, combining their strengths in a strategic decision to give themselves the critical mass and power necessary to stand a better chance of competing with Oxford, Cambridge, London and the major American universities. It helped matters that the two universities were both research-intensive institutions and shared broadly the same missions. However, there were a number of very sensitive issues to overcome. First, there was the name of the new institution. It was vital that staff, particularly those in the smaller institution (UMIST), did not feel that they were the subject of a takeover. Subsequently staff members from both institutions were invited to express preferences from a list of 10 possible names, the preferred choice being the University of Manchester. In order to avoid accusations of a 'takeover', the 'double dissolution' model under which both existing university charters were dissolved and a new charter created for the new integrated university was seen by both parties as the best way of delivering this, despite this being a more expensive

Exhibit 2.2 The crests and logos of, from left to right, the Victoria University of Manchester, UMIST and the merger of the two, the University of Manchester.
Source: The University of Manchester, with permission.

and complex procedure than merely adapting the existing charter of one of the partners. The two existing universities disappeared and a new one was simultaneously created.

Corporate communication was, of course, vital. The signs and symbols that expressed the corporate identity of the universities were all replaced in a very short period of time to ensure the new marks were in place for the official merger date. This involved a huge exercise and the replacement of, in certain cases, old and expensive examples of identity, e.g. plate glass windows displaying the old UMIST and Victoria University coats of arms. The plan was to ensure that staff felt part of the new university as soon as possible and one way to undermine this would have been to take several years to replace the visible representations of identity that are on display every day in the workplace.

It was recognised throughout that the support of the academic staff of both universities was essential to the merger going forward. If the academic staff had turned against the proposal it would not have happened. Considerable time and effort were spent in seeking to prevent such an outcome. In addition, some particularly sensitive issues, such as consideration of the name of the merged university and its academic structure, were delayed until after the decision to merge had been taken. It was vital that the process did not become bogged down in the minutiae that could sabotage the overall process.

The merger of these two great old institutions demonstrates that it is possible to create a new corporate identity as long as due consideration is given to the sensitivities of key employee groups and there is a commitment to corporate communications to ensure quickly that old visible symbols do not compromise the new institution.

Question

Consider the organisation you work for, or one with which you are familiar. Identify the elements of the corporate identity that would be most difficult to change (and why) if your company were to merge with or be taken over by another organisation.

This chapter seeks to explore the scope of corporate reputation. It has examined identity and image and their relationship to reputation and looked at the different relational forces that can impact a corporate reputation. The examination of the scope of corporate reputation continues with an examination of the different criteria that stakeholders use to assess an organisation's reputation.

Criteria that influence corporate reputation

How do we judge the corporate reputation of a particular organisation?

So how do we judge the corporate reputation of a particular organisation? Figure 1.1 detailed the four criteria that Charles Fombrun suggests help organisations build strong and favourable reputations: credibility, reliability, trustworthiness and responsibility. These four areas are undoubtedly key tenants and underpin the reputation of any organisation. However, we should perhaps be thinking more widely, especially as this chapter wishes to examine the scope of corporate reputation. We can consider reputation in terms of the criteria detailed in Figure 2.3.

The list of factors upon which an organisation can establish its reputation is detailed in the following. It is by no means an exhaustive list but it covers a comprehensive range of the fundamental criteria inherent in the field of corporate reputation. Brands may excel in one particular area, e.g. customer service, and this may be the pillar upon which their reputation is built. The ideal scenario is, of course, to be seen to excel in all areas and therefore have a comprehensive or total reputation.

1. Product/service quality (including value)

The Reputation Institute devised a reputation quotient system (see Chapter 4), which measures the degrees of commercial reputation, and, within this, product or service quality proves the

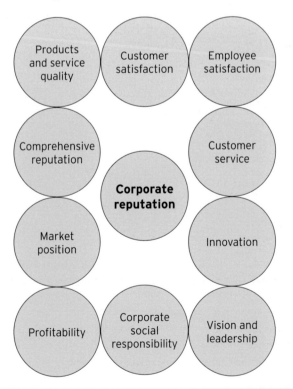

Figure 2.3 Criteria that influence corporate reputation.

most crucial factor. This reinforces the intuitive presumption that the fundamental premise which underpins a favourable reputation of any company would be the standard of its raw material, its central offering, its *raison d'être*, its essence.

> The fundamental premise which underpins a favourable reputation of any company is its central offering

Herein also lies the potentially problematic, and rather abstract, notion of value, i.e. the importance that we ascribe to a product. Product or service quality is not only based on the calibre of the product/service, but is also assessed according to the price/quality relationship. This refers to the perception by most consumers that a relatively high price is a sign of good quality. Therefore the more we spend on a product, the higher the quality we expect that product to be.

A company that has consistently adapted its product mix in order to maintain its position as one of the world's leading brands is McDonald's. For more detail see this book's supporting website (www.pearsoned.co.uk/roperfill).

2. Employee satisfaction

Employee satisfaction is a measure of how happy workers are with their job and their working environment. It is important from a reputational point of view for employees to be content, as happy workers are more likely to be more productive, have lower absenteeism and be more loyal to the company (Ind, 1997, 1998; Hart & Murphy, 1998; see Chapter 3 for greater detail on employee satisfaction).

3. Customer satisfaction

Customer service is a difficult term to define. It could be described as the fulfilment of customers' requirements or needs. Of course, satisfaction is a very personal concept and will mean

> Customer service is a difficult term to define.

different things to different people. The services marketing literature suggests that customer service is based upon a comparison of an individual's expectations versus their perception of the actual experience (Parazuraman *et al.*, 1988).

The John Lewis Partnership has finished top of retail analysts Verdict's list of Britain's Best Retailers for the last 3 years. The company has finished either first or second in every poll since the year 2000. The survey rates retailers in terms of range, price, convenience, quality, service, ambience, facilities and layout. Similarly, consumer magazine *Which?* named John Lewis top online retailer in 2010, thus demonstrating the company's all-round performance. A panel of 14,000 *Which?* subscribers put the partnership in first place in a number of categories, including home and garden, electrical, baby and toddler, and toys and games categories. In 2009, John Lewis also took two of the top three places in the UK Consumer Satisfaction Index from the Institute of Customer Service.

John Lewis's commitment to customer satisfaction is clear. A look at its website (www.johnlewispartnership.co.uk) shows that customer satisfaction is at the top of the mind of the company. It states:

> We treat customers as individuals and take them through their purchases from start to finish: we are delighted that so many customers remark on our Partners' friendliness and helpfulness.
>
> We also use formal methods of research and feedback, such as customer surveys, panels, focus groups, online feedback forms and regular mystery shopping. These help us monitor levels of customer satisfaction and give us a broad spectrum of customer opinion to respond to.

Of course, an organisation that demonstrates a commitment to customers has to demonstrate a similar commitment to their employees (see Viewpoint 3.4, p. 67, for an insight).

4. Customer service

The Institute of Customer Service defines customer service as 'the sum total of what an organisation does to meet customer expectations and produce customer satisfaction'. It could also be thought of as the ability to provide a service or product in the way that it has been promised.

First Direct Bank is an organisation that excels in an area of business that has recently been much maligned. It is the UK's most recommended bank; that is, its existing customers act as an advocate for the bank by recommending it to others. Starting as a telephone bank in 1989 it set new standards by being the first UK bank to offer 24-hour call centres. Customers nowadays may take 24-hour provision for granted but over 20 years ago it was a groundbreaking innovation in escalating the standards of customer service. First Direct has also complemented its call centre operation with internet banking. First Direct claims that one of its customers recommends it to someone else every 6 seconds.

5. Innovation

An innovation is a new way of doing something: a new or original product or process.

An innovation is a new way of doing something; a new or original product or process. A brand may have a good reputation for innovation. By its nature this means that a brand's capacity for imagination and change must be a permanent feature of its make-up. An organisation that has showed its capacity for innovation from day one is MTV (see Viewpoint 2.4).

Viewpoint 2.4	Moving culture with MTV

MTV has unswervingly managed to remain relevant to audiences since its launch in 1981. Whilst its original purpose was solely to play music videos, its progressive universal exposure and popularity over three decades has converted it into a medium of culture, expression and advertising. It has revolutionised the music industry, becoming the hub of the music scene.

The channel has singlehandedly propelled rock stars to fame. With a willingness to play black music videos, it helped to remove the colour barrier in music, notably by playing the videos of that great pioneer of music video as an art form, Michael Jackson. In the early 1990s, in particular, MTV was a conduit that projected musicians and their videos to the forefront of the industry, serving as a prime marketing tool for the industry.

The channel has always possessed the power to shape mainstream musical tastes through its musical selections. MTV helped bring more controversial genres of music such as hip hop and gangsta rap to mainstream audiences. A channel that has such influence on musical preference must be viewed as a rich source of culture.

MTV has facilitated the process of globalisation of the music industry. In recent times, its focus has shifted from music, instead prioritising non-music reality TV programmes. While music videos were featured for up to 8 hours daily in 2000, they appeared on average for just 3 hours per day in 2008. However, as with its music, MTV has popularised and pioneered certain types of TV programmes, ranging from adult animations (such as *Beavis and Butthead* and *Celebrity Deathmatch*) to reality TV (such as *Real World* and *The Osbournes*), dating shows (such as *Singled Out*) and prank shows (such as *Jackass* and *Punk'd*). Other channels have consequently begun to broadcast similar programmes under different titles.

Managing the reputation of a brand such as MTV is far from easy. Criticised by the Christian right in the US as well as conservative media watchdog groups for airing morally questionable material, it must also ensure that it does not alienate its target audience of young consumers by being seen as a censor. Thus, MTV is gripped in a continuous dilemma to appease groups from all corners of society that have widely differing interests, a seemingly impossible task. Consequently, it is trapped in a reputational limbo, attempting to entertain the younger masses whilst also trying to avoid offending more traditional groups. In spite of this, it continually defines and redefines society's trends within popular culture.

Exhibit 2.3	Over its 30-year history MTV has constantly shifted its focus in order to stay relevant.

Source: © MTV Networks Europe. All Rights Reserved. Reproduced with permission.

MTV has continually made efforts to promote social, political and environmental activism in young people (principally by its 'Think MTV' campaign), exhibiting MTV's dedication to making positive changes in the fabric of society. Being in tune with the nuances of this culture, MTV carefully selects figureheads that can reach its audiences. An example was when MTV worked with P. Diddy's 'Vote or Die' campaign, designed to encourage young people to vote. This also underlines the reputation held by the channel as a forward-thinking entity that passionately projects the sentiments and ideas of its target audience.

Question

Think of three examples of innovative companies. Why are they considered to be innovative and is it possible to sustain an innovative culture over the long term?

6. Vision and leadership

Inspirational leaders have a vision of where they want their business to go. They have the ability to inspire others with this vision and provide a direction for them to share and follow. True leaders are able to articulate their vision going beyond a bland mission or vision statement and instead underpinning the entire culture of the successful organisation.

> Inspirational leaders have a vision of where they want their business to go.

By 'leadership' we mean more than just 'management' of the organisation. Leaders have the ability to be able to influence others to follow them in achieving their cause no matter how difficult this may seem. Winston Churchill is considered Britain's greatest ever Prime Minister due to his inspirational leadership qualities during the Second World War.

Regarding companies, Richard Branson is credited with great motivating qualities that have led to great success for his businesses. For more detail see this book's supporting website (www.pearsoned.co.uk/roperfill).

7. Corporate social responsibility

Corporate social responsibility (CSR) is really a form of self-regulation by the organisation that ensures that ethical behaviour underpins its business model. An organisation practising CSR would take responsibility for its actions relating to its

> Corporate social responsibility (CSR) is really a form of self-regulation by the organisation.

employees, the wider environment, consumers, its suppliers and all other stakeholder groups. As an example, a company would ensure that its suppliers did not employ child labour in countries without the regulatory and legal protection offered to workers in the western world. CSR is examined further in Chapters 5 and 12.

8. Profitability

One clear measure of business success, but certainly not the only one, as this book will demonstrate, is profit. For example, from a UK start-up company in 1984, Vodafone is now the world's leading mobile telecommunications company and the 10th most profitable company in the world according to *Fortune* magazine. Considering its relative youth and the fact that it set up in business in direct competition with long-established national telecommunications providers who were establishing their own mobile networks, this is a remarkable success story. It posted a profit of $13.7 billion in 2009, its success perhaps reflecting its reputation for unrivalled network coverage.

9. Market position

Certain brands become 'front of mind' for particular occasions or product purchases. For example, people who require computer software many first think of Microsoft; for those seeking a cheap flight, Ryanair may be considered first. It should be noted that, as times change, so must the position of the brand. The brand must always have relevance for customers even if that means fundamentally altering its offering. Even a brand that has held great emotional significance for generations of customers is at the mercy of an unsympathetic market. Being unable to adapt to the times can result in a diminishing reputation.

> **The brand must always have relevance for customers.**

10. Comprehensive reputation

The ultimate goal must be for an organisation to be known as having a strong all-round reputation encompassing all of the categories detailed above. Examples of companies that fall into this highly desired category are detailed in Chapter 8.

It is important to note that reputations can decline over the years and before the company knows it, it is too late to reverse the downward trend. This point is emphasised by the demise of one of the great brands of the 20th century, Woolworths (see Viewpoint 2.5).

Viewpoint 2.5 | **Declining reputation at Woolworths**

One company that categorically failed to exploit the emotional feeling held towards it by a considerable part of the nation was Woolworths, a huge retailer that finally foundered and went into administration towards the latter end of 2008. One of the great brands of the British high street was dead at the age of 99, the last store closing on 6 January 2009; the closure of the company led to the loss of 30,000 jobs.

Its reputation management over the last 30 years appeared almost non-existent, completely neglected throughout the decades in which it could have attempted to resurrect itself. It faced two principal predicaments as an organisation. It certainly made minimal efforts to overturn its dowdy, antiquated image, which had become entrenched by the 1990s and proved particularly unattractive to younger consumers. This was a shame as it was one of the great innovators in its earlier years. It was one of the first retailers to put merchandise out for the public to browse through and handle without the necessity of a salesperson being present. The store also pioneered the use of lunch counters, a forerunner of the modern day food court.

Exhibit 2.4 Woolworths: (a) in its heyday; (b) on the eve of closure.
Source: (a) Mirrorpix; (b) Press Association Images/David Davies.

Over the years it consistently lost market share to its more tightly focused competitors. Woolworths gained something of a reputation as a store that was a 'Jack-of-all-trades', but sadly, a master of none. An increasingly drab image, unfavourable secondary locations and a poor product catalogue all contributed to consign Woolworths to its inevitable fate. If we follow the Reputation Institute's assertion that product/ service quality is the most important factor, then Woolworths' poor product inventory may be pinpointed as the primary cause of its downfall. Commentators latterly remarked that it had simply become a huge pick'n'mix stall.

Whilst it cannot be denied that Woolworths lacked functionality in terms of its purchasing policy and product portfolio selection, compounded by its locational difficulties (Woolworths became a symbol of the decline of the secondary units/retail spaces that it inhabited), it certainly held emotional resonance as a brand. Edna Sherman, 62, from Everton, Liverpool, was one of the last customers allowed inside on the final day of trading.

She said: 'People in there are fighting to get at empty shelves, there is nothing left. I've been shopping at Woolies all my life. I remember going to the pick and mix when I was a girl and lately I would buy clothes for my grandchildren. There was always a bargain to be had at Woolies, I just don't understand where it all went wrong.' An indication of the affection in which Woolies was held was that the stores' final bag of pick'n'mix was sold on eBay for £14,500.

Ultimately the lack of clarity relating to the brand and its position in the market fuelled its problems and, together with increasingly sophisticated (and mobile) customers and more specialised competition, led to Woolies' demise in image and reputation.

Question

Woolworths, like many department stores, declined as more tightly focused stores took their market share. Is it still possible to be a successful 'all-rounder' in the 21st century? Provide examples to support your argument.

Chapter summary

In order to consolidate your understanding of the scope of corporate reputation, below are the key points summarised against each of the learning objectives.

1. Outline the difference between shareholders and stakeholders

Company shareholders are part-owners of the organisation. They are individuals, or more often corporations, who own shares of a company's stock. Defining stakeholders can be more difficult. They are wide-ranging groups that have an interest in the organisation.

Stakeholders will include the shareholders themselves, employees, customers, local government, national government, media, trade unions, financial institutions, investors, suppliers, regulators as well as local communities and the general public.

2. Consider the relationship between corporate identity, corporate image and corporate reputation

Corporate identity comes from within the organisation. Corporate identity answers questions such as 'Who are we?', 'What do we stand for?', 'What is our core purpose?', and 'What does it mean to be involved in this company?' (van Riel & Fombrun, 2007).

The result in the mind of the external stakeholder is the corporate image. Of course, the corporate image is often projected to external audiences using corporate communications. Balmer & Wilson (1998) explain that the effective management of corporate identity will result in a favourable corporate image and that over time this will result in a positive corporate reputation (the overall view of the organisation).

3. Understand the building blocks of corporate reputation

There several building blocks that together constitute the corporate reputation management process: the corporate personality, identity, image, communication and corporate reputation. The inter-relationships and quality of the linkages between these blocks help to shape the strength of the organisation's reputation and the nature of any gaps or discontinuities in the process.

4. Discuss the forces that impact upon an organisation

The organisation will be influenced by a range of external, internal and relational forces. External forces can be considered in terms of the PESTLE framework and are largely uncontrollable. Internal forces such as the corporate strategy, culture and use of resources, including financial, management and employee expertise, are more controllable and can be adapted to the different contexts. Relational forces concern the way an organisation competes, interacts and conducts itself within relationships. Relational forces also encompass the associations it is perceived to make through partnerships and behaviour with other organisations.

5. Identify the criteria that influence our view of the corporate reputation of an organisation

There are many different factors that may influence our view of an organisation. The ideal is to have a strong overall or comprehensive reputation, but a company may have built its reputation upon one of the following pillars: product or service quality; employee satisfaction; customer satisfaction; customer service; innovation; vision and leadership; corporate social responsibility; profitability; and market position.

Discussion questions

1. Provide definitions of the terms corporate identity, corporate image and corporate reputation.
2. Write a paragraph about an organisation of your choice where there is a strong connection between employees and the company.
3. It could be argued that the traditional *heavy* industries had a stronger connection with their employees than does the modern corporation. What can the modern firm do to foster a strong connection with its staff?
4. Choose an organisation and write notes on how the five different identities of Balmer & Greyser's (2002) AC²ID Test may apply to your chosen company.
5. What is meant by the relational forces that impact upon an organisation?
6. List as many criteria as you can that will influence the way in which the corporate reputation of an organisation is judged.
7. We have provided 10 criteria that influence a corporate reputation. Provide an example of a brand that excels in each of these criteria.
8. For an organisation with which you are familiar, draw a diagram outlining the stakeholders of the organisation and their relative importance.
9. Provide an example of an organisation that has had to reconsider its identity following a merger or acquisition. How has it dealt with this problem?
10. Outline the relationship between the personality, identity, image and corporate reputation of an organisation. Use an example to illustrate your points.

References

Aaker, D.A. (1996). *Building Strong Brands.* New York: The Free Press.

Abosag, I., Roper, S. & Hind, D. (2012). Examining the relationship between brand emotion and brand extension among supporters of professional football clubs. *European Journal of Marketing*, in press.

Abratt, R. (1989). A new approach to the corporate image management process. *Journal of Marketing Management* 5(1), 63–76.

Agrawal, A. & Jaffe, J. (2000). The post merger performance puzzle. *Advances in Mergers and Acquisitions* 1, 119–156.

Albert, S. & Whetten, D.A. (1985). Organisational identity. In: Cummings, L.L. & Staw, B.I.M. eds. *Research in Organizational Behaviour*, pp. 263–295.

Balmer, J.M.T. (1998). Corporate identity and the advent of corporate marketing. *Journal of Marketing Management* 14(8), 963–996.

Balmer, J.M.T. & Gray, E.R. (2003). Corporate brands: what are they? What of them? *European Journal of Marketing* 37(7/8), 972–997.

Balmer, J.M.T. & Greyser, S.A. (2002). Managing the multiple identities of the corporation. *California Management Review* 44(3), 72–86.

Balmer, J.M.T. & Greyser, S.A. (2003) *Revealing the Corporation.* London: Routledge.

Balmer, J.M.T. & Wilson, A. (1998). Corporate identity: there is more to it than meets the eye. *International Studies of Management and Organisation* 28(3), 12–31.

BBC (2010). 'Final Woolworths stores shut down'. Online: http://news.bbc.co.uk/1/hi/7811187.stm. Accessed: 4 August 2010.

Bernstein, D. (1984). *Company Image and Reality: A Critique of Corporate Communications.* London: Holt, Rinehart & Winston.

Bickerton, D. (2000). Corporate reputation versus corporate branding: the realist debate. *Corporate Communications* 1, 42–48.

Cartwright, C. & Schoenberg, R. (2006). Thirty years of mergers and acquisitions research: recent advances and future opportunities. *British Journal of Management* 17(1), S1–S5.

de Chernatony, L. (1999). Brand management through narrowing the gap between brand identity and brand reputation. *Journal of Marketing Management* 15(1–3), 157–180.

de Chernatony, L. (2001). How suited is a brand's strategy to its environments? *Proceedings of the 5th International Conference on Corporate Reputation, Identity and Competitiveness,* Paris.

de Chernatony, L. (2001). *From Brand Vision to Brand Evaluation.* London: Butterworth-Heinemann.

de Chernatony, L. & Harris, F. (2000). Developing corporate brands through considering internal and external stakeholders. *Corporate Reputation Review* 3(3), 268–274.

de Chernatony, L. & Segal-Horn, S. (2003). The criteria for successful services brands, *European Journal of Marketing* 37, 7/8, 1095–1118.

Colvile, R. (2011). Sony PlayStation hack: a glimpse into the world of online crime. *The Telegraph.* Accessed: 28 April 2011 www.telegraph.co.uk/technology/sony.

Daily Telegraph (2010). 'McDonald's Chicken McNuggets branded "healthy" by Weight Watchers.' Online: http://www.telegraph.co.uk/health/healthnews/7359902/McDonalds-Chicken-McNuggets-branded-healthy-by-Weight-Watchers.html. Accessed: 20 July 2010.

Davies, G., Chun, R., da Silva, R.V. & Roper, S. (2001). The personification metaphor as a measurement approach for corporate reputation. *Corporate Reputation Review* 4(2), 113–127.

Davies, G. & Miles, L. (1998). Reputation management: theory versus practice. *Corporate Reputation Review* 2(1), 16–28.

Fombrun, C.J. (1996). *Reputation: Realizing the Value from the Corporate Image.* Boston: Harvard Business School Press.

Gaines-Ross, L. (2008). *Corporate Reputation: 12 Steps to Safeguarding and Recovering Reputation.* New Jersey: Wiley.

Gregory, A. (1997). An examination of the long run performance of UK acquiring firms. *Journal of Business Finance & Accounting* 24, 971–1002.

Gray, E.R. & Balmer, J.M.T. (1998). Managing corporate image and corporate reputation. *Long Range Planning* 31(5), 695–702.

Harris, F. & de Chernatony, L. (2001). Corporate branding and corporate brand performance. *European Journal of Marketing* 35(3/4), 441–456.

Hart, S. & Murphy, J. (1998). *Brands: The New Wealth Creators*. Basingstoke: Macmillan Business.

Hatch, M.J. & Schultz, M. (1997). Relations between organizational culture, identity and image. *European Journal of Marketing* 31(5/6), 356–365.

Hatch, M.J. & Schultz, M. (2001). Are the strategic stars aligned for your corporate brand? *Harvard Business Review* February, 128–134.

Hatch, M.J. & Schultz, M. (2003). Bringing the corporation into corporate Branding. *European Journal of Marketing* 37(7/8), 1041–1064.

Ind, N. (1997). *The Corporate Brand*. Basingstoke: Macmillan Business.

Ind, N. (1998). An integrated approach to corporate branding. *The Journal of Brand Management* 5(5), 323–329.

John Lewis Partnership (2010). Online: http://www.johnlewispartnership.co.uk/Display. aspx?MasterId=1c4e8a06-26bb-4452-a574-378d4e0d82e4&NavigationId=629. Accessed: 26 July 2010.

Kennedy, S.H. (1977) Nurturing corporate images: total communication or ego trip. *European Journal of Marketing* 31(1), 120–164.

Kitching, J. (1974). Winning and losing with European acquisitions. *Harvard Business Review* 52, 124–136.

Markwick, N. & Fill, C. (1997). Towards a framework for managing corporate identity. *European Journal of Marketing* 31(5/6), 396–409.

Olins, W. (1989). *Corporate Identity: Making Business Strategy Visible Through Design*. London: Thames & Hudson.

Parasuraman, A., Zeithaml, V.A. & Berry, L.L. (1988). SERVQUAL: a multiple item scale for measuring consumer perceptions of service quality. *Journal of Retailing* 64(1), 12–40.

Porter, M.E. (1985). *Competitive Advantage*. Free Press: New York.

Pringle, H. & Gordon, W. (2001). *Brand Manners: How to Create the Self-Confident Organization to Live the Brand*. Chichester: Wiley.

Roper, S. & Davies, G. (2007). The corporate brand: dealing with multiple stakeholders. *Journal of Marketing Management* 23, 74–90.

Rostand, A. (1994). Optimizing managerial decisions during the acquisition integration process'. Paper presented to *14th Annual Strategic Management Society International Conference*, Paris.

Schoenberg, R. (2006). Measuring the performance of corporate acquisitions: an empirical comparison of alternative metrics. *British Journal of Management* 17(4), 361–370.

Simmons, J. (2006), *The Invisible Grail: How Brands Can Use Words to Engage with Audiences*. London: Marshall Cavendish Business.

Smith, H.J. (2003). The shareholder vs. stakeholder debate. *Sloan Management Review*, Summer, 85–90.

The Times (2010). 'Tesco faces revolt from suppliers'. Online: http://business.timesonline. co.uk/tol/business/industry_sectors/retailing/article5062774.ece. Accessed: 4 August 2010.

van Riel, C.B.M. & Fombrun, C.J. (2007). *Essentials of Corporate Communication*. Abingdon: Routledge.

Whetten, D.A. (1997). Theory development and the study of corporate reputation. *Corporate Reputation Review* 1(2), 26–34.

Wilson, A. (2001). Understanding organisational culture and the implications for corporate marketing. *European Journal of Marketing* 35, 353–368.

Wilson, R. (1997). Corporate branding. *The Journal of Brand Management* 4(5), 303–310.

Chapter 3

The significance of corporate culture

One of the important building blocks of corporate reputation, introduced in Chapter 2, is the corporate personality. This refers to the particular traits, disposition, way of working and overall essence that characterise an organisation. A key part of an organisation's personality is the prevailing culture.

Understanding the corporate culture and the way it impacts on corporate reputation is critical. This is because reputation is embedded in the people who work for an organisation.

Aims and learning objectives

The aim of this chapter is to consider the importance and purpose of corporate culture, its relationship to the corporate brand and its impact upon corporate reputation.

The learning objectives of this chapter are to:

1. Discuss where the responsibility for corporate reputation lies
2. Define and explore the characteristics of corporate culture
3. Consider strong and weak corporate cultures
4. Recognise the differing types of corporate culture that exist within organisations
5. Explain the difficulties associated with cultural change
6. Link culture with the values of the brand
7. Consider the relationship to the employer brand.

Introduction

Increasingly, organisations and the media refer to the importance of corporate reputation. However, questions arise about who is responsible for an organisation's reputation. Some would argue that a head of reputation or corporate affairs should be appointed. Others suggest that everyone in an organisation has a responsibility to manage and develop an organisation's reputation and no formal department or structure is required. Perhaps the importance of an organisation's reputation indicates that the CEO should take direct responsibility in order to signal the criticality of maintaining a strong reputation.

> The CEO should take direct responsibility for maintaining a strong reputation.

What is clear is that whoever is charged with the responsibility of managing corporate reputation needs to understand the nature of the organisation's personality, and in particular its corporate culture. This chapter examines the various issues associated with corporate culture, including an exploration of the various dimensions and characteristics of corporate culture, the different types of culture, some of the issues associated with cultural change and the linkage between culture and brand values.

Who is responsible for corporate reputation?

Where does responsibility for the corporate reputation lie? Is it enthusiastically maintained by the chief executive officer (CEO) and does, therefore, the value of reputation emanate from him or her to all levels of management and staff? The CEO should set the tone for the importance of a positive corporate reputation for the firm. If this is the case then reputation management is not merely a branch of the PR department's brief. Gaines-Ross (2008) states that CEO reputation is inextricably linked with the reputation of the firm and that CEOs are far more in the public eye than in previous years.

How should a firm react to reputational issues? Griffin (2008) discusses the fact that there is a lot more hostility in the media and in society than there has been previously. The media often take a dogmatic approach and organisations often find themselves wrong-footed because they are reactive and appear passive in the face of resistance. He cites the example of protesters against supermarkets who 10 years ago didn't want out-of-town retailing and now don't want supermarkets in town centres. These groups, whom Griffin claims hold a minority opinion, are fundamentally against supermarkets and the concept of these large stores and so anything the supermarkets do will be criticised. Griffin (2008) encourages management to consider 'What exactly are the people who oppose supermarkets trying to achieve?' (p. 62). He suggests that taking on opponents on the substance of their debate may be better than trying to keep a low profile. The worry about a major crisis, the traditional concern of reputation management, is blinding management to the smaller but significant reputational threats they face every day.

Seizing the initiative is therefore recommended by Griffin. Companies should be open about their plans and how they intend to be a good corporate citizen. In such aggressive times, companies should not allow others to dominate the media agenda. Ryanair, for example, has been very aggressive in its condemnation of extra taxation on airline passengers, accusing the UK government of increasing indirect taxation and dressing

> Companies should not allow others to dominate the media agenda.

this increase up as a green tax. This is an example of a company that is determined to get its own side of the argument across, whether people like it or not. It may be criticised for being aggressive, but it is not subject to any more criticism than other companies who take a more passive line with the media and pressure groups.

The point is that an anti-corporate stance has taken hold. As people in the west have become richer, the populations worry more about abstract issues in which they are not directly related, for example poverty and child labour in the developing world. The ultimate example of this is in the US where counselling for children and even pets is widespread. The less people have to worry about, the more they worry. This displacement activity is often directed at companies (Griffin, 2008).

As demonstrated in some of the examples in this book, a good deal of criticism related to organisations is justified. However, there is a point to be made about the impact on employees and staff morale. If a company chooses to be strong and stands up for itself rather than be a punch-bag for the press or opposition groups, then this may well have a beneficial impact upon employees. Lobbying and behind-the-scenes activities are not a replacement for a strong and confident public position on issues, as it leaves the organisation's reputation in the hands of others.

> A key area is the corporate culture that has helped to shape that reputation.

A key area to think about when considering the reputation of an organisation is the corporate culture that has helped to shape that reputation. Before we discuss this issue, consider the corporate culture of a well-known British corporate brand, Dyson, in Viewpoint 3.1.

Viewpoint 3.1   Dyson – culturally determined and innovative

Dyson is a company with a commitment to innovation embedded in its culture. Such has been its impact in the vacuum cleaner market that its specific innovation in this field has revolutionised an entire industry. Prestigious accolades, including the International Design Fair prize in Japan, awarded to the Dyson vacuum, confirm the vacuum's standing as an original and creative innovation. In 1997 James Dyson, the firm's founder, received the Prince Philip Designers Prize and by 2005 he was elected as a Fellow of the Royal Academy of Engineering.

Dyson is a company underpinned by the concept of innovation, with its website detailing both the design heroes and icons of James Dyson, whose commitment to the notion of innovation is such that he has both built a Dyson School in the hope of 'creating a new generation of inventors' and established prizes to the sum of £10,000 for budding new architects.

Creating an innovative company often entails being a risk-taker and having a natural feel for what the public want. Dyson defied the key marketing logic that insists upon obeying market research, ignoring the

Exhibit 3.1   James Dyson poses with some of his bladeless Dyson Air Multiplier fans.
Source: Courtesy of Dyson.

feedback from both the public and retailers and opting to follow his personal intuition that his machines were novel and positively unusual. Dyson was clear that in the field of new technology, consumers' lack of expertise often leaves them incapable of imagining a desired product. Hard work is also part of the Dyson story. Fifteen years produced over 5,000 prototypes before the launch of the Dyson DC01 vacuum cleaner. Within 22 months it became the best-selling cleaner in the UK.

The company has diversified into the realm of hand dryers, washing machines, bladeless fans and 'Ballbarrows' (one of Dyson's original inventions), showing that thoughtful and innovative design can improve products that we have been using for decades. The 'ContraRotator' washing machine is reputed to have required a million man-hours and £25 million to be launch-ready in 2000. Not everything turns to gold, however, as the washing machine, although a significant improvement on traditional models, proved too expensive to manufacture to be a viable profitable product.

As a company, it has seemingly accomplished the virtually impossible: to convert a vacuum cleaner into a quasi-glamorous product through its visually compact and satisfying structure. Fashion designer Sir Paul Smith even began to retail the cleaner in his London clothes store. Dyson is also a company that takes advantage of innovative self-promotion, both extending and eliminating conventional boundaries of marketing. Dyson products are currently displayed at museums across the globe, including the Victoria & Albert Museum in London, the San Francisco Museum of Modern Art, the Georges Pompidou Centre in Paris and the Powerhouse Museum in Sydney. Such quirky facts lend the brand a quasi-mythical aura and, in doing so, emphasise the necessity to avoid corporate complacency when market leader (by 2002 the company had captured 38 per cent of the British market). Indeed, this proactivity has ensured that profits have soared from £35 million to £190 million between 2000 and 2010. Doubling operating profits in the last 12 months, Dyson has shown that it is possible to buck the recession.

Question

To what extent is the innovative culture of Dyson linked to its founder? How could this culture be maintained if the founder were to step down from his hands-on role?

Source: Various, including www.dyson.co.uk.

Is reputation management embedded in the culture of the organisation?

A clear point that all readers should take from this book is that reputation is not an optional extra to be tacked on to an organisation. A strong reputation and reputation management process should be at the core of all organisations.

Reputation is not an optional extra to be tacked on to an organisation.

This takes us back to one of the great, often self-inflicted, problems of marketing and management, namely that of over-promise and under-delivery. Any potential damage to reputation should be considered before corporate communication programmes are launched. Corporate reputation should be deliberately built instead of the company worrying about damage to an existing reputation. Again, if this mindset is

Corporate reputation should be deliberately built.

adopted then clearly reputation management is embedded within the culture of the organisation. A clear strategy for managing different stakeholder groups should form part of this proactive approach to reputation management. Is activity that leads to the enhancement of the reputation of the firm built into the reward structures of the company? It needs to be if the firm wants to get reputation management into the culture of the organisation.

Are people within the organisation comfortable about raising issues that they perceive may lead to reputational risk, or is the culture of the firm to keep quiet and not to be seen to be criticising or rocking the boat?

What is corporate culture?

Determining the corporate culture can be complex and something that may only be possible using qualitative research. The purpose of trying to investigate the culture of a particular company is to determine the attributes within the company that determine and drive corporate behaviour. The point is that it is the culture that determines how people behave within a firm. Do they act in the long-term interests of the organisation, and of society, or do their actions reflect a more short-term and perhaps selfish orientation? A very simple way to define culture is 'the way we do things around here' (Deal & Kennedy, 1982).

> A very simple way to define culture is 'the way we do things around here'.

Corporate culture emerges and is shaped and reinforced over time. It informs people about the values of a business, it shapes their behaviour and guides problem-solving and ways of communicating. It is necessary for an organisation to have a clear corporate culture, especially as an organisation grows. This is because the values associated with earlier owners and leaders, transmitted through their personalities and entrepreneurial spirit, may no longer be appropriate. In larger concerns it is possible that some individual staff members never meet senior management. This means they take their behavioural cues from the attitudes and actions of others.

> Corporate culture assists brand discipline.

Corporate culture assists brand discipline and ensures that the brand is not damaged or weakened by brand extensions or new ventures. The corporate brand and corporate brand management can really help mature organisations to stay focused.

Defining corporate culture

Within the field of organisational studies, corporate culture is a particular area of study that explores the psychology, attitudes, experiences, beliefs and values of an organisation. Certain rituals and symbols can be used by an organisation to help demonstrate and cement the culture of the workplace.

Edgar Schein is generally accepted as having coined the term corporate culture. He describes culture using the metaphor of an iceberg with much of the culture hidden below the surface. Schein's (1999) definition of corporate culture has three levels:

1. **Artefacts and behaviours** – these can be objects, words or deeds. These are the visible, above-the-surface demonstrations of culture that can be clearly observed. The use of particular forms of language and the dress code of the staff can be part of the artefacts of culture. These are tangible and identifiable elements of an organisation.

   The history of the company will be included within this level, and perhaps the splendour (or lack) of the offices from which the company works. Technical expertise, the prevailing attitude towards technology and, of course, the firm's products and services will also be included. The stories and even the myths about an organisation will be a key part of the artefacts.

   However, although easy to observe, such artefacts may be difficult to interpret.

2. **Espoused values,** below the water surface at a tacit level and therefore they are not necessarily spoken, although a company may well have its values printed on cards for staff, displayed on the walls of its headquarters and, of course, visible on the website. The values manifest themselves in the organisation's belief system.

> Espoused values manifest themselves in the organisation's belief system.

   Of course, it is likely that those who lead the organisation will have a strong impact upon the espoused values of the firm. The founder of a firm would initially set out the firm's values which then become assimilated over time within the organisation.

   Espoused values can be represented by the philosophies, strategies and goals of the organisation.

3. **Assumptions**, also below the water surface, reflect the shared values within the organisation. To really understand culture we need to get to the deepest levels, the assumptions and beliefs. They can be so well integrated in an organisation that they are difficult to recognise even from within the organisation. They are clearly below the surface in the iceberg metaphor. Such assumptions impact upon those areas that are given priority within a company. Indeed, Schein informs us that assumptions grow out of values until they become taken for granted within the organisation and drop out of awareness.

> Assumptions reflect the shared values within the organisation.

The fact that assumptions drop out of popular awareness is the reason why it is difficult for the outsider to easily grasp a corporate culture. The assumptions and beliefs are so deeply embedded that they do not need to be referred to.

It is the combination of these three levels that constitute the culture and indeed the communication climate (see Chapter 10) that exists within an organisation. It is this dynamic that shapes the way people behave towards each other and other stakeholders.

Figure 3.1 puts this into perspective. The three parts of corporate culture should be interrelated. We certainly must be able to understand all three levels before we can claim to understand a corporate culture. For Morgan (1997) there are three basic questions about corporate culture that need to be answered:

- What are the shared frames of reference that make the organisation possible?
- Where do they come from?
- How are they created, communicated, and sustained?

Morgan describes organisational culture as 'the set of beliefs, values, and norms, together with symbols like dramatized events and personalities that represents the unique character of an organization, and provides the context for action in it and by it'.

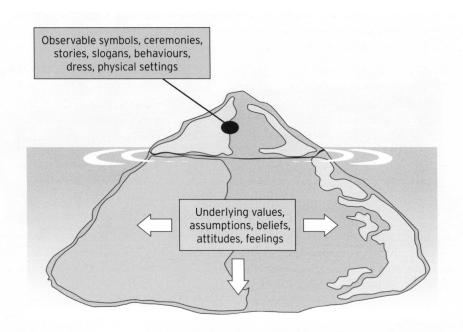

Figure 3.1	Levels of organisational culture.

Source: Schein (1999), John Wiley & Sons Ltd (UK), with permission.

There are many other definitions and interpretations of organisational culture, but there is considerable agreement over the importance of several points. These concern the collective experience, routine, beliefs, values, goals and system. These are learned and re-learned, passed on to new employees, and become a key part of a organisation's personality.

Strong and weak cultures

The benefit of organisational or corporate culture is that it quickly teaches people how they are expected to behave within an organisation. Is there a strong culture in place that has staff responding to a clear set of organisational values and passing these on to others? This could be said to be a strong culture. A weak culture may be one that relies on a set of rules and bureaucratic procedures in order to impose its will on employees. A weak culture can be less efficient and more expensive as, in effect, behaviour within the firm needs to be policed.

Corporate culture quickly teaches people how they are expected to behave within an organisation.

A strong culture is one where most of the members share the same organisational beliefs and values. Members unite around these values and behave in the desired manner implicitly. A weak culture may encourage individual thought. This is not necessarily a bad thing, particularly in innovative companies where new ideas are welcomed. Certainly a strong culture is one that will exert more influence on employees than a weak one.

A weak culture may encourage individual thought.

| **Exhibit 3.2** | Marks & Spencer has a strong corporate culture, which can be difficult to change. |

Source: Marks and Spencer plc (company), with permission.

Deal & Kennedy (1982) report research from US companies that claims that consistently high performance is a trait of companies with strong cultures. The famous work by Peters & Waterman (1982), *In Search of Excellence*, also points out that shared common values and a strong culture are a mark of successful companies. However, as pointed out in Chapter 1, the success of many of these companies in the Peters & Waterman study was short-lived. We recommend caution in claiming, as many authors do, that strong cultures are inherently good and weak cultures bad for an organisation.

It may become a problem to have a strong organisational culture. Marks & Spencer (M&S) struggled to become a more imaginative and innovative retailer when their market position weakened several years ago. They had spent decades recruiting people who would not 'rock the boat' but were happy to be directed and implement the chairman's wishes. We know that organisations need to recruit people who complement the existing culture. If the culture needs to be changed then the organisation may need to recruit people with a different type of personality. The M&S example demonstrates that a strong culture can be very difficult to change. This type of cultural embeddedness can lead to a variety of strategic challenges for an organisation, some of which cannot be resolved quickly.

> It may become a problem to have a strong organisational culture.

Organisations do not have a single culture. The dominant culture is often supported by various subcultures. So, it is possible that a weak culture persists because of the number of subcultures that exist within an organisation. Different departments may exhibit strong cultures but there is no unifying culture within the firm. This can be a problem when creating a coherent corporate brand. Also, in an age of mergers and acquisitions, problems with both dominant cultures and subcultures can arise when the employees of two organisations are brought together, in what might be considered an arranged marriage.

The types of organisational culture

Furnham & Gunter (1993) refer to the functions of organisational culture as internal integration and co-ordination. Their literature review of the field led them to the conclusion that the internal integration aspect involves socialising new members into the organisation, creating the boundaries for the organisation and fostering the feeling of identity, belonging and commitment to the organisation amongst its people.

The co-ordinating function of culture refers to differentiating the firm in order to have a competitive edge, enabling the firm to make sense of the environment in terms of what is acceptable behaviour.

Goffee & Jones (1996, 1998) outline four forms of organisational culture: networked, mercenary, fragmented and communal (Table 3.1). These four organisational types appear in matrix form with two dimensions or axes. The first is *sociability*, the amount of sincere friendliness amongst members of the organisation. A high level of communication is observed in a sociable firm, with people sharing ideas and fostering a strong team spirit.

> Sociability is the amount of sincere friendliness amongst members of the organisation.

The second dimension is *solidarity*, and is a measure of the ability of the workforce to pursue shared objectives, regardless of personal ties. The solidarity of the culture allows members to act as one. There is likely to be a lower tolerance of poor performance in an organisation focused on solidarity and it is likely to be more ruthless. The matrix is reproduced in Figure 3.2.

> Solidarity is a measure of the ability of the workforce to pursue shared objectives.

Table 3.1	The four types of organisation
Type of organisation	**Explanation**
The networked organisation (highly sociable and low in solidarity)	A highly social workplace where people socialise with each other inside and outside of work demonstrates a networked organisation. People may get a job here through people they know. The normal hierarchies may be circumnavigated to suit particular individuals or groups.
	The downside to this can be a very politicised workplace with cliques and in-crowds. Leaders can struggle to break through such cliques and impose their will. Such organisations will be mature, as these relationships do not happen overnight.
The mercenary organisation (low sociability and high solidarity)	This organisation is at the opposite end of the spectrum. Communication is business-based rather than social, and work and social life are clearly separate. The goal is to defeat the enemy (competitors). Such organisations will respond quickly to opportunities and threats. Employees not deemed to be pulling their weight will be quickly dispensed with. A long-hours culture will exist in the mercenary organisation.
	They may be successful but employees may lack loyalty to such companies as they feel no great personal empathy. Merchant banks are examples of mercenary organisations.
The fragmented organisation (low sociability and low solidarity)	Low consciousness of organisational membership may exist in the fragmented organisation. Employees may believe they work for themselves or have greater identity with professional groups. Universities are examples of such an organisation. Retiring director of Manchester Business School, Professor John Arnold, described managing the school as 'like being in charge of 200 sole traders!'
	When asked what they do for a living someone may reply 'a lawyer' rather than that they work for a local authority. Working from home may be popular in the fragmented firm and people often work alone rather than as a group. It is difficult to get agreement on how individuals should be judged (low solidarity) and proposed methods are often fiercely criticised all round. Such organisations may have slid into this quadrant by considerable downsizing and the closure of large offices in favour of working from home. BT (British Telecommunications) is an example of such a company.
The communal organisation (high sociability and high solidarity)	Perhaps best represented (but by no means all the time) by a small, fast-growing start-up business. Founders and employees may be close friends, however everyone needs to work hard and pull in the same direction to ensure the firm succeeds. Employees are likely to have shares in the company. Strong companies are high in both cultural contexts although it may be very difficult to achieve this state in many businesses. Innocent Drinks (see Viewpoint 8.2) could be considered an example of a communal organisation.

Source: Based on Goffee & Jones (1996).

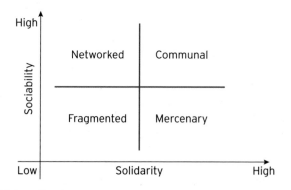

Figure 3.2 The four dimensions of culture.
Source: Goffee & Jones (1996), Harvard Business School Publishing, with permission.

Goffee & Jones state that one segment is not better than or superior to another. What is important is to ensure that the culture is appropriate for the market and competitive situation in which the firm operates.

It may well suit us to work in a sociable environment and the ease of communication may help creativity be fostered. Individuals may work harder than necessary and may also therefore go the extra mile for customers. Friendship can, however, lead to the tolerance of poor performance and there may be an overly exaggerated demand for consensus which slows down and distorts the decision-making process.

Solidarity is often exhibited by professional bodies such as doctors or lawyers, who will close ranks if they feel threatened. The culture that exhibits solidarity will have a high degree of strategic focus. It can engender trust among employees who see that everyone is judged by the same standards. This can lead to strong commitment in ensuring the corporation's goals are met (Goffee & Jones, 1996). Rigid job descriptions and the development of turf wars as individuals protect the boundaries of their own roles can be a downside of a culture that leans towards solidarity.

It should be noted that the literature surrounding corporate culture is vast and there are many variations on Goffee & Jones's interpretation of culture. Wallach (1983), for example, suggests that there were three main types of organisational culture: bureaucratic, supportive and innovative. Zammuto & Krakower (1991) produce their own matrix based upon having an internal or external focus on one axis and the balance between control and flexibility on the other axis. This is known as the Competing Values Framework. Mintzberg & Quinn (1988) identified five different ideologies (cultures) that complemented different types of organisation.

Cultures may change but not always for the better. The Football Association has professionalised itself to a considerable degree over recent years but questions remain about how successful this has been (see Viewpoint 3.2 for a glimpse of the issues).

> **Cultures may change but not always for the better.**

Viewpoint 3.2   Offside at the Football Association

The Football Association (FA) purports to be 'a world-class organisation with a winning mentality', self-styled rhetoric that, at best, is unsubstantiated and, at worst, would be deemed vacuous and tasteless by the bulk of the nation, in light of the glaring lack of success delivered by the national team at major tournaments. Whilst there are various barometers of achievement, the accomplishments of the national side may be pinpointed as the ultimate (and certainly most obvious) benchmark of the FA's success. Since the 1966 World Cup (the only major trophy won) England has only reached the semi-final stage of major tournaments on two occasions (World Cup, Italy, 1990; European Championships, England, 1996), modest achievements according to the ambitious targets/standards set by the organisation. The humiliation of the national team at the 2010 World Cup was the latest in a long line of spectacular failures.

Furthermore, the off-field profit yielded by the national team (marketed as a brand) is not relative, and it could be said is inverse, to the on-field performance, with the fact that the England national shirt is the world's highest-selling replica belying the small amount of success enjoyed by the side on the field. Sport is considered a meritocracy, yet the FA does not appear to espouse such values. The failing of England's youth policy has proven a decisive factor in allowing other nations to overhaul England's standing in world football whilst the fraction of money invested into the game at grassroots level has been minuscule in comparison to that injected into the top level of the sport. Another problem for the value system is the FA's corporate prioritisation (clearly in evidence at the expensively rebuilt Wembley stadium), which also characterises most Premiership clubs, permitting the most affluent (yet often the least committed) fans to occupy the most impressive panoramic vantage points at grounds nationwide.

The FA has facilitated and overseen a situation that has rendered the game less accessible to the 'everyday' citizen by gradually out-pricing them. It should be noted that in Spain and Germany (also infinitely

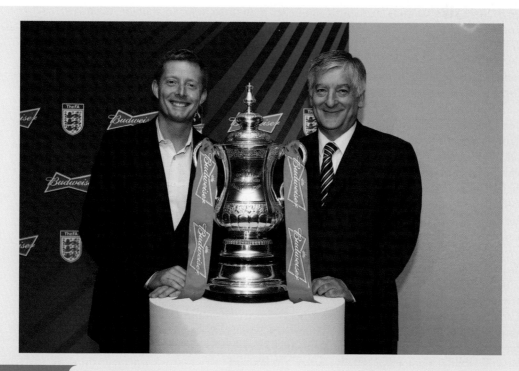

Exhibit 3.3   FA Chairman David Bernstein and Chris Burggraeve of AB InBev unveil Budweiser as
the FA Cup lead partner at Wembley Stadium in London on 16 June 2011.
Source: © Mark Thompson/The FA/Getty Images.

more successful as national teams than England) price points are set much more with the ordinary fan in mind. The absence of obvious English candidates for the job of coach of the national team (another problem that the FA must take responsibility for) resulted in the appointment of England's first foreign coach in 2001, Sven-Göran Eriksson, a selection that generated ambivalence amongst the nation's partisans. With the precedent fixed, the FA deemed it acceptable to appoint Fabio Capello in 2007. Despite being by far the best remunerated manager at the World Cup, more failure ensued.

On a rudimentary level, through the endorsement of football (a societal entity), the FA should hypothetically attempt to benefit society, though it appears to gauge success according to revenue generation even when this is palpably not in the interests of the core supporters of the game. Whilst the FA generates huge sums, it has allowed the grassroots of the game to decline enormously over the years. The general perception of the organisation is not a positive one, reviled as it is by a considerable number of English football fans who hold the game so dear. In order to improve its reputation it must begin to question its core values as both an institution and a brand, attaching primacy to its obligations as an institution rather than to its potential as a money-spinning corporate brand.

Question

What type of culture do you think exists at the FA? How could the culture be changed?

Brown & Turner (2008) talk of the danger of hubris, of management becoming over-confident of their own and their company's performance. They state that those organisations that demonstrate a consensus cluster, where the perceptions of the company and its results reflect the external perception, have the strongest financial performance.

The difficulty of changing cultures

Clearly corporate culture is a complex phenomenon. There may be problems within the organisational culture that require attention. One potential problem is that the company's values are ill-defined and there is a gap between the assumptions and the espoused values. There could well also be differences between the espoused values and the actual values demonstrated.

Culture mainly comprises tacit knowledge that is felt implicitly. New members of staff can, of course, be inducted into the organisation and informed about the rules and the culture, but it can take some time for this to become truly assimilated. It is when they see the example set by senior managers and colleagues that they will have a true idea of the type of behaviour that is expected of them. A senior manager may trot out the usual clichés about his door always being open but really give off an aura of 'ask no questions'.

> Culture mainly comprises tacit knowledge that is felt implicitly.

The deeper meanings that form the assumptions and beliefs of the employees are expressed as norms and values, and this shapes behaviour. So it is the culturally influenced behaviours that lead to the visible artefacts that are seen by all. Schein (1999) argues that when the new values, demonstrated by artefacts, are changed and are able to demonstrate their worth to members, then members absorb these ideas into the tacit, deeper levels of culture that constitute the values and assumptions. Over time this is how cultural change takes place. This is a difficult process as any new artefacts will always be absorbed and understood by members, using the existing cultural values and behaviours. Interpretation and negotiation are involved and changing culture never quite has the end result that the initiator expects. Employees need to be clear about the practical advantages these new values will offer them.

> Changing culture never quite has the end result that the initiator expects.

Many organisations like to think that they are innovative, but to what extent does the prevailing culture support this perception? What is the response of employees to new ideas and how are errors handled within the firm? Staff will not be willing to act creatively if they feel their mistakes will be punished. Hatch & Shultz (2008) discuss the work they have done with Johnson & Johnson and discuss that firm's credo, which states that 'employees must feel free to make suggestions and complaints' (p. 127). Clearly this is a key part of Johnson & Johnson's values.

In difficult economic circumstances, it may seem a good idea to move from a networked to a more results-oriented mercenary culture. Many public sector workers in the UK complain that this has been the case here, with a 'league table culture' dominating in schools, hospitals and universities. The danger is that in making many employees more accountable to concrete measures of success, e.g. the number of pupils passing examinations, the loyalty that employees have previously felt towards their institution may be eroded. Staff may be less willing to volunteer for additional duties if they feel that they are being judged in a detached fashion in key areas of their work. Cultural change is heavy with risk.

Goffee & Jones (1996) make recommendations for managers looking to adjust the amount of sociability or solidarity in their organisation. If the board wishes the firm to become more sociable, it can promote the sharing of ideas, interests and emotions and increase social interaction by arranging gatherings outside of the workplace. It can reduce the formality between employees, perhaps relaxing the dress code or altering the way space is allocated according to rank. Removing tiers of management, making the organisation flatter, moving to open-plan offices, ensuring the perks and conditions of service are uniform and genuinely demonstrating care to employees experiencing personal difficulties are all ways of moving the organisation to a more sociable structure.

Alternatively, management may be concerned that there is not sufficient solidarity within the organisation. To remedy this, managers may develop competitor awareness through formalised briefings, creating a greater sense of urgency by ensuring corporate objectives are well known, are repeated and have a measureable outcome. The will to win needs to be encouraged to ensure that employees become more results-focused.

> The organisation should recruit
> people who can help to move the
> culture towards the new ideal.

Of course, people are the key here and the human resources department should ensure that the organisation recruits people who can help to move the culture towards the new ideal. Training is a key way of ensuring that existing employees move towards the type of culture that is desired. An example of an organisation that has had to make considerable changes to its culture over recent years is London's Metropolitan Police (see Viewpoint 3.3).

Viewpoint 3.3   Is the culture nicked at the Met?

The murder in 1993 of black teenager Stephen Lawrence at a bus stop in south London would have wide-ranging implications for the organisational culture of the Metropolitan Police Service (MPS) that no one at the time could have envisaged. After the initial investigation, five suspects were arrested but never convicted. It was suggested during the course of the investigation that the murder had a racist motive, that Lawrence was killed because he was black, and that the handling of the case by the police and Crown Prosecution Service was affected by issues of race, leading to an inquiry.

Conducted by Sir William Macpherson, the inquiry found that the original police investigation had been incompetent and there had been 'the collective failure of an organisation to provide an appropriate and professional service to people because of their colour, culture or ethnic origin', which 'can be seen or detected in processes, attitudes and behaviour, which amount to discrimination through unwitting prejudice, ignorance, thoughtlessness, and racist stereotyping, which disadvantages minority ethnic people'. The report found that there had been a failure of leadership by senior MPS officers and that recommendations of the 1981 Scarman Report, compiled following race-related riots in Brixton and Toxteth, had been ignored.

Crucially the report made a total of 70 recommendations for reform – the overall aim being the elimination of racist prejudice and disadvantage and the demonstration of fairness in all aspects of policing. This

Exhibit 3.4	The Metropolitan Police Service in London underwent significant cultural change after the murder of black teenager Stephen Lawrence in 1993.

Source: Alamy Images/Ashley Cooper.

phrase meant that a culture existed that allowed a certain use of language and behaviours that became endemic within the force. Police forces were brought under the Race Relations Act, from which they were previously exempt, therefore criminalising racist statements made in private. Metropolitan Police Chief Sir Paul Condon said the report had brought 'shame on the police'. He said he would respond to the report with a crackdown on any form of racism in the force, with a rapid response murder inquiry force and with a research programme looking at how to improve policing.

Monitoring change was necessary to ensure it was taking place. This included police liaison with black and Asian communities, race awareness training and, efforts to tackle race crime and racist behaviour. Indicators such as monitoring the number of racist complaints against the police, recruitment of black and Asian officers and support in ethnic communities were implemented. Community engagement and professional development, including ongoing training, kept the issue current. The creation of a more representative workforce and the recognition of minority staff police associations within the MPS were initiated.

Reports have followed over the years that questioned the success of the MPS in implementing the Macpherson recommendations. However, by 2010 The Race and Faith Enquiry Report commissioned by London Mayor Boris Johnson stated, 'The MPS in 2010 feels incomparably more open, welcoming and progressive than the MPS of 1993. Many examples of a shifting and more open culture were recognised.'

An indication of what a long-term job changing culture can be is also clear in the report – '. . . it is only through further maturity and sophistication that the culture of the organisation will become sufficiently flexible for the constantly shifting nature of its staff to feel really confident and at home'.

Question

Find examples of three organisations that you feel have a culture that is out of sync with their market position. How should they go about changing their culture?

Actions speak louder than words in the difficult issue of cultural change. Of course, if a company is asking its employees to 'live the brand', then the senior management of the firm must set and live by the same high standards themselves. If they don't, then the message is seen to be insincere, lacking credibility and unlikely to be actioned.

Consider the money that is spent on rebranding exercises in the hope of turning around a company's fortunes. Clearly, from what we have discussed so far about the importance of culture, it should be obvious that merely changing the tangible symbols of a brand will not change the culture. A rebranding exercise is about more than considering the symbolic devices such as the corporate logo, letterheads and livery. So, a change to the visible elements does not mean that there will be a change to the tacit values and assumptions.

> Merely changing the tangible symbols of a brand will not change the culture.

Changing the visible elements is just an expensive quick fix. It is important that the HR policies of the organisation are a true expression of the corporate brand, its values and assumptions. What is being done within the firm to ensure that employees engage in brand-relevant behaviour? Is there a reward for doing so and how is this behaviour disseminated to the rest of the employees as a worthwhile example? Chapter 2 outlined the special role of employees within the corporate brand and the discussion of culture again emphasises their crucial importance to the brand.

> Changing the visible elements is just an expensive quick fix.

Culture and values of the brand

There is a clear link between the culture of an organisation and the brand that is produced. A lot of research into culture finds that it is the organisational values that are seen as being the clearest manifestation of culture (Parker & Bradley, 2000). This book emphasises the critical importance of values to the corporate brand (see Chapters 6 and 8) as the clear point of differentiation around which stakeholders can rally. In an era where the business world is often criticised and many products and services appear to be very similar, is it possible for customers to appreciate the culture embedded in the values of a brand? If so, then the culture of the brand can be appreciated externally as well as being a unifying force internally.

The headquarters (or a flagship building) of the corporate brand could potentially be an example of the power and prestige of the company. This could be an iconic building like the BT Tower in central London. The HQ can also say something about the values of the firm. Tesco's head office is a very modest 1960s built concrete office block on an industrial estate in Chesham, just off the M25. The value system of Tesco is represented by their humble HQ. It demonstrates that they will not spend money lavishly on themselves, and that the firm's money only gets spent on areas that generate revenue for the company, i.e., where the customers are. On occasions this may cause problems for the brand in terms of recruitment, as potential employees may be unimpressed by the place where they are expected to work. With a marketing strategy that is very customer-focused, the corporate HQ of Tesco reflects their waste-not-want-not approach to business.

The dress code at Asda is to dress down on a Friday, but crucially staff are encouraged to wear predominantly clothes from the George range, Asda's own label. Events and entertainment are often laid on for staff at their HQ in Leeds and such events will conclude with all staff singing the company song. If you are the sort of person who cringes at the idea of singing a corporate song then Asda is probably not the place for you to work, however strong the culture.

Many organisations reflect on their history and use corporate storytelling to express the *raison d'être* and personality of the organisation. Storytelling is not about telling stakeholders that you provide excellent customer service or some other easily repeatable bland strapline. James Dyson (see Viewpoint 3.1, p. 54) became frustrated by his vacuum cleaner's inability to vacuum properly and this led him to amending it from materials found around his house. This is the beginning of the story of innovation and determination to overcome difficulties that underpins this successful corporate brand.

Corporate storytelling helps demonstrate the importance of the brand.

The most effective corporate stories have a simplicity that is very powerful. Success stories are important, as are stories that celebrate the history of a brand, outlining its reason for being. Corporate storytelling helps demonstrate the importance of the brand both internally and externally and hints at what may be lost if the brand were to disappear.

To what extent is there an emotional bond to help lay a solid platform for a corporate story? For example, Southwest Airlines is based on fun and friendliness, and Volvo's market position and its reputation are largely built around pioneering safety in car manufacture.

The corporate story helps a firm to bond with its employees and creates a position for the company against competitors. Nationwide (as a mutual building society rather than a bank) positions itself in opposition to the caricature of the uncaring bank manager in its advertising. This attempts to give it some uniqueness in a homogeneous market, which is becoming more and more difficult to achieve, as companies are often run by accountants and contain very similar corporate structures. Again, therefore, the values and culture as explained by the corporate story can cement the position of the brand in the minds of stakeholders. Ideas and issues concerning storytelling are explored further in Chapter 10.

Employee satisfaction

If values and culture are important to a brand and culture comes from within the organisation, then naturally contented employees are vital. Employee satisfaction is important and, as Davies *et al.* (2003) point out, reputation comes from within and thus it is important to ensure employee satisfaction, as this leads to customer and stakeholder satisfaction and an enhanced reputation. Heskett *et al.*'s (1994) 'service-profit chain' claims an empirical link between employee and customer satisfaction.

For a service to be successful, front-line staff must have a high regard for the company, the service provided and the environment in which they work, otherwise they will not communicate appropriate messages to their stakeholders. An example of a brand that achieves this harmonious state is John Lewis (see Viewpoint 3.4).

> **Front-line staff must have a high regard for the company.**

Viewpoint 3.4 Everyone satisfied at John Lewis!

John Lewis Partnership hires a motivated cohort of staff, enhanced through their system in which each employee receives a share of the business's annual profit. This incentive scheme epitomises the notion of the internal customer and thus has staff actively buying into the company culture as a profitable venture.

Employees are known as partners and every partner receives a share of the profit. This is calculated as a percentage of salary, with the same percentage for everyone, from top management down to the shop floor. The bonus has varied between 9 and 20 per cent of the partners' annual salaries since 2000. In 2010, partners shared a bonus of £151 million, 15 per cent of annual salary.

In 1999, in response to a fall in profits, there were calls from some partners for the business to be demutualised and floated on the stock market. If implemented, each partner would have been guaranteed a windfall of up to £100,000, in order to compensate them for their share of the business. In the end, no one on the Partnership Council agreed with the idea and only one member spoke in favour of a referendum on the issue. This story helps outline the shared value system of the company.

The scheme commenced as early as 1920 when John Lewis's son expanded earlier power-sharing policies by sharing profits among the employees. When he died, Spedan Lewis (son of the original founder) bequeathed the company to his employees. Proud of being British, John Lewis has supported the textile industry in the north-west of England for a number of decades before recently being forced to sell two factories due to lack of profitability. However, it still operates one manufacturing business in Lancashire.

Every employee influences the business through branch forums, which discuss local issues at every store, and the divisional John Lewis and Waitrose councils. Partners also elect at least 80 per cent of the Partnership Council's 82 representatives, while the chairman appoints the remaining number. The Partnership Council also elects five of the directors on the partnership board (which is responsible for the commercial activities), while the chairman appoints another five. The two remaining board members are the chairman and the deputy chairman. This structure ensures that every non-management partner has an open channel for expressing his/her views to management and the chairman. Additionally, the John Lewis Partnership publishes a weekly in-house magazine, called *The Gazette* (the oldest in-house magazine still being published in the UK). Each John Lewis branch also has its own weekly magazine, called *The Chronicle*.

John Lewis has an extensive programme of social activities for its partners, including two large country estates with parklands, playing fields and tennis courts; a golf club; a sailing club with five cruising yachts; and two country hotels offering holiday accommodation for the partners. In addition to this, upon completing 25 years of service for the company, partners are given a paid 6-month break. It is little surprise that this inclusive, staff-oriented culture has led John Lewis Partnership to acquire a reputation as an exalted employer. This strong internal identity helps to foster an external reputation that is the envy of many of its competitors.

Question

Is employee or customer satisfaction the most important aim of management?

Source: Various, including www.johnlewispartnership.co.uk.

The employer as brand

If, as discussed, culture is a key area for management and employees are a vital part of a brand, then recruiting and retaining staff of the right calibre will impact upon the success of the brand. Like everything else, the competition for the best people is a market. In order to give themselves the best chance of recruiting the best people companies have developed what is referred to as 'employer branding'.

Some experts still see employer branding as a 'slippery concept' (CIPD, 2007, p. 7). Ambler & Barrow (1996) have been widely credited with introducing the concept of employer branding, defined as 'the package of functional, economic, and psychological benefits provided by employment, and identified with the employing company' (p. 8). Other definitions of the concept include Lloyd's (2002) 'sum of a company's efforts to communicate to existing and prospective staff that it is a desirable place to work'. Backhaus & Tikoo (2004) see it as the 'process of building an identifiable and unique employer identity' and Sullivan (2004) as 'a targeted, long-term strategy to manage awareness and perceptions of employees, potential employees, and related stakeholders with regards to a particular firm'.

> The aim of employer branding is to provide a 'total work experience' that is distinctive and desirable for employees.

The aim of employer branding is to provide a holistic experience (Gaddam, 2008), designed to create and maintain a 'total work experience' that is distinctive and desirable for employees (Ewing *et al.*, 2002; Lloyd, 2002; Mosley, 2004). Its goal is also to incorporate the organisation's core 'brand essence' (Mosley, 2004) into relevant work activities and provide a means of identification for existing employees (Barrow & Mosley, 2005). This seeks to align the core brand essence with the external messages that are disseminated to potential employees and other stakeholders (Ambler & Barrow, 1996). By harmonising the internal and external messages of the brand (see Chapter 2) reputation is enhanced.

An organisation's core brand essence is made up of its values and culture and these are displayed in its mission, brand personality and overall defining characteristics that signify 'what it is' and 'the way things are done in the organisation' (Martin, 2008, p. 19). An organisation's core brand essence can be interpreted as its 'identity' as outlined in Chapter 2 and is taken to represent an organisation's core, distinctive and enduring attributes (Albert & Whetten, 1985; Gioia *et al.*, 2000; Argenti & Druckenmiller, 2004), as perceived and understood by members of the organisation (Hatch & Schultz, 1997; Davies & Chun, 2002).

Employer branding therefore involves the delivery of the employment value proposition or promise (Berthon *et al.*, 2005; Carrington, 2007; CIPD, 2007; Moroko & Uncles, 2008) made to potential and actual employees by the organisation. The employment value proposition outlines the package of benefits that employees would receive as a result of their employment with the organisation. In effect, this becomes a psychological contract between the employees and the organisation. The psychological contract represents the mutual beliefs, perceptions and informal obligations between the employer and employees. Clearly as the contract is informal rather than formalised in writing, it is indicative of the trust that exists between the two parties. This contract should have a positive effect on behaviour at work, linked, of course, to the prevailing culture of the firm, and on the firm's performance.

Clearly there is an inherent danger here. Gaps between the image of the company that the public form and the identity that is perceived by the employees can have a detrimental impact on reputation (Ambler & Barrow, 1996; Martin *et al.*, 2005). Gaps between the employment promise and that, which is delivered, will noticeably decrease job satisfaction, employees' trust in the organisation, as well as job performance (Lester *et al.*, 2002; Suazo, 2009). The point, therefore, is that there must be consistency in all areas for the brand to be successful.

> Employer branding, therefore, serves to distinguish an organisation from its competitors as the employer of choice.

Employer branding therefore, serves to distinguish an organisation from its competitors as the employer of choice, as it provides employees with a distinctive and attractive total work experience. Employer branding can be measured, to some extent, by league tables published (for example) in the UK by *The Sunday Times*' Best Companies to Work For (see Chapter 4) and by *Fortune*'s list of best employers in the US. A company that appears to emphasise the employer brand and has a culture that has led to its exponential growth to one of the internet's great success stories is Google (see Viewpoint 3.5).

Viewpoint 3.5	**To find a great place to work . . . Google it!**

Founded as recently as 1998, Google is now a huge global brand. Most famous for its search engine (but now having developed its business into so much more), the company processes over one billion search requests each day. Google is renowned for its informal corporate culture, manifested externally by its quirky and ever-changing versions of its own corporate logo. In 2007 and 2008, *Fortune* magazine had Google at the top of its workplace preference list. Since then it has occupied an impressive fourth place. Google's corporate ethos encapsulates such anti-corporate ideology as 'you can make money without doing evil', 'you can be serious without a suit' and 'work should be challenging and the challenge should be fun'.

Hiring is based on three principles – 'it's tough to get into Google; all hires are talent; we cherish our culture'. Once recruited, an 'on-boarding' process takes place. A new recruit is allocated a 'buddy' for a year; hence the culture of the firm is protected and maintained.

Google's impressive headquarters in Mountain View, California, has been entitled 'the Googleplex'. It has received plentiful publicity owing to the unique, vibrant work environment engendered by the complex which has consequently rendered it a much sought-after site of employment. The lobby is embellished with a piano, lava lamps, old server clusters, and a projection of live search queries currently being requested by net users across the globe on the wall. Exercise balls and bicycles fill the hallways. There is a modern-day version of Cadbury's (Viewpoint 2.1) recreational facilities. Recreational amenities are innovative and plentiful, including a state-of-the-art gym, a massage room, assorted video games, a baby grand piano and various amusements (namely foosball, pool tables and ping pong). In addition to the recreation room, there are numerous restaurants serving food of multinational varieties, and snack rooms stocked with various foods and drinks.

As an alternative motivation technique (called 'innovation time off'), all 'Googlers' (a playful term attached to Google engineers which serves to reinforce the identity of both the brand and its employees) are urged to spend 20 per cent of their work time on projects that interest them. The scheme (and thus underlying philosophy) has paid tangible dividends, with some of Google's novel services, such as Gmail, Google News, Orkut, and AdSense deriving from these individual projects. The implication for management at a brand like Google is that 'structured liberty' is a good thing in order to enhance expression in the workplace, since authoritarianism could inevitably prove counterproductive, stifling creativity and invariably provoking dissent in the work ranks.

Finally, in a noble bid to avert becoming overtly corporate through maintaining the initial core values upon which the company was established, Google has designated a chief culture officer in 2006, specifically named so that the company does not lose its distinctive value system. The CCO also serves as the director of human resources.

Considering all the above, it is not surprising, therefore, that Google continues to be regarded, both by the job-hunting public and its officially published ranking, as the zenith of employers.

Question

What are the factors that may threaten an innovative culture such as that at Google?

Newer organisations and particularly those that have come to prominence via the expansion of the internet may seek to differentiate themselves by their culture. To them work is not a chore but a calling and a place where fun is to be had. There are considerable benefits of creating a fun work environment, not least increased employee loyalty and creativity.

In the *most admired company* league tables, what constitutes employer branding often appears under the heading of quality of management and people management.

Quality of management and people management

One of the key areas indicating corporate success according to Brown & Turner (2008) when detailing Britain's most admired companies is *quality of management*.

In the most admired lists this characteristic comprises three factors:

- the profile of the CEO and how well he or she manage stakeholders
- how clearly the CEO articulates the company's strategy
- how the CEO/chairman is perceived as delivering against this strategy.

High-profile past and present CEOs include such luminaries as Jack Welch (General Electric), Bill Gates (Microsoft), Steve Jobs (Apple) and Richard Branson (Virgin), John Browne (BP), Stuart Rose (Marks & Spencer) and Justin King (Sainsbury's). Clearly such individuals are of great importance to the culture, and therefore reputation, of their corporate brands.

Procter & Gamble is an example of a company that scores highly for its quality of people management. It has a managerial philosophy of 'building from within' and fostering 'an exclusive culture'. It achieves this accolade despite the fact it is a very large company with 135,000 employees in 80 countries.

Another category of the most admired index that impacts very much upon culture is 'ability to attract, develop and keep talented people'. This is 'people management', is referred to as 'talent management' by Brown & Turner (2008), and clearly can be included within employer branding.

Is the talent of staff seen as a corporate asset within an organisation in the way that more tangible assets are? Britain has a well established long-hours culture. Which companies actively involve themselves in their employees' work-life balance, thereby reducing workplace stress?

Is the talent of staff seen as a corporate asset?

A company that demonstrates such a commitment to its staff may be said to have demonstrated a supportive and forward-thinking culture.

It is interesting to contrast the UK culture with that of another European country, Sweden. In Sweden managers are seen more as facilitators or coaches who offer advice and suggestions, and decisions tend to be made by consensus rather than by giving orders. Sweden has been named in a European Union study as having among the most flexible working hours in Europe, allowing employees to strike a better balance between work and home life (www.sweden.se). Swedes consider that such flexibility makes good business sense, as creativity is stimulated and productivity increased amongst satisfied and committed employees.

Commitment to staff in the modern, flatter organisation that has fewer tiers of management and therefore decreased opportunity for promotion can be more difficult to decipher. Employees often see commitment in these flatter organisations in terms of the quality of training that they are offered by their employer (Roper & Davies, 2010).

These complex relationships can perhaps best be explained by the circular relationship shown in Figure 3.3.

The key components are the values and value system of the organisation.

Satisfied employees articulate and demonstrate the brand values.

The key components are the values and value system of the organisation. These lead to a culture that ensures the best employees can be recruited and, crucially, retained. Satisfied employees articulate and demonstrate the brand values to customers and stakeholders who, in turn, support these values and continue to endorse and recommend the brand to others. It is this constant process of reinforcement that makes a corporate brand strong and sustains competitive advantage.

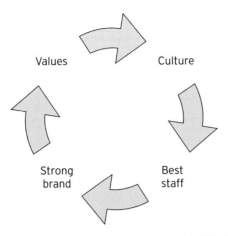

| **Figure 3.3** | The relationship between values, culture and the brand. |

Chapter summary

In order to consolidate your understanding of the significance of corporate culture, here are the key points summarised against each of the learning objectives.

1. Discuss where the responsibility for corporate reputation lies

Responsibility for corporate reputation must lie at the top of the organisation. If there is no commitment at the top then it is unlikely that a culture will develop that will seek to build and maintain a favourable reputation.

Certain commentators on the subject insist that a proactive role should be taken by companies rather than simply allowing themselves to be chastised by an unfriendly media. Corporate reputation management means just that – it is about ongoing management, not just responding when a crisis has occurred. Corporate reputation is not an additional extra that should be the preserve of the PR department.

2. Define and explore the characteristics of corporate culture

Corporate culture is a complex phenomenon and one that may take quite some time to uncover. A culture will develop and be reinforced over a period of time. Corporate culture is a field of study that describes the psychology, attitudes, experiences, beliefs and values of an organisation.

It is often useful to think of corporate culture in terms of the metaphor of an iceberg, with much of the culture invisible at first glance. Edgar Schein tells us that corporate culture is made up of three levels – artefacts and behaviours, espoused values and assumptions – that reflect the shared values of the organisation. Assumptions can be so embedded in an organisation that they go without saying. This means they can be difficult for observers to identify.

Morgan describes organisational culture as 'the set of beliefs, values and norms, together with symbols like dramatised events and personalities, that represents the unique character of an organisation, and provides the context for action in it and by it'.

3. Consider strong and weak corporate cultures

A strong culture is one that will be clearly recognisable and one that has staff members responding to a clear set of organisational values and passing these on to others. All members of the organisation will clearly pull in the same direction as they have bought into the shared values of the company.

A weak culture is one where rules and bureaucracy may be necessary to enforce the desired behaviour. Many commentators insist that a strong culture is the sign of a successful organisation. This can be true, but it can also be difficult to change a strong culture, if needed. A weak culture is one where individual thought is more likely. This, however, may be desirable in an organisation that is creative and innovative.

It may be the case that individual departments have strong cultures but the overall culture of the firm is weak.

4. Recognise the different types of corporate culture that exist within organisations

Goffee & Jones (1996, 1998) outline four forms of organisational culture: networked, mercenary, fragmented and communal. Which type of company you are depends upon the amount of sociability or solidarity there is within the organisation. A sociable firm will have considerable communication and there will be a lot of shared activity both inside and outside of the workplace.

A company that displays solidarity is one in which the members are able to come together and work in the same direction in order to achieve specific corporate goals. This company may be more ruthless than its sociable counterpart. The important thing is to ensure that the culture that exists is one that suits the prevailing market conditions.

5. Explain the difficulties associated with cultural change

Because cultures form and are reinforced over time, they can be very difficult to change. At the more extreme end, certain commentators point out that if you wish to change your culture then you must change your staff. Certainly new values will have to be explained and understood by all if they are going to be embraced. Of course, new values are assimilated using the old value system and therefore cultural change is risky and may not have the exact effect that was desired.

Goffee & Jones (1996, 1998) suggest that tweaking the amount of sociability or solidarity that is exhibited by the firm, in order to better reflect market conditions, may be the best way to go about changing culture. Training is a key way of ensuring that existing employees move towards the type of culture that is desired.

6. Link culture with the values of the brand

Values are a key part of any corporate brand. Our products and services may be easily imitated by competitors but they will find it considerably more difficult to imitate our culture. The key link in both culture and brands, therefore, is the values/value system of the company.

Having an authentic corporate story is a good starting point and can be used to demonstrate the personality and *raison d'être* of the brand. This can cement the importance of the brand internally and externally and let us know what might be lost if the brand no longer existed.

7. Consider the relationship to the employer brand

Culture comes from within the firm. So do the employees, and ensuring they are happy is a key way to ensure that they reflect the correct and consistent message to customers. In this way a virtuous circle is created and corporate reputation is enhanced. Employer branding is really the attempt to ensure that the best staff are able to be recruited and crucially maintained. It aims to provide a total work experience that is distinctive and desirable for employees.

In this way the core brand essence of the firm is encapsulated and then projected onwards to all stakeholders.

Discussion questions

1. Provide a definition of corporate culture.
2. For an organisation of your choice, write a paragraph outlining the corporate culture of that organisation as you see it.
3. Why is the metaphor of the iceberg used when explaining corporate culture?
4. Provide examples of artefacts that could be important to the culture of an organisation.
5. Goffee & Jones (1996) outline four dimensions of corporate culture. Provide an example of an organisation that fits the description of each of these four dimensions.
6. Why is it so difficult to change a corporate culture?
7. What steps could be taken by management to ensure that an attempt to change the corporate culture was successful?
8. What is employer branding and what is the link between this and corporate branding?
9. What steps can management take to ensure that reputation management is embedded within the culture of the organisation?
10. In what circumstances may it be a disadvantage for an organisation to have a strong culture?

References

Albert, S. & Whetten, D. (1985). Organizational identity. In: Cummings, L. & Staw, B., eds. *Research in Organizational Behavior*. Greenwich, CT: JAI Press, pp. 263–295.

Ambler, T. & Barrow, S. (1996). The employer brand. *Journal of Brand Management* 4(3), 185–206.

Argenti, P. & Druckenmiller, B. (2004). Reputation and the corporate brand. *Corporate Reputation Review* 6(4), 368–374.

Backhaus, K. & Tikoo, S. (2004). Conceptualizing and researching employer branding. *Career Development International* 9(4/5), 501–517.

Barrow, S. & Mosley, R. (2005). *The employer brand: Bringing the best of brand management to people at work*. Chichester: John Wiley & Sons Ltd.

Berthon, P., Ewing, M. & Hah, L. (2005). Captivating company: dimensions of attractiveness in employer branding. *International Journal of Advertising* 24(2), 151–172.

Brown, M. & Turner, P. (2008). *The Admirable Company*. London: Profile Books.

Carrington, L. (2007). Designs on the dotted line *People Management Magazine* (18 October), 36–39.

Chartered Institute of Personnel and Development (CIPD) (2007). *Research insight: Employer Branding – The latest fad or the future for HR?* Online: http://www.cipd.co.uk/NR/rdonlyres/56C8377F-256B-4556-8650-8408B0E07576/0/empbrandlatfad.pdf. Accessed: 12 January 2009.

Davies, G. & Chun, R. (2002). Gaps between the internal and external perceptions of the corporate brand. *Corporate Reputation Review* 5(2/3), 144–157.

Davies, G., Chun, R., da Silva, R. & Roper, S. (2003). *Corporate Reputation and Competitiveness*. London: Routledge.

Deal, T.E. & Kennedy, A.A. (1982). *Corporate Cultures: The Rites and Rituals of Corporate Life*. Harmondsworth: Penguin Books.

Dowling, G. (1994). *Corporate Reputations: Strategies for Developing the Corporate Brand*. London: Kogan Page.

Ewing, M., Pitt, L., de Bussy, N. & Berthon, P. (2002). Employment branding in the knowledge economy. *International Journal of Advertising* 21, 3–22.

Furnham, A. & Gunter, B. (1993). *Corporate Assessment: Auditing a Company's Personality.* London: Routledge.

Gaddam, S. (2008). Modelling employer branding communication: the softer aspect of HR marketing management. Hyderabad: *The Icfai University Press*, pp. 45–55.

Gaines-Ross, L. (2008). *Corporate Reputation: 12 Steps to Safeguarding and Recovering Reputation.* New Jersey: Wiley.

Gioia, D., Schultz, M. & Corley, K. (2000). Organizational identity, image, and adaptive instability. *Academy of Management Review*, 2(1), 63–81.

Goffee, R. & Jones, G. (1996). What holds the modern company together? *Harvard Business Review*, November–December.

Goffee, R. & Jones, G. (1998). *The Character of a Corporation.* London: Harper Business.

Griffin, A. (2008). *New Strategies for Reputation Management: Gaining Control of Issues, Crises and Corporate Social Responsibility.* London: Chartered Institute of Public Relations.

Hatch, M.J. & Schultz, M. (1997). Relations between organizational culture, identity and image. *European Journal of Marketing* 31(5–6), 356–365.

Hatch, M.J. & Schultz, M. (2008). *Taking Brand Initiative: How Companies Can Align Strategy, Culture and Identity through Corporate Branding.* San Francisco: Jossey-Bass.

Heskett, J.L., Jones, T.O., Loveman, G.W., Sasser, W.E., Jr., Schlesinger, L.A. (1994). Putting the service-profit chain to work. *Harvard Business Review* 72(Mar–Apr), 164–174.

Lester, S., Turnley, W., Bloodgood, J., & Bolino, M. (2002). Not seeing eye to eye: differences in supervisor and subordinate perceptions of and attributions for psychological contract breach. *Journal of Organizational Behavior* 23, 39–56.

Lloyd, S. (2002). Branding from the inside out. *BRW* 2(10), 64–66.

Martin, G. (2008). Employer branding – time for some long and hard reflections? Online: http://www.managingpeoplebook.com/userimages/revised_reflections_paper_june_14th.doc. Accessed: 2 July 2009.

Martin, G., Beaumont, P., Doig, R., Pate, J. (2005). Branding: a new performance discourse for HR? *European Management Journal* 23(1), 76–88.

Mintzberg, H. & Quinn, J.B. (1988). *The Strategy Process.* Harlow: Prentice-Hall.

Morgan, G. (1997). *Images of Organization.* Thousand Oaks, CA: Sage Publications.

Moroko, L. & Uncles, M. (2008). Characteristics of successful employer brands. *Journal of Brand Management* 16(3), 160–175.

Mosley, R. (2004). *Employer Brand Leadership, A Roadmap.* Online: http://www.webdms.net/dms/uploaded_files/pib/pib.mdb/downloads/Employer%20Brand%20Roadmap.pdf. Accessed: 15 May 2006.

Parker, R. & Bradley, L. (2000). Organisational culture in the public sector: evidence from six organisations. *The International Journal of Public Sector Management* 13(2), 125–141.

Peters, T. & Waterman, R.H. (1982). *In Search of Excellence: Lessons from America's Best Run Companies.* London: Profile Books.

Roper, S. & Davies, G. (2010). Business-to-business branding: external and internal satisfiers and the role of training quality. *European Journal of Marketing* 44(5), 567–590.

Schein, E. (1999). *The Corporate Culture Survival Guide: Sense and Nonsense about Culture Change.* San Francisco: Jossey Bass.

Suazo, M. (2009). The mediating role of psychological contract violation on the relations between psychological contract breach and work-related attitudes and behaviors. *Journal of Managerial Psychology* 24(2), 136–160.

Sullivan, J. (2004). Eight elements of a successful employment brand. *ER Daily*, 23 February.

Wallach, E. (1983). Individuals and organisation: the cultural match. *Training and Development Journal* 12, 28–36.

Zammuto, R.F. & Krakower, J.Y. (1991). Quantitative and qualitative studies of organizational culture. *Research in Organizational Change and Development* 5, 83–114.

Chapter 4
Measuring corporate reputation

Measuring the strength and quality of an organisation's reputation is an important task. One of the first steps in the measurement process is to undertake a reputational audit to determine how stakeholders currently perceive the organisation. It is from this point that reputation strategies can be legitimately formed.

Various commercial and academic methodologies have been developed to measure corporate reputation. Some, however, have serious issues that cast doubt on what they are actually measuring. Despite these issues, it is clear that attempting to measure an organisation's reputation is a positive action, and one that cannot be ignored, although it often is.

Aims and learning objectives

The aim of this chapter is to examine the various approaches used to measure corporate reputation.

The learning objectives of this chapter are to:

1. Consider whether an attempt should be made to measure corporate reputation
2. Explore the idea of reputational audits
3. Consider some of the broad indicators of corporate reputation
4. Review some of the specific tools used to measure corporate reputation
5. Introduce the idea of measuring reputation by assessing the corporate character of the organisation.

What price your reputation?

Tiger Woods is golf's first billion-dollar man. Since turning professional he has earned a staggering eight-figure sum from the sport. Although the prize money earned through winning tournaments has hardly been insubstantial, his main career earnings have come from commercial endorsements from brands eager to link themselves to his unparalleled success as the world's number one player. The first 10 years of his professional career realised $100 million in prize money and a staggering $668 million in endorsement earnings (Sirak, 2008). His undoubted skill allied to a seemingly blemish-free private life made Woods a great commercial partner. All of this was to come crashing down, however, at the end of 2009 when allegations and subsequent confessions about his private life surfaced.

Reputation is difficult to put a price on.

As will be discussed, reputation is difficult to put a price on. However, perhaps the case of Tiger Woods allows us to do this. Corporate sponsors Accenture and AT&T dumped him as an endorser. This reputational sanction cost him a combined $18–25 million a year, according to Robert Tuchman of Premiere Global Sports, as reported in *USA Today*.

Christopher R. Knittel and Victor Stango of the University of California conclude that between the car accident and Woods' announcement of an 'indefinite leave' from golf on 11 December 2009, sponsors' shareholders lost $5–12 billion in wealth relative to shareholders of firms he does not endorse. They conclude that not only are the losses substantial but Woods' sports-related sponsors seem to suffer more than his other non-sports related sponsors. This could indicate some of the difficulties of reputational association as outlined in Chapter 1. While his top five sponsors (Accenture, Nike, Gillette, Electronic Arts and Gatorade) lost 2–3 per cent of their market value after the incident, his core sports-related sponsors, EA, Nike and PepsiCo (Gatorade), lost over 4 per cent.

The reputational audit

The corporate reputation of an organisation rests with the CEO.

Dowling (2006) explains that the corporate reputation of an organisation rests with the CEO and is shared with other board members. He states that the three main elements of a reputational audit are as follows:

- The beliefs and expectations of stakeholders are the point against which the company is judged. They set the emotional benchmark against which a company is compared. Also, comparing a company with its rivals in the marketplace allows a performance benchmark to be set.
- The business model of a company defines the primary operational levers of control and the major sources of reputation risk.
- The business philosophy and values espoused by a company define its moral compass (see Chapter 6 for a discussion of the importance of values to a brand).

Dowling emphasises the importance of continually assessing the sources of reputational risk to an organisation.

The purpose of a reputational audit is to assess where a company is in terms of its corporate reputation.

The purpose of a reputational audit is to assess where a company is now in terms of its corporate reputation. In the light of this we now discuss some of the most important measures of corporate reputation from both an academic and a commercial perspective.

Fombrun (1996) suggests that companies show their commitment to certain business functions by staffing a department that is committed to that function, e.g. customer service or

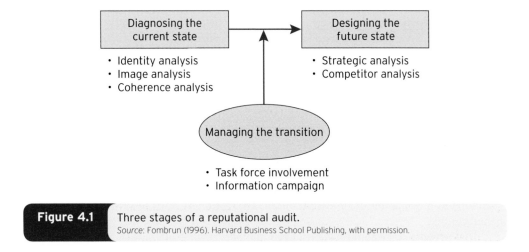

Figure 4.1 Three stages of a reputational audit.
Source: Fombrun (1996). Harvard Business School Publishing, with permission.

public relations. He proposes that the appointment of a chief reputational officer within companies would cement the importance of reputation management within an organisation.

Fombrun presents three stages of a reputational audit (see Figure 4.1):

- **Stage 1: Diagnosing the current state** – a diagnostic review of the company's current identity, images and reputation
- **Stage 2: Designing the future state** – a strategic analysis of trends, plans and competitive positioning that defines the company's desired future state
- **Stage 3: Managing the transition** – a review of the company's plans for managing the transition towards the future state.

The broad indicators of corporate reputation

It is interesting that there are many accountants who do not consider that it is possible to quantify the impact of branding, advertising and marketing communications. In view of the considerable influence accountants appear to have on company boards, this is a clear reason why such activities have often been seen not as an investment but as a cost to the business. This mindset leads inevitably to a reduction in the effort given to these factors when an economy falters. However, seeing as these activities are designed to increase the familiarity and favourability of an organisation, it must be said that they are able to have an impact on 'creating the reputational assets' of the company (Fombrun & van Riel, 2004, p. 32). It could be said therefore that branding activity per se will help and impact upon the reputational capital of a business.

Fombrun & van Riel (2004) consider reputational capital to be one of four measures that should be used to deconstruct the market value of a company: physical, financial, intellectual and reputational capital (see Table 4.1 for an explanation). The first two are straightforward accountancy-based measures which could be clearly identified in a company's balance sheet and are therefore easy to measure. Intellectual capital is as difficult to measure as reputation. Fombrun & van Riel (2004) therefore suggest another quantifiable measure of reputation – the income from the lease of the corporate name, i.e., licensing agreements. The larger the share of royalties from the lease of the name, they argue, the higher the reputation. They state that royalty licences can range between 8 and 14 per cent of projected sales. In 2010, for example, product merchandise sales at Disney grew to $2.7 billion largely based upon the success of *Toy Story 3* plus the acquisition of the Marvel comics brand.

> Fombrun & van Riel (2004) consider reputational capital to be one of four measures that should be used to deconstruct the market value of a company.

Table 4.1	Four measures of an organisation's market value
Type of capital	**Explanation**
Physical	The replacement of the company's non-financial tangible assets
Financial	The liquid financial assets of a company
Intellectual	The value of a company's know-how
Reputational	The value of the company's brands and stakeholder relationships

Source: Based on Fombrun & van Riel (2004).

Traditionally, much of this income is produced directly by licensing the Disney brand to other manufacturers.

A drop in share price could be considered another, albeit crude, measure of reputational capital. How does the share price of a company react to a crisis? The BP share price fell from a 52-week high of £6.55 to a low of £3.02 at the low point of the fallout from the Deepwater Horizon drilling rig explosion in April 2010. By December 2010 it had recovered to £4.60. At one point the share price had dropped below the book value (assets minus liabilities, not including issues such as branding and reputation) of the company, a situation previously unheard of for the oil giant.

Other well known financial measurements and ratios could be used as crude (non-specific) measurements of a corporate reputation. Examples of these are provided in the following sections.

Return on investment (ROI)

Return on investment is a performance measure used to evaluate the efficiency of an investment or to compare the efficiency of a number of different investments. To calculate ROI, the benefit (return) of an investment is divided by the cost of the investment; the result is expressed as a percentage or a ratio.

The ROI formula:

$$ROI = \frac{(\text{gain from investment} - \text{cost of investment})}{\text{cost of investment}}$$

In this formula 'gains from investment' refers to the proceeds obtained from selling the investment of interest. ROI is a very popular metric because of its versatility and simplicity. That is, if an investment does not have a positive ROI, or if there are other opportunities with a higher ROI, then the investment should not be undertaken.

Shareholder value

Shareholder value is the value delivered to shareholders because of management's ability to grow earnings, dividends and share price. In other words, shareholder value is the sum of all strategic decisions that affect the firm's ability to increase efficiently the amount of free cash flow over time. Of course, here lies the difficulty that helped lead to the banking crisis. Achieving a balance between responsibly growing shareholder value and recklessly attempting to increase profits at all costs has proved difficult for many companies that previously held blemish-free corporate reputations.

> Shareholder value is the value delivered to shareholders because of management's ability to grow earnings, dividends and share price.

The banking crisis has reflected the reputational demise of Britain's top banks. For many years a blue-chip stock, many banks have joined a club they would not have wished to be members of – the 90 per cent club. RBS share price as at 13 March 2009 was 22.4p, down

94 per cent from its peak of the previous year. In December 2010 it stood at 41.4p. Lloyds bank shares lost 91 per cent and Barclays 88 per cent of their value. HSBC was seen as one of the strongest banks, but still suffered a 61 per cent fall. Standard Chartered lost 54 per cent of its peak share price (Evans, 2009). The speed with which the share price recovers after a crisis can also be informative about the strength of an organisation's reputation. It will be an interesting exercise to monitor the share price of the companies mentioned here and assess the nature, speed and extent of their recovery.

Media comment

It may be that the brand's media reputation is higher than its reputation with customers. The company may need to work on one or the other. It was mentioned in Chapter 1 how difficult it can be to protect one's reputation from onslaught, particularly by the newer forms of social media. Deephouse (2000) discusses media reputation, defined as the overall evaluation of a firm presented in the media. His work indicates that media reputation is a resource that increases the performance of commercial banks. However, it should be noted that this work was conducted well before the banking crisis (see Viewpoint 1.4). The Reputation Institute provides a 'media reputation index' (MRI) for large organisations that compares companies with its rivals. The MRI measures the number of stories, tone, number of impressions, and the average impact and net effect of media coverage of the six dimensions of the Reputation Quotient, discussed later in this chapter.

The media can have a disproportionate impact on a company's reputation. Coverage in newspapers or on consumer affairs television programmes such as BBC's *Watchdog* can very quickly undermine a painstakingly built corporate reputation.

> The media can have a disproportionate impact on a company's reputation.

Viewpoint 4.1 | BA's terminal reputation

Opened in a blaze of publicity in spring 2008, Terminal 5 at Heathrow Airport was billed as offering the ultimate in passenger experience. The main building in the complex is the largest free-standing structure in the UK. Terminal 5 is currently used as a global hub exclusively by British Airways (BA). The terminal is designed to ultimately handle 35 million passengers a year. The building cost £4 billion and was many years in the planning. There was considerable controversy (and a very long public inquiry) into whether it was appropriate to build a new terminal at what many consider to be an already overcrowded and poorly located airport or whether the resource should go to competitor airports such as Stansted. Terminal 5 was a huge undertaking involving 16 major projects and 147 sub-projects. These projects include several new buildings and a railway station. Furthermore, in order for these buildings to be constructed, a new control tower had to be built.

When opening the new terminal the Queen described it as 'a 21st-century gateway to Britain'. What should have been a triumph for BA soon descended into a reputational disaster for the company. It quickly became apparent that the new terminal was not operating smoothly, and BA cancelled 34 flights and was later forced to suspend baggage check-in altogether. Over the following 10 days, some 42,000 bags failed to travel with their owners and over 5,000 flights were cancelled. *The Sun* indicated that 90 per cent of bags would never be reunited with their owners. In July 2008 the poor start became a reputational horror show for BA as negative news coverage abounded. Nightly updates on major television news programmes together with front-page headlines harangued the beleaguered company. It was nearly 2 weeks before BA was able to operate its full schedule from Terminal 5 and it was forced to postpone the transfer of its long-haul flights from Terminal 4 to Terminal 5. The difficulties were later blamed on a number of problems with the terminal's IT systems, coupled with car parking, including staff being unable to report for work due to a lack of parking and, indeed, being unable to find the car parks! All these stories combined to give the impression of a company unable to cope with its own business.

Exhibit 4.1 London Heathrow's Terminal 5.
Source: Alamy Images/Kevin Allen.

The Guardian claimed that 900 bags per day were still being lost at Terminal 5 and damningly that travel insurers were so concerned that they were withdrawing cover for lost baggage at the new facility. A spokesperson for Direct

At one point, it was claimed 900 bags per day were being lost at Terminal 5.

Line said: 'It is a general principle of all insurance that it only covers unforeseen chance events. Once something becomes widely known like this, it is no longer unforeseen.'

British Airways had to launch an advertising campaign to assure the public that things were working normally again. The company reported that the chaos surrounding the opening of Terminal 5 had cost an initial £16 million only days into the unfortunate opening. The costs were incurred mainly by the cancellation of 300 short-haul flights, the firm said. However, the true cost of reputational damage cannot be measured in terms of a few missed flights. Analysts at Deutsche Bank forecast the problems at Terminal 5 would persist into the summer and would cost the airline about £150 million in total and damage long-term reputation at a time when competition on transatlantic routes was intensifying.

Clearly the press were not prepared to see these issues as teething problems as indicated by BA, and the media reputation of the company was dealt a huge blow.

Question

To what extent are the problems that a service organisation has to manage in defending its reputation greater than those of a goods manufacturer?

The financial value of reputation

Research by Fombrun & van Riel (2004) provides evidence of a link between reputational ratings and market value. They suggest that a 10 per cent improvement in reputation is worth between 1 and 5 per cent of a company's market value. They state that reputational capital is a subset of market value – together with physical, financial and intellectual capital. However, one of the difficulties of measuring reputation financially is that it negates discussion of not-for-profit (NFP) organisations. Reputation is just as important to NFPs.

> Reputational capital is a subset of market value.
>
> Reputation is just as important to not-for-profit organisations.

However, even for profit-oriented organisations, the link between reputation and financial performance is unclear. Koch & Cebula (1994) found that firms with stronger financial performance had higher rankings for corporate reputation. These authors attribute 30 per cent of the variance in the rankings to financial factors. Kowalczyk *et al.* (2003) report on the findings of several studies attempting to link financial performance with reputation and conclude that financial measures account for approximately half of the variance in the data.

Putting to one side questions to do with research methodologies, sample sizes and frames, a key question remains: does reputation drive financial performance or is it more likely that a good financial performance causes respondents to rank reputation more highly?

The development of measures of corporate reputation

The key models for the measurement and management of corporate reputation have evolved over the last two decades out of an earlier focus on corporate identity. Much early work on corporate identity focused upon the physical manifestation of identity with an emphasis on graphic design. This has broadened into an understanding of the significance of organisational behaviour, communications and symbolism in influencing the views of internal and external audiences.

> Models for the measurement and management of corporate reputation have evolved over the last two decades out of an earlier focus on corporate identity.

Schemes for the measurement of corporate identity focused only on internal stakeholders. Balmer's Affinity Audit was a qualitative method involving employee interviews, observation and analysis of company documentation to assess how closely the dominant systems of values and beliefs within the organisation accord with its stated corporate mission and strategy. A quantitative measure of identity is The Rotterdam Organisational Identification Test (ROIT), which measures the effect of antecedents such as employee communication, perceived organisation prestige, job satisfaction, goals and values and corporate culture upon the employees' identification with their company. Both methods measure the strength of employees' identification with the organisation, using an investigation of the organisation's corporate personality as a prerequisite to an understanding of its corporate identity (van Riel & Balmer, 1997).

Chun (2005) and Bromley (2000) both highlight the problems caused by overlapping or interchangeable use of key terms, particularly identity, image, reputation and personality. As discussed in detail in Chapter 2, there does now appear to be a consensus, in the literature on reputation, that identity means the view held by the internal stakeholders, image means the external picture and reputation is the combination of both. Chun (2005) endorses this classification and identifies three distinct approaches to the analysis of corporate reputation, namely evaluative, impressional and relational.

The contributions of Balmer & van Riel discussed above fall into the impressional school, where reputation is assessed in terms of the perceptions or impressions of a particular class of stakeholder (in this case employees). The evaluative school places its focus on the financial value of reputation and would be more interested in share price, ROI and other clear financial measurements. Only the more recently developed relational school adopts a multiple stakeholder approach. This examines the relationships between the perspectives of different stakeholder groups and gives equal value to both the internal and external reputation perspectives.

Approaches to measurement suffer from the same definitional confusion and one-dimensional focus. Measures producing a 'good/bad' classification are uninformative, particularly when outcomes fail to correlate with financial performance. Focusing on particular attributes such as social responsibility or competence gives a fuller picture but adds no understanding of their relative importance to particular stakeholders.

Reputation involves the assessment of multiple stakeholders.

As already established, reputation involves the assessment of multiple stakeholders. Two measures achieve this, Fombrun's Reputation Quotient, recently developed as the RepTrak measure for 'Global Pulse' rankings, and the Corporate Personality Scale developed by Davies *et al.* (2004), now termed the Corporate Character Scale.

Specific tools of reputation measurement

A key theme within the literature on corporate reputation is that of measurement. Establishing a good reputation is important to business success, but how exactly can the strength of that reputation be measured? How can it be measured and what are the factors that need to be measured?

What are the factors that need to be measured?

There are a number of specific measures intended to assess a particular market sector, for example a number of rankings exist of business schools that are used by many applicants to arrive at a shortlist of schools they wish to apply to. Trade magazines tend to run annual 'beauty contests' to decide the 'best' organisation in certain fields. The most well-known measures of corporate reputation are considered in the following sections.

Fortune's 'Most Admired Companies'

There are a number of general measures of corporate reputation, many focusing on the ranking of corporations (Fombrun, 1998). The most widely known is from the business magazine *Fortune*, which annually polls business executives and analysts as to the reputation of leading companies. Such measures have been criticised because the criteria for assessment have no theoretical foundation, are overly focused on financial performance and because the sample universe for reputation surveys is narrow (executives and business analysts) and excludes most stakeholders, specifically employees and customers. The Enron scandal of 2002 is an example of the fragility of reputation based upon financial measures alone and also, of course, in the case of Arthur Andersen, an example of how ephemeral a positive reputation can be.

Enron was voted number five in the 2002 *Fortune* list even as the company collapsed into scandal and criminal proceedings that would result in senior executives being jailed. They also took their accounting firm, Arthur Andersen, one of the largest in the world, down with them, the reputational association being too much for Andersen to take.

Fortune's supposed strength could also be said to be its weakness.

Empirical data have been collected since 1982 and tables are produced annually. *Fortune*'s supposed strength could also be said to be its weakness. Data are gathered from a large group of managers, analysts and directors of major companies. The survey currently covers 25 international industries and 39 primarily US market industries. Companies are rated from 0 to 10 on nine key reputational attributes (in order of importance):

1. Quality of management

2. Financial soundness

3. Quality of goods and services

4. Ability to attract, develop and keep talented people

5. Value as a long-term investment

6. Capacity to innovate

7. Quality of marketing

8. Community, social and environmental responsibility

9. Use of corporate assets.

In order to create a top 500 overall list of the most admired companies respondents are asked to select the 10 companies they admire most in any sector. The overall ranking survey differs from the industry survey. A strong position in the industry survey, therefore, doesn't guarantee a high ranking in the overall survey (Davies, 2011).

Ten thousand respondents complete *Fortune*'s annual survey (US) from the largest 1,000 companies (ranked by revenues) and the 25 largest US subsidiaries of foreign-owned companies. A single question has been added which asks respondents to list the top 10 companies that they admire. Critics of the survey point to its over-reliance on the financial performance of the so-called most admired companies. The people who fill out the survey (senior executives at large corporations) are probably judged on their own financial performance and so, likewise, they also judge others on this criterion. This could therefore be said to produce a very narrow definition of reputation. It is also internally focused in terms of the limited scope of the stakeholders that it surveys. Such stakeholders may be less concerned about the social responsibility that a company displays than would be other members of the general public for example. The sample frame utilised for the study is unlikely to do anything other than reinforce the status quo. In addition, the ranking method and the context are irrelevant for medium-sized charities. Reputation is just as important to not-for-profit organisations as it is to private sector companies but this is not reflected in this well-known study.

> Ten thousand respondents complete *Fortune*'s annual survey.

> Critics of the survey point to its over-reliance on financial performance.

Fryxell & Wang (1994) criticise the *Fortune* index and its over-reliance on financial performance. They use confirmatory factor analysis in order to show that all but one of the items from *Fortune* (community and environmental responsibility) is directly influenced by the respondent's perception of the financial viability of the organisation. A further criticism of *Fortune* is that only US companies (and domestic subsidiaries of large multinationals) are included. Below is a list of the top 10 companies in the *Fortune* 500 index.

Companies ranked 1st–10th position respectively by revenue in the *Fortune* 500 index:

- **2010:** (1) Wal-Mart, (2) Exxon Mobil, (3) Chevron, (4) General Electric, (5) Bank of America, (6) ConocoPhillips, (7) AT&T, (8) Ford Motor, (9) JP Morgan-Chase, (10) Hewlett-Packard.

- **2009:** (1) Exxon Mobil, (2) Wal-Mart, (3) Chevron, (4) ConocoPhillips, (5) General Electric, (6) General Motors, (7) Ford Motor, (8) AT&T, (9) Hewlett-Packard, (10) Valero Energy.

- **2008:** (1) Wal-Mart, (2) Exxon Mobil, (3) Chevron, (4) General Motors, (5) ConocoPhillips, (6) General Electric, (7) Ford Motor, (8) Citigroup, (9) Bank of America, (10) AT&T.

Source: Based on data from CNNMoney.com

Within these lists there is some evidence of a halo effect, which suggests that once a company is on the list it may stay there. For example, Ford made a $2.7 billion loss in 2010, cut its US workforce by 33,000 and lost its place as America's number two motor manufacturer to Japanese rival Toyota. However, it still achieved the number 8 position in the *Fortune* index.

The survey could be said to be a self-fulfilling prophecy, one that merely encourages votes for the most financially successful corporations. van Riel & Fombrun (2007) also criticise the scale for its lack of academic rigour in scale development. They say that although the financial 'halo' cannot be discounted, aspects such as media visibility, advertising expenditure and charitable contributions also impact upon reputation. They say, however, that there are serious reservations about relying on the *Fortune* scale as a clear measure of corporate reputation. Enron won the innovation category every year between 1996 and 2001! As was later revealed, its real innovative zeal was in its approach to accounting methods.

> There are serious reservations about relying on the *Fortune* scale as a clear measure of corporate reputation.

Brown & Turner (2008) point out that in the 25 years between 1983 and 2008 there have been eight overall winners of the US Survey – IBM, Rubbermaid, Coca-Cola, General Electric, Dell, Apple, Merck and Wal-Mart. More than 45 companies have won the individual categories and there has been a rise in new entrants – Google, Whole Food Markets and Kinder Morgan, for example. GE has won most overall awards and Merck the most individual awards – over 30, but none now for 15 years. There has been rapid movement up and down the league tables as demonstrated by IBM. This amply demonstrates the fragile and even ephemeral nature of corporate reputation. IBM in 1994 had sunk to as low as 354th place.

A brand that inspires considerable loyalty is Adidas, placed fourth place in the 2010 apparel sub-division and is the subject of Viewpoint 4.2.

Viewpoint 4.2   Reputational heritage assists Adidas

Adidas is an example of a brand that has stayed relevant whilst leveraging its undoubted heritage. The German sportswear company famous for its footwear also produces bags, shirts, watches, eyewear and other sports and clothing-related goods. Founded in 1924 as Gebrüder Dassler Schuhfabrik (Dassler Brothers Shoe Factory) it changed its name to Adidas in 1948 following an acrimonious split between Adi Dassler and his brother Rudolf, who founded Puma in the same year.

The history of the brand allows and encourages this nostalgia. Innovators in marketing as well as design, the company gave away their first pairs of free shoes to the athletes of the 1928 Olympic Games in Amsterdam. Adi Dassler persuaded legendary US athlete Jesse Owens to wear his spiked running shoes at the 1936 Berlin Olympics. Owens' four gold medals led to a huge boost in demand for the company's products. Adidas produced revolutionary lightweight football boots with previously unheard-of screw-in studs for the 1954 West German World Cup squad. The team returned home with the trophy after overcoming strong favourites Hungary in the final. Adidas started developing high-performance match balls in 1963, when most balls were heavy, brown and became easily waterlogged and heavy in wet conditions. The company has manufactured the balls for every World Cup tournament since 1970. In 1971 both Muhammad Ali and Joe Frazier wore Adidas in their much-publicised showdown, one of heavyweight boxing's most celebrated fights.

Such a rich history has allowed the Adidas brand to demonstrate its greatness by simultaneously offering contemporary and highly technical sportswear together with classic products from its past to the market. It has relaunched vintage-style football boots, training shoes and balls from the World Cups of yesteryear. Featuring the iconic three stripes motif, the designs remain faithful to the original, though the fabric of the boots is as per the modern version. Adidas also produce duplicates of their classic casual trainer collection. In highly modern Adidas stores, both the contemporary and classic kits are placed alongside each other, a juxtaposition of eras that allows the company to cater to all sections of the market. For example, classic trainers such as Gazelles, Sambas or Stan Smith are now worn by middle-aged consumers who were teenagers

Exhibit 4.2   Dwight Howard of the Orlando Magic basketball team shows off his association with Adidas in Paris.
Source: adidas Group, with permission. The 'Trefoil logo' is a registered trade mark of the adidas Group, used with permission.

when these shoes were originally on the market in the 1970s. Younger consumers also buy them and acknowledge the credibility of the brand by wearing its retro products.

The importance of the brand to sports is also emphasised by its popularity and importance in popular culture, notably its association with music. The company and its clothing – especially the trefoil logo T-shirt – became indelibly linked with 1970s fashion, and during the early years of rap music's ascendancy, Adidas became the first fashion brand name to find itself connected with hip-hop cool. The retro range are worn by fans and musicians alike and homage was paid to them in hip-hop legends Run DMC's 1986 track, 'My Adidas'.

Question

Which other brands can you name that have a rich heritage that has allowed them to build a strong reputational platform?

Source: Based on various sources including www.adidas.com.

Financially motivated measurement methods similar to those of Fortune operate in Europe, Asia and Japan, including the *Financial Times*' 'Europe's Most Respected Companies', *Management Today*'s 'Britain's Most Admired Companies', *Asian Business*'s, 'Asia's Most Admired Companies', and an audit of reputation by *Manager-Magazin* in Germany.

'Britain's Most Admired Companies'

The British version of the 'most admired' scale is produced for *Management Today* (previously *The Economist*) and was started in 1990. Very similar categories to the *Fortune* scale are surveyed in Britain. One distinction is that quality of marketing is surveyed, whilst in the US this is subsumed within quality of products and services. Brown & Turner (2008, p. 6) state that tracking these criteria over time helps us to learn 'what works and what doesn't in building and maintaining a reputation'.

A difficulty of these scales is how
quickly they can fluctuate.

Perhaps a difficulty of these scales is how quickly they can fluctuate. As Brown & Turner (2008) point out, Marks & Spencer started 2008 as Britain's most admired company, but due to difficulties during the year then dropped out of the top 20 altogether. However, they find an 'indisputable' correlation between being an admired company and financial performance.

In the UK there have been eight
overall winners since 1990.

In the UK there have been eight overall winners since 1990 – Shell, Marks & Spencer, Glaxo, Rentokill, Cadbury Schweppes, Tesco, Reuters and BP. Financial soundness together with quality of management are shown to be the two most important categories for the most admired companies. Again this can change quickly, as witnessed by the banking crisis and the subsequent fallout that has sullied the reputation of both the banks and the rules and regulations under which they operate. It may well be a monopolistic position in the marketplace that allows a company to represent financial soundness.

A sceptical view would question the nature of the respondents to these surveys. That they are able to rank the quality of management (i.e. themselves) and the financial soundness (what they are mainly targeted to achieve) in front of the quality of goods/services, surely the most important factor for customers, is slightly bizarre.

The importance of six sigma and the zero defect approach pioneered by the Japanese has great impact here. Performing well in the products and services category isn't just a case of conforming to standards. These days it also requires an evangelical approach to communication about standards of service and product quality. The case of Richer Sounds in Viewpoint 4.3 demonstrates the type of service necessary in order to develop an outstanding corporate reputation.

Viewpoint 4.3 | Reputational highs at Richer Sounds

Richer Sounds is a retailer and e-tailer of hi-fi, home entertainment and flat-screen TV equipment based in the UK, and is successful in presenting a 'total reputation' (see reputational categories in Chapter 2).

The chain is entirely owned by Julian Richer, the founder and managing director of the company. He began at the age of 14 by buying and selling hi-fi separates while still at school. By the age of 17 he had three employees and, in 1978, when he was 19, Richer Sounds formally began trading with the opening of his first shop at London Bridge.

The following key facts substantiate Richer Sounds' profitability/customer satisfaction and market leadership. First, over the past two decades the store has been featured in the *Guinness Book of Records* for the highest sales per square foot of any retail outlet in the world. Secondly, the company now trades from 51 stores in 39 towns/cities nationwide, with 10 in London alone, and is the biggest hi-fi retailer in the country.

Historically, Richer Sounds has been known for selling budget audio equipment, but in recent years it has responded to a shift in the electronics retail market and expanded its range from the purely audio to encompass plasma and LCD TVs as well as complete home cinema and entertainment solutions. An installation service has also been developed, covering home quotations, wall-mounting TVs and building complete home theatres for customers.

The salespeople are hi-fi enthusiasts (employee satisfaction) and therefore work in an arena about which they are naturally passionate, and refute 'hard sell' tactics. Richer Sounds empowers employees to ensure

Richer Sounds' employee suggestion
scheme is widely acknowledged as
one of the most successful.

they are able to take decisions that best help the customer. Its suggestion scheme is widely acknowledged as one of the most successful in terms of the number of suggestions received per employee and has become the model for a number of other businesses, including the Halifax Bank and Asda supermarkets. In terms of tangible accolades, Richer Sounds was adjudicated as the best British-owned company to work for by *The Sunday Times* in 2002. In May 2010 it was awarded the accolade of best retailer from consumer magazine *Which?*

Richer Sounds' location strategy confirms that the notion of value is of paramount importance. Shops tend to be on the edge of main shopping areas in order to keep costs down and pass savings on to their customers.

Exhibit 4.3   Richer Sounds' home page.
Source: www.richersounds.com, with permission.

The core philosophy of the company is encapsulated by the motto 'Biggest brands, best prices, expert advice & take it home today', which is emblazoned on every shop front and is featured in all ads and in-store literature.

Richer encourages customers to proactively shape the shopping experience, asking for their feedback, both positive and negative. Stores provide freepost cards that are sent directly to Richer himself. Shoppers get to rate their visit via a questionnaire attached to every receipt, and Richer responds personally to any negative feedback. The company's sense of responsibility towards the community (CSR) has also received recognition. Richer Sounds currently donates a generous 15 per cent of its profits to charitable organisations, a higher percentage than most other British companies.

> Richer Sounds currently donates 15 per cent of its profits to charitable organisations.

Question

Select five different stakeholder groups. Compare and contrast the criteria upon which these groups would assess a company's corporate reputation.

Source: Based on various sources, including www.richersounds.com.

Table 4.2	Britain's Most Admired Companies		
	2010	**2009**	**2008**
1	Unilever	BSkyB	Diageo
2	Serco Group	Tesco	Johnson Matthey
3	Royal Dutch Shell	Johnson Matthey	Unilever
4	BSkyB	Cadbury	BSkyB
5	Whitbread	GlaxoSmithKline	Tesco
6	Berkeley Group	Rolls-Royce	Stagecoach
7	Rolls-Royce	BP	Rolls-Royce
8	Tesco	Marks & Spencer	Man Group
9	BG Group	Diageo	Kingspan Group
10	Aggreko	Cobham	3i

Again, difficulties with the method and sample used to collate Britain's Most Admired Companies can be observed. The fact is that the banks (until very recently) have always scored well for financial soundness but have never registered in the quality of products and services (a customer-oriented) category (see Table 4.2).

Do the 'most admired' scales measure reputation?

As discussed, a criticism of many of these scales is that most focus on only one type of stakeholder, that is senior executives at large, usually public limited companies. Considering that most definitions regard corporate reputation as a collective term encompassing the views of all stakeholders, these most admired surveys are guilty of misrepresentation. Neither the lists themselves nor the criteria used are relevant to any general evaluation of the reputation of companies outside of this context. In particular, the US scale is claimed to assess reputation, yet in reality it only assesses image, and image among one group of stakeholders. Is it sufficient to use such limited peer group audiences and claim that this assesses reputation? It is difficult to think how an organisation could use these surveys to improve itself and its own performance. A scale that allows improvements to be made and then monitors that improvement would perhaps be more useful.

Defenders of these scales would argue that it is the singular purpose of this narrow band of stakeholders to be fully aware of what is happening within their industry. It could be argued that their views are far more significant and relevant than those of customers, for example, who perhaps have never visited or done business with any of the other companies in the industry. For example, how might customers be able to offer a view or a judgment as to which supermarket is better that the others if they have never been into a Tesco or a Morrisons, possibly for the simple reason that there aren't any where they live.

In addition, the scales take no account of smaller privately owned companies. Hence Richer Sounds, considered in Viewpoint 4.3, doesn't feature in Britain's 'most admired' lists. If the public were asked their opinion of the most admired companies, would they pick Richer Sounds and John Lewis or Aggreko and Cobham, which are listed? Amongst students at our universities, straw polls indicate that Mars remains a prestigious employer of choice. Many students continue to indicate that it would be their first-choice graduate position. Mars, however, being a privately owned company, does not appear in the 'most admired' lists. Again the methodology is shown to be weak.

The 'most admired' scales take no account of smaller privately owned companies.

Despite these critical points, both the US and UK 'most admired' scales are probably the widest known measures of corporate reputation.

Various other published surveys purport to measure the best companies in which to work if you are a woman or a member of a minority group. All organisations work under the critical eye of the media and social criteria are often used to rate firms and provide an indicator of their reputation. Social criteria include the numbers of women and minorities in the workforce, treatment of gay staff, environmental performance and the ethical policies of the company. Interest in social responsibility is not a fad but is indicative of a deeper change in the relationship between stakeholders and companies. According to Lewis (1999) the number of customers who equate an organisation's profitability with a positive reputation has halved since the 1970s. Still there is scope for some improvement here. Heavily implicated in the global financial crisis, Goldman Sachs was well placed in the 2009 list.

> Far more often social criteria is used when rating firms.

Shultz *et al.* (2001) criticise such ranking systems stating that they do not produce the truth about firms' reputations. Rather they claim that rating systems contribute part of what reputation can be said to be. Black & Carnes (2000) attempt to measure the market value of corporate reputation. They are not able to do this but find that internally generated intangibles, which are not currently recognised as assets, do contribute to the value of the firm and are viewed as assets by investors. This casts doubt on the worth of purely financially based measures of reputation.

Measuring tangible and intangible facets of corporate reputation

Caruana (1997) uses qualitative and quantitative research to establish the attributes that form a corporate reputation. He reduces a scale from an initial 34-item to a 14-item tool. The scale is still, however, functional in its make-up, concentrating mainly on financial and sales performance, and considers reputation from a single stakeholder perspective, albeit an important one: the customer.

Due to criticisms of the *Fortune* index, academic authors have attempted to analyse the link between reputation and financial performance in order to generate a more robust method. Kowalczyk *et al.* (2003) report on some of these attempts and propose a measure of their own based upon that of Brown & Perry (1994). They attempt to measure which of five financial variables (sales, risk, return on assets, growth and market-to-book value), has the highest explanatory power over the reputation dimensions of the *Fortune* Most Admired survey. They find the highest value attributable to market-book value. They also find that past reputation scores are a significant predictor of current reputation scores. This suggests there is some 'stickiness' to a corporate reputation. Although this study moves forward from the *Fortune* survey, it is again financially based. It could be argued that market value

> There is some 'stickiness' to a corporate reputation.

minus book value equates to the added value of the brand or the value of an organisation's reputation. This measure of reputation is, however, dependent upon the stock market and general economic confidence. Problems in these areas could quickly erode any surplus value. So again the question needs to be asked, is this reputation or merely the halo effect of financial success?

Cravens *et al.* (2003) are concerned about the omission of key intangible assets from financially driven measures. They are cautious, however, about the dangers of having a value that is derived more from conceptual than from physical assets. To illustrate this problem, they cite the fall of dot.com companies. Between 1995 and 2000 stock markets rose spectacularly on the back of new internet-based companies. Investors overlooked more traditional measures such as price:earnings ratio in favour of the attractiveness of new technology. Of course, without actual profits, the dot.com boom was the classic house built on sand. When nervousness set in, the huge boom in stock prices collapsed and many dot.coms went bust in the resulting shakedown. The most spectacular example was Boo.com which spent $188 million in just 6 months in an attempt to create a global online fashion store. It went bankrupt in May 2000 having never made a profit.

Cravens *et al.* (2003) cite reports from both governments and business groups around the world calling for the rebalancing of accounting measures with an assessment of the value of intangible assets in reputation. Their aim is build a reputation index that reports positive as well as negative aspects of reputation, i.e. intangible liabilities as well as intangible assets. The aim of this would be to put some sort of value on negative stories emanating about an organisation as well as measuring positive aspects of reputation.

Cravens *et al.* (2003) are influenced by strategic tools such as the balanced scorecard and the knowledge capital scorecard, which aim to provide a more comprehensive attempt to measure the success of an organisation through both financial and non-financial means. Using information gleaned from many other reputational surveys, Cravens *et al.*'s Reputational Index relates to products, employees, external relationships, innovation and value creation, financial strength and viability, strategy, culture and intangible liabilities. The Reputational Index assigns a weighted score to individual components in order to produce an aggregate measure of corporate reputation. The tangibles are given by far the highest scores of between 30 and 60 per cent weighting. Financial strength is given a lower score of 0–10 per cent and, interestingly, culture is given a very low weighting of between 1 and 0 per cent. This is a surprising finding as surely a strong and positive culture can contribute very strongly to a good corporate reputation.

> A strong and positive culture can contribute very strongly to a good corporate reputation.

The work of Cravens *et al.* (2003) is a useful contribution to the literature on reputation measurement as it recognises the value of intangible assets that are not really dealt with by the US and UK 'most admired' lists. However, their work does not progress beyond the conceptual stage and no fieldwork has been reported.

Work by Sabate & Puente (2003) provides a useful summary of the attempts to measure the impact of financial performance on reputation. They report on a number of studies conducted over the past 15 years. These include those that have identified a relationship between financial performance and reputation, those that have been more ambitious and attempted to indicate the direction of causality between the two studies, and those that support both directions of relationship, i.e. outline a circular relationship between performance and reputation. They remark that considerable progress has been made in this area; however, they criticise the lack of appropriate theoretical frameworks and the use of inappropriate methodological tools. Consistency is called for amongst studies so that results can truly be compared.

Harris-Fombrun Reputation Quotient

It should be noted that consumer responses in research that developed the Reputation Quotient (RQ) showed that there was little impact upon evaluation of reputation based upon the criteria of financial performance and leadership. This is interesting considering the criticisms of the 'most admired' scales and their over-reliance on financial success.

> The public consider product and service quality and innovativeness as key drivers of reputation.

The public consider product and service quality, and innovativeness as key drivers of reputation (Fombrun & van Riel, 2004). The company's workplace environment and social responsibility are significant predictors of how consumers rate a corporate reputation. The difference in emphasis between consumers and managers is revealing.

The RQ has been used to measure reputation in 26 countries. This system measures reputation by asking respondents to measure companies on 20 items which group around six dimensions:

1. Emotional appeal
2. Products and services
3. Vision and leadership
4. Workplace environment
5. Financial performance
6. Social responsibility.

Respondents complete a seven-point Likert scale. Items were generated mainly from existing media rankings and then additional items were added from the literature on image and reputation (Davies, 2011). The result is a survey with factors very similar to *Fortune*, with the addition of an emotional element.

The survey claims to measure the attitudes of employees, investors and customers, rather than being limited to executives. However, only the public have actually been used to validate the scale. The RQ model, however, demonstrates the importance of moving away from strictly financial measures (and those firms that benefit most from them) when determining reputation.

In an analysis of the six dimensions in the above list, the originators suggest that ratings for products and services, workplace environment, social responsibility, vision and leadership and financial performance each contribute to emotional appeal, which in turn creates reputation. Interestingly vision and leadership contribute negatively to emotional appeal, and financial performance is not significantly correlated. Being financially successful appears to dominate reputation in the eyes of the business community, but in the eyes of employees and customers this dimension does not appear to be significant.

The RQ has been utilised in many different countries. Its creators maintain that there is a hidden price to pay for having a poor reputation. A weaker reputation generates lower regard from investors, and hence lowers the company's market value.

> A weaker reputation generates lower regard from investors, and hence lowers the company's market value.

Schweizer & Wijnberg (1999) state that the development of trust and the formation of the perception of corporate reputation can be 'cognition-based' or 'affection-based'. Processing technical details such as product information or the annual report would be a cognition-based impression, whereas the formation of a relationship with an organisation's employees is an example of affection-based reputation. Clearly both are important and should be capable of measurement by models of corporate reputation.

Existing criteria from *Fortune* and other business publications' measures of reputation from around the world were used to compile the study, e.g. *Asia Business*, *Management Today* (UK), *Manager Magazin* (Germany). Harris & Fombrun claim that it is a wider measurement of reputation amongst stakeholders (e.g. consumers, investors, employees) but there must be a rider here. The RQ scale has not been empirically validated with any of these diverse stakeholder groups, only with consumers. In most countries, the products and services dimension is the most powerful predictor, followed by social responsibility and the workplace environment. Financial performance is not of great concern to the consumers and nor is leadership, dimensions that score very highly amongst the managerial groups.

Reputation Institute's RepTrak

A development of the RQ is the RepTrak Model and the Global Pulse study, launched in March 2006. The fieldwork from this study shows that a company's reputation is influenced by:

Exhibit 4.4	Rolls Royce - consistently appears in the 'Most admired' lists and would score highly in RepTrak's Products and Services dimension.
	Source: Pearson Education Ltd./Naki Kouyioumtzis.

- Stakeholders' experience – peoples' personal experiences with the company
- Corporate messaging – the company's corporate communication and initiatives
- Media coverage – how and what the media is covering about the company
- Internal alignment – the company's employees' strategic alignment.

The study is based around 23 key performance indicators grouped around seven core drivers derived from quantitative and qualitative research.

Some empirical difficulties had surfaced over the years with RQ, and the aim of RepTrak was to rectify these. Many of these problems boiled down to an issue that is common in many scales, that of multi-colinearity. This means that the respondents do not really see all of the factors as separate entities but that more than one of them can mean the same thing. When this happens, the entire validity of the scale can be called into question. For example the variable 'emotional appeal' correlated very highly with the independent variable 'overall reputation'. This suggests that they are components of a single dimension.

The seven dimensions of RepTrak are shown in the outer circle of Figure 4.2. The impact of these seven dimensions is assessed on an overall measure of affect constructed from four items that appear at the centre of the model (see Figure 4.2), overall reputation (esteem) and three emotional attributes – admiration, trust and feeling. It

Note that the emotional dimensions of RepTrak are at the centre of the model.

is the addition of this affective dimension that differentiates RepTrak from the RQ. Note that the emotional dimensions are at the centre of the model. This indicates the importance of the value system of a brand, as outlined in Chapter 6, and its resonance for consumers.

However, the RepTrak model is not particularly well explained, even in books by its creator, van Riel & Fombrun (2007), and leaves many questions unanswered. The issue of the scales validation amongst multiple stakeholder groups remains unanswered. The dimensions of RepTrak also appear to be very similar to the much-admired scales with the addition of an emotional element.

Cultural differences can also be observed through the work of Hatch & Shultz (2008). They report the importance of national attitudes upon RepTrack. They say, for example, that Danes regard corporate citizenship to be the main determinant of corporate reputation, where as Americans correlated reputation with the quality of a firm's product and services.

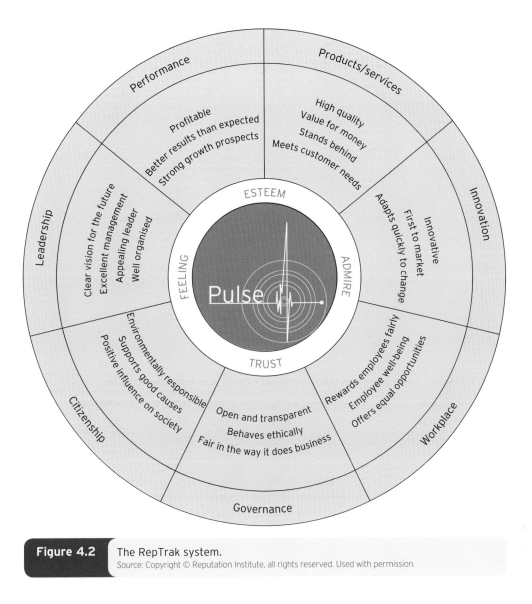

Figure 4.2 The RepTrak system.
Source: Copyright © Reputation Institute, all rights reserved. Used with permission.

The Corporate Character Scale

Measures of corporate reputation fall into two main areas: cognitive and affective (Davies, 2011). Cognitive measures assess an organisation in terms of more direct measures, e.g. the product quality, rating as an employer or rating of a company as a suitable investment. In affective measures it is the feelings of respondents towards the company that are most important.

> Measures of corporate reputation fall into two main areas: cognitive and affective.

Davies *et al.* (2001, 2004) devised a scale capable of measuring both the internal and external perspectives of corporate brands. The scale uses the personification metaphor, i.e. 'brand as person'. Respondents are asked to imagine that the organisation they are assessing has 'come to life' as a human being. The personality or 'character' of the organisation can then be assessed in a similar manner to human personality. The scale was built by using not just marketing and branding literature but also that of organisational behaviour together with writing about culture and the measurement of culture to gain potential dimensions of a corporate character. The corporate character is therefore used as a measure of affect, enabling the

Table 4.3	The seven dimensions of corporate personality

Dimensions	Personalities
Agreeableness	Warmth – friendly, pleasant, open, straightforward Empathy – concerned, reassuring, supportive, agreeable Integrity – honest, sincere, trustworthy, socially responsible
Enterprise	Modernity – cool, trendy, young Adventure – imaginative, up to date, exciting, innovative Boldness – extrovert, daring
Competence	Conscientiousness – reliable, secure, hardworking Drive – ambitious, achievement-oriented, leading Technology – technical, corporate
Ruthlessness	Egotism – arrogant, aggressive, selfish Dominance – inward-looking, authoritarian, controlling
Chic	Elegance – charming, stylish, elegant Prestige – prestigious, exclusive, refined Snobbery – snobby, elitist
Informality	Casual, simple, easy-going
Machismo	Masculine, tough, rugged

Source: Davies et al. (2004).

respondent to assess the reputation of a brand. It represents an inventory of both the dimensionality and content of traits that are used by customers and employees to distinguish organisations.

Seven dimensions of 'corporate character' were identified.

Considerable qualitative work helped to build the scale following an extensive literature review. The scale was rigorously tested and validated by researching 15 organisations with a total sample of over 4,600 respondents. Seven dimensions of 'corporate character' were identified: agreeableness, competence, enterprise, chic, ruthlessness, informality and machismo (see Table 4.3).

Each dimension has its own traits. For example, agreeableness is made up of three traits – warmth, empathy and integrity. Respondents assess the brand by responding to a Likert scale from 'strongly disagree' to 'strongly agree', e.g. do they feel that the brand is friendly, pleasant, open, etc.? They may consider that the brand expresses more negative personality traits, e.g. it is more arrogant, aggressive and selfish.

Measures of satisfaction were added to assess which of the factors of corporate character has the greatest influence on satisfaction.

The benefits of the Corporate Character Scale as a method of assessing reputation are that it is possible to assess multiple stakeholder groups simultaneously and then assess where gaps exist between the stakeholder views. This is important in view of the criticisms of the narrow perspectives of the 'most admired' scales. Its also considers the negative aspects of the corporate personality and does not pretend that there is only a positive aspect to branding and reputation. A firm may well have a reputation for ruthlessness, for example.

The Corporate Character Scale can assess where gaps exist between the stakeholder views.

One of the benefits of the Corporate Character Scale over the 'most admired' scales is that it can not only be used to measure the views of multiple stakeholders but also to examine the character and reputation of corporate brands from the not-for-profit sector. A shining example of such a brand is Médecins Sans Frontières (see Viewpoint 4.4).

Viewpoint 4.4 — Médecins Sans Frontières (Doctors Without Borders)

According to its website, Médecins Sans Frontières (MSF) is an independent humanitarian medical aid organisation. They are committed to providing medical aid where it is most needed, regardless of race, religion, politics or gender and also to raising awareness of the plight of the people they help.

In 1970 a group of French doctors joined an international aid mission to help victims of Nigeria's civil war. They were frustrated by government interference in humanitarian aid and felt they were being silenced when they wanted to tell the world about the atrocities they witnessed.

To speak out about the plight of victims, and seeking an independent, impartial way to provide care where they saw the greatest need, they joined a group of French journalists who were committed to the same principles and founded MSF in 1971.

The organisation started life as a group of medics travelling to remote corners of the world, providing medical aid to victims of wars and natural disasters. Over time the organisation grew, employing more people in the countries where it worked. Now MSF has offices in 19 countries, including the UK. Of the 27,650 total field positions, 91 per cent of the staff are hired locally in the countries of intervention. Headquarters staff represent 4 per cent of the total staff. In 1999, in recognition of its 'pioneering humanitarian work on several continents', MSF was awarded the Nobel Peace Prize.

> Médecins Sans Frontières was awarded the Nobel Peace Prize in 1999.

Corporate branding centres on the values of the brand. Consider the charter of MSF in this regard. All of its members agree to honour the following principles:

> Corporate branding centres on the values of the brand.

- Médecins Sans Frontières provides assistance to populations in distress, to victims of natural or man-made disasters and to victims of armed conflict. They do so irrespective of race, religion, creed or political convictions.

- Médecins Sans Frontières observes neutrality and impartiality in the name of universal medical ethics and the right to humanitarian assistance and claims full and unhindered freedom in the exercise of its functions.

- Members undertake to respect their professional code of ethics and to maintain complete independence from all political, economic or religious powers.

- As volunteers and members understand the risks and dangers of the missions they carry out and make no claim for themselves or their assigns for any form of compensation other than that which the association might be able to afford them.

In countries where health facilities are insufficient or even non-existent, MSF collaborates with authorities such as the Ministry of Health to provide assistance. MSF rehabilitates hospitals and clinics, runs vaccination programmes, performs surgery, operates feeding centres for malnourished children, provides psychological support and runs water and sanitation projects. MSF also works in remote health care centres and slum areas and provides training to local personnel.

Exhibit 4.5 — The logo of Médecins Sans Frontières.
Source: Médecins Sans Frontières, with permission.

The total income for 2010 was €943.3 million. 91 per cent of this was from private sources, 7 per cent from public institutions, and 2 per cent from other. There were 5.1 million individual private donators last year worldwide. This admirable organisation sends 26,000 doctors into 60 countries where help is desperately needed. The biggest category of expense is the staff operating in the field: about 50 per cent of expenditure comprises all costs related to national and international staff (including plane tickets, insurance, accommodation, etc. 58 per cent of expenses go to Africa, 21 per cent to the Americas, and 18 per cent to Asia, with Europe and Oceania taking 1 per cent each.

To be able to speak and act freely, MSF remains independent of any political, religious or economic powers. It has only once in its history requested military intervention, during the 1994 genocide in Rwanda.

Question

Which items of the Corporate Character Scale (Table 4.2) would MSF score most highly upon?

Source: Based on www.msf.org.uk.

Best Companies to Work For

This book has emphasised the importance of employees to the corporate brand. In view of this we should really consider the staff perspective and offer this internal perception as a way of considering reputation. Produced annually in the UK by Best Companies Ltd. for *The Sunday Times* newspaper, the '100 Best Companies to Work For' list is derived from the views of employees and the policies and processes of employers. It identifies best practice and ranks companies chiefly according to their performance in eight key factors of staff engagement.

The survey captured the views of over 230,000 employees in 2010 across all participating companies. Surveys are distributed to a randomly selected group of staff. At least 40 per cent of surveys have to be returned for a company to be eligible. The survey contained 70 questions, measuring eight equally weighted workplace 'factors' that have been identified from extensive research within the UK:

- Leadership (the heads and senior managers of the company)
- My manager (the local management on a day-to-day basis)
- Personal growth (opportunities to use skills and advance)
- Well-being (balancing work–life issues)
- My team (immediate colleagues)
- Giving something back (giving back to society and to the community)
- My company (the company and the way it treats staff)
- Fair deal (pay and benefits).

The '100 Best Companies to Work For' survey captured the views of over 230,000 employees in 2010 across all participating companies.

The results for 2010 are shown in Table 4.4. It is interesting to see the internal perspective on reputation headed not by a large public limited company as with the 'most admired' lists but by a charity (see Viewpoint 4.5). This helps demonstrate the fact that some of the best corporate brands are public sector or not-for-profit brands.

Table 4.4	Best Companies to Work For – 2010	
Rank	Employer	Sector
1	P3	Charity
2	Luminus	Community housing
3	Beaverbrooks	Jewellery retailer
4	Office Angels	Recruitment consultancy
5	Napp Pharmaceutical Holdings	Pharmaceuticals
6	New Charter Housing Trust Group	Housing association
7	W L Gore & Associates	Creative technologies
8	Sewell Group	Retail and estates management
9	Richmond Group	Financial services
10	Lindum Group	Construction and developer

Source: With permission from Best Companies Ltd.

Viewpoint 4.5   A delight to work at P3

The 2010 winner of Best Company to Work For was social inclusion charity P3, an organisation that is all about people, potential and possibilities. It is the first time a charity has taken the title.

P3 has been around for nearly 40 years, working in some of the most deprived areas of the UK helping vulnerable people rebuild their lives through its services and long-term support. Like last year's winner, Beaverbrooks, the key to P3's victory lies not in big pay and bonuses – the average salary of a support worker is just over £17,000 and only six of the 262 staff earn more than £35,000 – but rather in its supportive, inclusive culture which promotes control, choice and independence for staff as well as clients. P3's website states their vision as 'to give people the practical skills and self-esteem that they need to sustain an independent and self-sufficient lifestyle by providing opportunities and support that help vulnerable people move on from social exclusion to inclusion'.

Chief executive Martin Kinsella says: 'People who come to work for us do not want to make a million pounds or be the next *X Factor* winner but to do something to make a difference.' Employees love working for the charity and would not leave tomorrow even if they were offered another job, giving positive scores of 88 per cent on both questions in our survey.

Remarkably, given the nature of the job and the fact that some employees have experienced the type of problems P3 helps to address, such as homelessness, mental health issues and even, in isolated cases, domestic violence, the organisation has the lowest levels of stress of all 100 firms on the list (88 per cent) and people don't feel taken advantage of (83 per cent).

The questions with the most improved scores from the previous year show an emphasis on supportive managers, unified working and effective management of stress and pressure.

Team-building days, training and access to bosses at all levels mean employees don't lack the support they need from managers (88 per cent, up 7 per cent in 2010, the biggest rise of all its scores), departments work well together and people feel they really can make that difference (74 and 87 per cent, both up 3 per cent). 'If you do not support your staff you can't support your clients,' says Kinsella, a social enterprise ambassador for the government. 'We have made it a great place to work. It is about a conscious effort to make it as good as it can be for no other reason than it makes sense. It's not rocket science.'

P3's biggest improvement in factor scores this year was in questions about bosses where it saw a 1.4 per cent increase overall, almost the same margin by which it took first place. The role of managers has emerged as one of the significant developments this year with My Manager replacing Leadership as the factor most closely correlated with a company's position on the list for the first time.

Question

Which is the most important group as far as the reputation of an organisation is concerned – employees or customers?

Source: Based on *The Sunday Times* 'Best Companies to Work For'.

Chapter summary

In order to consolidate your understanding of the measurement of corporate reputation, here are the key points summarised against each of the learning objectives.

1. Consider whether we can and should attempt to measure corporate reputation

Reputation is hard-earned and easily undone. Because of this it has always been considered difficult to measure corporate reputation. However, in order to gain the attention the subject needs at board level, it is important that we make an attempt to measure and preferably provide some quantitative measurement of reputation.

In the case of Tiger Woods, attempts have been made to quantify the loss of earnings both by him and by the companies that endorse him as a result of his reputational difficulties.

2. Explore the idea of the reputational audit

The purpose of a reputational audit is to assess where a company is now in terms of corporate reputation. Fombrun states that we must, diagnosing the current state of the company, design the future state that we would like to see and manage the transition to this future ideal.

The reputational audit should determine who in the organisation is responsible for the corporate reputation. Commitment to the subject can perhaps be demonstrated by the appointment of a chief reputational officer.

3. Consider some of the broad indicators of corporate reputation

Many accountancy-based measures are considered to be broad indicators of corporate reputation, e.g. return on investment, share price and shareholder value. The amount of media commentary about an organisation (and the nature of it) is another measure. Attempts have been made to establish the financial value of having a positive corporate reputation.

Whether reputation drives financial performance or a good financial performance causes respondents to rank reputation more highly is a difficult question. Many of the financially based measures fail to address this question.

4. Review some of the specific tools used to measure corporate reputation

Measurement of reputation can fall into three schools of thought according to Chun (2005): evaluative, impressional or relational. The most well-known measures of a corporate reputation are the *Fortune* 500 index from the US and its British equivalent, 'Britain's Most Admired Companies'.

There is doubt over the methodology used to compile these scales, in particular the narrow sample used and the halo effect whereby respondents are often influenced by the financial success of the top companies. There are other problems with such scales, e.g. they only cover publicly quoted companies and there is no thought given to non-profit organisations when the lists are compiled.

Charities and non-profits are considered in the employee perspective with the *Sunday Times*' Best Companies to Work For list. RepTrak is an international survey very similar in make-up to the 'most admired' lists, although it contains the addition of an important emotional element.

5. Introduce the idea of measuring reputation by assessing the corporate character of the organisation

The Corporate Character Scale is an instrument capable of measuring both the internal and external perspectives of corporate brands. The scale uses the personification metaphor, i.e.

'brand as person'. Respondents are asked to imagine that the organisation they are assessing has 'come to life' as a human being. The personality or 'character' of the organisation can then be assessed in a similar way to human personality.

Seven dimensions of 'corporate character' were identified: agreeableness, competence, enterprise, chic, ruthlessness, informality and machismo.

Discussion questions

1. What are the four measures that Fombrun & van Riel (2004) suggest can be used to deconstruct the market value of a company?
2. Why is it not sufficient to measure reputation purely by using accounting methods such as ROI or shareholder value?
3. Write notes outlining the advantages and disadvantages of the *Fortune* 'Most Admired Companies' list as a method of measuring reputation.
4. Corporate reputation is said to be a sticky concept. What is meant by this?
5. Which are the most important groups to survey when assessing the corporate reputation of an organisation?
6. Consider the Corporate Character Scale. Would it ever be beneficial for a company to have a reputation for ruthlessness?
7. Not one of Britain's 'Best Companies to Work For' appear in the top 10 of 'Britain's Most Admired Companies'. Why would there be such a gap?
8. Should we attempt to put a financial value on a corporate reputation?
9. Consider the nine reputational attributes upon which the *Fortune* index is calculated. In which order would you put the nine attributes? Justify your choice.
10. It is said there is a halo effect associated with corporate reputation. What is this and what are the dangers of the halo effect to an organisation?

References

Black, E.L. & Carnes, T.A. (2000). The market valuation of corporate reputation. *Corporate Reputation Review* 3(1), 31–42.

Bromley, D.B. (2000). Psychological aspects of corporate identity, image and reputation. *Corporate Reputation Review* 3(3), 240–252.

Brown, B. & Perry, S. (1994). Removing the financial halo from *Fortune*'s Most Admired Companies. *Academy of Management Journal* 37, 1347–1359.

Brown, M. & Turner, P. (2008). *The Admirable Company*. London: Profile Books.

Caruana, A. (1997). Corporate reputation: concept and measurement. *Journal of Product and Brand Management* 6(2), 109–118.

Chun, R. (2005). Corporate reputation: meaning and measurement. *International Journal of Management Reviews* 7(2), 91–109.

CNNMoney.com *Fortune* 500 List. Online: http://money.cnn.com/magazines/fortune/fortune500/2010/full_list/. Accessed: 18 April 2011.

Cravens, K., Oliver, E.G. & Ramamoorti, S. (2003). The reputational index: measuring and managing corporate reputation. *European Management Journal* 21(2), 201–212.

Davies, G. (2011). The meaning and measurement of corporate reputation. In: Burke, R.J., Martin, G. & Cooper, C., eds. *Corporate Reputation: Managing Threats and Opportunities*. Surrey: Gower Publishing Ltd.

Davies, G., Chun, R., da Silva, R.V. & Roper, S. (2001). The personification metaphor as a measurement approach for corporate reputation. *Corporate Reputation Review* 4(2), 113–127.

Davies, G., Chun, R., da Silva, R. & Roper, S. (2004). A corporate character scale to assess employee and customer views of organizational reputation. *Corporate Reputation Review* 7(2), 125–146.

Dowling, G. (2006). Reputation risk: it is the board's ultimate responsibility. *Journal of Business Strategy* 27(2), 59–68.

Deephouse, D.L. (2000). Media reputation as a strategic resource: an integration of mass communication and resource-based theories. *Journal of Management* 26(6), 1091–1112.

Evans, R. (2009). 'Bank shares: bargain or basket case?' *Daily Telegraph*, 11 March.

Fombrun, C.J. (1996). *Reputation: Realizing the Value from the Corporate Image*. Boston: Harvard Business School Press.

Fombrun, C.J. (1998). Indices of corporate reputation: an analysis of media rankings and social monitors' ranking. *Corporate Reputation Review* 1(4), 327–340.

Fombrun, C.J. & van Riel, C.B.M. (2004). *Fame and Fortune: How Successful Companies Build Winning Reputations*. New Jersey: FT Prentice Hall.

Fryxell, G.E. & Wang, J. (1994). The Fortune corporate reputation index. *Journal of Management* 20(1), 1–14.

Hatch, M.J. & Schultz, M. (2008). *Taking Brand Initiative: How Companies can Align Strategy, Culture and Identity Through Corporate Branding*. San Francisco: Jossey-Bass.

Koch, J.V. & Cebula, R.J. (1994). In search of excellent management. *Journal of Management Studies* 31(5), 681–699.

Kowalczyk, S.J., Malmberg, A. & Eng, J. (2003). The underlying constructs of Fortune's corporate reputation. *Proceedings of 7th International Conference on Corporate Reputation and Competitiveness*, Manchester, UK.

Lewis, S. (1999). Measuring corporate reputation. *Templeton College Paper*. London: MORI.

van Riel, C.B.M. & Balmer, J.M.T. (1997). Corporate identity: the concept, its measurement and management. *European Journal of Marketing* 31(5/6), 340–355.

van Riel, C.B.M. & Balmer, J.M.T. (2004). *Fame and Fortune: How Successful Companies Build Winning Reputations*. New Jersey: FT Prentice Hall.

van Riel, C.B.M. & Fombrun, C.J. (2007). *Essentials of Corporate Communication*. Abingdon: Routledge.

Sabate, J.M. & Puente, E. (2003). Empirical analysis of the relationship between corporate reputation and financial performance: a survey of the literature. *Corporate Reputation Review* 6(2), 161–177.

Schultz, M., Mouritsen, J. & Gabrielsen, G. (2001). Sticky reputation: analysing a ranking system. *Corporate Reputation Review* 4(1), 24–41.

Schweizer, T.S. & Wijnberg, N.M. (1999). Transferring reputation to the corporation in different cultures: individuals, collectives, systems and the strategic management of corporate reputation. *Corporate Reputation Review* 2(3), 249–266.

Sirak, R. (2008). 'The Golf Digest 50'. *Golf Digest*, February. Online: http://www.golfdigest.com/magazine/2008/02/gd50. Accessed: 18 April 2011.

Minicases for Part 1

The following minicases are designed to help readers consider some of the issues explored in this part of the book. The questions that follow each case should be attempted and outline answers can be found on the supporting website.

Minicase 1.1 — Ericsson – from product supplier to solution provider: how corporate reputation can facilitate business transformation

Dr Chris Raddats: University of Liverpool

Ericsson is a provider of telecommunication (telecom) products and services whose roots date back to 1876. The company is Swedish and its history is characterised by international expansion, with the firm now having customers in more than 180 countries. It is perhaps best known for its joint venture, Sony Ericsson, a market leader in mobile phone handsets, and is the inventor of Bluetooth technology. However, its largest business is supplying products and services to telephone providers (companies that provide mobile and fixed line telephone services to individuals, homes and businesses). Ericsson's customer offerings traditionally centred on the products at the heart of telephone providers' networks. As in many industries involving expensive and complex products, telephone providers generally expect a number of services to accompany any purchase of network products, such as installation to get the products working, training on how to use and maintain the products and a help desk in case of problems.

Historically telephone providers bought these services from their product suppliers (e.g. Ericsson), although there were often variations in what was provided by different suppliers in terms of the services offered, how they were priced and their quality. Some of Ericsson's competitors viewed services as an extension of the product sale, which were almost guaranteed to be sold no matter what the price or quality. Ericsson, however, saw services not only as an opportunity to enhance the performance of their products but also as a way to build deeper relationships with customers and strengthen their corporate brand. These enhanced customer relationships enabled Ericsson to better understand the challenges that telephone providers faced and, consequently, which new services could be developed that might assist them to address these challenges. This has helped to change Ericsson's reputation in the eyes of its customers from a product supplier to a valued provider of services as well.

Two trends occurred in the industry in the early 21st century. First, after the 'dot.com crash' the telecoms market dramatically changed, as established telephone providers saved money by extending the life of their existing products rather than purchasing new ones. In consequence their strategic focus was directed towards reducing their cost base, and a large proportion of their costs was spent on technical staff. One approach was to outsource their technical support services to product suppliers. Secondly, market liberalisation created more competition, leading to the emergence of a new breed of telephone provider happy to subcontract network-related activities to existing product suppliers, enabling them to focus on growing and managing their customer base. Ericsson was one of the first companies to recognise these trends.

Product suppliers like Ericsson were well placed to take advantage of these two trends because of its perceived product expertise and reputation as a valued services provider, making it the obvious choice for many telephone providers. Equally, these contracts were often long-term and business-critical, meaning that Ericsson's corporate longevity and financial strength were a reassurance to its customers that it would still be around in the long term to fulfil its contractual obligations. Ericsson's international focus also supported this transition, with telephone providers often requiring a consistent level of pan-national services delivery. Ericsson has services teams around the world within the Ericsson Global Services business unit, which comprises the industry's largest services workforce, numbering 45,000 personnel. This separate business unit has enabled a services culture and mindset to develop within the company whilst a global services capability means that best practice can be shared around the company and success stories in one part of the world used to build credibility with potential customers in other countries. For example, Ericsson ▶

won the contract to manage the 3 mobile network and its IT infrastructure in the UK.

Networks are complex and rarely comprise products from just one supplier, so telephone providers generally have to manage multiple product suppliers. Given the high cost of managing multiple suppliers and possible variations in services from each, telephone providers started to envisage a situation where a lead supplier would take over the direct provision of services on less important products within their networks. Ericsson's product heritage and reputation for services often made the company the preferred choice to be the lead supplier for telephone providers looking to consolidate their services activities. Today Ericsson offers a wide range of services on products from different suppliers and is the global market leader in this field, supporting its claim to be the only company able to build, operate and manage any network, regardless of the products currently in place, anywhere in the world.

Industry experts perceive the company to have one of the best reputations in the industry built on a number of key tenets: its longevity and financial strength, product heritage, global presence, services capabilities on products from many suppliers and track record of successful contracts. By setting up Ericsson Global Services the company has been able to manage services as a discrete business, with a distinct services culture, that has invested appropriately in personnel, processes and technology. Ericsson's corporate reputation has changed from that of product supplier to provider of product and service solutions. It is well placed to grow as telephone providers across the world increasingly focus on brand-building by designing new offerings for individuals, homes and businesses and leaving the running of their telephone networks to specialist partners.

Questions

1. What reputational issues might there be for telephone providers in getting their product suppliers such as Ericsson to build, operate and manage their networks? Are there any aspects of its business that a telephone provider should not outsource?

2. Could Ericsson use its strong industry reputation and expertise to become a telephone provider itself? What might be the advantages and disadvantages of this strategy?

Minicase 1.2 — Harley-Davidson – balancing corporate image and corporate reputation

Jonathan Shrager

Harley-Davidson (H-D) is an example of a brand in which there is a considerable affinity between the brand itself and its users, reflecting the harmony between its corporate image and corporate identity. When image and identity are tightly bound, the result can be a very positive corporate reputation and this is certainly the case with Harley. Originally founded in 1903 the company produces large motorcycles (above 750cc). It says something about the image of the brand and what the brand name means to its customers that it sells in large numbers internationally when really its products are designed for the (straight) open roads of the United States. It is the deliberate retro style of H-D bikes that differentiates them from perhaps more efficient and practical Japanese models.

The H-D website is filled with ideas and images of the uniqueness associated with H-D ownership. The company also looks to exploit the importance of the brand community, which is the sense of belonging that comes with ownership of a Harley. Numerous benefits are afforded by setting up an online user profile, with the company promising to deliver an enhanced online experience. Whilst the terminology conveys the impression that the customer is reaping all the benefits, the advantages are reciprocal, with H-D gathering invaluable customer information.

The website is one of the most comprehensive on the internet, offering all the necessary requirements for riding a motorcycle. The company even tends to the most basic details, aside from the rather standard option to customise or tailor their bikes to individual preferences: H-D assists in the process of learning to ride a bike (by locating bike schools), offers insurance to riders, and even helps to budget the cost and finances for each potential customer. There is an interesting point to all this. This information (often for beginners) demonstrates the newer demographic for H-D of middle-aged customers with high disposable income who have never previously owned a bike heading straight to the top of the food chain with their first venture into the biking world. Previous generations would have worked their way up to a Harley after many years of riding. Similarly, there is a section devoted to the Harley women-riders' community again emphasising a more recent demographic shift for this iconic brand.

The website offers a forum upon which the community members can view organised bike events, wherein H-D riders travel en masse. Alternatively, the website has a Ride-Planner which not only assists in the mapping out of individual rides but also offers discounts to members on a variety of hotels nationwide. Hiring bikes/purchase of second-hand bikes is also catered for. These events revolve around the individuality of owning a Harley, and thus provide a sense of shared belonging or community to those that attend. Harley's declaration that 'It's all about the experience' demonstrates that whilst the brand and the experience are inextricably linked, it is the experience offered by H-D that overrides even the product itself. H-D riders are a classic example of the concept of a brand community, a deeper level of association between users of the brand, their relationship with other users and the company itself (see Chapter 8).

Harley-Davidson has also created a Harley Owners Group for those enthusiasts who want to officially pledge their allegiance to the brand. Referred to as a family of members on the website, its strapline is 'Over a million brothers and sisters; bound by the passion to ride'. These family overtones intensify the notion of a united Harley community. Reinforcing this family or community feel, H-D is a company that demonstrates its brand values by showing its dedication to both national and local charitable aid. Its support for the Muscular Dystrophy Association is a nationwide project that began in 1980 and since then, the H-D family of customers, dealers, suppliers and employees has raised more than $65 million to aid research and programme services for children and adults with muscular dystrophy. The funds raised support life-saving research, comprehensive medical care for children and adults with neuromuscular disease, and MDA summer camps. Harley workers are also encouraged to raise finds for local charities near to their Milwaukee base.

Harley-Davidson's convincing and powerful rhetoric asserts and promises to 'contribute a better life to all those who live in their communities'. Thus, H-D promotes itself as a compassionate organisation that proactively endeavours to help on both a national and a local scale, an all-encompassing charitable feat which conveys the outward image of a corporation with a community-friendly culture. In turn, this must certainly serve to endear an already devoted customer base to the company.

The brand's history and classic images provide a key insight into its core appeal, which is closely related to the psyche of its users. It is cool, edgy and rebellious yet at the same time has a huge following amongst those members of society who do not consider themselves to be any of these things. Its appeal across the cultural spectrum is demonstrated by two cult films in which H-D bikes are lionised. *Easy Rider* is a classic counter-culture film whose stars, Peter Fonda and Dennis Hopper, ride customised Harleys and are most definitely on the wrong side of the law, rejected by mainstream American society. *Electra Glide in Blue*, on the other hand, sees a motorcycle cop (Robert Blake) driving his H-D Electra Glide around Arizona's iconic roads through Monument Valley. The film is sometimes referred to as a cops' version of *Easy Rider*.

So, ridden by rebels and law-enforcers alike, H-D manages to appeal to both the non-conformists in society and those who enforce the law. In some ways, this is its most impressive accomplishment, its ability to fuse the image and identity of the brand in order to build its reputation amongst all sections of society.

Questions

1. Outline the elements that make up the corporate identity and corporate image of H-D. How do these elements link with each other?

2. The demographic profile of H-D riders has changed considerably over the last 20 years. In what way has it changed and how might this affect the corporate reputation of the brand?

Part 2
Corporate branding

Chapters 5-8

This part of the book is concerned with exploring and understanding what is meant by corporate branding.

Chapter 5 provides a contextual reflection on the nature and purpose of corporate branding, before making important links between branding and reputation. Following an exploration about branding and corporate social responsibility (CSR), and the co-creation of brands, the chapter finishes with a discussion about the emotional power of brands, a topic that is picked up again later in the book.

Chapter 6 follows on from the ideas explored in the previous chapter and sets out for readers what corporate brands are, through a definition and an examination of the importance of and reasons behind the rise in corporate branding activity at both practitioner and academic levels. An assessment of the advantages and disadvantages of corporate branding is followed by a consideration of the differences between product brands and corporate brands. The chapter closes with a critical learning point, namely the gaps that can emerge between a brand's corporate identity and its corporate image.

Chapter 7 is about how brands are measured and what they are worth. This involves a discussion about brand equity and the methods used to measure corporate brands. This in turn gives rise to the role and nature of brands outside of the 'corporate' world. This leads to a consideration of branding and reputation in the third sector and the implications for measurement in this context.

In Chapter 8 we consider how brands might evolve and how some of them provide benefits for society as well as for themselves. Topics explored include wider definitions of corporate brands to include celebrity brands and country brands, brand authenticity, brand communities, anti-branding movements and the difficulties associated with managing brands in the 21st century. The chapter and part closes with some thoughts on the future of branding.

Finally Part 2 closes with two minicases designed to allow readers to consider some of the issues about how branding and its management can be best understood.

Case 1   David Beckham – the individual as a corporate brand

Case 2   Warburtons – a brand built on family values

Chapter 5
The branding-reputation dilemma

Understanding what brands are and what they mean is important when appreciating the scope and significance of corporate brands. Indeed, the link between a brand and corporate reputation can be considered from either perspective. This in turn leads to questions about corporate social responsibility and the role this concept might play within the brand as a promotional device or at a deeper level, as part of corporate citizenship. These questions and ideas concerning the concept of the corporate brand are introduced in this chapter, and are then dealt with in more detail in Chapter 6.

Aims and learning objectives

The aim of this chapter is to consider the relationship between corporate reputation and branding.

The learning objectives of this chapter are to:

1. Define what is meant by a brand
2. Make the link between branding and reputation
3. Introduce the notion as the brand as a repository for the organisation's reputation
4. Discuss reputation and corporate social responsibility (CSR)
5. Investigate the co-creation of brands
6. Discuss the emotional power of brands.

Branding background

The use of branding was prominent long before the term was first used or properly defined. Ancient Greek and Roman civilisations lived in cities and tradesmen promoted their wares by means of written information (Hart & Murphy, 1998) in order that the public would be aware that there were products and services available at a particular address. The association of the name of a craftsman or shopkeeper with his skill or wares was established at this time and, of course, continues to the present day.

> The use of branding was prominent long before the term was first used or properly defined.

Archaeological finds show that shopkeepers used pictorial signs to symbolise and advertise their goods during Roman times. This symbolism was particularly relevant in a society with low levels of literacy, something that has been a feature of all societies up until the 20th century. In the modern age, symbolism is still an important feature of branding, both for reasons of literacy in the developing world and as shorthand for busy consumers in industrialised nations. The term 'branding' itself comes from the earliest examples of organised farming (Kochan, 1996). Norse farmers would put their own mark on cattle as a means of identification and to signify ownership (see Exhibit 5.1). The term brand comes from the Norse word *brandr*.

Society remained in a fragmented state for many centuries to come and the sophistication of branding developed only slowly. Symbolic branding featured prominently in the design of pub signs in Britain from Shakespearean times onwards. However, the real starting point for the development of modern brands and brand management was the industrial revolution. Low & Fullerton (1994) point out various macroeconomic factors that allowed innovative companies to lay the foundations of modern brand strategy.

> The real starting point for the development of modern brands and brand management was the industrial revolution.

Exhibit 5.1 Branding cattle – Norse farmers were among the first to put their own mark on cattle. The term brand comes from the Norse word *brandr*.
Source: Getty Images/Jonathan S. Blair/National Geographic.

Improvements in transport and communications ensured that national distribution became easier. The improvements in production processes allowed mass production and corresponding economies of scale to take effect and this, combined with consistent quality in the manufacturing process, allowed producers to persuade customers that they could rely on their products time and again. Packaging improvements meant that, as well as providing necessary protection, manufacturers could make their products instantly recognisable and begin the cycle of consumers asking for the product by name and therefore repeat purchase. Newspapers provided mass communication and were supported by the establishment of the advertising industry as a legitimate form of persuading customers to support a brand.

Different routes to market, including the first department stores and mail order, were a move towards self-selection by consumers, thereby weakening the power base of the existing distribution channel and the shopkeeper and increasing the importance of individual purchase decisions by consumers. The rise of the middle classes in the wake of the industrial revolution ensured that there was a growing group of more prosperous and better-educated consumers waiting to take advantage of the new brands.

Legal factors, such as the recognition of trademarks, have assisted in the building of brands. As time has developed the law has extended to allow the trademarking and copyrighting not just of names but also of shapes and colours used in packaging, thus further protecting the difference and added value inherent in a branded good.

Brands are now recognised on balance sheets.

Brands are now recognised on balance sheets as assets in the same way that tangible assets such as buildings are assigned a value. Rank Hovis McDougall valued their brands at £678 million on their 1988 balance sheet, a move that has been replicated by other companies (de Chernatony & McDonald, 1998). Nestlé's purchase of Rowntree for £2.4 billion was considerably above the market capitalisation of the company of around £1 billion (Egan, 1998). The point is that the company is not simply about processes and tangibles; the brand has a valuable relationship with its customers that would exist even if the tangible assets of the company were destroyed.

Definitions of a brand

What is the difference between an ordinary, undifferentiated product and a brand? Commodity markets are characterised by a lack of perceived differentiation by the consumer about the choices available to them (King, 1984). Various forms of fuel, e.g. petrol or gas, would be an example of such a marketplace and customers often come to their purchase decisions on the basis of price and availability. The consumer does not perceive any added benefit in buying one product as opposed to another. With nothing to differentiate them, manufacturers are vulnerable to competitors with a lower cost base or superior distribution network. A brand is

A brand is a manufacturer's way of adding value and giving its product or service an individuality that sets it apart from the rest.

a manufacturer's way of adding value and giving its product or service an individuality that sets it apart from the rest. A weak brand will face problems when there is insufficient differentiation to counter the threat of competition. British Gas has lost significant market share following the liberalisation of its market, ending its monopoly position. Gas is seen by many as a commodity, with price the only significant differentiator. An inability to offer added value through superior customer service or brand image has left British Gas in a vulnerable situation following a change in its macro-environment. This organisation fails the (difficult) test set by Kapferer (2008), who suggests that brands ask themselves what would be lost in the marketplace if their brand did not exist.

Branding, however, is more than merely a method of differentiation. In their seminal paper 'The product and the brand' in the *Harvard Business Review*, Gardner & Levy (1955) describe a brand as a 'complex symbol that represents a variety of ideas and attributes'. Customers build up a set of associations with the brand that they are unable to do with an undifferentiated product. Over a period of time the consistent quality and security represented by a brand, encouraged by advertising and promotional messages, allow it to develop an identity of its own. Product differences and packaging allow easy identification, leading to repeat purchase and the development of a relationship, either conscious or subconscious, between the consumer and the organisation. Kim (1990) describes branding as the 'attribution of social and symbolic meaning to a product'. Such meanings can be passed on to others, of course, and the branding of an item allows easier description both in advertising terms and, perhaps more importantly, by word of mouth.

Brands, therefore, are more than the core product and represent more to the consumer than the rational reason behind the need for and selection of the core product. It is the collection of tangible and intangible factors that are used to distinguish brands that allow a premium price to be charged for them (see Figure 5.1). A product tends to be very closely associated with the technologies that have been used to create it, whereas a brand is associated with the core customer satisfactions necessary for success (Egan, 1998). In this way a brand may continue to succeed even when the technologies and products offered by the organisation change over time. A full and clear appreciation of consumers and the markets in which they exist is necessary to develop and maintain a successful brand. Hart & Murphy (1998) insist that a brand is a 'synthesis of all the elements, physical, aesthetic, rational and emotional', and that product attributes must be 'coherent, appropriate, distinctive and appealing to consumers'.

So what is a brand? A brand provides something that is different and relevant; it is a promise, a summary of the mental associations and emotions that are top of mind when a name is thought of or mentioned. Names can be real or coined but they can be a very powerful sign and must be capable of projecting a brand's cues. Product parity is very common as the features and benefits of a product can be replicated and improved, but it is the brand that brings true distinction and differentiation. Brands provide a shortcut for stakeholders, so messages should be simple and uncluttered. An organisation should ensure that the brand idea is clear; if it is complex or contradictory, then the shortcut understanding is lost and brand development becomes problematic.

> **A brand provides something that is different and relevant.**
>
> **It is the brand that brings true distinction and differentiation.**

What makes a strong brand? What is the driver of that brand? Is there a message about the band that can be conveyed cohesively and consistently? Having a strong brand driver will focus the long-term vision of the brand. It helps to establish its difference from competitors and helps to point the way for new brand initiatives. A strong brand can provide a clear direction

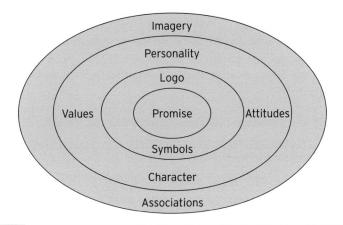

Figure 5.1   The intangible nature of a brand.

and can help to shape and underpin the way employees should behave and represent the brand. It directs all strategic and creative expressions of the organisation (Adamson, 2006).

Much of the existing literature focuses on product branding and appears to assume that branding is a subject appropriate to consumer goods only. This is disappointing and an aim of this book is to redress this balance. By discussing the move away from product branding to the consideration of the company as a brand or corporate branding, and considering ideas concerning the co-creation of brands, branding can be considered across the consumer, business-to-business and corporate landscapes.

Characteristics of brands

A key characteristic of brands is that they enable differentiation from the common herd. Kotler *et al.* (2004) refers to six levels of meaning that a brand is able to deliver. Table 5.1 explains each of these six meanings.

Kochan (1996) concentrates on values but explains that there are three tiers of brand values, namely functional, expressive and central values. The functional values represent the perform-ance of the product and reflect the rational reason for purchase, i.e. a meal satisfies hunger. Competitors can replicate functional elements. This therefore leads on to expressive values, which say more about consumers and their self-image, e.g. Calvin Klein represents a lifestyle statement. Kochan, however, states that it is the central values that are most important. Such values reflect 'the core of the consumer's central beliefs'. The most powerful example of this concept is when brand values embody national or international trends, e.g. Body Shop (see Viewpoint 2.2, p. 32), whose values reflect the importance of morality in a world of mass consumption.

Competitors can replicate functional elements.

Randall (2000) defines brands as containing four characteristics – functions, differences, personality/image and source. These characteristics tie in with the work of Kotler and Kochan. The first three characteristics have already been recognised; sources are very similar to central values in that they ask what the company stands for.

de Chernatony & McDonald (2003) argue that brands consist of four levels – generic, expected, augmented and potential. It is at the augmented level that branded goods are expected to differentiate themselves, e.g. First Direct, through exceptional levels of customer

Table 5.1	Levels of brand meaning
Brand meaning	**Explanation**
Attributes	Product attributes such as the high level of safety features within a Saab motor car
Benefits	What customers are interested in, i.e. they feel more secure on overcrowded roads in their Saab
Values	The brand is in tune with the values of consumers, i.e. consumers feel that they are individuals and express this through their choice of car
Culture	The brand may represent a certain culture. The Saab represents Swedish culture: organised, safe, high quality
Personality	If the car were a person it would be professional, intelligent and solid
User	The primary target, the type of person who consumes the brand – a solid middle-aged business person in this instance

Source: Based on Kotler *et al.*, 2004.

service. It is the potential level which goes beyond this and stretches the brand to new efforts on behalf of its customers, e.g. consideration of individual customer needs by airlines.

Brands consist of four levels – generic, expected, augmented and potential.

Types of branding

The different types of branding in the marketplace are well summed up by Randall (2000), who identifies nine of them (see Table 5.2). This is an interesting yet confusing list. In an effort to break down brands into compartments, Randall and other authors are blurring definitions. What, for example, is the difference between an umbrella brand and a company or family brand? All serious brands seek protection through law as much as is possible. So, what is the difference between a corporate brand and a licensed brand? There are many ambiguities within this list, a theme identified by Goodyear (1993). She complains that definitions of branding fail to identify which bit of a product's identity is the brand and questions if it is a singular concept. With regard to the Carlton motor car produced by Vauxhall, a part of General Motors, she asks at which level do the brand's values originate?

Table 5.2	Types of brand
Type of brand	**Explanation**
Product brand	A single product or service, e.g. Mars bar.
Line or range brands	A group of products displaying similar packaging, quality and price, e.g. Boots No.7 range
Umbrella or pillar brands	This type of brand gives protection to several sub-brands, e.g. Birds Eye Foods
Company, family or source brands	e.g. Ford or Sony
Endorsing company, corporate or banner brand	The company name appears to lend weight but is not the main brand, e.g. Nestlé and Kit Kat
Designer labels	Armani, Ferrari
Griffes or haute couture brands	These refer to a signature, e.g. design houses
Licensed names	e.g. the Disney Corporation
Retailers' brands	Store name brands and generics

Source: Based on Randall (2000).

The list produced by Randall (2000), although comprehensive to the point of being over-elaborate and ambiguous, still makes very little of the corporation as a brand. We believe this is an important oversight and explore corporate branding in the context that it is now the principal area of branding.

Moving towards corporate branding

Trying to define the term 'brand' and seek universal agreement has been problematic, yet this task is still being addressed by academics. de Chernatony & Riley (1998) undertook a

Trying to define the term 'brand' and seek universal agreement has been problematic.

	Table 5.3	Definitions of a brand

	Brand definition	Antecedents	Consequences
1.	Legal instrument	Mark of ownership. Name, logo, design. Trademark	Prosecute infringers
2.	Logo	Name, term, symbol, design. Product characteristics	Identify, differentiate through visual identity and name. Quality assurance
3.	Company	Recognisable corporate name and image. Culture, people, programmes of organisation define corporate personality. CEO is brand manager	Evaluate over long time horizon. Product lines benefit from corporate personality. Convey consistent message to stakeholders. Differentiation: proposition, relationship
4.	Shorthand	Firm stresses quality not quantity of information	Rapidly recognise brand association. Facilitate information processing, speed up decisions
5.	Risk reducer	Confidence that expectations being fulfilled	Brand as a contract
6.	Identity system	More than just a name. Holistic structured with six integrated facets, including brand's personality	Clarify direction, meaning, strategic positioning. Protective barrier. Communicate essence to stakeholders
7.	Image	Consumer-centred. Image in consumers' mind is brand 'reality'	Firm's input activities managed using feedback of image to change identity. Market research important. Manage brand concept over time
8.	Value system	Consumer relevant values imbue the brand	Brand values match relevant consumer values
9.	Personality	Psychological values, communicated through advertising and packaging, define brand's personality	Differentiation from symbolism: human values projected. Stress added values beyond functional
10.	Relationship	Consumer has attitude to brand. Brand as person has attitude to consumer	Recognition and respect for personality. Develop relationship
11.	Adding value	Non-functional extras. Value satisfier. Consumers imbue brand with subjective meaning they value enough to buy. Aesthetics. Enhanced through design, manufacture, distribution	Differentiate through layers of meaning. Charge price premium. Consumer experience. Perception of users. Belief in performance
12.	Evolving entity	Change by stage of development	Change by stage of development

Source: de Chernatony & Riley (1998). Copyright © Westburn Publishers. Reprinted by permission of Taylor & Francis Ltd.

comprehensive review of over 100 articles on branding from both a trade and an academic perspective. They reinforce the point made earlier that definitions tend to overlap with each other. Their review disaggregates the meaning of a brand into 12 definitions and then lists the subsequent antecedents to, and consequences of, the brand construct. Their table is replicated in Table 5.3.

de Chernatony & Riley (1998) go further than other writers in the area. By attempting to collapse some of the definitions, they make redundant some of the terms used previously. For example, they state that company, identity system, image, value system, personality, relationship and added value can be combined to form a common antecedent of a brand's personality.

Their paper is also useful due to the categorisation of input and output features of brands. Legal instrument, logo and company are input-oriented, whilst shorthand, risk reducer, image, value system, personality, relationship and adding value blend input and output measures. de Chernatony & Riley argue that consumers and the firm's staff are the two key stakeholders and that 'the firm's activities (input) and consumers' perceptions (output) emerge as the two main boundaries of the brand construct'.

Consumers and the firm's staff are the two key stakeholders.

The organisation should not merely be considered as an input feature. A successful brand, particularly if it is a corporate brand, should be considered as an input and an output feature. Indeed, if a company is the brand, as opposed to a fast-moving consumer goods (fmcg) organisation, then if the brand has no 'output', i.e. customers are not aware of the values that the company name represents, then it could be argued that the organisation does not have a brand at all. It is the harmonisation of the input and output process that is at the centre of good branding, and particularly corporate branding practice. Today, it is the reputation of the company that must become the branding focus for management.

> It is the reputation of the company that must become the branding focus for management.

Goodyear (1996) discusses the progress of branding and how branding is perceived around the world. She discusses 'classic branding', a feature of more mature industrial nations, as consisting of four stages:

- Unbranded – e.g. commodity goods
- Brand as a reference – brand used for identification, very often the maker's name, becomes a guarantee for quality
- Brand as personality – focus on emotional appeal
- Brand as icon – brand taps into higher-order values of society.

Goodyear (1996) then develops this theme with her 'continuum of consumerism' by referring to postmodern branding, consisting of two elements. The first is the brand as a company, where the need is to focus on corporate benefits and to develop a holistic view of the brand. The second element considers brand as policy. Here, company brands are aligned to social and political issues, where consumers 'vote' on issues through companies.

Brands have become so important that consumers vote for brands in the way we vote for political parties. This suggests therefore that the corporate brand is now the main emphasis of brand management.

> Consumers vote for brands in the way we vote for political parties.

The importance of trust to a brand

A strong brand with a positive reputation must be trusted by its stakeholders. Brands that are trusted are more able to diversify into other areas, often unrelated, than those that are not trusted (Ind, 2003). The reason for this is that if consumers appreciate the value set of an organisation, they are more likely to transfer this trust (of the value set) into other offerings by the same brand. A good and effective corporate brand reduces customer risk. Willmott (2001) suggests that trust is based upon three core elements – honesty, fairness and openness – and describes these elements collectively as 'transparency'.

Keller & Aaker (1998) consider important organisational associations of which trustworthiness is vital:

- Corporate expertise – the ability to competently make and sell its product/service offering
- Corporate trustworthiness – the extent to which a company is thought to be honest, dependable and sensitive to consumer needs
- Corporate likeability – the extent to which a company is thought to be likeable, prestigious and interesting.

Traditionally, marketing has been used by organisations as a top-down process. A more contemporary view acknowledges that customers are more difficult to identify and attract. They are sceptical about business and cannot be effectively categorised into huge groups (segments) that the top-down process encouraged. For example, segmentation by white/blue collar workers, social or income groups is impractical. Consumers use a vast range of media

Table 5.4	Top 10 Superbrands

Top 10 Superbrands 2009/10

1. Microsoft
2. Rolex
3. Google
4. British Airways
5. BBC
6. Mercedes-Benz
7. Coca-Cola
8. Lego
9. Apple
10. Encyclopaedia Britannica

Source: Copyright © Superbrands (UK) Ltd, with permission.

and their lives are hectic, fast-paced and full of devices that reduce their concentration levels. Consider the impact of the free *Metro* newspapers given away in UK cities in the morning, for example. This product has helped to reduce the news to bite-size chunks whereby the whole paper can be read in 20 minutes.

The commercial world is cluttered and complex.

Brands help to simplify the decision-making process.

The commercial world is cluttered and complex, as evidenced by the fact that each consumer is exposed to between 3,000 and 10,000 commercial messages each day, according to *Advertising Age*. The inevitable consequence is that consumers become desensitised. One way of simplifying this complexity and reversing the process for stressed consumers is through the development of trust they can place in a brand. Brands help to simplify the decision-making process for individuals, and trust plays a critical part. The top 10 'Superbrands' have all built up a relationship of trust with their consumers (Table 5.4). Number 10 in the list is discussed in Viewpoint 5.1.

Viewpoint 5.1	Encyclopaedic brand adaptation

The *Encyclopaedia Britannica* is the oldest, and widely considered to be the most scholarly, of all encyclopaedias. It was first published between 1768 and 1771 in Edinburgh, Scotland. Aimed at educating children and adults, it has for centuries been a first point of reference for innumerable scholars.

Like the best corporate brands, the *Encyclopaedia Britannica* has adapted to the changes that have taken place in society and the wider environment. For literally centuries this merely meant its huge editorial team updating its references and sources for new editions. The 15th print edition was current between 1974 and 1994. In 1995 the brand realised that it would die quickly if it stuck to the print-based structure that had previously served it so well. So, since then *Encyclopaedia Britannica* has introduced products for optical media and, of course, the internet (www.britannica.com). New products have followed under the Britannica name, notably during the CD-Rom era at the start of the 21st century when *Britannica* challenged and eventually saw off the threat from the multimedia encyclopaedia, Encarta.

For 200 years now *Encyclopaedia Britannica* has enjoyed a reputation for scholarly excellence that is unparalleled, particularly in the difficult art of summarising knowledge. The online version contains more than 120,000 articles and is updated regularly. It also contains daily features, updates and links to news reports from *The New York Times* and the BBC. The overwhelming majority of Britannica's revenues now come from online subscriptions – both institutional, e.g. schools, libraries and universities, and individual

(a)

(b)

Exhibit 5.2 (a) Encyclopaedia Britannica's corporate headquarters in Chicago; (b) The company's consumer web page.

Source: (a) © 2007 William J. Bowe, reproduced by permission; (b) © 2011 Encyclopaedia Britannica Inc.; with permission.

consumers. This transition has been vital to the brand's survival as a generation has grown up expecting a search engine to be its first source of new information.

Of course, challenges remain, most notably from the free online encyclopedia Wikipedia. *Britannica* alludes to its most recent competitor on its website whilst simultaneously differentiating itself, asking: 'Are you fed up with trawling through numerous search engines and sites where anyone can update pages which can lead to incorrect information? Are you looking for expertly written, fact checked and professionally edited knowledge?'

After praise from heads of state and some of the great names of science and literature over literally centuries (C.S. Forester and George Bernard Shaw, for example – both claimed to have read the *Britannica* in its entirety) its inclusion in the Superbrands list is a somewhat modest accolade but it shows how a 240-year-old brand can reinvent itself and remain contemporary.

Question

Evaluate the reasons why brands such as *Encyclopaedia Britannica* survive over the long term, whereas other, once great brands no longer exist.

The link between branding and reputation

Brand management is increasingly focused around the company as the brand.

The study and practice of brand management are increasingly focused around the company as the brand, as opposed to the product brand (e.g. Olins, 2000; Hatch & Schultz, 2001; Kowalczyk & Pawlish, 2002; Knox & Bickerton, 2003; Kapferer, 2004). Corporate branding allows organisations to use their culture and values as a marketing device and as a promise of value to the marketplace. With a corporate brand, the organisation itself becomes the focus, including its employees, its activities, its policies and, most importantly, its values. The corporate brand allows a company to bring its values to the forefront of its activities in a way that cannot be achieved by merely concentrating on the product offering. As demonstrated by companies such as Harley-Davidson, the clear value system of the brand, its principles and corporate behaviour allow a greater emotional connection between the brand and like-minded individuals. As such values are difficult to imitate, sustainable points of differentiation and competitive advantage can be achieved.

Values are difficult to imitate.

Brands that are trusted in one strategic area, based on its principles and value system, are more likely to be trusted in other, possibly diverse, business areas. A good example of a corporate brand that has diversified in this fashion is Tesco (see Viewpoint 8.1, p. 185). It is possible that there is greater risk here for the corporate brand as it is presenting itself as only one entity to its stakeholders and the reputation of the organisation, therefore, becomes very important.

However, the literature is often ambiguous about the link between the corporate brand and corporate reputation. Dowling (1994) considers reputations as extensions of the corporate brand. de Chernatony & Harris (2000) link corporate branding with reputation when they say that by encompassing all stakeholders' evaluations, 'reputation is a representative evaluation of a brand's identity'. The opinions of different stakeholders are important and not just those belonging to one group, e.g. customers. de Chernatony & Harris are influenced by Kapferer's (2008) prism, presented in Figure 5.2.

The opinions of different stakeholders are important.

Kapferer identifies six elements of a brand – physique, personality, culture, relationship, reflection and self-image – and these are used to consider the meaning of a brand, from both an internal and an external perspective. Brands are a combination of the tangible attributes,

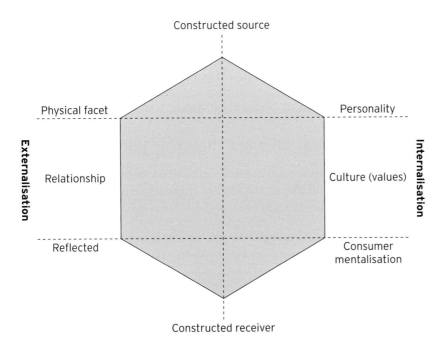

Constructed source

Physical facet

Personality

Externalisation

Internalisation

Relationship

Culture (values)

Reflected

Consumer mentalisation

Constructed receiver

Figure 5.2 Brand identity prism.
Source: Kapferer (2008).

e.g. the physical aspects, and the intangible attributes (Reizbos, 2003), such as personality and culture. Of these, brand culture and values are of great importance to the corporate brand.

de Chernatony & Harris (2000) consider corporate brand management to be about narrowing the gaps between the components of identity among staff in order that a strong and coherent identity is developed. Furthermore, the gaps between brand identity and its reputation amongst stakeholders should also be narrowed and be a focus for managerial action. Their theory is that the narrower these gaps are, the stronger a brand's performance will be. The better employees relate and contribute to the brand identity, the more consistent will be the presentation of the brand identity. Davies & Miles (1998) also suggest the importance of identifying gaps between the internal and external perspectives of a brand, which may erode reputation.

Relationships are a significant part of Kapferer's prism and de Chernatony & Harris (2000) propose that the greater the contact between an organisation and its stakeholders, the greater the congruence between its identity and reputation. Corporate communication plays an important role in narrowing these gaps, a topic explored in Part 3 of this book.

These authors also state that a brand's reputation will be more favourable, the more congruent the brand's identity is with the self-image of stakeholders. This reinforces the seminal work of Martineau (1958). Similarly, the greater the extent to which a brand's core values merge with the values of stakeholders, the more favourable will be the reputation. This is in line with Goodyear's (1996) idea of consumers 'voting' for products in the way that they once voted for political parties; that is, they express their trust in the brand and align the brand closely with their own values and view of the world.

Kowalczyk & Pawlish (2002) describe reputation as a measure of the quality of the corporate brand. They propose that the corporate brand has two main dimensions: recognition,

Reputation is a measure of the quality of the corporate brand.

i.e. the extent to which a brand is known; and quality, defined as the positive or negative image of the brand. According to Kowalczyk & Pawlish (2002), therefore, reputation is broadly the same as the external brand image.

Note the difficulties outlined in Chapter 2 here, whereby different authors place emphasis on different areas. For example, de Chernatony & Harris stress identity and Kowalczyk & Pawlish stress image. Argenti & Druckenmiller (2004) also take an external view, saying that reputation is the collective representation of many different stakeholder perspectives. They indicate that if the corporate brand promise is experienced, consistently, then reputation will be strengthened.

> **Reputation is the collective representation of many different stakeholder perspectives.**

Branding and reputation – are they the same thing?

Fombrun & van Riel (2004) warn against thinking that brand and reputation are synonymous. Reputation is concerned with the assessments of multiple stakeholders about a company's ability to fulfil their expectations, fuelled by a brand's promise. It follows that a company may have a strong brand yet a weak reputation. For example, Nike is considered to be a strong brand yet its reputation scores in public reputation surveys are often low due to its association with child labour issues in the developing world.

> **A company may have a strong brand yet a weak reputation.**

Fombrun & van Riel (2004) believe that branding is a subset of reputation management. This is because branding affects the likelihood of a favourable purchase, whereas reputation affects the likelihood of supporting behaviours from all stakeholder groups. This may be a strict interpretation simply because external groups do not always dissect and demarcate distinctions and definitions so clearly. We prefer to think of the brand as the repository of the organisation's reputation.

Fombrun & van Riel (2004) use a magnet as a metaphor of reputation, i.e. that corporate reputation helps to attract all kinds of stakeholders. Davies *et al.* (2003) state that they are not the same thing, but that a corporate brand is central to and contributes to reputation. The brand is the focal point of their Corporate Reputation Chain, forming the basis of the various stakeholders' views, which in turn contribute to a company's reputation (see Figure 5.3).

In summary, the corporate branding and corporate reputation concepts should not be considered to be synonymous, but neither are they two separate concepts. There can be no doubt that they are closely interlinked and interact with each other, helping to support each other (Ettenson & Knowles, 2008). However, in practice, as Abimbola & Kocak (2007) observe, consumers find it difficult to separate the two.

The brand as a repository of the organisation's reputation

There are still many arguments among researchers about what the exact relationship is between the brand and the reputation of an organisation. One perspective states that corporate

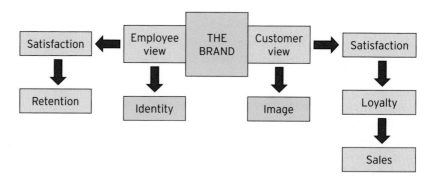

Figure 5.3 The Corporate Reputation Chain.
Source: Davies *et al.* (2003). Routledge, with permission.

reputation is a core component of the corporate brand (Herbig & Milewicz, 1993; Fombrun & van Riel, 1997; Bickerton, 2000; Dowling, 2001; Dowling & Weeks, 2008).

According to Herbig & Milewicz (1993), a positive reputation needs to be developed and clearly established if a brand is to be successful and profitable. Moorthy (1985) considers the brand name to be a repository for the reputation of the organisation. An example of this is where the quality of one product may be transferred to another through the brand name. Therefore, in the case of a corporate brand that establishes all of its products under the same corporate name, such as L'Oréal, the products may benefit from a 'halo effect' of the company's reputation. L'Oréal is owned by Procter & Gamble.

> The quality of one product may be transferred to another through the brand name.

Knox & Maklan (1998) are of the view that reputation is one of the four elements that make up a corporate brand. The other three components are the product/service performance, the product brand, and the customer portfolio and networks within which the brand operates. However, other academics take the opposite view and believe a corporate brand is one of the core components of the corporate reputation. They see the brand as a vital aspect in the management of the reputation (Fan, 2005).

Many authors take the view that reputation and corporate branding are interlinked concepts, with one leading to the other. Authors such as Abimbola & Kocak (2007), Schwaiger (2004) and Balmer & Gray (2003), for example, suggest that by nurturing and effectively managing the corporate brand, corporate reputation can be significantly enhanced and strengthened. Authors such as Kitchen & Laurence (2003) and Argenti & Druckenmiller (2004), on the other hand, place a greater importance on reputation and emphasise the use of branding to help develop it. How do these views differ?

By considering the brand to be the repository of the organisation's reputation, individuals can cut through the myriad information and decisions that need to be made. It simplifies a purchase decision, thereby reducing the choice (or repertoire) set. The higher the risk that is attached to a decision, the more important the reputation of the brand is in reducing that risk.

Of course, branding is about the intangible elements of an organisation over and above its tangible assets. The book-to-market value ratio is often used to emphasise the intangible value of brands. In other words, the company's total tangible assets less its total liabilities would make up its book value. The intangibles, including its brand, make up the market value. If the market value of the firm is significantly above its book value then this can be attributed to the power of the brand itself. If the brand is worth more than the tangible assets of the company, as with Coca-Cola, for example, then damage to the reputation can easily lead to the destruction of the majority of the company's value. Protecting these intangible assets is therefore of great importance.

> The book-to-market value ratio is often used to emphasise the intangible value of brands.

Brands, reputation and corporate social responsibility

The issue of corporate social responsibility (CSR) needs to be addressed as this is often seen as a response to the call for greater transparency by companies. Increasingly, over recent years CSR has been used as an outlet for firms to build reputational capital with stakeholders (see Viewpoint 5.2).

> CSR has been used as an outlet for firms to build reputational capital with stakeholders.

Viewpoint 5.2 | FC Barcelona/Aston Villa FC

Barcelona Football Club is a sporting giant, the second most successful Spanish football club of all time, surpassed only by Real Madrid. It boasts upward of 50 domestic titles and has amassed 10 European trophies, as befitting a club that possesses the largest stadium in Europe (with a capacity of 98,772). Its striking success is perhaps more impressive in light of the fact that it remains unquestionably one of the principal global sporting exponents of charity, showcasing an extraordinary altruism within the context of a sport that has progressively become financially dominated. Indeed, its admirable ethos pertains to all facets of the organisation. It has acquired the title of 'the people's club', with the fans' involvement clear as they vote on who will be the club's president every 4 years.

A month after the Spanish civil war began, Barça's left-wing president, Josep Sunyol, was murdered by Franco's soldiers near Guadarrama. Perhaps as a result of this incident, the club symbolises a resistance to established order, with its stadium, the Nou Camp, proving one of the few places where Catalan could be spoken freely during the Franco dictatorship. Hence, for the citizens of the region, the club means more than a mere sport, elevating FC Barcelona to a higher plane of significance. Many Spaniards view the club as a staunch defender of rights and freedoms. This defiance is paralleled only by its unswerving refusal to comply with the financial goals of many other top clubs. It was for many years the only major club not to allow a corporate sponsor to tarnish the significance embodied by the Barça shirt.

Barcelona finally accepted its first ever shirt sponsor in 2006, an agreement with UNICEF that guarantees a donation of £1.5 million to the charity on an annual basis. The fact that Manchester United is currently accruing £20 million per annum via a contract agreed with American insurance giant AON puts Barcelona's policy into context. The club provides both revenue and publicity to a worthy charitable cause at a cost of over £20 million per season to itself. Surely this is a case of corporate social responsibility (CSR) in action.

It is encouraging that other clubs are looking to emulate such an unprecedented display of charity. For example, Aston Villa have secured a similar arrangement with the Acorns Hospice, a well-known charity in the Midlands that seeks to support local children who, due to their illnesses, are not expected to reach adult

Exhibit 5.3 | FC Barcelona striker Lionel Messi poses with children upon his appointment as a UNICEF goodwill ambassador.
Source: © Josep Lago/AFP/Getty Images.

life. This often involves providing 24-hour care as well as support for parents and families. Villa already had an established relationship with Acorns and has previously raised more than £100,000, through payroll-giving (regular donations given directly from people's salaries) and bucket shakes, to pay for 230 beds at the cost of £450 a day. Players had become regular visitors to the Selly Oak Acorns, one of its three hospices. The move to a shirt deal, however, was a radical step, and provided crucial publicity for an organisation that is itself unable to afford advertising. Children's hospices usually only receive about 5 per cent of their funding direct from the government, meaning there is a constant battle to raise revenue or risk bed closures. The 2-year agreement (2008-2010), therefore, was an unparalleled move in the money-driven Premier League and, again, an example of true CSR in action.

Question

Find three examples of CSR campaigns that you are aware of. How strong is the link between the brand in question and the CSR campaign?

McWilliams & Siegel (2001) refer to CSR as a concept which enables organisations to move beyond the extent of their normal business operations, take initiatives that contribute to the betterment of the society, and take part in activities that go beyond an organisation's self-interest. The European Commission (2001, p. 366) describes CSR as 'a concept whereby companies integrate social and environmental concerns in their business operations and in their interaction with their stakeholders on a voluntary basis'. CSR helps to ensure that a business monitors and ensures its support for the law, ethical standards and international norms.

Of course, many organisations now understand the strategic importance of CSR and attempt to use it as a point of differentiation over their competitors. CSR is really a link between the world of business and the community at large. It could be described as strategic philanthropy and it perhaps works best where there is a clear connection between the company concerned and the beneficiary of its CSR activity. Governments of many countries, together with non-governmental organisations, now expect large organisations to do business in a way that contributes to the betterment of their own nation's social and economic needs. There is now an expectation that sustainability, for example, will be written into a company's agenda. The move towards carbon-neutral stores at Marks & Spencer and the lower carbon footprint of newly built Tesco stores are examples of this type of behaviour.

> CSR is really a link between the world of business and the community at large.

Porter & Kramer (2006) outline four reasons why companies engage in CSR:

- **Moral obligation:** companies engage in CSR because they think it is their duty to be a good corporate citizen.

- **Sustainability:** firms participate in CSR in an attempt to ensure that there are sufficient resources and customers in the future to allow the business to continue benefiting. This might be considered to be enlightened self-interest.

- **Licence to operate:** organisations need to ensure that they fulfil the legal, moral and ethical codes that are necessary to operate in their various marketplaces.

- **Reputation:** many firms hope to build their reputational capital by engaging in CSR. The company is portrayed as responsible and ethical, which leads to a higher reputation, higher profitability and an increased share price.

Kotler & Lee (2005) take a pragmatic view of the reasons why a company has a CSR agenda. First, CSR activity helps to increase market share and sales. Secondly, engaging in CSR is likely to generate a more positive attitude in the minds of its stakeholders and so improve brand positioning. Linked to this is the need to create a positive image. Leverage of their CSR activity

Employees will feel pride in being associated with firms that engage in CSR activities.

can help organisations to gain positive coverage in the media. This should not be underestimated of course, as this can boost employee morale and assist in ensuring employee retention. Employees will feel pride in being associated with firms that engage in CSR activities.

Many enterprises feel that engaging in CSR helps them reduce their operating costs, which can result in higher profits. It helps firms reduce their marketing costs, as companies engaging in CSR receive free publicity, as a direct outcome of being socially responsible.

Does CSR positively affect the corporate reputation of an organisation?

Proponents of CSR argue that there is a strong business case for it and that corporations benefit in many ways by operating with a wider perspective than their own immediate, short-term profitability. Critics argue that CSR distracts from the fundamental economic role of businesses, the Milton Friedman argument that started this book. Others argue that it is nothing more than a superficial attempt to paper over the cracks or, perhaps worse, that it is an attempt to deflect government attention and regulation from powerful global companies.

Often reputational results are understood in terms of broad targets, such as having a reputation for behaving responsibly towards the community in which a firm operates (Mutch & Aitken, 2009). Certain studies have put forward the view that the more a firm talks about its social and ethical objectives, the more prone they are to draw critical attention (Ashforth & Gibbs, 1990). There is even the possibility that by overemphasising a commitment to CSR, people may think a company is trying to hide something (Brown & Dacin, 1997). As with those firms that most closely follow the marketing concept, firms involved in CSR are more often the target of negative reactions from consumers than the not-for-profit beneficiaries (Dahl & Lavack, 1995).

Firms should have CSR institutionalised within their operations.

Research suggests that firms should have CSR institutionalised within their operations rather than running CSR for promotional purposes. The idea is to take care of environmental and social concerns, for example, and to integrate these into the business in the same way that financial concerns are present.

Promotional CSR, on the other hand, is more concerned with the short-term benefit that firms can reap. Organisations may be criticised for not involving their stakeholders while developing a CSR programme. Although consumers may not expect a firm to instigate a CSR programme merely for altruistic purposes, it is very important for them to believe that the campaign is honest (i.e. the amount stated is actually donated) and non-exploitative (i.e. the amount donated should not be trivial).

Margolis & Elfenbein (2008, p. 20) report that 'research over 35 years shows only a weak link between socially responsible corporate behaviour and good financial performance'.

Starbucks is an example of a company that has shown commitment to CSR programmes whilst still attracting criticism (see Viewpoint 5.3).

Griffin (2008, p. 137) takes a more sceptical view of CSR. He says that CSR is just a defence mechanism, trying to defend the corporation from a hostile world, a world that dislikes and distrusts it. He claims that CSR is 'managed reactively, defensively and entirely on the territory of others'. This means that CSR is defined with very negative concepts in mind, and it is about preventing adverse things from happening, which suggests that businesses are inherently bad and seek to reduce this perception via CSR.

Griffin (2008) claims that there are two reasons for the use of CSR:

1. Companies are afraid that today's CSR issues will turn into lawsuits tomorrow and they are basically getting their defence in first. For example, food companies are blamed for obesity and manufacturers or airlines being made answerable for climate change.

Viewpoint 5.3 | Starbucks' rise with CSR

Starbucks has played a pioneering role (particularly in the UK) within the burgeoning worldwide coffee market. The coffee boom witnessed in the US has palpably transferred itself to the UK, a very much under-developed market prior to Starbucks' arrival in Britain. Its popularity in Britain has now reached such a magnitude that it increasingly shares the traditional mantle of tea as the nation's favourite hot beverage, especially among younger generations.

In the UK, each of the coffee-house franchises actively fosters a unique image. Starbucks nurtures a more American brand of coffee shop whilst Costa and Caffè Nero exploit an Italian image. This taps into the popular notion that Italy is the birthplace and rightful home of this global phenomenon. Each establishment charges premium prices and thus the selection is based more on preference than on cost.

Back in 1971, Starbucks was originally a purveyor of coffee-related products (e.g. coffee beans and equipment), finally becoming an actual coffee shop when young entrepreneur Howard Schultz, who joined the company in 1982 as director of marketing, bought out the company in 1987. Hereafter, a rapid expansion ensued, with 165 US-based outlets by 1992.

Starbucks' rate of international expansion has been nothing short of breathtaking. It is the largest coffee-house company in the world, with over 17,000 stores in 49 countries, including around 11,000 in the United States, nearly 1,000 in Canada and more than 800 in Japan. The first store outside the US or Canada opened in the mid-1990s, and overseas stores now constitute almost one-third of Starbucks' stores. By November 2005, London had more outlets than Manhattan. Schultz, Starbucks' CEO, announced company plans to establish 900 new stores outside the US in 2009 and in 2010 announced that its fastest-growing market, China, would be the focus of thousands of new Starbucks' stores.

Certain leading bookstores have capitalised upon the patent link between coffee breaks and free time, and the potential that this time affords. Harking back to the original cafés located in France, traditionally (and still presently) treated as rendezvous points for the pontifications of philosophers, artists and intellectuals, Starbucks' outlets have partnered Barnes & Noble in the US in order to tap into this scholarly connection.

As a global organisation, Starbucks is scrupulous in its corporate behaviour, with a meticulously devised CSR programme making it renowned for being environmentally friendly, cemented by its number 15 rank on the US Environmental Protection Agency's list of Top 25 Green Power Partners for purchases of renewable energy (www.starbucks.com). The US government approved Starbucks as the first company dispensing food or drink products in recyclable packaging. Furthermore, its Product Red goods enable the provision of AIDS medicine for 3,800 people per year and it has launched a volunteer programme in which employees will rebuild part of New Orleans 3 years post-Hurricane Katrina. Like most coffee houses it has also shown itself to be committed to the Fairtrade cause, as almost 70 per cent of the coffee used by Starbucks around the world comes from the sixth major producer in the world, Guatemala, a pro-organic producer. It is the largest buyer of Fairtrade coffee in the United States (the world's largest market). Note, however, that Starbucks' commitment to CSR does not save it from considerable criticism from commentators and the anti-globalisation movement.

Question

What are the objectives of Starbucks' CSR programmes? How will the organisation know if these programmes have been a success?

2. They have always done it – corporate philanthropy is the idea of giving something back and they like to be seen as good corporate citizens. This could be as simple as a financial donation or as complicated as the building of an entire community, such as Bournville (Cadbury's) or Port Sunlight (Lever Bros – William Lever) (see Viewpoint 5.4).

Corporate philanthropy is the idea of giving something back.

Viewpoint 5.4   CSR – old and new perspectives and dilemmas

Griffin (2008), makes the point that companies like Lever Bros and Cadbury's have always conducted CSR and questions its value. Is this a fair comment? These companies, as with cases from the industrial revolution where schools were built by non-conformist Methodist mill owners in the UK, are examples of a fundamental ideology often based upon religious beliefs that really shows modern-day CSR up for what it is. Men like George Cadbury and Joseph Rowntree were industrial giants and philanthropists and often based their good works upon their religious convictions. There was a great tone of paternalism amongst these men – almost like fathers looking after their children. Their philanthropy puts many contemporary CSR programmes to shame.

In a similar vein, the founder of the Ford Motor Company, Henry Ford, was also noted as an employer for paying his workers well above the industry's going rate. He expected them to work hard for their wages but he knew that looking after his staff was vital to the company's success. Ford was also happy to make smaller profits on his cars in order that more US citizens could afford to buy one. The price of Ford cars reduced by half between 1908 and 1916 despite demand outstripping supply. Ford was criticised in America and harangued by shareholders and the business press, such as *The Wall Street Journal*, for allowing social improvement to hamper his pursuit of profits (Willmott, 2001).

The devastation of former industrial areas such as South Wales and the north-east of England when the coal mining industry was shut down in the 1980s was not just in employment terms but also in the simultaneous decimation of a large part of the social network, i.e. the support the industry gave to sports, choirs, bands, etc. Coal mining and other heavy industries of the past placed themselves at the heart of their communities in a way that CSR is struggling to do.

Looking at the situation in the second decade of the 21st century, we seem to have travelled through 180°, with the state having to move in to protect us from the excesses of capitalism and so-called market forces. Similarly, the state itself does not seem willing or able to provide the infrastructure needed in many communities. Surely this provides the opportunity for CSR?

However, at the same time, the value of CSR to the reputational capital of the organisation is strongly questioned. Griffin, for example, discusses the amount of work that Coca-Cola has put into its Global Water Challenge aimed at improving sanitation, hygiene education and access to clean water in developing countries, yet as a global icon Coke is still one of the brands that is lambasted by anti-globalisation protestors. Similarly Tesco's huge Computers for Schools CSR programme and its development of the £25 million Sustainable Consumption Institute at Manchester University are doing little to protect the brand from accusations of anti-competitive practices and its contribution in reducing the UK to a collection of 'clone towns'. As noted in Viewpoint 5.3, Starbucks commits itself to Fairtrade coffee yet is similarly held up as an out-of-control monster also reducing us to clone town status. It is a target for anti-capitalists and action groups (see, for example, www.ihatestarbucks.com).

The food industry has allowed itself to take the blame for the obesity crisis in the western world. CSR, though, seems to be a quasi-legal requirement, with governments the world over insisting on CSR programmes, often as a price for allowing expansion into developing markets. If CSR does become a legal requirement, this will further undermine it as a reputation-enhancing area for a business.

Question

To what extent should organisations ditch specific CSR initiatives in favour of being a good corporate citizen?

CSR or citizen brands?

As discussed in the previous section, there is considerable debate as to the benefit of CSR programmes to the organisation. In a similar vein, the CSR component of the 'Most Admired Companies' indices is not considered that highly by those who complete the surveys. Ninety per cent of the *Fortune* 500 companies provide CSR reports for the attention of stakeholders, yet CSR is the lowest rated category of all those included in the most admired surveys (Brown & Turner, 2008). This, of course, may change in future years as stakeholder's expectations about the ethical standards of business increase.

Similarly, instead of dealing with individual CSR issues, Willmott (2001) talks of engendering 'citizen brands'. This is over and above companies merely doing good deeds such as supporting worthwhile causes. Instead of focusing on their responsibilities, brands should be focused on their relationship with society. Willmott believes that being a citizen brand encapsulates three major issues: branding, core values and corporate citizenship. This moves away from the add-on effect that CSR often gets lost in and emphasises a more political dynamic of the corporate brand and its level of importance in society.

> Brands should be focused on their relationship with society.

A strong corporate brand needs not just to integrate its internal and external stakeholders but to integrate itself with society at large. It is not enough to be seen as paternalistic, handing over a small percentage of its profits to charities. For the brand to really engage, it must form a relationship with society. Willmott (2001) claims that it is more important that a brand understands and cares about the issues of society. The wider concerns of society are here to stay and the public probably now look to businesses for reassurance and action on these issues more than they do to the state. The citizen brand puts society at the heart of the business rather than, say, the customer.

> The citizen brand puts society at the heart of its business.

The concept of the citizen brand is again a clear indication that the corporate brand needs to be clear in its values and not be shy in promoting and reinforcing these in all of its activities. The idea of being a good corporate citizen or a citizen brand lies in not seeing these wider environmental issues as obligations but rather as something by which mutual benefit can be gained by the organisation and the world at large.

Forbes magazine produces a list of the '100 Best Corporate Citizens' each year. Now in its 11th year, the 2010 winner was Hewlett-Packard. It reports that behaviour as good corporate citizens is improving. Companies in the list can be slapped with a yellow card if official legal action is ongoing against them. Pfizer was issued with a red card this year and removed from the list due to its pleading guilty to illegal marketing activity for one of its pain-killing drugs, which attracted a fine of $2.3 billion.

The triple bottom line

The shift in the debate as to where the responsibilities of business lie is reflected in the concept of a triple bottom line (TBL). Practically, TPL accounting means expanding the traditional reporting framework to take into account ecological and social performance in addition to financial performance. It is often referred to as people, planet and profit, as set out at Figure 5.4.

'People' relates to fair business practices that benefit the labour force, their communities and regions, such as the Fairtrade initiative. 'Planet' refers to sustainable environmental practices. A company practising TBL will endeavour to reduce its ecological footprint. The use of recyclable materials in manufacture and consideration of proper disposal of the product after use will be key considerations of the TBL company. 'Profit' cannot be interpreted as a simple traditional corporate accounting figure. A more appropriate measure is the economic value created by the organisation after deducting the cost of all inputs, including the cost of the capital tied up. Profit under the TBL description needs to be seen as the real economic benefit enjoyed by society. What is the positive impact that is made on the economic environment in which the firm is operating?

> A company practising TBL will endeavour to reduce its ecological footprint.

The phrase 'triple bottom line' was coined by John Elkington in 1994. It was later expanded and articulated in his 1998 book *Cannibals with Forks: the Triple Bottom Line of 21st Century Business*.

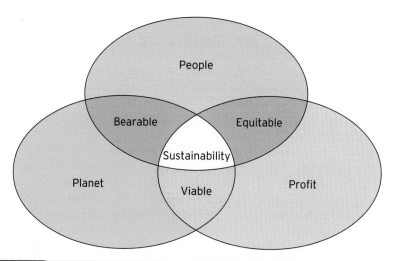

Figure 5.4 The triple bottom line.

Sustainability itself was first defined by the Brundtland Commission of the United Nations in 1987.

The concept of TBL demands that a company's responsibility be to stakeholders rather than to shareholders. In this case, 'stakeholders' refers to anyone who is influenced, either directly or indirectly, by the actions of the firm. According to stakeholder theory, the business entity should be used as a vehicle for co-ordinating stakeholder interests, instead of maximising shareholder (owner) profit. The Co-operative Bank is an example of a brand that has differentiated itself via an ethical, more socially aware approach (see Viewpoint 5.5).

Viewpoint 5.5 Triple hit for The Co-operative Bank

Originally formed in 1972 but not becoming a full clearing bank (and therefore able to issue its own cheques) until 1975, The Co-operative Bank is unable to compete with the other UK clearing banks on the basis of size. However, it has found a much more effective form of market segmentation due to its ethical policies. It launched its ethical stance in 1992 and is unique in consulting its customers about which sectors it will and will not do business in. A huge number of customers (80,000) responded to a detailed questionnaire in autumn 2008 covering topics from human rights and animal welfare to ecology and international development. The bank introduced new pledges as a result:

- A refusal to lend to firms engaged in fossil fuel extraction has been extended to include those distributing fuels that have a high impact upon global warming, including biofuels and unconventional oil sources.

- Its arms trade policies are to include the boycott of companies involved in the manufacture of indiscriminate weapons such as cluster bombs and depleted uranium munitions.

- A policy on animal experimentation for cosmetic/household purposes is also to cover activities connected with exploitation of great apes – as they are humans' closest living relatives. The ban doesn't involve those involved in animal experimentation for health purposes.

All this means that Co-op has declined more than £1 billion of business over the years as it felt that such relationships would compromise the bank's ethical standards. In June 2005 the bank closed the account of the evangelical Christian group, Christian Voice, due to its views on homosexuality. The Co-op said that the group's 'discriminatory pronouncements . . . were . . . incompatible with the position of the Co-operative Bank which publicly supports diversity and dignity'. The bank has refused business from companies involved in the fur trade, exploitation of labour practices (e.g. use of child labour) and nuclear power amongst others.

The **co-operative** bank
good with money

Ecological impact

98%

invested in renewable energy

of our customers want their money

Part of The **co-operative** financial services

Exhibit 5.4	The Co-operative Bank has differentiated itself via an ethical, more socially aware approach to business.
	Source: The Co-operative Bank, with permission.

However, this policy has helped underpin a strong business performance. Commercial lending went up from £571 million (1992) to £4.4 billion (2008), an average increase of 14 per cent per year. There has been a 65 per cent increase in current account opening. The company states that one-third of its customers are attracted as a direct result of its ethical policy and credentials. Co-op and Smile are in the top three banks for customer satisfaction according to consumer magazine, *Which*?

Interestingly, the bank has put a value on its ethical stance. It estimates that 24 per cent of its profits are directly linked to its ethical stance; that is the additional revenue that it gains purely from its ethical position in the marketplace.

Question

The Co-op Bank's corporate brand is closely linked to its ethical stance. Consider three examples of corporate brands and outline the values that underpin them.

Source: Various sources, including Papworth (2009).

Investigating the co-creation of brands

In Chapter 6 corporate brands are defined and discussed in detail. This chapter has discussed the importance of brands but it is essential now to consider the broader landscape in which contemporary branding occurs. This involves moving away from the dyadic producer–consumer micro-level approach to branding to one that looks deeper at the culture, where the impact, influence and power of brands are inescapable. There needs to be a focus on the gap between managerial intent and market response, a space that is inherent in much of the traditional practice and theory of brand management.

> Consumers (or other stakeholders) by their actions and involvement contribute to creating the brand.

In this newer perspective, the consumer is not treated as a malleable, passive individual who can be bent to the will of the brand but as a creator of the brand to the same extent as the company. This is what is meant by 'co-creation' of the brand. It is a recognition that consumers (or other stakeholders) by their actions and involvement contribute to creating the brand and what it means, together with the company. Those in favour of the co-creation approach to branding are critical of the top-down approach exercised by more formal brand management organisations.

Balmer (2006) discusses corporate brand cultures and the communities from which the brand emerges. He introduces the idea of 'corporate faith communities' and deals with the complexity of brand architecture, culture and custodianship that form part of the intricacy of the corporate brand and the myriad relationships that exist within the corporate brand. Balmer states that the real power of the brand comes from the emotional ownership which resides in the corporate brand community.

> Neither managers nor consumers have total control over brand meanings.

Bergvall (2006) also discusses the multi-level interactions of brands using the term 'brand ecosystems'. Bergvall makes an excellent point that 'neither managers nor consumers have total control over brand meanings'. Discussing a brand ecosystem reflects the move towards a networked society where the relationships between brands and consumers are far more developed and interwoven than the traditional perspective of the company producing a brand which the consumer then obediently purchases.

This bond between the brand and the consumer is reinforced by the company Innocent, for example, who display unusual messages received by customers on their products. This provides entertainment, and gives the impression of a down-to-earth company comfortable with its position and its relationship with customers who help to co-create the brand. Not for them the corporate-looking and -sounding CSR report. Real thought goes into the production of their website (www.innocentdrinks.co.uk), further reinforcing the brand message and giving the real impression of a company enthusiastic about its product and brand. Labels are changed regularly because customers do actually read them. How many other fast-moving consumer goods companies would this apply to?

The emotional power of brands

Askegaard (2006) presents the idea of brands as a global ideoscope, arguing that brands and branding have a profound impact on the marketplace and the consumers within it. He borrows the term ideoscope from work outlining central ideas derived from the Enlightenment, e.g. democracy, welfare, freedom. Such is the impact of market-based institutions on our entire lives that brands have become a fundamental method of structure in the prevailing status of a market-based system that dominates the world. Again confirming the confusion of present-day culture, this has taken place in a society that often claims to be anti-branding.

What this refers to is the social construction of brand meaning, the symbolic use of brands and brand relationship to personal self-interest. This means that brands have developed beyond the stage whereby they are merely products or services, but are a fundamental part of the fabric of our lives. Ultimately, Askegaard (2006) claims that the meaning of things, places and people is created by people's linkage to brands. The globalisation of consumer culture provides the platform for this growth, and brands have become a central metaphor for both corporate and consumer identity formation. Brands have led the way to a new form of consumption – mall-based, chain stores and internet shopping showing the homogenised way forward. In certain cases, brands have adopted a semi-spirituality and even quasi-religious overtones that have elevated them to a far higher emotional level than previously seen. This theory is examined using both global and local brands as examples.

Brands form part of the stories that help to explain post-modern life. Western societies have moved away from traditional sources of power, such as religion and politics, to economic sources, in which brands have filled the gaps. This

> Brands form part of the stories that help to explain postmodern life.

has happened to such an extent that the use of symbolic spheres that were once the preserve of religion is now happening – the French retail giant Carrefour, for example, now organises both weddings and funerals. Corporate brands are taking over managerial responsibilities previously organised by central and local government, for example in the running of towns and cities. There has been a move, therefore, of brands from the sphere of management to the sphere of government, further emphasising their huge power and central position in our lives.

These themes will be developed further in Chapter 8 where the future of brands is discussed.

Chapter summary

In order to consolidate your understanding of the link between corporate reputation and branding, here are the key points summarised against each of the learning objectives.

1. Define what is meant by a brand

A brand is a complex set of associations with which the consumer can identify and provides differentiation from mere products. A brand represents quality and security together with considerable emotional attachments and benefits for the consumer. A brand attributes social and symbolic meaning to a product.

A brand provides something that is different and relevant; it is a promise, a summary of the mental associations and emotions that come to mind when a name is conjured up or mentioned. Kotler *et al.* (2004) talks of the six levels of meaning that a brand is able to deliver. He states that a brand consists of attributes, benefits, values, culture and personality and reflects the user.

2. Make the link between branding and reputation

As we have moved towards corporate branding, so the reputation of the brand has become ever more important. The values of the company are key here in differentiating the brand and providing competitive advantage. The brand and the reputation are related but it is important to understand that they are not the same thing. It is possible to have a strong brand but a poor corporate reputation. It is thought that gaps between the internal identity and the external image of a brand will negatively affect the reputation.

3. Introduce the notion as the brand as a repository for the organisation's reputation

There is a debate about the relationship between the brand and the reputation. One perspective states that corporate reputation is a core component of the corporate brand and that a positive reputation needs to be developed and clearly established if the brand is to be successful and profitable. The other perspective is that it is the corporate brand that is one of the core components of the corporate reputation and that the brand is a vital aspect in the management of the reputation.

This book takes the view that the brand is the repository of the organisation's reputation.

4. Discuss reputation and corporate social responsibility (CSR)

Corporate social responsibility takes place when an organisation takes initiatives that contribute to the betterment of society at large and goes beyond the organisation's self-interest. Most well-known brands will now participate in some form of CSR programme(s). They hope to build some reputational capital from their CSR activities. However, CSR is often viewed with cynicism by the public and there is very mixed evidence that it actually benefits the organisation conducting the CSR programme.

In light of this, it may be best for companies to concentrate on the longer-term view and become good corporate citizens.

5. Investigate the co-creation of brands

The corporate brand has multiple stakeholders. As such, it must move away from thinking simply about the producer–consumer model whereby the company produces the brand and the consumer compliantly purchases it. It is more useful to think of a brand as being co-created and that consumers can often be as much creators of the brand as the company. This approach reflects the importance of brands to society and how the interaction with brands often forms a central part of a consumer's life.

6. Discuss the emotional power of brands

As indicated by the idea of co-creation, it is clear that many brands have developed to the stage that they are a fundamental part of the fabric of our lives. In certain cases, brands have adopted a semi-spirituality and even quasi-religious overtones that have elevated them to a far higher emotional level than previously seen. As western societies have moved away from traditional sources of power, i.e. religion and politics, brands have filled in the gaps. Such is the emotional resonance and power of brands that they now guide many consumers through key stages of their lives, including birth, marriage and funerals. Brands are present from the cradle to the grave.

Discussion questions

1. Summarise the key developments in society that have led to the prominence of brands.
2. What proportion of a brand is made up of emotional elements and what proportion of practical elements? Justify your thinking.
3. Make notes on the concept of consumers 'voting' for brands.
4. How would you describe the link between branding and reputation?
5. Why may reputation be considered more important for corporate brands than product brands?
6. Explain how the book-to-market value ratio can be used to highlight the intangible value of brands to a company.

7. Many companies are criticised despite taking part in various CSR-related activities. Provide three examples of companies that could genuinely said to be good corporate citizens.

8. Many brands now claim to be co-created by the company and its consumers. How appropriate is the role of consumers in the co-creation of a brand?

9. Explain the concept of the triple bottom line as outlined by Elkington (1998).

10. If asked to discuss the issue of the social construction of brands, what key points would you like your audience to take away?

References

Abimbola, T. & Kocak, A. (2007). Brand, organization identity and reputation: SMEs as expressive organization. *Qualitative Market Research: An International Journal* 10(4), 416–430.

Adamson, A.P. (2006). *Brand Simple: How the Best Brands Keep it Simple and Succeed.* New York: Palgrave Macmillan.

Argenti, P.A. & Druckenmiller, B. (2004). Reputation and the corporate brand. *Corporate Reputation Review* 6(4), 368–374.

Ashforth, B.E. & Gibbs, B.W. (1990). The double edge of organizational legitimation. *Organization Science* 2, 177–194.

Askegaard, S. (2006). Brands as a global ideoscape. In: Schroeder, J.E. & Salzer-Morling, M., eds. *Brand Culture.* Abingdon: Routledge, pp. 91–102.

Balmer, J. (2006). Corporate brand cultures and communities. In: Schroeder, J.E. & Salzer-Morling, M., eds. *Brand Culture.* Abingdon: Routledge, pp. 34–49.

Balmer, J.M.T. & Gray, E.R. (2003). Commentary: corporate brands: what are they? What of them? *European Journal of Marketing* 37(7/8), 972–997.

BBC (2010). Microsoft 'is king of UK brands'. Online: http://news.bbc.co.uk/1/hi/8149460.stm. Accessed: 22 September 2010.

Bergvall, S. (2006). Brand ecosystems: multi-level brand interaction. In: Schroeder, J.E. & Salzer-Morling, M., eds. *Brand Culture.* Abingdon: Routledge, pp. 186–197.

Bickerton, D. (2000). Corporate reputation versus corporate branding: the realist debate. *Corporate Communications: An International Journal* 5(1), 42–48.

Brown, M. & Turner, P. (2008). *The Admirable Company.* London: Profile Books.

Brown, T.J. & Dacin, P.A. (1997). The company and the product: corporate associations and consumer product responses. *Journal of Marketing* 61(1), 68–84.

de Chernatony, L. & Harris, F. (2000). Developing corporate brands through considering internal and external stakeholders. *Corporate Reputation Review* 3(3), 268–274.

de Chernatony, L. & McDonald, M. (2003). *Creating Powerful Brands*, 3rd edn. London: Butterworth-Heinemann.

de Chernatony, L. & Riley, F.D. (1998). Defining a 'brand': beyond the literature with experts interpretations. *Journal of Marketing Management* 14(5), 417–443.

de Chernatony, L., Riley, F.D. & Harris, F. (1998). Criteria to assess brand success. *Journal of Marketing Management* 14(7), 765–781.

Dahl, D.W. & Lavack, A.M. (1995). Cause-related marketing: impact of size of cause-related promotion on consumer perceptions and participation. *Winter Educators Conference: Marketing Theory and Applications*, vol. 6. Chicago: American Marketing Association, pp. 476–481.

Davies, G., Chun, R., da Silva, R. & Roper, S. (2003). *Corporate Reputation and Competitiveness.* London: Routledge.

Davies, G. & Miles, L. (1998). Reputation management: theory versus practice. *Corporate Reputation Review* 2(1), 16–27.

Dowling, G.R. (2001). *Creating Corporate Reputations: Identity, Image and Performance*. Oxford: OUP.

Dowling, G.R. (1994). *Corporate Reputations*. London: Kogan Page.

Dowling, G. & Weeks, W. (2008). What the media is really telling you about your brand. *MIT Sloan Management Review* 49(3), 28–34.

Egan, C. (1998). Chasing the holy grail: a critical appraisal of the brand and the brand valuation debate. *The Journal of Brand Management* 5(4), 227–244.

Elkington, J. (1998). *Cannibals with Forks: the Triple Bottom Line of 21st Century Business*. Gabriola Island, BC: New Society Publishers.

Ettenson, R. & Knowles, J. (2008). Don't confuse reputation with brand. *MIT Sloan Management Review* 49(2), 19–21.

European Commission (2001). Green Paper. *Promoting a European Framework for Corporate Social Responsibility*. Brussels: European Commission.

Fan, Y. (2005). Ethical branding and corporate reputation. *Corporate Communications: An International Journal* 10(4), 341–350.

Fombrun, C. & van Riel, C. (1997). The reputational landscape. *Corporate Reputation Review* 1(1), 5–13.

Fombrun, C.J. & van Riel, C.B.M. (2004). *Fame and Fortune: How Successful Companies Build Winning Reputations*. New Jersey: FT Prentice Hall.

Gardner, B.B. & Levy, S.J. (1955). The product and the brand. *Harvard Business Review*, March–April, 33–39.

Goodyear, M. (1993). Reviewing the concept of brands and branding. *Marketing and Research Today*, May, 75–79.

Goodyear, M. (1996). Divided by a common language: diversity and deception in the world of global marketing. *Journal of the Market Research Society* 38(2), 105–122.

Hart, S. & Murphy, J. (1998). *Brands: The New Wealth Creators*. Basingstoke: Macmillan Business.

Hatch, M.J. & Schultz, M. (2001). Are the strategic stars aligned for your corporate brand? *Harvard Business Review*, February, 128–134.

Herbig, P. & Milewicz, J. (1993). The relationship of reputation and credibility to brand success. *Journal of Consumer Marketing* 10(3), 18–24.

Ind, N., ed. (2003). *Beyond Branding: How the New Values of Transparency and Integrity are Changing the World of Brands*. London: Kogan Page.

Kapferer, J.N. (2008). *The New Strategic Brand Management*. London: Kogan Page.

Keller, K.L. & Aaker, D.A. (1998). Corporate-level marketing: the impact of credibility on a company's brand extensions. *Corporate Reputation Review*, 1 (August), 356–378.

Kitchen, P.J. & Laurence, A. (2003). Corporate reputation: an eight-country analysis. *Corporate Reputation Review* 6(2), 103.

Kim, P. (1990). A perspective on brands. *Journal of Consumer Marketing* 7(4), 63–67.

King, S. (1984). *Developing New Brands*, 2nd edn. London: J.W.T.

Knox, S. & Bickerton, D. (2003). The six conventions of corporate branding. *European Journal of Marketing* 37(7–8), 998–1016.

Knox, S. & Maklan, S. (1998). *Competing on Value: Bridging the Gap between Brand and Customer*. London: FT-Prentice Hall.

Kochan, N. (1996). *The World's Greatest Brands*. Basingstoke: Macmillan Press.

Kotler, P. & Lee, N. (2005). *Corporate Social Responsibility: Doing the Most Good for Your Company and Your Cause*. Hoboken, NJ: Wiley.

Kotler, P., Wong, V., Saunders, J. & Armstrong, G. (2004). *Principles of Marketing*, 4th European edition. New Jersey: FT-Prentice Hall.

Kowalczyk, S.J. & Pawlish, M.J. (2002). Corporate branding through external perception of organizational culture. *Corporate Reputation Review* 5(2/3), 159–174.

Low, G.S. & Fullerton, R.A. (1994). Brands, brand management, and the brand manager system: a critical-historical evaluation. *Journal of Marketing Research* 31, 173–190.

Margolis, J.D. & Elfenbein, H.A. (2008). Doing well by doing good: don't count on it. *Harvard Business Review* 86(1), 19–20.

Martineau, P. (1958). The personality of the retail store. *Harvard Business Review* 36, 47–55.

McWilliams, A. & Siegel, D. (2001). Corporate social responsibility: a theory of the firm perspective. *Academy of Management Review* 26(1), 117–129.

McWilliams, A., Siegel, D.S. & Wright, P.M. (2006). Corporate social responsibility: strategic implications. *Journal of Management Studies* 43(1), 1–18.

Moorthy, K.S. (1985). Using game theory to model competition. *Journal of Marketing Research*, 22 (August), 262–282.

Mutch, N. & Aitken, R. (2009). Being fair and being seen to be fair: corporate reputation and CSR partnerships. *Australasian Marketing Journal* 17(2), 92–98.

Olins, W. (2000). How brands are taking over the corporation. In: Schultz, M. *et al.*, eds. *The Expressive Organization: Linking Identity, Reputation, and the Corporate Brand* (77–96), Oxford University Press, New York.

Papworth, J. (2009) 'No monkey business with biofuels and apes'. *The Guardian*, 7 February. Online: www.guardian.co.uk/money/2009/feb/07/. Accessed: 10 February 2011.

Porter, M.E. & Kramer, M.R. (2006). Strategy and society. *Harvard Business Review* 84, 78–92.

Randall, G. (2000). *Branding: A Practical Guide to Planning Your Strategy*. London: Kogan Page.

Riezebos, R. (2003). *Brand Management: A Theoretical and Practical Approach*. Harlow: FT Prentice Hall.

Schwaiger, M. (2004). Components and parameters of corporate reputation – an empirical study. *Schmalenbach Business Review* 56(1), 46.

Willmott, M. (2001). *Citizen Brands: Putting Society at the Heart of Your Business*. Chichester: John Wiley.

Chapter 6
The rise of corporate brands

Much has been written about brands, although many texts still focus on the classic product brands and fast-moving consumer goods organisations. However, over recent years it is the corporate brand that has come to the fore. The rise of the service industry and a change in corporate strategy are closely connected with this change of emphasis.

Corporate brands require new strategies and different ways in using resources and communicating with stakeholders. Indeed, a whole new focus is necessary in order to leverage the opportunities that corporate brands represent.

Aims and learning objectives

The aim of this chapter is to examine what a corporate brand is and to consider the varied nature of corporate branding in practice.

The learning objectives of this chapter are to:

1. Define and discuss corporate brands
2. Consider the rise in importance of corporate brands
3. Appraise the rise of the service industry and the company as a brand
4. Explore the difference between product brands and corporate brands
5. Evaluate the gaps that occur between a brand's corporate identity and the corporate image
6. Assess the advantages and disadvantages of corporate branding.

Introduction

The rise of the corporate brand presents new issues and challenges for both brand owners and stakeholders. In this chapter we discuss the crucial importance of values to a corporate brand and explore the differences between corporate and product brands. In addition to this, we examine the problems that may be created by any gaps that might exist between the views held by different stakeholders of a brand.

In the 21st century even the most ardent of product brand-oriented organisations have decided that their future strategy is best served by an increased exposure to the principles of corporate branding (see Viewpoint 6.1 on Unilever).

Viewpoint 6.1 | Unilever develops its profile

Unilever is a product brand organisation that may be considered the ultimate brand manager. Together with Procter & Gamble it could be considered the company that invented modern brand management, back in the 1920s. It owns such well known brands as Knorr Foods, Wall's and Ben & Jerry's ice cream, Lipton, Brooke Bond teas, Cif, Comfort, Domestos and Persil, amongst many others. Selling its products in 170 countries, employing over 160,000 staff and with a turnover of nearly €40 billion, it is one of the world's great corporations.

Since March 2009 Unilever has been using the corporate brand name and logo in all of its product brand advertisements. This signals a shift from a product towards a corporate branding strategy. Whilst this will serve to reassert their tenure over a broad range of products, it amplifies the importance of reputation management uniformly for all the business units listed under its portfolio. There is an inherent risk here, although evidently Unilever has recognised the prospective benefits for their corporate brand and reputation. Extensive research revealed that consumers in the UK and Ireland have relatively low awareness and knowledge of the organisation, despite being very familiar with its product brands, which the company is looking to overhaul with immediate effect. The organisation provides a frank account of its motivation to implement the conversion to 'signature' corporate branding, highlighting, among other factors, that 'it makes good business sense'.

> **Unilever has been using the corporate brand name and logo in all of its product brand advertisements.**

The use of a corporate brand helps to unite a diverse group of products and stakeholders around a defining theme. The Unilever website outlines the philosophy that underpins their corporate brand:

'In the future, our brands will do even more to add vitality to life. Using our strong roots in science, we will focus our brands on meeting your growing needs for:

- *a healthy lifestyle*
- *more variety, quality, taste and enjoyment*
- *time, as an increasingly precious commodity*

We are also committed to the vitality of the environment and the communities in which we operate. The environment provides us with our raw materials and the ingredients we need to make our products and our communities are the homes where our consumers and employees live and thrive.

We believe that doing business in a responsible way has a positive benefit. We create and share wealth, invest in local economies, develop people's skills and share our expertise. We also work in partnership with governments, international agencies (such as UNICEF) and non governmental organisations (such as WWF). Through these partnerships we play our part in helping address some of the world's big social and environmental concerns, such as health, hygiene and nutrition.

We haven't got all the answers - but we're committed to making a difference.'

Clearly if one of the world's great product brand organisations recognises the benefits of adopting a corporate branding strategy then this is a strong signal that we are clearly in the age of corporate branding.

Unilever have, over recent years, rationalised their product portfolio enormously, reducing their portfolio from approximately 1,600 to 400 'power' brands, and are ensuring that the corporate brand behind them receives due recognition. This is a reversal of the previous strategy that aimed at marketing separate product brands with the intention of ensuring the customer did not know that they came from the same group. The cost of managing and maintaining multiple product brands is high – the corporate brand helps with the synergy of the entire portfolio.

Question

What are the benefits and risks for Unilever associated with adopting a corporate branding strategy?

Source: Based on www.unilever.co.uk.

Defining corporate brands

Back in 1991, King stated that it was increasingly difficult to split the product and service element of a company's offering. Because of this he predicted that 'increasingly the *company brand* will become the main discriminator'. King states that customers will increasingly differentiate on their assessment of 'the whole company culture' rather than evaluating the functional benefits offered by the organisation. Brand-building will thus be much more closely aligned with the principles of services marketing than with the marketing strategy that led to the dominance of the classic consumer brands.

McDonald *et al.* (2001) stated that customers will feel greater confidence when trying a brand that draws upon the name of a well established firm. Since the mid-1990s the term 'corporate brand' has been increasingly utilised (Balmer, 1995), due in part to the growth of the service industry where the name of the company is the only brand name used in the market. Corporate branding is also a more appropriate perspective for organisations whose main objective may not be profit, i.e. charities, healthcare organisations and universities.

There has been a consequent widening of the discussion of corporate brands in the academic literature (Balmer, 1995; 2001a; Aaker, 1996; Ind, 1997, 1998; de Chernatony, 1999; Knox *et al.*, 2000; Gray & Balmer, 2001; Hatch & Schultz, 2001; McDonald *et al.*, 2001; Balmer & Gray, 2003; Knox & Bickerton, 2003).

Aaker (1996) makes the point that it is increasingly difficult to differentiate one service or product from another. With a host of me-too products and seemingly endless choice, consumers are faced with the dilemma of product parity – how do they differentiate between one product and another? A possible solution to this problem is to base the brand identity on the company that is behind the brand. Aaker states it is the 'particular set of values, culture, people, programs and assets/skills' that helps to provide the differentiation that goes into producing the unique product or service (p. 115). In other words, it is the corporate brand that is the new and significant differentiator.

> It is increasingly difficult to differentiate one service or product from another.

> It is the corporate brand that is the new and significant differentiator.

van Mesdag (1997) reports that customers have responded very positively to ever-broadening product ranges from corporate brands. Japan has always been used to the idea of corporate branding where often huge conglomerates market a vastly different range of products and services under one corporate brand name. In the UK, Virgin is an example of a corporate brand under the umbrella of which a diverse range of goods are sold, from soft drinks to financial services and from rail travel to pop concerts. Vick (1993) breaks the meaning of corporate branding into four areas – appearance, performance, trust and value. Wilson (1997) recognises the need for long-term planning in corporate branding and that reputation needs to be at the top of the organisation's agenda. He insists that staff be tuned in to corporate service standards and that salient brands are those where the staff clearly understand and share the vision of the company.

Hart & Murphy (1998) and Ind (1997) take a more positive view, stating that strong corporate brands are able to recruit and retain the best people; they have a long-term focus, are able to move easily into new markets and their company name is the factor that binds together the goodwill generated by the business's operations. Hart & Murphy insist that a corporate brand must reflect the vision and values of the company and that these should reflect the personality of board members and senior managers downwards. They state that leadership, buy-in and communication are essential to the successful management of a corporate brand. According to Argenti & Druckenmiller (2004), a corporate brand covers an entire company and also conveys expectations of what the company will deliver in terms of products, services and customer experience. Ind (1997) states that there are three core attributes that define the corporate brand: intangibility, complexity and responsibility.

> Strong corporate brands are able to recruit and retain the best people.

> A corporate brand must reflect the vision and values of the company.

Intangibility. As with services we cannot physically pick up the corporate brand, and areas such as its history, culture or values may be remote to those other than employees (intangibility). Without knowing any of this, we are at the mercy of the media telling us stories, often unflattering ones, about companies from which we draw simplistic conclusions about the strength of a brand or its reputation. This is the problem with image – it is often considerably different from the real identity of the organisation. The task of the corporate brand is to remove this intangibility as much as possible, to provide a consensus opinion on what the brand represents and to consistently communicate this with stakeholders.

Complexity. The corporate brand is a complex entity. It may involve many staff, different divisions, different countries and different decision-making bodies. Amongst all this, there may well be different cultures, adding to the difficulty of managing a corporate brand.

Responsibility. Ind (1997) states that the corporate brand has a broad social responsibility or ethical imperative. Certain brands, of course, compete on their ethical stance. Notably, both Ben & Jerry's and The Body Shop have been taken over by large corporate brands in recent years. Innocent drinks are a more recent incarnation of the ethical brand. The customers and suppliers (who must pass an ethical test) have bought into the value system of these companies that goes way beyond the traditional responsibility of generating profits and value for shareholders.

Ind (1998) agrees that it is 'clearly articulated and communicated values' that lead to successful corporate brands. He criticises the short-term approach towards staff by many organisations, especially when it is the employees who have the power to make or break a brand. Branding involves emotion and there must be a strong emotional attachment between the employees and their company, before a strong corporate brand will emerge and thrive. He goes on to state that among the biggest barriers to the emergence of a strong corporate brand are unsympathetic cultures and disinterested leaders. An unsympathetic culture will lead to reputational problems for the organisation. de Chernatony *et al.* (2003) inform us that the values of the corporate brand are a key part of the organisation's reputation. These values must come from within the organisation.

Values, culture and personality

Stakeholders must be able to understand what it is that is different about a particular corporate brand.

As with product brands, stakeholders must be able to understand what it is that is different about a particular corporate brand. The repetition that can be seen in mission or vision statements shows how many organisations do not achieve this. Consider the duplication in the following mission statements:

- We aim to be the best telecommunications organisation in the world
- Our purpose is to provide the best solutions to our customers' communications needs
- To become the most respected and profitable insurance company in the United States.

So, unsurprisingly, everyone wants to be the best. If brands want to be admired or even loved, then they are not likely to achieve this by these safety-first approaches. They must inspire positive values and associations.

On many occasions, the stated values are merely those of the founders of the organisation. In Nike's case it was a passion for running, as the founders and early employees were also running enthusiasts who were disappointed by the lack of specialist footwear to allow them to run on roads. Nike as a brand was seen as breaking the mould. The culture of being invented by actual enthusiasts has led to the 'just do it' strapline and the free spirit of the initial culture has led to the sponsorship of stars who do not just excel at their chosen sport but also display an anti-establishment persona. Examples include Eric Cantona and Ian Wright from football, Shane Warne from cricket and, of course, Michael Jordan from basketball.

One key difficulty for management is maintaining the values as the company grows older and larger and when the original founder moves on or dies. The values and assumptions of the organisation are the glue that holds the elements of the corporate brand together (Ind, 1997).

McDonald *et al.* (2001) also highlight the crucial importance of employees to the success or otherwise of a corporate brand. The interactions that customers have with customer-facing staff will have huge ramifications for the corporate brand. The attitude of employees towards the brand is also crucial and can have an effect upon customer perception of the brand. Smyth *et al.* (1992) say that corporate branding is of assistance to a company as it can help unify the behaviour of employees through the way in which a brand is presented to customers. Aaker (1996) agrees when he says that brand strength is dependent upon the extent to which the perceptions of the brand are consistent, positive and shared by customers.

Corporate culture is important in building a corporate brand.

de Chernatony (1999) discusses the move toward corporate branding and also emphasises the importance of corporate culture in building a corporate brand. He says that corporate culture manifests itself as the corporate personality and that stakeholders recognise the values of the brand from their interactions with the employees of the brand.

Balmer (1998) states that a strong corporate brand requires a clear corporate mission and philosophy, that a brand's personality and identity needs to be understood and that the stakeholder's perspective of these perceptions needs to be measured. Balmer points out that when considering the corporate identity of an organisation it is necessary to look beyond the traditional four Ps of the marketing mix and include six additional Ps: philosophy, personality, people, performance, perception and positioning. It is becoming clear that both the internal and external perceptions of the brand are crucial. Clear measurement of these would be to the advantage of management.

Corporations should have a set of basic core values that form and define the brand, and all these values are 'intrinsic to the firm and part of its core ideology' (Uggla, 2006, p. 786).

> Corporations should have a set of basic core values that form and define the brand.

Brand promise

Ambler & Styles (1996) and Judson *et al.* (2009) refer to the importance of the promise conveyed by the corporate brand. Certain authors use the expression 'covenant' to convey the same meaning (Johansson & Hirano, 1999; Mitchell, 1999; Tilley, 1999). Balmer (2001a,b) argues that a covenant between a company and its major stakeholder groups is at the core of the corporate brand. Balmer & Gray (2003) refer to the corporate brand as a collection of promises encompassing the brand's physical and emotional benefits to buyers.

Balmer & Greyser (2007) outline what they call the six Cs of corporate marketing (Table 6.1). Within this they regard the corporate brand as a covenant and this helps to engender a deep loyalty. This covenant also relates to the emotional relationship that stakeholders have with the brand and perhaps to the co-creation of brands, as discussed in Chapter 5. Because of this emotional connection, corporate brands can create a strong sense of loyalty, trust and legitimacy towards the organisation for consumers (Balmer, 2001a).

> The corporate brand is a covenant which helps to engender a deep loyalty.

The shift from marketing individual product brands to corporate brands has led certain authors to refer to a 'paradigm shift' towards corporate branding.

Branding, whether the emphasis is product or corporate, needs to demonstrate consistency over a period of time in order to engender trust in stakeholders. Despite huge environmental change over the decades, Disney is an example of a brand that has delivered consistently high-quality offerings to successive generations (see Viewpoint 6.2).

Table 6.1	The six Cs of corporate marketing	
Six Cs	**Reputational element**	**Meaning**
Character	Corporate identity	What we indubitably are
Communication	Corporate communication	What we say we are
Constituencies	Marketing and stakeholder management	Whom we seek to serve
Covenant	Corporate brand management	What is promised and expected
Conceptualisations	Corporate reputation	What we are seen to be
Culture	Organisational identity	What we feel we are

Source: Balmer & Greyser (2006). Emerald Publishing Group Ltd, with permission.

Viewpoint 6.2 — Disney across the eras

Disney is an example of a corporate brand that has maintained its standards of excellence for over 80 years. It is the largest media and entertainment organisation in the world. Founded in 1923 by Walt and the lesser known Roy Disney, it made its name through animated films, progressing over the years to become a huge film studio, owner of a worldwide network of theme parks and, more recently, television channels, e.g. ABC and ESPN. The Walt Disney Studios distribute motion pictures under Walt Disney Pictures, which includes Walt Disney Animation Studios, Pixar Animation Studios and Disney Toon Studios, Touchstone Pictures, Hollywood Pictures and Miramax Films. In 2009 it moved to acquire another huge brand – Marvel Comics and its portfolio of over 5,000 characters, including Spider-Man, X-Men, Captain America and the Fantastic Four.

Disney World theme parks have also received much acclaim for their employee network and customer management. Disney was an innovator in setting the standards for the modern theme park, beginning in 1952. Its parks can be found in France, Hong Kong, Japan (Tokyo) and its native United States. It prioritises attracting the right staff, rigorously preparing them to perform, and then motivating employees. It is simultaneously a generous and no-nonsense employer. Red Pope (a long-time Disney observer and writer) comments that its resounding success stems from its handling of staff. Disney World may be deemed one grandiose theatre, with the company adopting showbusiness terminology at all junctures possible to create an intense sense of spectacle. The commitment expected from employees is indicated by the fact that they are known as 'cast members' rather than staff or personnel, the employees facilitating the experiential element for customers so vital to their company.

Disney is a prime example of a corporate brand that has provided consistently excellent service for just shy of a century. It has remained massively successful, irrespective of the hugely changing social and economic setting of the 20th century. When one considers the changing nature of childhood over the decades, it is remarkable that the Disney Corporation is seemingly always able to tap in to the imaginations of children. From *Snow White and the Seven Dwarves* as far back as 1937 to *Peter Pan* in 1953, *Bedknobs and Broomsticks* in 1971, *Toy Story* in 1995 and *A Christmas Carol* in 2009, it is a story of unrelenting success.

Its pioneering use of merchandising started in 1929 with the iconic Mickey Mouse character; this was at a time when the term hadn't been heard of.

Disney's unwavering consistency is an indispensable attribute and has helped the construction of a sturdy, durable reputation.

Question

Consider other examples of long-standing corporate brands. What are the factors that have led to their prolonged success?

The halo of the corporate brand

Corporate brands seek a level of trust and commitment both from customers and employees. Brands seek affection and love but few get it. Simmons (2006) explains how the straplines used by brands have reflected this move, developing from the functional and straightforward, i.e. 'Persil washes whiter', 'towards empathetic attempts to engage with the aspirations of a brand's audience' (p. 20) and the example of Microsoft™ and its strapline: 'Where do you want to go today?'

There is no point at all in trying to build and project brand values if these are not held or practised by the people who represent the brand. Consistency of communication can only take place if there is a clear understanding of what the corporate brand is and what it stands for.

Why are some corporate brands able to get it right and really create the added value that ensures that the stakeholder sees them as a cut above the opposition? Hatch & Schultz (2008) say that it is the degree to which organisational identity has been made the foundation for corporate brand management that is the key differentiator.

In defining a corporate brand, therefore, the word corporate implies organisations, both profit and non-profit making, and the company as a whole, not its individual parts or products and services. The idea of cohesion is therefore important, that of people coming together (Ind, 1997) and working towards common goals. The difficulty is that organisations are diverse by nature. If they are spread over several sites, and of course several countries, then it is easy for them to be different things in different places thus defusing the power of the brand.

> The word 'corporate' implies organisations, both profit and non-profit making.
>
> The idea of cohesion in an organisation is important.

So, the idea of the corporate brand is to 'personalise the company as a whole in order to create value from the company's strategic position, institutional activities, organisation, employees and portfolio of products and services' (van Riel & Fombrun, 2007). The corporate brand throws a 'favourable halo' over everything that the company does and allows it to make the most of its reputation.

The corporate brand is a 'visual representation of a company that unites a group of products or businesses and makes it known to the world through the use of a single name, a shared visual identity, and a common set of symbols' (van Riel & Fombrun, 2007, p. 107). 'The process of corporate branding consists of the set of activities undertaken by the company to build favourable associations and positive reputation with both internal and external stakeholders.' (van Riel & Fombrun, 2007).

So, along with the above we may define the corporate brand as 'a systematically planned and implemented process of creating and maintaining favourable images and consequently a favourable reputation of the company as a whole by sending signals to all stakeholders by managing behaviour, communication and symbolism' (van Riel, 2001 cited in Einwiller and Will, 2002, p. 101). The reference to behaviour is the most important word in this definition as it underpins what we would most like to impress upon you when defining a corporate brand. That is, a corporate brand is defined by its core values.

Hatch & Schultz (2008) talk about three waves of corporate branding. The first wave features a marketing mindset which treats corporate branding as a giant product brand, e.g. advertising alone would be enough to revive and support it. The second wave concentrates on a corporate mindset making branding a multi-functional activity. So, marketing, HR and other commercial functions join together to manage the brand. However, the importance of stakeholders, they claim, has led to the third wave, the enterprise mindset. This concerns the interests and expectations of the full range of stakeholders, and, when included, the corporate brand becomes a strategic asset.

The growth of the service industry and corporate branding

All company names are, to some extent, corporate brands and this is especially true for services in particular (Kay, 2006). The rise of the corporate brand has to a large extent been linked to the rise of the service industry. Over 70 per cent of the UK workforce is employed in the service industry and it contributes 75 per cent of gross domestic product.

> The rise of the corporate brand has to a large extent been linked to the rise of the service industry.

Many authors agree that what separates the marketing of products from that of services are the IHIP factors, i.e. intangibility, heterogeneity, inseparability and perishability. The presence of these factors makes marketing more difficult than for tangible products. Customers can pick up and examine products and so determine quality issues before purchase. In the absence of these tangible and visible clues, it is the values and reputation of the service provider that help to provide reassurance. There is a clear link, therefore, between the growth of service-related offerings and the move towards corporate branding strategy.

The traditional 4 Ps of the marketing mix are extended to 7 Ps in the services marketing mix. Physical evidence, and, in particular, process and people are mix elements that directly relate to the concept of a corporate brand. We have repeatedly emphasised the importance of the employees of the organisation embracing the culture and values of the firm in order to truly differentiate it.

The people who represent or deliver a brand are always on duty. In talking to friends they will discuss their organisation, and any negative signals will say something about the organisation to their friends. Think of overhearing people's conversation in the pub or in the street when they are discussing their workplace. Are they positive or negative about their organisation? If people do not feel engaged with the brand then their working life is probably not as rewarding or satisfactory as it should be. Employees, when engaged, are a good source of new ideas for a brand, and so a virtuous circle is formed. It is likely they will help to move customers up the loyalty ladder so that they too become advocates for the brand.

Similarly, brand processes should demonstrate a clear commitment to superior customer service and emphasise the point that the whole company culture is centred upon the satisfaction of the most important stakeholders.

A difficulty in managing a service and a corporate brand is that, unlike a product brand, there are multiple brand signals that need to be maintained. There are multiple touchpoints whereby a customer can contact and interact with a brand. All of these touchpoints are an opportunity to enhance the brand experience for customers and other stakeholder groups, and to demonstrate and reinforce the brand values. These may need tiny adjustments as we progress in order to present the seamless experience that the customer wants. Inability to do this may result in a poor brand experience for the customer. So, the servicescape, i.e. the place where the service is delivered and experienced by the customer, encompassing the atmosphere, the colours, the aroma, the staff and the quality of the interactions with customers, all affect the corporate and the service brand. The corporate brand is the synergistic sum of all the parts of the service.

McDonald *et al.* (2001) discuss services and corporate brands. They point out that it is possible to transform a commodity into a strong corporate brand and use Tesco and Sainsbury's as examples that have gone from strength to strength, whereas the high street banks have failed to differentiate themselves and therefore remain commodities.

Differences between product brands and corporate brands

Managing the corporate brand requires a wider perspective.

Managing the corporate brand requires a wider perspective compared with the marketing communications focused product brand. Hatch & Schultz (2001) encourage companies to engage with the idea of corporate branding in order to correct both consumers' and practitioners' perceptions of branding. Rather than being merely product-focused, corporate branding insists upon the use and implementation of a value foundation from which the brand is seen to summarise the additional values that are intrinsic in, or associated with, the corporation, its products and services (Tilley, 1999; Urde, 1999). The development of values held internally and manifested to external stakeholders ensures that the corporate brand is a guarantee of quality and an insurance against risk (Balmer & Gray, 2003).

Responsibility for the brand lies with the whole organisation not just the marketing department.

Responsibility for the brand lies with the whole organisation, not just the marketing department. The perspective is on the long term and the values are real, not merely contrived for advertising purposes. There are wider communication channels whereby all the actions of the organisation's activities help to communicate the corporate brand values. Issues such as identity, corporate strategy and vision from the perspective of multiple stakeholders within the wider macro-environment help to differentiate the modern corporate brand from the product brand (Balmer, 2001a). Corporate brands build associations based upon their heritage and future vision (Olins, 1989). Ind (1997) discusses the importance of social responsibility or the ethical imperative of the corporate brand. The organisational structure, physical design and culture help to support the meaning of the corporate brand internally and externally (Hatch & Schultz, 2003). The philosophy underpinning the corporate level brand allows the principles to apply also to cities, regions and even countries (Ind, 1997). Chapter 8 deals with the wider associations of corporate branding.

The importance of employees is emphasised within the corporate branding literature (Ind, 1997; Wilson, 1997, 2001; de Chernatony, 2001; Harris & de Chernatony, 2001; Hatch & Schultz, 2001, 2003; Balmer & Gray, 2003). Employees, through their attitudes and behaviours, can make or break the corporate brand. They interact with customers and any negative attitudes will soon have an impact upon the customer's experience of the brand. They need to be tuned in to the corporate culture and salient corporate brands will be those where the staff clearly understand and share the vision of the company.

> Employees, through their attitudes and behaviours, can make or break the corporate brand.

Balmer (2001a) discusses the importance of the move towards corporate branding and corporate marketing. The importance of satisfying a larger group of stakeholders rather than just customers is a key reason behind this change in emphasis. He states that questions of corporate brand and corporate reputation management have become principal concerns for organisations and their managements. The one-dimensional approach of product branding is replaced with a more rounded emphasis. The management of the corporate brand is the responsibility of the chief executive rather than that of a middle manager. All staff members have a responsibility to maintain the corporate brand as opposed to the product or brand manager's responsibility for the product brand. There is a strategic rather than a marketing-oriented approach to the management of the corporate brand and the values of the corporate brand are based upon those of the founder plus a mix of corporate or other subcultures rather than the possibly more contrived values of the product brand.

Compared with a product brand, the corporate brand contains a much wider range of associations (Keller, 2008). The corporate brand, therefore, can be seen as a more powerful way for firms to express themselves in a pattern that is not necessarily related to their specific products or services (Keller, 2008; Kapferer, 2002). The goal of the corporate brand is to create meaning and value through various relationships between the company and its various stakeholders. The task of product branding is to build a separate image for each product.

> Compared with a product brand, the corporate brand contains a much wider range of associations.

Due to multiple stakeholder involvement and ownership, the corporate brand cannot be left to the marketing department; it involves the entire organisation and it must start with the chairperson/CEO. A corporate brand needs to be a holistic entity that permeates every area of the business. It must therefore be communicated using a cross-functional team approach (Alloza, 2008). This provokes issues of integration and communication structure, which are explored in Part 3 of this book.

The brand architecture of an organisation can help us to understand the difference between product and corporate branding. Table 6.2 illustrates the differences between product and corporate branding.

Of course, the visible corporate communication of a brand is important and is explored later in this book. However, it is crucial to see corporate branding as being much deeper than just the symbolism associated with logos, livery, straplines and the design of web pages. Corporate brands are the concern of multiple stakeholders, rather than a simple fixation with the needs of customers.

> Corporate brands are the concern of multiple stakeholders.

Table 6.2	Differences between product and corporate brands	
Brand issue	**Product brand**	**Corporate brand**
Scope and scale	One product or service, or a group of closely related products	The entire enterprise, which includes the corporation and all its stakeholders
Origins of brand identity	Advertisers' imagination informed by market research	The company's heritage, the values and beliefs that members of the enterprise hold in common
Target audience	Customers	Multiple stakeholders (includes employees and managers as well as customers, investors, NGOs, trade unions, partners, communities, politicians and financial markets)
Organisational behaviour	Behaviour of the company and interactions often invisible to the consumer	Organisational behaviour becomes visible at the level of customer–employee interactions. Organisational behaviour is very transparent
Responsibility	Product brand manager and staff, marketing, advertising and sales departments	CEO or executive team, typically from marketing, corporate communications, HR, strategy, design or development departments
Planning horizon	Life of product	Life of company. Long-term and strategic

Source: Adapted from Hatch & Schultz (2008).

The heritage and history of the organisation are the very essence of corporate branding.

One key criticism of modern brand management is the all too frequent rush to rebrand. Rebranding is often seen as a panacea to a company's difficulties or in the modern era, is fuelled by takeovers and mergers. Often such rebranding does not take account of the heritage and history of the organisation, the very essence of corporate branding. When thinking about the surfeit of rebranding activity in the marketplace, consider this. Would you change your child's name every 5 years because you have become bored with it? Of course not, so why do management believe brands can be swapped and changed with impunity?

As corporate brands do not have the tangible product-related symbols of a product brand, they must therefore transmit brand signals or cues in other ways. In the case of First Direct, this is achieved through the attention given to customer service and delighting the customer during each transaction; at Dell computers it may be the ordering process; at Marks & Spencer, the no-quibble refund differentiated its quality from other retail brands for a generation of shoppers. All of these key areas are the opportunity to provide positive messages about your brand.

The corporate brand, therefore, conveys to customers and other stakeholders what the company will deliver in terms of products, services and customer experience. It helps to remove intangibility and define what the company says it is and what it wants to be and encapsulates the promise of the brand. This serves to set up customer expectations about the brand.

A company engages in corporate branding when it markets itself as a brand (Argenti & Druckenmiller, 2004) and positions itself to target all stakeholders simultaneously (Hulberg, 2006). What will vary will be the strength of the brand.

Corporate brands appear in many different guises.

Corporate brands appear in many different guises unlike their more simplistic product brand cousins. An example to demonstrate this is provided in Viewpoint 6.3.

Viewpoint 6.3 Mixing ingredient brands

An interesting approach to corporate branding is to employ an ingredient branding strategy. Prevalent since the 1990s, the idea is to build a mutually beneficial relationship between brands and to brand what otherwise might have been considered as commodities, quite probably unknown to the general public. Ingredient branding adds credibility and value to products and commodities.

Intel has built its corporate brand by identifying itself as 'Intel Inside'. This mark of quality meant that Intel no longer had to introduce new product brands each time it upgraded its chips – 286, 386, Pentium etc. It also gave greater belonging to employees as people knew who Intel was when asked. The strategy helped de-commoditise the company and the esteem of the workforce rose as the company became synonymous with the computer itself. It has been a hugely successful strategy, resulting in Intel becoming one of the world's top 10 brands according to brand research agency Interbrand. How many other brands of microchip are you able to name?

The use of ingredient brands can positively affect consumer preference and choice. Other highly successful examples of ingredient branding include Gore-Tex, a waterproof breathable fabric used in high-performance outdoor clothing by brands such as Berghaus and The North Face. Gore-Tex has become a guarantee of quality and the truly waterproof nature of various outer garments to customers who look for the Gore-Tex trademark when choosing. Similarly, Nutrasweet is the brand name for the artificial sweetener 'aspartame', and provides a low-calorie alternative to sugar in many food and beverage products. It is used in more than 5,000 products and consumed by 250 million consumers worldwide, most notably as an ingredient in Diet Coke, Diet Pepsi and Equal sweetener. A Sunkist sticker on an orange gives the customer a guarantee of the quality contained within the product.

In order for ingredient branding to succeed, the ingredient must be highly differentiated (often through branding activity) and is frequently patented. It may be that the ingredient is a technically complex product that can only be understood by the average customer as part of a finished consumer product. Other examples of ingredient branding would be Dolby noise reduction systems in audio equipment and Teflon in non-stick kitchenware.

It should be noted that this strategy may not work for premium brands as customers expect the best components to be used in such brands anyway. IBM, for example, has resisted the Intel Inside approach as it feels that to use this strapline would undermine the generic quality of its entire product offering.

Question

Corporate brands are far more diverse than product brands. How many different types of corporate brand are you able to identify?

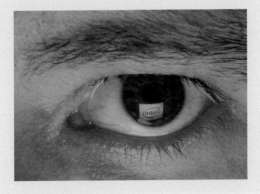

Exhibit 6.2 Intel has built its corporate brand by identifying itself as 'Intel Inside'.
Source: Alamy Images/bildbroker.de.

The rise of corporate brands

Having defined corporate branding, we now need to understand why corporate brands have become so prominent. The amount of information that is available and the growing cynicism about companies means that a corporate brand can build attractive associations, often in the shape of brand personality, with the organisation's stakeholders. To an extent the volume of accessible information today can make people less trusting of organisations. The NHS is a good example that illustrates this point. As a credence-based service we previously had to rely on the medical professional to diagnose our health problems and then to prescribe a course of treatment to cure us. Now we do not have to take their word for it. The internet provides a library of information on illnesses and can also direct us to the best possible treatment. News stories tell us how individuals in the UK are demanding drugs to treat cancer that are not regularly prescribed, usually due to their high cost. How do the public know about these alternatives? Simple: they have been on the internet researching the most successful drugs used to treat the same condition in the US. In the UK the demand by patients of the US drug Herceptin to treat breast cancer illustrates this point. The corporate brand must be capable of overcoming these areas of information overload and declining levels of trust.

A corporate brand can build attractive associations.

The challenge of presenting a coherent offering to multiple stakeholders can be tackled by delivering an effective corporate brand and thereby managing both the corporate identity and corporate image (Einweiller & Will, 2002). Of course, in contemporary society and a global marketplace, it makes sense to present a coherent corporate brand in all markets, e.g. Samsung.

The difficulty of living in an age of perceived product parity is that consumers have difficulty distinguishing a clear differentiation between one product and another. If this is the case then they are likely to make their choice on the basis of the best available price. The ethereal values of the corporate brand provide a basis upon which no two brands are identical. A strong corporate brand will demonstrate values that are difficult for competitors to imitate. Strategically it is the longevity of the corporate brand that provides the durability that many other resources of the organisation fail to deliver.

A further benefit of corporate branding is the benefit from economies of scale, e.g. the savings on marketing communications that can be achieved, as opposed to marketing brands individually. Similarly, launching new products and brands under the umbrella of the corporate brand will help with these economies. Using consistent messages and the use of media are discussed in later chapters of this book.

Strong corporate brands can also assist the organisation to recruit suitable partner organisations.

Another advantage enjoyed by strong corporate brands is their ability to attract, recruit and retain the best employees (Balmer & Gray, 2003; Leitch & Motion, 2007), and to provide employees and customers with reassurance (Melewar & Walker, 2003). The corporate brand also adds value to the balance sheet of the organisation (Leitch & Motion, 2007). Strong corporate brands can also assist the organisation to recruit suitable partner organisations (Barney & Hansen, 1994).

Olins (2000), a noted corporate identity expert, endorses corporate branding, stating it allows corporations to construct a singular identity in the international arena. The corporate brand also provides a focus around which diverse areas of the company, often separated by geography, function or even culture, can rally. It is the value system of the brand that can create depth and texture for the corporate brand across countries and markets (Aaker, 1996). Corporate brand values allow a brand to capitalise on pre-established brand knowledge and equity in the minds of consumers (Keller, 2002, 2003), and be leveraged. In this way the pre-established reputation of the corporate brand is capitalised through a process of image transfer (Riezebos, 2003; James, 2005). In this way consumers are more

Consumers are more confident in choosing a new offering that belongs to a well-established corporate brand.

confident in choosing a new offering which belongs to a well established corporate brand. Such values have allowed corporate brands such as Tesco to move seamlessly into areas such as financial services.

Chapter 7 deals with the measurement of corporate brands. However, whilst discussing the reasons for the rise of corporate brands, it should be pointed out that it has been claimed that launching a new product under the banner of a corporate brand can save 26 per cent on the costs of launching a new stand-alone product, and the success rate for the new product increases by 20 per cent (Newman, 2001). Research also tells us that corporate brands can add substantial value to the company's product policy and that linking the product and corporate brands will be beneficial to both the product and the organisation (Uehling, 2000). This would explain Unilever's move towards corporate brand endorsement (see Viewpoint 6.1, p. 135). Mitchell (1997) further argues that, given the development of global systems in finance, communication, marketing, branding etc., and the interconnectedness of the business world, the corporate entity has more significance than the products and services it produces.

Traditionally, corporations and their brands have conducted themselves without transparency. Indeed, it could be argued that sheltering the manufacturer behind a raft of unrelated brand names is a clear example of this lack of transparency. Today, stakeholders demand access to the company behind the brand and take a much keener view of what they signify and their policies and practices (Kapferer, 1997; Mitchell, 1999; Knox & Bickerton, 2003). Bernstein (2009) claims that brand communication is considered less meaningful to a consumer if it excludes information about the company. The practice of hiding behind the brand, a form of corporate anonymity, is increasingly unacceptable. Previously it was thought that if a brand is detached from its corporate owner, any brand failure will not harm the company or its other brands. However, today the brand and the company are synonymous in the minds of consumers. The corporate brand is the vehicle through which reputable business can be demonstrated.

Corporate branding is therefore not only about differentiating the organisation, it is about belonging, and even co-creation of the brand as mentioned in Chapter 5. The corporate brand expresses the values that attract key stakeholders to the organisation and encourages a sense of belonging to it (Hatch & Schultz, 2003).

Thus the corporate name has been transformed from a trade name that described an entity, e.g. an industry, a product or service, into the far more important corporate brand, a rallying point for all stakeholders and the focal point for corporate communications.

> The corporate brand is a rallying point for all stakeholders and the focal point for corporate communications.

Consumers today are saturated by advertising and are overloaded with product messaging. The public filter out the majority of this information, as they are unable to process it all. The building of a broader strategy based upon a corporate brand enables the organisation to cut through this surfeit of advertising and truly position the company within the macro-environment.

Viewpoint 6.4 offers an illustration of the diversity of corporate brands and their objectives.

Viewpoint 6.4 | **Building the corporate brand: Abu Dhabi and Manchester City FC**

The Abu Dhabi investment fund, controlled by billionaire Sheikh Mansour bin Zayed Al Nahyan, purchased Manchester City FC for £150 million in late 2008. Heavy investment in new players and also in improving the club's training facilities, pitch, staff offices, stadium, supporter experience and other infrastructure has so far seen this initial investment rise to nearly £0.5 billion.

The prospective investment power permitted by such owners was vocalised by the group head himself, who has vowed to make the club 'the biggest in the Premier League'. However, it would be naive to regard the takeover as beneficial only to City, given the patent advantages that Abu Dhabi will seek to secure from the ownership.

The football club, firmly placed in the world's most popular division, will be harnessed as a conduit through which Abu Dhabi will aspire to gain worldwide exposure and subsequently improve its worldwide status and reputation, representing a prime exercise in rapid corporate brand-building.

This brand architecture is typified by the prompt establishment of Etihad (the national airline of the UAE, owned by the group) as the official club sponsor, a step that greatly reinforces Abu Dhabi's corporate brand. Etihad has replaced Thomas Cook travel as City's shirt sponsors, as Thomas Cook is a corporation whose outlook is very much focused nationally rather than globally, as desired by the new owners. The Abu Dhabi group will undoubtedly aim to bolster its reputation by every possible avenue afforded by the football club. It is improbable that the Sheikh will make a direct return on his investment in City; however, it is the publicity for the Adu Dhabi brand that is the wider objective here.

However, the brand-building must be a reciprocal process. Whilst Abu Dhabi will capitalise upon City's position in the most popular league in world football in terms of viewing figures, hence procuring the intended worldwide exposure, City will also develop into a global brand with a reputation for success on the pitch that is epitomised by close neighbours (and fierce rivals) Manchester United. This will attract more world-class players, and in turn increase the media attention afforded the team, culminating in more of their games being televised globally. Logically, it follows that the fan base will increase particularly in the UAE, and in the Middle East generally, where football remains the most popular sport.

Good corporate branding reflects a clear value system. The association between City and Abu Dhabi in the manner of good corporate branding reflects a clear value system. Sheikh Mansour and the Emirates' rulers are acutely aware that what happens in east Manchester will receive enormous media attention, and so must reflect honourably on Abu Dhabi itself.

'There is an appreciation of the association the club have with Abu Dhabi that we hold very dearly,' City chairman Khaldoon al-Mubarak explained. 'There is almost a personification of the club with the values we hold

Exhibit 6.3 Photocall to mark the signing by Etihad Airways of an initial 3-year partnership deal with Manchester City FC to be the official shirt sponsor.
Source: © Richard Heathcote/Getty Images.

as Abu Dhabi. These are loyalty, commitment, discipline, long-term thinking, respect, appreciation of history. We are acknowledging that how we are handling this project is telling a lot to the world about how we are.'

Khaldoon added: 'The UAE is different from other Arab countries. People think the Arab world is one, but it is not. This is showing the world the true essence of who Abu Dhabi is and what Abu Dhabi is about.'

Having lived in the shadow of the more well known Dubai for years, the purchase of City is the highest profile investment by Abu Dhabi, Inc. to build its corporate brand. It should, however, be noted that Mansour bought City privately, with his own money. He saw City as a club rich in tradition, including traditional under-achievement, with a large, bloody-mindedly loyal fan base and a brand new stadium. Manchester City, though, has been turned into an embodiment of the Abu Dhabi 'brand', because of the huge media attention the deal generated.

Other Abu Dhabi investments include stakes in global banking giants, a multi-billion-pound investment in Daimler-Benz, a Formula One racetrack and space tourism.

Question

Is it fair to describe football clubs as corporate brands?

Source: Based on Conn (2009).

Strategic problems: gaps in the corporate brand

Hatch & Schultz (2008) state that getting the right connection between the I (the internal view of the company) and the we (the external reflection of who we are) is crucial to corporate brand success. Mistakes can be made in the orientation of the brand. It is quite possible to have a dysfunctional organisational identity by concentrating too much on projecting an identity without listening to stakeholders, referred to as narcissism, or by responding to every stake-holder demand or latest market trend (referred to as hyper-adaptation) and therefore losing internal direction.

Hatch & Schultz (2003) tell us that the brand promise must resonate strongly with the actual brand experience provided by the organisation. The same authors have developed a Vision–Culture–Image (VCI) Alignment Model (2008) (see Figure 6.1). They argue that the more coherence between the strategic vision – what it is that managers wish to accomplish in the future, what has always been known or believed by employees (organ-isational culture) – and what external stakeholders expect/desire from the company (stakeholder images), the stronger the brand will be. Gaps between these dimensions of the corporate brand will create problems and lead to underperformance. Considering VCI ensures that a more integrated and enterprise-wide (multi-stakeholder) approach is taken to corporate brand management.

> The brand promise must resonate strongly with the actual brand experience.
>
> Gaps between these dimensions of the corporate brand will create problems.

Hatch & Schultz (2001) state that the vision, images and culture should be considered as pieces of a jigsaw. When spread out on the table they are incoherent, but put together in the proper order they can build a strong positive reputation for the organisation. Hatch and Schultz advise us to answer the questions in Figure 6.1 to check the gaps in our corporate brand alignment.

Recall the discussion of image (external) and identity (internal) from Chapter 2. The corporate image should be a reflection of the corporate identity. The corporate brand name should be the link between the corporate identity, i.e. its internal culture, values and beha-viour, and the corporate image, i.e. the stakeholders' perceptions of the brand. The difficulty is that although the corporate brand may wish to project a single image, in reality the brand may project several different brand images to different stakeholder groups.

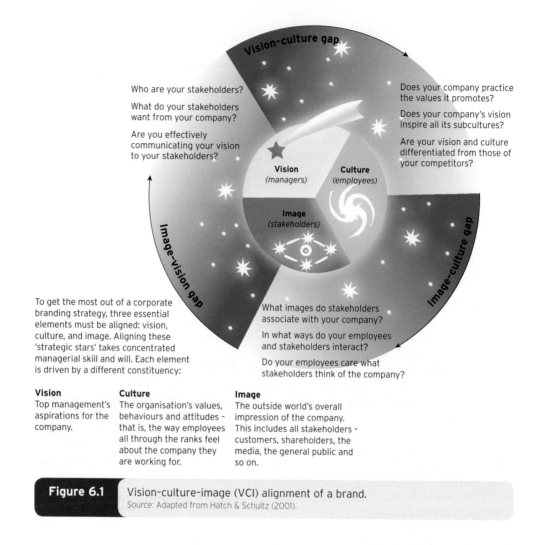

Who are your stakeholders?

What do your stakeholders want from your company?

Are you effectively communicating your vision to your stakeholders?

Does your company practice the values it promotes?

Does your company's vision inspire all its subcultures?

Are your vision and culture differentiated from those of your competitors?

Vision-culture gap

Image-vision gap

Image-culture gap

Vision (managers)

Culture (employees)

Image (stakeholders)

To get the most out of a corporate branding strategy, three essential elements must be aligned: vision, culture, and image. Aligning these 'strategic stars' takes concentrated managerial skill and will. Each element is driven by a different constituency:

What images do stakeholders associate with your company?

In what ways do your employees and stakeholders interact?

Do your employees care what stakeholders think of the company?

Vision
Top management's aspirations for the company.

Culture
The organisation's values, behaviours and attitudes – that is, the way employees all through the ranks feel about the company they are working for.

Image
The outside world's overall impression of the company. This includes all stakeholders – customers, shareholders, the media, the general public and so on.

Figure 6.1 Vision-culture-image (VCI) alignment of a brand.
Source: Adapted from Hatch & Schultz (2001).

Shared values between stakeholders will help to unify and strengthen the corporate brand.

Shared values between stakeholders will help to unify and strengthen the corporate brand. Ind (1997, 1998), de Chernatony & Harris (2000) and Pringle & Gordon (2001) refer to the importance of alignment between employee values and their behaviour and the expectations of customers. In this case then the causes of satisfaction with the brand should be the same amongst differing stakeholder groups.

Corporate brands require clear corporate missions and philosophies.

Strong corporate brands require clear corporate missions and philosophies; the brand's personality and identity need to be understood and each stakeholder's perspective of these perceptions needs to be measured (Balmer, 1998). The existence of gaps emerging between differing stakeholders' perspectives of the corporate brand (Aaker, 1996; de Chernatony, 1999; Bickerton, 2000; Harris & de Chernatony, 2001) is deemed to be a threat to the corporate brand and must be guarded against. What these authors are saying is that the corporate brand should mean the same thing to different stakeholder groups.

The difficulty of a corporate brand experiencing gaps between differing stakeholder groups is outlined by Roper & Davies (2007). They examine a university business school from the separate perspective of its staff, students, senior management and partners (usually companies providing work placement for students). Significant gaps are observed between the different perspectives of the university brand. Their work considers the impact of gaps between perspectives

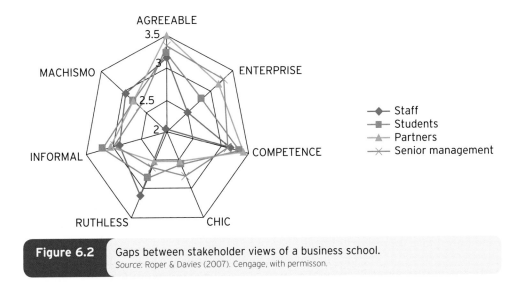

Figure 6.2	Gaps between stakeholder views of a business school.

Source: Roper & Davies (2007). Cengage, with permisson.

of the brand and the response of senior management to these gaps. Using the Corporate Character Scale set out in Chapter 5, to assess a university brand, the gaps existing between the various stakeholders' opinions are shown in Figure 6.2.

The research of Roper & Davies (2007) revealed not only gaps between differing groups of stakeholders but also statistically significant gaps in the views of the brand between genders. The two external groups find that the school is more agreeable, more enterprising, more competent and more chic than do the staff. Partners rate these attributes more highly than students, who rate them more highly than staff. Academic staff consider the school to be more ruthless and less informal than the other groups. Female stakeholders would appear to have a more positive view of the corporate brand of the business school and this is reflected amongst all three stakeholder groups (staff, students, partners). Senior management in general had a higher opinion of the brand than other stakeholders. They are, of course, heavily involved in it and well rewarded for working there.

Davies & Chun (2002) warn that it is important that the most positive view of the brand is held by the employees. They argue that a lower employee opinion of the corporate brand can lead to lower satisfaction and poorer financial performance in

> It is important that the most positive view of the brand is held by the employees.

the private sector. Employees positively oriented towards the brand will pass on the positive messages to external stakeholders, thus allowing the overall opinion of the brand to rise. The university example referred to previously is a public sector organisation and it may be that gaps are not as crucial in the not-for-profit sector, particularly universities, where the staff culture encourages internal criticism of their own institution. However, the university could well be storing up problems for the future due to these gaps and this would need to be monitored.

Success and failure of corporate branding

Can stakeholders appreciate the history of the organisation, its set of values and, of course, its reputation? The strongest corporate brands make great play of their heritage. Several long-standing brands actually have museums that help to celebrate the heritage of the brand. Note that these are actual museums, not merely visitor centres. A great example of this is the BMW museum in Munich, a celebration of a truly great brand and a clear example of the pride that the brand brings, not just to employees but also to the region of Bavaria.

> The strongest corporate brands make great play of their heritage.

Of course, as mentioned earlier, the wave of mergers and acquisitions we have witnessed are another reason for the growth in importance of corporate branding. The merged identity is necessary to get stakeholders on board with the new company. Nestlé is a corporate brand that has subsumed some great old product brands such as Rowntree Macintosh (KitKat, Aero, Polo, Fruit Pastilles and Quality Street, amongst others) in the UK and Chambourcy in France under its global corporate brand.

However, the large car companies are perhaps an example of where corporate branding has not succeeded. Is this because there has not been a proper attempt to implement it? Is Ford worried about the negative impression it may make in the marketplace if it is considered too big and too powerful, i.e. that it is actually reducing consumer choice? Ford owns Lincoln, Mercury, and has a stake in Mazda and Aston Martin. It has recently sold Volvo, Jaguar and Land Rover. Of course, these great individual product brands have been built over many decades and a corporate brand cannot be seen to just take over instantaneously. The problem here could also be that some of the product brands are actually more powerful (e.g. Aston Martin, Land Rover) than the corporate brand.

There are arguments for and against the adoption of a corporate branding strategy.

In summing up the contribution of the corporate brand, it would be fair to say that there are arguments for and against the adoption of a corporate branding strategy. van Riel & Fombrun, (2007) provide the following arguments in favour of corporate branding:

- The corporate brand creates a clear sense of internal coherence and simplifies internal co-operation.
- The corporate brand helps demonstrate the strength and size of the organisation to outsiders.
- It is cheaper to maintain a corporate brand than a range of different product brands.

However, opponents would argue:

- Investing in the corporate brand implies that large sums have been wasted in building the product brands. The counter-argument is that the move to corporate branding is just a development in strategic thinking as time has progressed and a response to the competitive environment becoming more difficult.
- Adopting a corporate brand can mean giving up a powerful local brand and perhaps losing market share. We would agree regarding local brands. There was some distress in the UK over the loss of great names such as Rowntree Macintosh and there has been some criticism of the way corporate brands like Nestlé have handled local brands. However, there is little evidence of any loss of market share.
- Using a single corporate name will limit distribution options. We are not sure how this is the case and what evidence there is for this claim.
- Size may appeal to financial audiences in the home market but will not help us with consumers in local markets elsewhere.
- Increased importance of the corporate brand will reduce the influence of business unit management.

van Riel & Fombrun (2007) consider how easy it will be to implement a corporate branding strategy. They say four key factors need to be considered:

- Strategy – the degree of relatedness amongst business units
- Organisation – the degree of centralisation and control exercised by HQ over the business units
- Employees – the degree of identification by employees with corporate HQ compared with business units

- Value – the expected performance and reputation gains to be obtained from the corporate brand.

In concluding this chapter, a demonstration of the diversity of corporate brands is provided by the excellent example of a not-for-profit brand, Chester Zoo, set out in Viewpoint 6.5.

Viewpoint 6.5 | Innovating Chester Zoo

Chester Zoo first opened to the public in 1931. It is one of the larger zoos in the UK and has strengthened its reputation over the years. A self-supporting charity that receives no government funding, it is the most visited wildlife attraction in Britain, with nearly 1.5 million visitors per annum. In 2007 *Forbes* magazine awarded Chester Zoo the accolade of being one of the top 15 zoos in the world. Even from the early days the zoo's founder, George Mottershead, wished to move away from the Victorian concept of zoos, that of animals behind bars in cages. Instead, a series of moats, ditches and islands and the recreation of more natural habitats for the animals were created.

The zoo now houses a large and diverse range of animals and species. Over half of the species at Chester appear on the International Union for Conservation of Nature's Red List of Threatened Species and many are threatened species or are kept as part of a managed captive breeding programme. Many threatened plant species are also kept at the zoo.

In an era where animal welfare has become an important issue, often aggressively supported by quasi-political groups, Chester Zoo has avoided the reputational issues suffered by other zoos by being at the forefront of education and conservation science.

The mission of Chester Zoo is 'to be a major force in conserving biodiversity worldwide'. Its website explains the motivations behind the organisation:

Chester Zoo significantly contributes to the protection of species and habitats through a combination of field and zoo-based conservation. By using the expertise of zoo staff and working with a wide range of national and international partners, we initiate and support a variety of conservation activities. We achieve our mission through the following channels: field conservation, education, conservation breeding, research and advance in animal welfare.

Exhibit 6.4 | Chester Zoo's 'Islands' is the first part of their Natural Vision project.
Source: Design and concept by Dan Pearlman www.danpearlman.com

An increasing number of species are threatened with extinction. It is estimated that a third of all animal and plant species face a high risk of extinction in this century. Chester Zoo . . . supports biodiversity conservation at home and around the world.

In early 2009 the zoo outlined its ambitious plans to continue its ground-breaking conservation work. A project entitled Natural Vision will create the only domed ecosystem in the UK: an African rainforest-themed sanctuary for a band of gorillas, chimpanzees, okapi (rare giraffe-like creatures) and a wide variety of tropical birds, amphibians, reptiles, fish and invertebrates. The animals will, of course, be able to move freely among the lush vegetation. The dome will be called the Heart of Africa. Further stages in the plan will be introduced until its completion in 2018, the culmination of years of planning and design.

Chester Zoo is a great example of a not-for-profit corporate brand that has, like all great brands, innovated over the decades and adapted as the environment and attitudes towards its core business have altered radically.

Question

Corporate branding has been embraced by the not-for-profit sector. What problems may be faced by a not-for-profit brand that would not trouble a profit-making firm?

Source: Based on www.chesterzoo.org.

Chapter summary

In order to consolidate your understanding of the rise of corporate brands, here are the key points summarised against each of the learning objectives.

1. Define and discuss the nature of corporate brands

We have moved towards an era of corporate as opposed to product branding. It is the values, culture and personality of the corporate brand that set it apart. The corporate brand is the covenant or promise between the stakeholders and the corporation. Due to this emotional connection, corporate brands aim to create a strong sense of loyalty, trust and legitimacy among consumers towards the organisation (Balmer, 2001a).

2. Consider the rise in importance of corporate brands

Consumers often see little difference between one product and another (product parity). In such instances, it is the values and culture of the corporate brand that differentiate the organisation from its competitors. A brand is no longer simply responsible for pleasing customers, instead having to satisfy multiple stakeholders. The single corporate entity is strategically felt to be the best way to deal with this.

The corporate brand provides a halo that allows the brand to move into often unrelated product and service offerings due to the trust it engenders. Tesco and Virgin are good examples of this phenomenon.

3. Appraise the rise of the service industry and the company as a brand

Approximately three-quarters of western countries' GDP can be attributed to the service industry. The IHIP factors make marketing of services more difficult than for tangible products. In the absence of these visible clues, the values and reputation of the service provider help to provide reassurance and therefore there is a clear link to the principles of corporate branding.

The importance of employees to the corporate brand mirrors that of their vital contribution to the service industry. The processes of the brand should demonstrate a clear commitment to superior customer service.

4. Explore the difference between product brands and corporate brands

The company's heritage, its values and beliefs are vital to the corporate brand and the whole company culture is vital. Corporate brands are far more visible than the more singularly focused product brand. Satisfying multiple stakeholders and not just customers is vital.

The behaviour of the corporate brand is much more evident to its stakeholders and it must be led by the CEO rather than built by the marketing department or its advertising agency. The corporate brand is strategic by nature and its time-frame is long-term.

5. Evaluate the gaps that occur between a brand's corporate identity and corporate image

Many authors warn of the problems inherent in gaps occurring between the internal (identity) and external (image) perceptions of the brand. Such gaps are likely to result in a weakened and confused offering to the market. Hatch & Schultz (2001, 2003) extend this discussion by warning brands to guard against gaps between the vision, culture and image of the brand.

It is considered that the employees of the organisation should have the most positive opinion of the brand. Employees will pass on these positive messages to external stakeholders, thus allowing the overall opinion of the brand to rise.

6. Assess the advantages and disadvantages of corporate branding

There are arguments for and against the adoption of a corporate branding strategy. The corporate brand creates a clear sense of cohesion, is cost-effective, allowing for economies of scale, and demonstrates the strength of the organisation to multiple stakeholders.

Critics of corporate branding claim that it undermines local brands and leads to a more centralised form of management that can become desensitised to the concerns of local consumers.

Discussion questions

1. Outline the differences between a corporate brand and a product brand.
2. How can the value system of the brand be maintained as the company becomes older?
3. Write notes about brand personality. Why has brand personality become important over recent years?
4. Put the 6 Cs of corporate marketing (Balmer & Greyser, 2006) in order of importance. Justify your viewpoint.
5. Why has the rise of corporate branding been linked to the rise of the service industry?
6. Select a corporate brand. Draw a diagram that identifies the stakeholders of that corporate brand and the relationships between these groups.
7. What are the risks involved for the firm pursuing a corporate branding strategy?
8. There are many different types of corporate brand, as they are more complex than product brands. Outline some different categories of corporate brand that you are aware of.
9. Write a paragraph explaining Hatch & Schultz's Vision–Culture–Image Alignment Model and its importance.
10. Why should management be concerned about gaps existing between the viewpoints of different stakeholders of the corporate brand?

References

Aaker, D.A. (1996). *Building Strong Brands*. New York: The Free Press.

Alloza, A. (2008). Brand engagement and brand experience at BBVA, the transformation of a 150 years old company. *Corporate Reputation Review* 11(4), 371–379.

Ambler, T. & Styles, C. (1996). Brand development versus new product development: towards a process model of extension decisions. *Marketing Intelligence and Planning* 14(7), 10–19.

Argenti, P.A. & Druckenmiller, B. (2004). Reputation and the corporate brand. *Corporate Reputation Review* 6(4), 368–374.

Balmer, J.M.T. (1995). Corporate branding and connoisseurship. *Journal of General Management* 21(1), 24–46.

Balmer, J.M.T. (1998). Corporate identity and the advent of corporate marketing. *Journal of Marketing Management* 14(8), 963–996.

Balmer, J.M.T. (2001a). Corporate identity, corporate branding and corporate marketing: seeing through the fog. *European Journal of Marketing* 35(3/4), 248–291.

Balmer, J.M.T. (2001b). The three virtues and seven deadly sins of corporate branding. *Journal of General Management* 27(1), 1–17.

Balmer, J.M.T. (2009). Corporate marketing: apocalypse, advent and epiphany. *Management Decision* 47(4), 544–572.

Balmer, J.M.T. & Gray, E.R. (2003). Corporate brands: what are they? What of them? *European Journal of Marketing* 3(7/8), 972–997.

Balmer, J.M.T. & Greyser, S.A. (2007). Corporate marketing: integrating corporate identity, corporate branding, corporate communications, corporate image and corporate reputation. *European Journal of Marketing* 40(7–8), 730–741.

Barney, J.A. & Hansen, M.H. (1994). Trustworthiness as a source of competitive advantage. *Strategic Management Journal*, 15(5), 175–190.

Bernstein, D. (2009). Rhetoric and reputation: some thoughts on corporate dissonance. *Management Decision* 47(4), 603–615.

Bickerton, D. (2000). 'Corporate Reputation versus Corporate Branding: The Realist Debate,' Corporate Communications, No. 1, pp. 42–48.

de Chernatony, L. (1999). Brand management through narrowing the gap between brand identity and brand reputation. *Journal of Marketing Management* 15(1–3), 157–180.

de Chernatony, L. (2001). *From Brand Vision to Brand Evaluation*. London: Butterworth-Heinemann.

de Chernatony, L. & Harris, F. (2000). Developing corporate brands through considering internal and external stakeholders. *Corporate Reputation Review* 3(3), 268–274.

Conn, D. (2009). 'From desert skyscrapers to Manchester City's sky blue land of riches'. *The Guardian*. Online: http://www.guardian.co.uk/football/2009/sep/18/manchester-city-abu-dhabi-mubarak. Accessed: July 2011.

Davies, G. & Chun, R. (2002). Gaps between the internal and external perceptions of the corporate brand. *Corporate Reputation Review* 5(2–3), 144–158.

Einweiller, S. & Will, M. (2002). Towards an integrated approach to corporate branding – and empirical study. *Corporate Communications: An International Journal* 7(2), 100–109.

Gray, E.R. & Balmer, J.M.T. (2001). The corporate brand: a strategic asset. *Management in Practice* 4, 1–4.

Harris, F. & de Chernatony, L. (2001). Corporate branding and corporate brand performance. *European Journal of Marketing* 35(3/4), 441–456.

Hart, S. & Murphy, J. (1998). *Brands: The New Wealth Creators*. Basingstoke: Macmillan Business.

Hatch, M.J. & Schultz, M. (2001). Are the strategic stars aligned for your corporate brand? *Harvard Business Review*, February, 128–134.

Hatch, M. & Schultz, M. (2003). Bringing the corporation into corporate branding. *European Journal of Marketing* 37(7/8), 1041–1064.

Hatch, M.J. & Schultz, M. (2008). *Taking Brand Initiative: How Companies Can Align Strategy, Culture and Identity through Corporate Branding*. San Francisco: Jossey-Bass.

Hulberg, J. (2006). Integrating corporate branding and sociological paradigms: a literature study. *Brand Management* 14(1/2), 60–73.

Ind, N. (1997). *The Corporate Brand*. Basingstoke: Macmillan Business.

Ind, N. (1998). An integrated approach to corporate branding. *The Journal of Brand Management* 5(5), 323–329.

James, D. (2005). Guilty through association: brand association transfer to brand alliances. *Journal of Consumer Marketing* 22(1), 14–24.

Johansson, J.K. & Hirano, M. (1999). Brand reality: the Japanese perspective. *Journal of Marketing Management* 15(1–3), 93–105.

Judson, K.M., Aurand, T.W., Gorchels, L. & Gordon, G.L. (2009). Building a university brand from within: university administrators' perspectives of internal branding. *Services Marketing Quarterly* 30, 54–68.

Kapferer, J.N. (1997). *Strategic Brand Management*, 2nd edn. London: Kogan Page.

Kapferer, J.N. (2002). *(Re)-inventing the Brand*. London: Kogan Page.

Kay, M. (2006). Strong brands and corporate brands. *European Journal of Marketing* 40(7/8), 742–760.

Keller, K. (2003). Brand synthesis: the multidimensionality of brand knowledge. *Journal of Consumer Research* 29(1), 595–600.

Keller, K.L. (2002). *Strategic Brand Management*. Upper Saddle River, NJ: Prentice-Hall.

Keller, K.L. (2008). *Strategic Brand Management: Building, Measuring, and Managing Brand Equity*, 3rd edn., New Jersey: Prentice Hall.

King, S. (1991). Brand Building in the 1990's, *Journal of Marketing Management*, 7, 3–13.

Knox, S. & Bickerton, D. (2003). The six conventions of corporate branding. *European Journal of Marketing* 37(7/8), 998–1016.

Knox, S.D., Maklan, S. & Thompson, K.E. (2000). Building the unique organisational value proposition. In: Schultz, M., Hatch, M.J. & Larsen, M.H. eds. *The Expressive Organization*. Oxford: Oxford University Press, pp. 138–153.

Leitch, S. & Motion, J. (2007). Retooling the corporate brand: a Foucauldian perspective on normalisation and differentiation. *Brand Management* 15(1), 71–80.

McDonald, M.H.D., de Chernatony, L. & Harris, F. (2001). Corporate marketing and service brands. *European Journal of Marketing* 35(3/4), 335–352.

Melewar, T. & Walker, C. (2003). Global corporate brand building: guidelines and case studies. *Brand Management* 11(2), 157–170.

van Mesdag, M. (1997). Brand strategy needs turning back to front. *Market Intelligence and Planning* 15(3), 157–159.

Mitchell, A. (1997). *Brand Strategies in the Information Age. Financial Times* report. London: Financial Times.

Mitchell, A. (1999). Out of the shadows. *Journal of Marketing Management* 15(1–3), 25–42.

Newman, K. (2001). The sorcerer's apprentice? Alchemy, seduction and confusion in modern marketing. *International Journal of Advertising* 20, 409–429.

Olins, W. (1989). *Corporate Identity: Making Business Strategy Visible Through Design*. London: Thames Hudson.

Olins, W. (2000). How brands are taking over the corporation. In: Schultz, M. *et al.*, eds. *The Expressive Organization: Linking Identity, Reputation, and the Corporate Brand*. New York: Oxford University Press, pp. 77–96.

Pringle, H. & Gordon, W. (2001). *Brand Manners: How to Create the Self-Confident Organisation to Live the Brand*. Chichester: Wiley.

van Riel (2001) cited in Einweiller, S. & Will, M. (2002). Towards an integrated approach to corporate branding – an empirical study. *Corporate Communications: An International Journal* 7(2), 100–109.

van Riel, C.B.M. & Fombrun, C.J. (2007). *Essentials of Corporate Communication*. Abingdon: Routledge.

Riezebos, R. (2003). *Brand Management*. Harlow: Financial Times-Prentice Hall.

Roper, S. & Davies, G. (2007). The corporate brand: a multi-stakeholder approach. *Journal of Marketing Management* 23(1–2), 75–90.

Simmons, J. (2006). *The Invisible Grail: How Brands Can Use Words to Engage with Audiences*. London: Marshall Cavendish Business.

Smyth, J., Dorward, C. & Reback, J. (1992). *Corporate Reputation*. London: Century.

Tilley, C. (1999). Built-in branding: how to engineer a leadership brand. *Journal of Marketing Management* 15, 181–191.

Uehling, J. (2000). Don't take your corporate brand for granted. *Brandweek* 41(21), 34–35.

Uggla, H. (2006). The corporate brand association base: a conceptual model for the creation of inclusive brand architecture. *European Journal of Marketing* 40(7/8), 785–802.

Urde, M. (1999). Brand orientation: a mindset for building brands into strategic resources. *Journal of Marketing Management* 15, 117–133.

Vick, E.H. (1993). The corporation as a brand. *Directors and Boards* 17(4), 57–58.

Wilson, R. (1997). Corporate branding. *The Journal of Brand Management* 4(5), 303–310.

Wilson, A. (2001). Understanding organisational culture and the implications for corporate marketing. *European Journal of Marketing* 35, 353–368.

Chapter 7
Measuring corporate brands

The development and management of corporate brands are recognised by many as critical elements in the management of corporate reputation. However, understanding and agreeing the exact contribution that a corporate brand can make to an organisation is not quite as clear-cut.

There have been many attempts to place a financial value on a corporate brand, and various measurement approaches have been proposed. Many might be deemed to be flawed due to methodological and financial biases. However, it is important that attempts are made to measure these brands and, in doing so, improve the way in which corporate brands are managed, regardless of the sector in which an organisation operates.

Aims and learning objectives

The aim of this chapter is to explore ways in which corporate brands can be measured.

The learning objectives of this chapter are to:

1. Consider what brands are worth and how they are measured
2. Assess the importance of brand equity and brand resonance
3. Evaluate the various methods used to measure corporate brands
4. Consider the importance of corporate branding and reputation in the third sector
5. Consider the problems of branding in the third sector
6. Provide details of the methods used to measure third sector corporate brands.

What are brands worth and how are they measured?

Chapter 4 dealt with the difficulties of measuring corporate reputation. In this chapter we turn to the equally challenging subject of measuring brands (see Viewpoint 7.1 on Amnesty International). Building a brand absorbs considerable time and financial resources, and management needs to be assured that there is a return on this investment.

Brands are made up of intangible assets.

There are various organisations that assess the value of the top brands. Of course, as we have discussed previously, brands are made up of intangible assets. It is often the value systems of corporate brands that differentiate them from the competition and such intangible assets cannot be assessed purely in financial terms. The extra value that a consumer gains from buying a brand is able to support a price premium for the brand owner. Isolating this premium into a monetary value is a difficult conundrum. Many consumers would in fact deny that they are willing to pay a premium for one brand over another, despite the fact that they do. This premium has always existed, although the terminology used is often different. When selling a shop, for example, an element of the purchase price would be made up of 'goodwill', a premium paid for the loyalty of the customer base. As an ongoing business, a brand should be able to calculate this goodwill, the reservoir of future earnings that can be relied upon based upon the asset of the brand itself.

Companies have attempted to place a value on these intangibles.

As brands have become more important than the products or services that they produce, so companies have attempted to place a value on these intangibles. Previously only tangible elements, such as ownership of patents, had a financial worth attached to them. Despite recognition of the importance of valuing brands, the process still remains more of an art than a science. The use of different methodologies can lead to different values for the same brand, as will be revealed.

Viewpoint 7.1   What value Amnesty International?

Amnesty International is a campaigning non-governmental organisation made up of ordinary people around the world. They claim 'our purpose is to protect people wherever justice, fairness, freedom and truth are denied'.

In 1961, British lawyer Peter Benenson wrote a newspaper appeal, 'The Forgotten Prisoners', calling for an international campaign to protest against the imprisonment of men and women for their political or religious beliefs. The appeal received a tremendous response. Within a month, more than a thousand readers had sent letters of support and offers of practical help. They also sent details of the cases of many more prisoners of conscience. Within 6 months, what started as a brief publicity effort was being developed into a permanent, international movement.

Amnesty traditionally focused on political prisoners (recognisable still from its original logo) but it now also campaigns on behalf of wider groups due to the changing patterns of human rights violations in the world. The organisation claims that the biggest threats to human rights are the mass violations committed during armed conflicts. Amnesty insists upon compliance with international laws and standards.

The values of the organisation are very clear, being 'international solidarity, effective action for the individual victim, global coverage, the universality and indivisibility of human rights, impartiality and independence, and democracy and mutual respect'. The aims of Amnesty are to promote the general awareness of human rights and to oppose specific abuses of human rights where they are encountered throughout the world. The principles of impartiality and independence were established from the beginning.

Amnesty's first mission was to Ghana in 1962 and led to the release of 152 political prisoners following pressure from the fledgling organisation. During the same year Amnesty sent an observer to Nelson Mandela's trial. International recognition followed from the United Nations and the Council of Europe. Of several hundred

Exhibit 7.1 Over its 50-year history Amnesty International has expanded its remit to include economic, social and cultural rights.
Source: Amnesty International, with permission. © Marie-Anne Ventoura.

human rights organisations in the world, Amnesty has the longest history and certainly the widest worldwide recognition. Its campaigning portfolio has grown over the decades. Its opposition to torture started in the 1970s and challenged not only rogue states but also established western governments such as the CIA in the United States. In 1977 the organisation received the Nobel Peace Prize in recognition of its stance on torture.

In the 1980s the growing number of refugees displaced by war and famine became a focus for Amnesty. By the 1990s Amnesty had grown to a membership of over 2.2 million in over 150 countries. Amnesty (like any strong brand) has continued to adapt and demonstrate its relevance in changing times and an increasingly complex world. In the 21st century it has turned to the challenges arising from globalisation and the huge aftermath of the 9/11 attacks of 2001. Amnesty has expanded its remit to include economic, social and cultural rights. Its reason for this is the growing power of companies and their hold over many governments, particularly in the developing world.

For an organisation still made up largely of volunteers, the impact of Amnesty International has been huge over its 50-year history.

Question

How do you measure the worth of a brand such as Amnesty International?

Source: Various, including www.amnesty.org.uk.

Grand Metropolitan was one of the first companies to attempt to value its brands. In 1988 it estimated its own worth at £565 million, including the Smirnoff Vodka brand that it had recently purchased. This was followed later the same year by Rank Hovis McDougall (RHD), which valued its own brands, such as Bisto, Hovis and Mr Kipling, at £678 million. This attempt at valuation was perhaps more important than the valuation by Grand Metropolitan, as these brands had not been purchased but were created by RHD over many decades. The balance sheet of the company was significantly increased by this (at the time contentious) valuation as the company's net assets at the time were only around £300 million.

In September 2010 the new ISO 10688 standard benchmark was agreed by the directors of ISO, thereby bringing in an internationally agreed brand valuation process. The ISO standard separates the primary criteria for brand valuation into three discrete areas – legal, financial and behavioural.

Legal. This refers to an assessment of the legal protection afforded to the brand in each geographical area and product or service registration category. These legal rights will, of course, vary between legal systems and need to be carefully considered when forming the brand valuation opinion.

Financial. The financial valuation is a complex issue that includes the following:

- **The market approach** measures value by reference to what other purchasers in the market have paid for similar assets. This really looks at what the brand might be worth if it were sold to another company.

- **The cost approach** measures value by reference to the cost invested in creating, replacing or reproducing the brand.

- **The income approach** measures value by reference to the economic benefits expected to be received over the remaining useful economic life of the brand. First, this involves estimating the expected future, after-tax, cash flows attributable to the brand. Secondly, these flows have to be reduced to their present-day value, using an appropriate rate of discount. This is very similar to the measurement approach currently used by Interbrand.

There are various suggested methods of calculating financial value, the recommended one being the 'royalty relief' method. This assumes that the brand is not owned by the branded business but is licensed from a third party. The value is deemed to be the present value of the royalty payments saved by virtue of owning the brand (Haigh, 2010).

The behavioural approach requires that the valuation must accommodate the market size, trends and the contribution the brand makes to the purchase decision. The attitude of all stakeholder groups to the brand and all economic benefits conferred on the branded business, by the brand, make up the behavioural criteria.

Haigh (2010) claims that approximately 25 years of debate have been ended by the provision of the ISO standard. However, we will see that there is still considerable licence allowed in the criteria listed above and in the methods.

Brand equity

The financial benefits provided by a brand name are a demonstration of brand equity. Brand equity refers to the marketing benefits and outcomes that accrue to a product due to its brand name compared with those that would accrue if the same product did not have the brand name. Brand equity manifests itself in increased market share, price premiums, customer recognition and positive brand associations (Figure 7.1). These lead to increased purchase intention and, therefore, enhanced lifetime value for the brand. A company with higher brand equity is likely to benefit from improved customer perceptions of its products, services and its general quality.

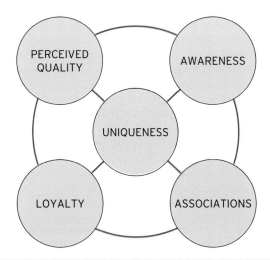

| **Figure 7.1** | Dimensions of brand equity. |

Brand equity is a well-known measurement and it does have the advantage of attempting to measure some of the intangible, more emotional, factors of a brand. The dimensions of brand equity seek to measure the rational and emotional value of brands. The standing of a brand with consumers can be measured through its sales volume, market share, pricing relative to competitors and similar rational economic measures. The uniqueness of the brand, and therefore its equity, is generated by four factors: awareness, association, loyalty and perceived quality.

> **Brand equity seeks to measure the rational and emotional value of brands.**

Awareness is a rational measure. Do consumers know the brand exists? Does it come to mind when a consumer identifies a need? Does problem recognition in the consumer decision-making process lead to the recall of particular brand names? Such brands that are at the top of the consumer's mind are therefore likely to be top of their choice set. Recall and recognition research can be used to measure brand awareness. This can be prompted, whereby respondents are presented with a list of brands (recognition), or unprompted, where respondents recollect brands solely from memory (recall).

> **Association is an emotional measure of the perceived brand value.**

Association is an emotional measure of the perceived brand value. This is the value-for-money, brand personality (i.e. the excitement and interest generated by the brand) and associations that can be reputational, such as trust. This aspect of brand equity focuses on the brand image. Free association tests and projective techniques are commonly used marketing research techniques. These are used to uncover the tangible and intangible attributes, attitudes and intentions about a brand (Keller, 1993). When the consumer thinks of a particular brand, what words or phrases come to mind? Are these positive or negative associations?

Loyalty represents a vital emotional level. Superior product and service quality leads to a virtuous circle whereby repeat business is assured from customers. This leads to higher sales and profit margins. At its highest level customers will not accept a substitute, insisting only on their preferred brand. These consumers also act as an advocate for that brand, encouraging others in their personal and/or professional networks to use it.

Perceived quality is a rational element that may be supplemented by emotion, i.e. brand innovativeness – as in the case of Apple, for example.

As with many issues in the field of marketing there are different interpretations of brand equity. Brand consultants and market research firm Ipsos include familiarity, uniqueness, relevance, popularity and quality in their interpretation of equity.

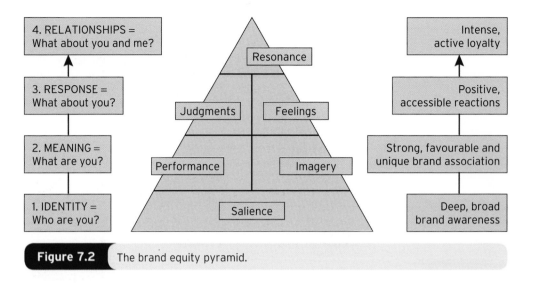

Figure 7.2 The brand equity pyramid.

Another measure of brand equity is the ability of the brand to introduce brand extensions.

Another measure of brand equity is the ability of the brand to introduce brand extensions. Extensions allow leveraging of existing brand awareness and associations and therefore reduce marketing communication expenditure. Brand equity can also be sold by licensing the brand as demonstrated by the Disney Corporation (see Viewpoint 6.2, p. 140).

Figure 7.2 illustrates the concept of the brand equity pyramid. Moving customers towards the top of the pyramid is highly beneficial for the brand. The left side of the pyramid focuses on the rational elements and the right side on the emotional connection with the brand. The brand that has real resonance for consumers fosters the intense and active loyalty that brings brand equity for the company.

Aaker (1996) claims that there is a strong empirical link between brand equity and stock market performance. One such brand that has exhibited strong performance and growth is Merlin Entertainment. You may not have heard of it, but the brands within its portfolio will be familiar to many (see Viewpoint 7.2).

Viewpoint 7.2   Thrills and spills as Merlin entertains

Merlin Entertainments is an excellent example of a corporate brand that has many well-known visitor attractions brands within its portfolio – both global and local. World-famous visitor attractions such as the London Eye, LEGOLAND, Madame Tussauds, SEA LIFE, Alton Towers Resort and Blackpool Tower are a few of the brands that the company owns or operates.

Like many corporate brands, its organisation is complex and it is therefore far happier for the public to identify with the much better known attractions under its control. Formed in 1999 via a management buyout of Vardon Attractions from Vardon plc, it is now owned by Blackstone, CVC, KIRKBI and Management. Merlin has demonstrated that it has grown its markets successfully. This alone shows the group's ability to maximise the potential of every one of its sites.

Operational management of the company is split into three business groups: LEGOLAND Parks, Midway attractions and Resort Theme Parks. These are supported by a unique 'backroom' organisation – Merlin Magic Making – which is responsible for looking for new sites and all the creative elements of the attractions from the creation of wax figures and LEGOLAND models to ride and attraction theming. The benefits of the corporate brand allow economies of scale across the different brands. These can be seen, for example, in marketing and media buying costs, but each attraction is individually accountable for its own profit and loss. The broad nature of the portfolio allows the corporate brand to be more resilient to volatility in individual markets.

Very successful organic growth by increasing profitability of its individual attractions and rolling out its midway brands globally – at a rate of 6/7 new openings a year supported by strategic acquisitions like

Exhibit 7.2	Legoland is just one of Merlin's many world-famous visitor attractions.

Source: Merlin Entertainment UK, with permission.

LEGOLAND Parks (in 2005), Gardaland (Italy's No 1 theme park, in 2006), The Tussauds Group (in 2007), and Sydney Attractions Group (in 2011) increased the scale of the business by over 20 times in seven years. Now market leader in Europe, it is second only to Disney on a global scale. The group currently comprises 75 (78 by the end of 2011) attractions in 17 countries across four continents, welcoming over 44 million visitors in 2010.

Whilst its visitor attraction brands are the customer-facing part of the business, Merlin itself uses its brand in two ways – first to link attractions providing important promotional and linked sales opportunities (like the Merlin Annual Pass currently available in the UK, where the group has 25 attractions, and in Germany), and to take an overarching approach to strategy and focus its objectives at financial and business markets. Merlin claims its strategy is to create a high-growth, international, destination-based family entertainment company with strong brands and a portfolio that is naturally hedged against external factors such as weather or localised market conditions.

One important part of Merlin's growth strategy is to grow its market by ensuring its theme park attractions are more than places for a day trip. The company intends to position all its theme parks as short break destinations in order to optimise their market reach and asset utilisation. Hotels and/or holiday villages are a clear market signal in achieving this, as is the addition of second gate midway attractions like SEA LIFE or waterparks, and Merlin plans to add new developments to its existing estate of six hotels and one holiday village on an ongoing basis. Hotels are already planned for LEGOLAND Windsor in the UK in 2012, and LEGOLAND California in 2013.

As a corporate brand its strategy must also deal with the needs of multiple stakeholders. To this end it states that its priorities are 'The delivery of memorable experiences to our millions of visitors underpinned by constantly monitored visitor satisfaction, world-class people development strategies, and the very highest customer service and health & safety standards'.

Expansion continues and early in 2011 Merlin expanded its portfolio in Asia Pacific, including the acquisition of the Sydney Aquarium, Sydney Wildlife World, Oceanworld Manly, Sydney Tower and the Koala Gallery in Australia, in addition to Kelly Tarlton's Underwater World in New Zealand. The group also announced plans for its first two attractions in Japan – a Madame Tussauds and a LEGOLAND Discovery Centre to open in Tokyo in 2012. Later in 2011 the Group opened its first new LEGOLAND Park since it acquired the brand – LEGOLAND Florida, with a second LEGOLAND Malaysia opening in 2012.

Question

Take two of the brands that operate under the Merlin corporate brand and compare your view of their brand equity.

Source: Various, including www.merlinentertainments.biz.

Measuring corporate brands

Interbrand's best global brands

So how are brands measured and valued? There are various well-known techniques. Interbrand is a brand consultancy that annually publishes a list of the top 100 global brands by value (see Table 7.1). Interbrand's method looks at the ongoing investment and management of a brand as a business asset. It takes into account all of the many ways in which a brand touches and benefits the company. The method claims to look at softer issues, from attracting and retaining talent to delivering on customer expectation.

Interbrand's method looks at the ongoing investment and management of a brand as a business asset.

Interbrand says its methodology has three key aspects that contribute to the overall assessment:

- **Financial performance.** This is a measure of the pure financial return for investors. Interbrand's financial assessments are derived from published annual reports, which allow them to examine brands' revenues, earnings and balance sheets. Additional publicly available data may be looked at, particularly for those brands that do not issue formal public accounts. This element determines the economic profit of the brand. Taxes are subtracted from net operating profit. From this a capital charge is subtracted to account for capital used to generate the brand's revenues.

- **Role of brand.** This is a measure of the portion of the decision to purchase that is considered to be attributable to the brand. This excludes other aspects of the offer, such as price or features. This criterion reflects the proportion of demand for a branded product or service that exceeds the demand for the same product or service if it was unbranded.

Brand strength is measured across 10 dimensions of brand activation.

- **Brand strength.** This is a measure of the ability of the brand to secure the delivery of expected future earnings. Brand strength is measured on a 0–100 scale across 10 dimensions of brand activation. Performance is judged relative to other brands in the industry, including global brands where appropriate. Interbrand claims that all 10 criteria are equally important. They bring together all aspects of a brand – its people, products, positioning and partners – to create a more holistic and accurate way of understanding and evaluating brands.

Interbrand's 10 measures of brand strength are set out in Table 7.2. The Interbrand study is interesting and well known. There are difficulties isolating the effect of the corporate brand

Table 7.1	Interbrand's top global brands, 2010	
Rank	Brand name	Brand value ($ million)
1	Coca-Cola	70,452
2	IBM	64,727
3	Microsoft	60,895
4	Google	43,557
5	GE	42,808
6	McDonald's	33,578
7	Intel	32,015
8	Nokia	29,495
9	Disney	28,731
10	Hewlett-Packard	26,867

Source: Interbrand, with permission.

Table 7.2	Ten measures of brand strength
Measure	**Explanation**
Commitment	A measure of an organisation's internal commitment to or belief in its brand. Commitment is the extent to which the brand receives support in terms of time, influence and investment.
Protection	This component examines how secure a brand is across a number of dimensions – from legal protection and proprietary ingredients to design, scale or geographic spread.
Clarity	The brand's values, positioning and proposition must be clearly articulated and shared across the organisation, along with a clear view of its target audiences, customer insights and drivers. It is vital that those within the organisation know and understand all of these elements, because everything that follows hinges on them.
Responsiveness	This component looks at a brand's ability to adapt to market changes, challenges and opportunities. The brand should have a desire and ability to constantly evolve and renew itself.
Authenticity	This component is about how soundly a brand is based on an internal capability. Authenticity asks if a brand has a defined heritage and a well-grounded value set, as well as if it can deliver against customers' expectations.
Relevance	This component estimates how well a brand fits with customer needs, desires and decision criteria across all appropriate demographics and geographies.
Understanding	Not only must customers recognise the brand, but there must also be an in-depth understanding of its distinctive qualities and characteristics, as well as those of the brand owner.
Consistency	This measures the degree to which a brand is experienced without fail across all touchpoints and formats.
Presence	This measures the degree to which a brand feels omnipresent and how positively consumers, customers and opinion formers discuss it in both traditional and social media.
Differentiation	This is the degree to which customers perceive the brand to have a positioning that is distinct from the competition.

Source: www.interbrand.com. Interbrand, with permission.

from the other intangibles and its effect upon market capitalisation and cash flow. How, for example, are the emotional and symbolic effects of a brand to be measured (Hatch & Schultz, 2008)? How is the impact on a brand of a workforce that is proud to represent the organisation to be measured? Although the Interbrand methodology claims to measure soft assets, the fact that the list is produced in order of financial value tells its own story. It can be argued that the emotional resonance of a brand lies outside economic analysis.

> The emotional resonance of a brand lies outside economic analysis.

The valuation that is placed on the brands on the list is also a contentious element. This can clearly be seen when we compare these valuations with those of another brand measurement tool, Millward Brown's BrandZ study.

Millward Brown/WPP BrandZ

As with the Interbrand study, this work demonstrates the value of branding to companies. Millward Brown claims that a brand is worth, on average, about a third of shareholder value. They argue that this is true for all sectors, and for corporate brands not merely consumer goods. Yet again an economic approach is taken.

> A brand is worth, on average, about a third of shareholder value.

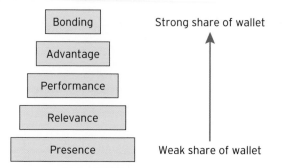

Figure 7.3 BrandZ brand dynamics pyramid.

The Millward Brown study includes WPP's BrandZ database, a huge record of consumers evaluating brands in a competitive context from categories that they actually shop in. Over a 10-year period, in excess of one million consumers and business-to-business customers in 31 countries have recorded their experience of over 21,000 brands. The study is restricted to market-facing brands, i.e. it will favour individual brands over corporate brands such as Unilever, Procter & Gamble and Nestlé.

The valuation process consists of the following three steps:

- **Branded earnings** – this is the intangible element, i.e. the proportion of a company's earnings generated 'under the banner of the brand'. So this is the intangible corporate earnings allocated to each brand, by country, based on secondary data, such as company and analyst reports, industry studies and revenue estimates.

- **Brand contribution** – how much of these branded earnings are generated due to the brand's close bond with its customers? This is the portion of intangible earnings attributable to the brand based on analysis of country, market and brand-specific consumer research (see the brand pyramid in Figure 7.3).

- **Brand multiple** – what is the growth potential of the brand-driven earnings? Financial projections and consumer data are analysed.

Now the brand value is calculated as following:

Brand value = branded earnings × brand contribution × brand multiple

For each brand, each person interviewed is assigned to one level of the pyramid depending on their responses to a set of questions. The brand dynamics pyramid shows the number of consumers who have reached each level. A brand pyramid is generated placing each user within one of five levels, from low to high, in terms of share of wallet. Using this methodology Millward Brown's list of the top global brands is as shown in Table 7.3.

Young & Rubicam's BrandAsset Valuator

The BrandAsset Valuator allows brands to be evaluated in comparison to their competitors.

The BrandAsset Valuator (BAV) is the result of many thousands of consumer interviews (over 714,000 at a recent count) conducted to assess over 44,000 brands in 72 countries since its conception in 1993. The hub of the survey instrument consists of 72 metrics measuring perception and evaluation of brands. BAV allows brands to be evaluated in comparison to their competitors. The four key dimensions are:

- differentiation – uniqueness (vitality of brand)
- relevance – degree to which brand meets personal needs (vitality of brand)

Table 7.3	BrandZ top 100 most powerful brands		
Position	Brand	Value ($ million)	Change in value from 2009 (%)
1	Google	114,260	14
2	IBM	86,383	30
3	Apple	83,153	32
4	Microsoft	76,344	0
5	Coca-Cola	67,983	1
6	McDonald's	66,005	−1
7	Marlboro	57,047	15
8	China Mobile	52,616	−14
9	General Electric	45,054	−25
10	Vodafone	44,404	−17

Source: Copyright © Millward Brown Optimor, with permission.

- esteem – degree to which consumers admire the brand (authority of brand)
- knowledge – degree to which brand is part of consumers' daily life (authority of brand); knowledge rather than awareness suggests a greater level of intimacy with the brand.

A brand should build the pillars in the order shown in Figure 7.4. Note the balance between the pillars and the importance of a ratio of 2 : 1, based on the future growth value of the brand.

The BrandAsset Valuator claims to indicate what must be done to keep a brand healthy. It indicates where the company can do better and therefore concerns itself with the future of the brand. Young & Rubicam say that these dimensions are consistently linked with a brand's ability to deliver revenues

> The BAV dimensions are consistently linked with a brand's ability to deliver revenues.

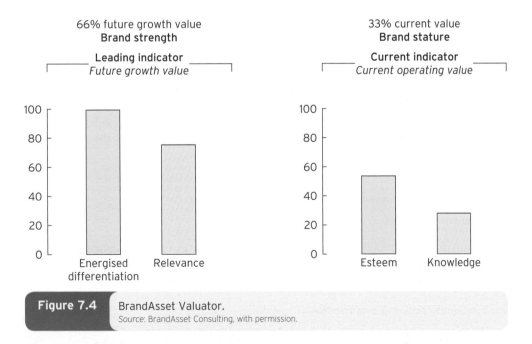

Figure 7.4   BrandAsset Valuator.
Source: BrandAsset Consulting, with permission.

and profits across industries and internationally. They produce a grid which plots the vitality of the brand against its authority, or its strength against its stature.

Healthy brands have a higher degree of differentiation than relevance.

The relationship between differentiation and relevance is an indicator of the brand's strength (Adamson, 2006). All healthy brands have a higher degree of differentiation than relevance. If the brand has greater relevance than differentiation then it may be becoming a commodity; uniqueness is in decline and price becomes the dominant reason for purchase. Esteem and knowledge are the factors that make up a brand's stature. Having higher esteem than knowledge indicates a brand with a high reputation – we admire it although we may know little about it. If the relationship is the other way around, this is more problematic. People may know a lot about the brand but not rate it that highly.

Harris Interactive's EquiTrend

Developed by the Brand and Communications Consulting practice at Harris Interactive, EquiTrend is another tracking study that measures and compares brand equity for over 1,000 brands in 42 categories. EquiTrend compares brands with their competitors and across categories determining the strengths and weaknesses of brands. The study evaluates the marketing communications used to support the brands.

EquiTrend is a 'snapshot' evaluation of engagement with a brand.

EquiTrend is a 'snapshot' evaluation of engagement with a brand. In order to obtain a well-rounded understanding of where and how a brand fits into the larger universe of brands, the study measures brand engagement in four areas:

- equity – a composite of familiarity, quality and purchase consideration
- connection – a composite of emotional connection, aspirational fit, practical fit and brand expectations
- commitment
- energy.

Behaviour, advocacy and trust are also measured by Harris.

Corebrand's Brand Power

Corebrand is a US firm that tracks the corporate brands of 1,200 firms in 47 countries. Respondents are senior business-to-business people from the top 20 per cent of US companies. Due to the seniority of the respondents, the sample size is limited to 400.

The Brand Power measurement, as with many advertising studies, deals with familiarity and favourability. Respondents are first asked to rate their familiarity with a series of companies and scores are weighted according to the average of the top three responses. Respondents who have a qualified level of familiarity are then asked to rate their favourability of those companies across three dimensions:

- overall reputation
- perception of management
- investment potential.

Familiarity and favourability data are combined to create 'brand power', a single measure of the size and quality of a corporate brand. This number provides a single measure of the size of a company's audience and its disposition towards the company. Coca-Cola, Johnson & Johnson, Harley-Davidson, Campbell's, UPS and Colgate-Palmolive have been highly placed in Corebrand's rankings over the years.

They state that having a stronger corporate brand image positively affects share price by some 5–7 per cent. The reliance on advertising spend will of course preclude the majority of B2B and many third sector brands from being assessed by the Corebrand model, despite the fact that this model claims to specifically measure corporate brands.

> Having a stronger corporate brand image positively affects the share price by some 5-7 per cent.

Difficulties with measuring brands

One of the difficulties with the methods discussed in the previous sections is that some of the methodologies used are not available to academics or others in order to allow independent analysis. The companies that create them wish to protect their own research and as a result there is a large element of secrecy about their methods and data. It should also be noted that these are commercial organisations whose aim is to make a profit from consultancy. This prevents them from revealing too much about their methodology as it is an asset they need to protect. As they wish to sign up new clients, it is hardly in their interest to undersell the value of their own measurement tools.

The Corebrand measure might be regarded as an old-fashioned approach, as it is very advertising-orientated. Twenty five years ago it would have been thought impossible to build a strong brand without the use of extensive advertising. In the more sophisticated era of the corporate brand, however, it is not appropriate to claim such a reliance on advertising. Google has built one of the world's top brands by word-of-mouth.

The reticence of accountants and others to attach valuations to a brand can be seen when comparing the different values given to the same brands by the two most important studies, Interbrand and BrandZ. Although some of the brands featured attract a very similar valuation, there are some huge discrepancies. BrandZ values Google at $114 billion whereas Interbrand values it at only $43 billion. How can one valuation not even be 40 per cent of the other? McDonald's is valued at $66 billion by BrandZ but only $34 billion by Interbrand. The international element of Interbrand's method excludes China Mobile from its list. This is a brand that only operates in its home market; however, the huge size of this market puts the company at number eight in the BrandZ list.

Some of the problems of brand valuation have led to warnings that these valuations are a bubble waiting to explode in the same way that the dot.com bubble burst. As with the financially oriented measures of corporate reputation outlined in Chapter 4, these measures, by their nature, exclude many of the best brands, those in the not-for-profit sector.

> The measures discussed exclude many of our best brands, those in the not-for-profit sector.

Brand personality

As an alternative to the financially driven measures of the brand, it may be more appropriate to consider some projective techniques instead. These may take the form of word association techniques or being asked to consider the brand as an animal or a relative (or even a pet) within a larger extended family or asking customers to engage in role-play rather than expressing feelings verbally. Such techniques may give a deeper understanding of the brand and where it is positioned in relation to its competitors.

Techniques like this can also be applied to not-for-profit brands. The most well known of these projective techniques is to use the 'brand as person' metaphor, i.e. a brand personality.

> The most well-known projective technique is to use the 'brand as person' metaphor, i.e. a brand personality.

Brands can be described as honest and sincere or dominant and selfish.

The theme that underpins much of the brand personality literature is the application of human characteristics to a brand. Many metaphors have previously been used to help our understanding, including brand as warrior, brand as family, brand as pilot, brand as partner and brand as seducer (Davies & Chun, 2003). Brand personality is a metaphor that allows a clearer insight into the implicit meaning of a brand. We ascribe human traits, either positive or negative, to a brand in order to express our feelings about it. Therefore, brands can be described as honest and sincere or as dominant and selfish, in the same way we would describe a person. In an academic context, metaphor is used in order to make sense of complex phenomena (Davies *et al.*, 2001). The brand as person is one of the most popular metaphors in the field of brand management (Hanby, 1999). Although first referred to by Martineau (1958), who discussed store personality, this term was quickly superseded by 'store image' in the literature. The concept was developed by King (1973), who insisted that the main difference between two similar yet competing brands lay in the different personalities projected by each brand. For example, King used the personality traits 'modern' and 'romantic' to describe the reputation of a furniture company.

In terms of developing the brand personality concept into a solid research methodology that could be repeated to measure different brands, Jennifer Aaker (1997) developed the five-factor model of brand personality. Aaker's approach mirrors that of human psychologists who believe that human personality can be described by just 5 dimensions. Known as the Big 5, many psychologists claim that every human being's personality is, to a greater or lesser extent, – 'open to experience', 'conscientious', 'extravert', 'agreeable' and 'neurotic'.

Aaker (1997) was intent on discovering the antecedents of brand personality. She describes brand personality as the 'set of human characteristics associated with a brand'. Customers form these associations during their direct and indirect contacts with a brand. Aaker's research produced the following dimensions of a brand's personality:

- Sincerity – down-to-earth, honest, wholesome, cheerful
- Excitement – daring, spirited, imaginative, up-to-date
- Competence – reliable, intelligent, successful
- Sophistication – upper-class, charming
- Ruggedness – outdoorsy, tough.

In all, 42 traits make up the five dimensions of Aaker's brand personality scale.

Aaker (1997) used her method to measure the personality of a variety of brands. The importance of this research rests on the suggestion by researchers that consumer preference and usage rate are influenced by empathy of the customer with the brand personality. This leads to greater levels of trust and therefore loyalty.

The Aaker scale was an important development, raising questions from which research into the internal and external views of corporate brands and their reputations took place, leading to the Corporate Character Scale outlined in Chapter 5. The use of language in Aaker's work indicates that the study is concerned with consumer brands and that it was only conducted amongst North American consumers.

The corporate character scale is capable of measuring corporate brands across many different market sectors.

The Corporate Character Scale built on Aaker's work on brand personality. This scale is capable of measuring corporate brands across many different market sectors, including the not-for-profit sector. It also examines the views of a single brand's multiple stakeholder groups, not just a consumer perspective.

Another flaw in Aaker's work is that her brand personality factors are all positive. A respondent could, of course, give low scores to a particular factor, indicating that they saw the brand in a negative light, but it is imperative to test for negative factors as well as positive. All human personalities have negative as well as positive traits and these had not been sufficiently well dealt with by the research preceding the Corporate Character Scale. The literature on marketing, branding, corporate reputation, advertising, organisational behaviour and human personality was consulted to rectify these omissions by Aaker.

Third sector corporate brands

The difficulties of measuring third-sector brands

As has been mentioned several times in this book, an important and under-represented sector in the branding literature is the not-for-profit sector or, as it is often now referred to, the third sector. The European Social Research Council (ESRC) defines the third sector as those non-governmental organisations that are value-driven and that principally reinvest their surpluses to further social, environmental or cultural objectives. The third sector may also be referred to as the civil society or the social economy. The name third sector is in reference to the two main sectors of the economy, the public and private sectors. It is the place between the state and the private sector.

> The third sector may also be referred to as the civil society or the social economy.

Particularly in an age of government spending cuts, the voluntary or not-for-profit sector is increasingly involved in the provision of vital public services and in providing funding for crucial areas that are underfunded by the state, e.g. medical research. The third sector is increasingly seen as vital to the health of society and the economy as a whole.

Of course, as economists would say, everything comes down to the allocation of scarce resources. Just as private companies compete for customers, so charities compete for donations. It is estimated that there are over 170,000 registered charities in the UK, for example, and 220,000+ voluntary organisations. In the US there are over 1.5 million not-for-profit organisations. There are different interpretations of what constitutes a non-profit organisation in different countries and this is down to cultural differences. Hospitals in the US, for example, would come under the non-profit heading, whereas in the UK the National Health Service, directly funded by taxpayers, is classified as a public sector organisation. Over 790,000 people are employed in the voluntary sector (Labour Force Survey, Office of National Statistics) in the UK. It is clearly a sector that deserves more emphasis than it has received from the perspective of the branding literature.

With such a large market and considerable 'competition', the task of the third-sector organisation should also be to build awareness, understanding and a connection with stakeholders in the same way that a commercial brand would.

Literature on third-sector branding

The payback for third-sector organisations lies in the benefits they provide for society rather than the profit they generate for shareholders. There is certainly considerably less literature available on branding in non-profits than in their commercial cousins. Early work on the subject found that much branding activity is transferable to and beneficial for non-profits (Tapp, 1996). Hankinson (2001) notes a slow acceptance of branding practice within the sector and that a brand orientation could help non-profits achieve their objectives. As reported above, there are a huge number of third-sector organisations competing for attention and, Ewing & Napoli (2005) report that management should be focused on gaining awareness for their brand.

> A brand orientation could help non-profits achieve their objectives.

An example of a brand from the third sector that has used branding to increase its awareness amongst its target audiences is Anthony Nolan (see Viewpoint 7.3).

Viewpoint 7.3 — Finding a match with Anthony Nolan

There are a huge number of charities out there and if there is no (or only very limited) awareness amongst the target audience then this severely limits the chances of the charity's objectives being met. Anthony Nolan is a UK charity that adopted a new corporate identity in 2010 in a bid to increase its appeal among younger people. The charity focuses on haematopoietic stem cell transplantation. It manages and recruits donors to one of the two bone marrow registers in the UK; the other register is the British Bone Marrow Registry run by the National Blood Service. It also carries out research to help make bone marrow transplants more effective.

In the rebranding process the Anthony Nolan Trust dropped the words 'the' and 'trust' from its name to become, simply, Anthony Nolan. It also adopted a radically different logo and strapline as part of a new 4-year strategy.

The charity runs the UK's largest stem cell register, which it uses to match donors with blood cancer patients in need of stem cell transplants. The new strategy aims to more than double the number of people on this register by 2014, from 400,000 to one million.

Anthony Nolan hopes to achieve this primarily by appealing more to younger people, particularly men, and it sees the new visual identity as a key part of the strategy. Its research has shown that awareness of the Anthony Nolan brand is good among people aged over 40, but less so among younger people. Men tend to be bigger and therefore produce more stem cells than women, so the charity is particularly keen for its new look to appeal to them.

(a)

(b)

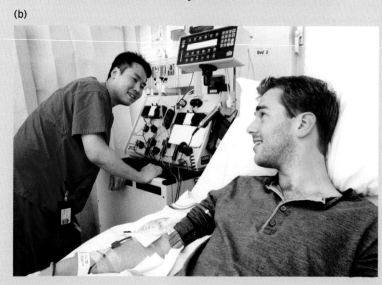

| Exhibit 7.3 | (a) The revised Anthony Nolan logo. (b) A donor (Mark Hill, 25) gives blood stem cells. *Source*: Anthony Nolan, www.anthonynolan.org, with permission. |

A new logo, strapline and website were designed to tackle this awareness issue. The old logo was navy blue with white lettering and featured a white daisy – the favourite flower of Anthony Nolan, in whose name the trust was set up. The strapline read 'taking back lives from leukaemia'.

The trust made the difficult decision to remove the flower, which, despite its historical meaning, did not explain what the charity does. The new look features a black-and-white logo with intersecting lines connecting the letters of the words 'Anthony Nolan' at various points. The new strapline 'Be a match, save a life' was chosen in order to clarify the purpose of the charity. Jess Ridout, brand project manager at the charity, says the old strapline was confusing and the words 'trust' and 'the' didn't add anything to people's understanding of the organisation. She says many health charities have blue branding and the black-and-white colouring sets Anthony Nolan apart.

Henny Braund, chief executive of Anthony Nolan, hopes the new look will give the charity a 'crisp, clean image'. The brand is also incorporated into the charity's website, which includes a 'join the register' tab at the top of every page, encouraging people to get involved.

There are signs of early success, as the rebranded Anthony Nolan was one of the highest new entries in the Charity Brand Index of 2010, placed at number 40.

Question

Under what circumstances should third-sector brands allocate a similar proportion of their income to branding/marketing activities as commercial brands?

Source: Various, including www.thirdsector.co.uk.

Schultz *et al.* (2005) are great advocates of corporate branding and recommend that third-sector organisations embrace a corporate branding strategy. Haigh & Gilbert (2005) point out that branding should be used to help third-sector corporations differentiate themselves from their competitors, whilst Meijer (2009) discusses the benefits of a favourable reputation in increasing the number of donors contributing.

In many ways third-sector organisations have a distinct advantage over commercial brands. Chapter 6 outlined the importance of values to the corporate brand and the *raison d'être* of the third-sector organisation is often for the benefit of a group in need or of society in general. This surely provides a crystal-clear set of values around which the employees can bond and makes the direction of the organisation unambiguous. Indeed, the values and culture of a charity or non-profit organisation can be used to identify potential new staff, those who hold similar values. Theoretically there would be no need to take the private company route of appointing brand ambassadors, as the closely aligned value systems of employees and organisation should make this unnecessary. Jaskyte (2004) says that non-profits should emphasise values through leadership and ongoing daily work to encourage employees' faith in the organisation.

> The values and culture of a charity or non-profit organisation can be used to identify potential new staff.

Brand equity in the third sector

Unsurprisingly the concept of brand equity is similarly neglected amongst third-sector organisations. Haigh & Gilbert (2005) believe there should be more emphasis on such monetary brand equity as a tool that could be used to create value for non-profits. It should be noted that finance in the third sector is there to help the organisation achieve its goals and is not an end in itself. In times of austerity, brand valuation can be central to the sustainability of the brand.

Quelch *et al.* (2004) consider the benefits of measuring brand equity in the third sector and state that these include the ability to recruit at multiple levels, i.e. staff, volunteers, board members, securing long-term corporate sponsors, recurring donations, and crucially, helping to increase their influence on government policy.

Brand awareness is as important in the third sector as in any other.

Certainly brand awareness is as important in the third sector as any other. If people are not aware of a charity then they will not donate to it. Associations drawn from the brand identity must also be positive to encourage the necessary interactions. Brand loyalty is also applicable in the third sector. Charities such as the National Society for the Prevention of Cruelty to Children (NSPCC) attempt to take donors down their own loyalty ladder. This involves converting the casual donor into a regular donor, perhaps through their monthly salary, and then to a legacy donor whereby even after death contributions to the charity continue via the will of the deceased donor.

Sargeant & Woodliffe (2007) impress on us the importance of shared values between donor and charity to encourage loyalty and that relationships are built between the two parties based upon trust. These authors also find that loyalty is engendered if the services of the organisation are of a high perceived quality, the fourth element of brand equity.

Interbrand goes someway towards adapting its methodology to consider non-profits in the third sector as reported later in this chapter. Most people have favourite charities or a particular cause that is close to their hearts; therefore Interbrand's assumption is logical. The brand of the third-sector organisation can also influence commercial companies to associate with or sponsor it rather than a rival.

Problems of third-sector branding

Many non-profit organisations have been slow to recognise the benefits of branding.

There are particular difficulties in branding a third-sector organisation that would not usually be encountered by a commercial brand. With this in mind many non-profits have been slow to recognise the benefits of branding. There may well be a rejection of branding by influential members of the management or boards of third-sector organisations as an overly commercial activity. Certainly in universities, there are many who reject such activity as being beneath an academic institution.

Even amongst those organisations that do embrace the branding concept, there may be a need to ensure that they don't look too professional. Oxfam is one of the biggest retailers in the UK and the NSPCC one of the biggest exponents of direct mail. However, slick mailouts may well not be appreciated by donors. Potential donors may consider that too much of their contributions are being spent on marketing activity than on worthy causes. Allied to this is the problem of relying on volunteer workforces as many charity shops do. Consistency, which embraces the behaviour of staff, is one of the hallmarks of a strong brand. It is far more difficult to insist upon standardised behaviour from individuals who are giving up their own time to work for a charity unpaid.

Non-profit organisations are more complex to manage due to the diverse nature of stakeholders.

Laidler-Kylander *et al.* (2007) confirm that non-profits are more complex to manage due to the diverse nature of stakeholders. The complex nature of stakeholders often means that it may be difficult to identify the true target of branding activity.

Is the third sector brand aiming at donors, recipients of donations, the general public, government bodies or all of these? Certainly differing approaches and messages will be required in targeting the differing groups.

Related to this is the difficulty of identifying a third-sector organisation's customers. For a commercial organisation the customer is the person who pays for the goods or services. Often the recipient of the good work by charities pays nothing towards the running costs of the charity. Customer identification is a difficult issue. University students are now expected to pay ever-increasing fees for their courses. This gives them the idea that they are customers. It could be argued that it is society that is the real customer of the work that universities do.

In contrast to commercial brands that target those whom they feel will fit their offering best, the third-sector brand's target may well be those who are the most resistant to its message. Action on Smoking and Health (Ash), for example, wants to encourage people to stop smoking but those who do smoke are most likely to avoid its negative messages about the impact of smoking. All this activity may be required when, as a result of the lack of marketing orientation in the third sector, there may not be an official budget allocated to brand-related activity.

These difficulties are perhaps a good reason why there should be more branding activity in the third sector, not less. Some of the difficulties of the third sector can be alleviated by the considered use of branding, as demonstrated by the National Childbirth Trust in Viewpoint 7.4.

Viewpoint 7.4   A new identity to reinvigorate the NCT

The National Childbirth Trust (NCT) was founded as a charity in 1961 to help rectify the lack of information available on the subjects of pregnancy and birth. This lack of information led to ignorance and fear and often to a feeling of isolation and lack of support among new and prospective mothers. The Trust's activities across the UK include antenatal and postnatal classes for expectant and new parents, local community activities for new parents such as Bumps and Babies groups, evidence-based information via online and print, breastfeeding counselling and lobbying for improvement across maternity services.

Since it was first conceived over 50 years ago, NCT has encountered problems due to misinterpretation. 'The logo was supposed to be the silhouette of a generic mother and baby, but people often thought it looked religious,' says Sally Horrox, Director of Corporate Communications at NCT. The size and shape of the logo also meant that it was difficult to reproduce in different sizes and formats.

There are 330 NCT branches throughout the UK and all were used to producing their own literature. This led to the classic branding problem of dilution of corporate identity through the different literature produced and also dissimilar tones of voice. The decentralised approach was causing problems. 'The NCT branding was stuck in the 1950s and 1960s whereas the organisation had moved on a long way,' says Horrox.

Members and volunteers were consulted before NCT was rebranded. There was some thought given to changing the name altogether. People thought that the charity was part of the National Health Service or misinterpreted its work and thought that it was a natural birth organisation. 'We discovered that the full name was actually more misleading and alienating for people than the initials, so we decided to retain some of the original brand and we became simply NCT.' The old logo had been open to widespread misinterpretation and the charity simplified it to a neutral graphic that would blend in well with the variety of contexts in which it would be used.

A style guide was devised for distribution to all NCT branches in order to standardise not just the graphics but the tone of voice used by the organisation on a national level. Together with the website redesign, the tone of the brand personality has changed. The brand is now seen as 'more of a big sister than a mother', says Horrox. Web traffic has increased by 25 per cent since the rebranding. The number of NCT members has grown to over 100,000 and Horrox believes that a large part is due to the brand's friendlier image. A brand audit found that consistency of brand in terms of logo, colour, photography and tone of voice was very strong across all audiences – parents, health professionals, external and internal stakeholders.

(a)   (b)

Exhibit 7.4   National Childbirth Trust logos: (a) old, (b) new.
Source: Courtesy of NCT.

Question

How would a brand audit differ between a third-sector brand and a commercial for-profit brand?

Source: Various, including *themarketer*, October (2009) pp. 20–23.

Measuring third-sector organisations

Interbrand

The problems detailed in the previous section, particularly the lack of financial resources, are one reason Interbrand states that third-sector organisations *should* attempt to value their brands. Brand consultants claim that such organisations are increasingly required to take a more commercial approach towards business partnerships in terms of sponsorship, licensing and commercially tendered contract services. They must therefore make the best of what they have.

The difficulty is that the standard approach used for valuing commercial brands requires a profit forecast and an expected return rate for a given owner, for example shareholders. This, of course, would not be applicable to non-profit brands. The methodology was adapted to consider the contribution to investable resources the brand makes in the context of a not-for-profit organisation. Central to the method is the concept of branded economic advantage, i.e. a measure of the extra money generated by the organisation that can be attributed to the success of its brand, across its various audiences.

> Branded economic advantage is a measure of the extra money generated by the organisation that can be attributed to the success of its brand.

This is made up of extra income and reduced costs. This considers the loyalty towards the non-profit brand and the affection in which it is held, and how these affect the economic choices people make. This might include volunteering, donating and even seeking to work for such organisations. The economic advantage of the brand can also influence business decision-makers when making choices as to which non-profit to form a partnership with. The sustainability of revenue to a non-profit is as much a mark of its strength as it would be to a commercially oriented brand. Can it sustain its revenues in the face of competition and in difficult economic circumstances?

The performance of the organisation's revenue and cost lines across a large number of comparable brands is assessed by Interbrand. The financial performance data of over 3,000 leading not-for-profit organisations is calculated. Although a league table is not produced in the way it is with commercial brands, the Interbrand methodology allows it to assign a valuation to particular non-profit brands. For example, The Royal College of Art brand was valued at £57 million at the end of 2008.

The Cone non-profit top 100

In the United States, strategy and communication agency Cone (www.coneinc.com), in collaboration with brand valuation consultants Intangible Business, value US non-profit brands. Their valuation is a combination of brand image, past revenue and propensity for future growth. Brand image is derived from a survey of 1,000 US citizens exploring the familiarity and relevance of non-profit brands to them. This is combined with other factors, such as media coverage and the percentage of revenue received from direct public support. The Cone list puts the YMCA of America at the top of its list with a valuation of $6,393 million. They claim that this methodology allows the brand to see whether there is untapped potential, or whether there's a disparity between the brand and its financial performance. When either significantly outperforms or lags behind the other, it is an indication that there is an unmet opportunity in potential revenue.

The Charity Brand Index

For the last 2 years *PRWeek* and *Third Sector* (www.thirdsector.co.uk), in association with Harris Interactive, have produced the Charity Brand Index, a comprehensive assessment of the UK's top charity brands based on a survey of more than 3,200 members of the public (see Table 7.4).

The report helps charities with the data they need to measure their effectiveness and compare their performance with other charities working in their cause area, as well as tracking their own performance year-on-year.

Table 7.4	Charity Brand Index, 2010	
Rank	**Rank 2009**	**Charity**
1	2	Cancer Research UK
2	5	BBC Children in Need
3	4	RSPCA
4	1	Macmillan Cancer Support
5	12	Great Ormond Street Hospital Children's Charity
6	8	Marie Curie Cancer Care
7	6	British Heart Foundation
7	19	Royal British Legion
9	3	NSPCC
10	9	British Red Cross

The in-depth survey assessed 150 charities on a wide range of measures, including:

- recognition of the charity
- willingness to donate
- attitudes towards their cause
- trust
- effectiveness of media relations and advertising
- understanding of their work.

Edelman Trust Barometer

The Edelman Trust Barometer shows average trust in four major areas across nations: business, government, non-governmental organisations (NGOs) and the media. As might be expected, there has been quite a dent made in these ratings over the last 3 years due to the global financial crisis, the reverberations of which are still being felt. In 2011 the US fell to fourth from the bottom, while 3 years ago it was in the top four. The UK ranks second from the bottom, jointly with Russia and ahead of Ireland. Trust in business in the UK was rated as 44 per cent.

> Trust in business in the UK was rated as 44 per cent.

The difficulty with these low rankings, according to Edelman, is that when an organisation is distrusted (less than 50 per cent support) the public will believe a negative story about it after hearing it only once or twice. Similarly, if a trust score is low then people need to hear a positive story several times before it is believed. This reflects the issue of aggregate or average reputation, as discussed in Chapter 1. Unlike many of the financially driven methods previously mentioned, Edelman rates financial performance at the bottom of 10 measures it uses to gauge corporate reputation.

Quelch *et al.* (2004) says that non-profits are under-utilising the public's high levels of trust in them. This would appear to be backed up by the findings of Edelman. The 2011 report finds that, globally, NGOs, which include non-profits and third-sector organisations, have a 61 per cent level of trust compared with 56 per cent for business, 52 per cent for government and 49 per cent for media institutions. This is perhaps further evidence of the need for branding in the third sector and the very solid base that it can be built from.

> Non-profit organisations are under-utilising the public's high levels of trust in them.

Chapter summary

In order to consolidate your understanding of the measurement of corporate brands, here are the key points summarised against each of the learning objectives.

1. Consider what brands are worth and how they are measured

Brands by nature have a large element of intangibility and this makes measuring them a difficult prospect. The reservoir of future earnings that can be relied upon based upon the asset of the brand itself is the focal point of brand measurement. There is debate about whether brand measurement is more of an art than a science. The introduction of the ISO 10688 standard is an attempt to normalise brand measurement.

2. Assess the importance of brand equity and brand resonance

Brand equity refers to the marketing benefits and outcomes that accrue to a product due to its brand name compared with those that would accrue if the same product did not have the brand name. Brand equity should lead to increased market share, price premiums, customer recognition and positive brand associations.

The dimensions of brand equity are awareness, associations, perceived quality and loyalty, leading to the uniqueness of the brand. Brand equity is made up of a combination of rational and emotional reactions from the consumer. The culmination of positive rational and emotional associations is brand resonance and this will foster the intense and active loyalty that brings brand equity for the company.

3. Evaluate the various methods used to measure corporate brands

There are a variety of branding consultancies that measure global brands producing top 100 lists of brands by value. Interbrand and Millward Brown's BrandZ are probably the best known. A financial value, the role that the brand plays and brand strength coalesce to form an overall value of the brand.

The difficulties in measuring brands can be seen in the discrepancies between the brands and the financial value attributed to these brands in the two lists. The Interbrand list has Coca-Cola at number one, whereas BrandZ has Google at the top with Coke coming in fifth.

We can, of course, resist the financial valuation of corporate brands and instead attempt to measure their brand personality or corporate character.

4. Consider the importance of corporate branding and reputation in the third sector

Some of our best service brands are non-profit, or third-sector, brands. The third sector is a term applied to NGOs which are value-driven and which principally reinvest their surpluses to further social, environmental or cultural objectives. Vital public services are often provided by third-sector organisations, e.g. medical research.

Of course third-sector organisations compete for scarce resources, e.g. donations, in the same way that commercial brands compete for customers' share of wallet. The branding literature finds that much branding activity is transferable to the non-profit sector. Although not resulting in financial profit, the criteria for assessing brand equity are just as appropriate for the third sector.

The values that led to the creation of the third-sector organisation are a clear focal point around which the employees can bond and therefore the direction of the brand should be clear and unambiguous. Branding will help recruit donors, employees and board members together with fostering positive associations.

5. Consider the problems of branding in the third sector

Third-sector organisations face particular problems not encountered to the same extent in the commercial world. There may be a distrust of branding and a lack of budget for it amongst many non-profits. They may also have to disguise in some way the monies that they do spend on branding activities in order not to alienate supporters.

Relying on a large volunteer workforce rather than paid employees can cause difficulties in managing the consistency of the brand. The true target of branding may not be as obvious and the need to satisfy multiple and diverse stakeholder groups can be complex for management. Customer orientation and identification are particular problems in the third sector. However, these problems are reasons why such organisations should perhaps concentrate more efforts on branding activity rather than less.

6. Provide details of methods of measuring third sector corporate brands

Although financial measurement of brands in the non-profit sector may not be appropriate, it is still attempted, certainly in the US. The UK consultancy Interbrand also values non-profit brands, aiming to measure the extra money generated by the organisation that is attributable to the success of its brand, across its various audiences.

The Charity Brand Index is a recent innovation and produces a list of the UK's top charity brands. Third-sector brands should also measure their brand personalities, as there could be scope for leveraging their positive personality traits. Such brands are likely to have a higher level of trust invested in them than commercial brands, an asset that is often under-utilised by the sector.

Discussion questions

1. It is said that brands are more important than the products or services they produce. Why is this?

2. ISO 10688 is a standard benchmark of a brand valuation process. What are its strengths and weaknesses?

3. What are the dimensions of the brand equity concept?

4. Compare and contrast the methodologies used by Interbrand and BrandZ to value brands.

5. Brand personality is an alternative method of measuring brands. What other 'projective techniques' allow us to measure brands?

6. Choose a not-for-profit organisation. What is it about this organisation that allows us to think of it as a brand?

7. Clear objectives and values can assist the creation of a third-sector brand. However, what are the difficulties of creating a brand in this sector?

8. Universities are examples of third-sector brands. How may universities measure their brand value?

9. Certain members of staff in third-sector organisations reject the idea that they should consider themselves as brands because it is overly commercial. How would you persuade them that they should embrace branding?

10. What are the advantages and disadvantages of using brand personality over a valuation method (e.g. Interbrand) when measuring brands?

References

Aaker, D.A. (1996). *Building Strong Brands*. New York: The Free Press.

Aaker, J.L. (1997). Dimensions of brand personality. *Journal of Marketing Research* 34, 347–356.

Adamson, A.P. (2006). *Brand Simple: How the Best Brands Keep it Simple and Succeed*. New York: Palgrave Macmillan.

Davies, G., Chun, R., da Silva, R.V. & Roper, S. (2001). The personification metaphor as a measurement approach for corporate reputation. *Corporate Reputation Review* 4(2), 113–127.

Davies, G. & Chun, R. (2003). The use of metaphor in the exploration of the brand concept. *Journal of Marketing Management* 19(1–2), 45–71.

Ewing, M.T. & Napoli, J. (2005). Developing and validating a multidimensional non-profit brand orientation scale. *Journal of Business Research* 58(6), 841–853.

Haigh, D. (2010). A new ISO standard on brand valuation? Online: http://www.businessreview europe.eu/blogs/economics/new-iso-standard-brand-valuation. Accessed: 26 January 2011.

Haigh, D. & Gilbert, S. (2005). Valuing not-for-profit and charity brands – real insight or just smoke and mirrors. *International Journal of Non-profit Volunteer Sector* 10(2), 107–119.

Hanby, T. (1999). Brands – dead or alive? Qualitative research for the 21st century: the changing perceptions of brands. *Journal of the Market Research Society* 41(1), 1–8.

Hatch, M.J. & Schultz, M. (2008). *Taking Brand Initiative: How Companies Can Align Strategy, Culture and Identity through Corporate Branding*. San Francisco: Jossey-Bass.

Hankinson, P. (2001). Brand orientation in the Top 500 fundraising charities in the UK. *Journal of Product & Brand Management* 10(6), 346–360.

Jaskyte, K. (2004). Transformational leadership, organisational culture, and innovativeness in non-profit organizations. *Non-profit Management & Leadership* 15(2), 153–165.

Keller, K.L. (1993). Conceptualizing, measuring, and managing customer-based brand equity. *Journal of Marketing*, 57(January), 1–22.

King, S. (1973) *Developing New Brands*. London: Pitman.

Laidler-Kylander, N., Quelch, J.A. & Simonion, B.L. (2007). Building and valuing global brands in the non-profit sector. *Non-profit Management and Leadership* 17(3), 253–277.

Martineau, P. (1958). The personality of the retail store. *Harvard Business Review* 36, 47–55.

Meijer, M. (2009). The effects of charity reputation on charitable giving. *Corporate Reputation Review* 12(1), 33–42.

Quelch, J., Austin, J.E. & Laidler-Kylander, N. (2004). Mining gold in not-for-profit brands. *Harvard Business Review* 82(4), 24.

Sargeant, A. & Woodliffe, L. (2007). Building donor loyalty: the antecedents and role of commitment in the context of charity giving. *Journal of Nonprofits & Public Sector Marketing* 18(2), 47.

Schultz, M., Antorini, Y.M. & Csaba, F.F. (2005). *Corporate Branding: Purpose/People/Process: Towards a Second Wave of Corporate Branding*. Køge: Copenhagen Business School Press.

Tapp, A. (1996). Charity brands: a qualitative study of current practice. *Journal of Non-profit and Voluntary Sector Marketing* 1(4), 327–336.

Chapter 8
The future for brands

We have discussed successful, and not so successful brands and the link between brands and corporate reputation. For the brands that want to be at the top of people's minds for reputation it is often not sufficient to be successful. So ingrained are brands now in every walk of life that it is expected that brands put something back into the communities and societies from which they earn their profits.

Brands must succeed in the face of fierce criticism and the anti-branding movement. Corporate brands must face up to many new challenges and be agile enough to take advantage of opportunities as they arise.

Aims and learning objectives

The aim of this chapter is to consider how brands may develop in the future.

The learning objectives of this chapter are to:

1. Consider those brands that have succeeded in developing a positive all-round reputation
2. Think about brands that do good for society as well as for themselves
3. Investigate wider definitions of corporate brands, e.g. celebrity brands, country brands
4. Consider the crucial importance of authenticity for a brand
5. Discuss the importance of brand communities
6. Consider the anti-branding movement and difficulty of managing brands in the 21st century
7. Summarise thoughts on the future of branding.

Brands with a comprehensive reputation

In the face of the challenges and issues facing brands, newer and more unusual forms of corporate brand have come to the fore and these are the subject of this chapter.

As discussed previously, brands are now more than the mere utility that products and services provide. Consumers are often left to differentiate between brands based upon the symbolic meanings rather than a brand's functional attributes. Undoubtedly there is a close relationship between corporate reputation and corporate branding. In Chapter 2 we outlined the criteria upon which the corporate reputation of a brand could be judged. These criteria – credibility, trustworthiness, reliability and responsibility – are shown graphically again in Figure 8.1.

> Customers often differentiate between brands based upon the symbolic meanings rather than a brand's functional attributes.

In many cases a corporate brand is likely to have a single strong competence or excel at one particular area and this can be the basis on which its reputation is built. However, in rarer cases, it may be possible for the brand to enjoy a positive overall or comprehensive reputation. An example of a brand that has risen to become the third largest retailer in the world exemplifies overall reputation. Tesco may be regarded as the ultimate corporate brand, a standing which necessitates its examination when discussing corporate reputation (see Viewpoint 8.1).

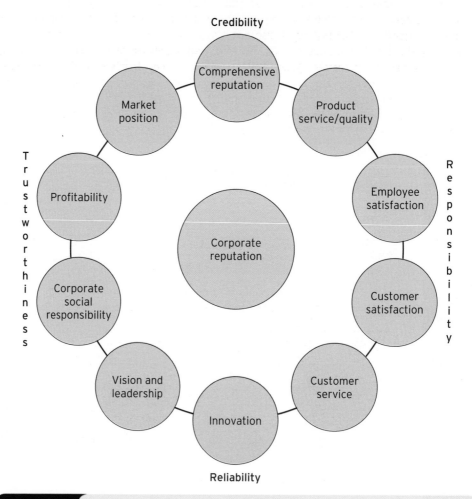

| **Figure 8.1** | Criteria that influence corporate reputation. |

Viewpoint 8.1   Every little helps Tesco's reputation

Tesco's profitability and market share figures make for impressive reading: with global annual profits exceeding £3 billion, it is the world's third largest retailer. Across all categories, over £1 in every £7 (14.3 per cent) of UK retail sales is spent at Tesco. The company is the UK's largest private sector employer (second in total after the NHS) and employs over 460,000 people worldwide.

Jack Cohen founded Tesco in 1919 when he began to sell surplus groceries from a stall in the East End of London (www.tescocorporate.com). The Tesco brand first appeared in 1924. During the 1950s and the 1960s, Tesco grew organically, but also through acquisitions, until it owned more than 800 stores. Under the leadership of managing director Ian MacLaurin, Tesco jettisoned the 'pile it high sell it cheap' ethos of Cohen which had left the company 'stagnating' having gained a 'bad image' (interview with Ian MacLaurin, 1998).

Throughout the 1990s, it rigorously pursued market development, both at home and abroad, and product development as it moved away from being just a food retailer and into profitable non-food items such as consumer electronics, clothing, entertainment, telecommunications (including mobile and fixed line) and an increasing range of financial services. Its place as number one in the UK market was cemented by the successful launch of its Clubcard loyalty scheme in 1995. The success of this marketing innovation not only usurped rival J. Sainsbury as the UK's leading retailer but provided the company with the personal details of some 15 million active members from which it has been able to grow its business further.

Tesco appeals to all segments of the market. One layer of this strategy has been Tesco's use of its own-brand products, including the upmarket 'Finest', mid-range Tesco brand and low-price 'Value'. It is testament to the Tesco corporate brand that its own-label products are trusted to the same extent as top fast-moving consumer goods (FMCG) brands. It also has a suitable retail store for every possible shopping occasion, including the traditional supermarket, the enlarged supermarket format (known as hypermarkets), the reduced supermarket format (Tesco Metro which were constructed for the high street), neighbourhood convenience stores (Tesco Express) and 'One Stop' newsagent-style shops. Tesco has become the local corner shop to many, a convenience store as well as a supermarket.

Tesco has embraced corporate social responsibility (CSR) with numerous outstanding initiatives, most notably a scheme that donated £92 million worth of technological equipment to schools up until 2004.

Exhibit 8.1   Tesco environment project in South Korea.
Source: Tesco Stores Ltd, with permission.

National and local charities are supported. In terms of its charitable contributions, in 2006, 1.87 per cent of its pre-tax profits went to charities/local community organisations. It has a clear commitment to sustainable retailing, opening carbon neutral stores, committing to a 30 per cent reduction in the carbon footprint of its products by 2010 and aiming to become carbon-neutral by 2050.

Tesco's market development has been nothing short of sensational. It has over 4,800 stores operating in 14 different countries. Tesco's international expansion strategy has recognised the absolute necessity of being attuned to local expectations in other countries by establishing joint ventures with local partners, such as Samsung Group in South Korea and Charoen Pokphand in Thailand (Tesco Lotus), and employing a high percentage of local personnel to fill management roles.

Question

To what extent does having a good reputation in one country help a company like Tesco to move into overseas markets?

Source: Various, including www.tescoplc.com.

The Tesco example demonstrates clearly the true value of the corporate brand and a strong reputation. That is, the confidence that people place in the name is such that people now bank and take out insurance policies (including car, travel, life, home and pet) with the company. With the collapse in faith of the mainstream clearing banks following the financial crisis, Tesco is seeking to move into mainstream retail banking. It will use its Clubcard data to identify its most likely customers. Customer decisions to adopt the Tesco bank will be based to a large extent on the transfer of brand values from the established retailer to the prospective banker.

Brands that do good

As already emphasised, the focal point of a brand should be its values and value system. For non-profit brands, doing good work for the community or other worthy cause may be the *raison d'être* of the organisation. Of course, commercial brands are there to declare profits, but that does not mean that they cannot combine this with 'doing good'. The best corporate brands are able to leverage their values to ensure that this is the case.

The focal point of a brand should be its values and value system.

At the extreme end of the 'doing good' continuum, for example, would be food company Newman's Own. The company was founded by the late actor Paul Newman in 1982. The actor and the Newman's Own Foundation donate all profits and royalties earned after taxes. All told, Newman has given more than $200 million to various charities of his choosing since 1982. Products include all-natural salad dressing, pasta sauce, salsa, lemonade and steak sauce. This may be an extreme case but it can help to influence mainstream brands with which we are all familiar. For example, since March 2003, McDonald's has offered Newman's Own all-natural dressings with its salads.

The Red brand was created in 2006 by rock star Bono and politician Bobby Shriver to raise awareness and money for the Global Fund to Fight AIDS, Tuberculosis and Malaria in Africa. Companies that are marketing their own specific line of Red products include Gap (clothing and bags), Apple (iPod), Motorola (Motorazr), Emporio Armani (sunglasses, watches, clothing), Converse (trainers) and American Express (credit card).

The companies plan to sell Red products for 5 years and donate up to 50 per cent of their profits from these specific Red lines to the Global Fund to provide AIDS medications in Africa. For example, American Express launched its no-fee 'red' Amex card in the UK only and promised that at least 1 per cent of every pound spent will go to the global fund. The benefit here is that corporate marketing budgets are much bigger than those of philanthropic organisations and the aim is that 'conscientious commerce will reward both our shareholders and the global community', according to John Hayes, American Express chief marketing officer (BBC, 2011).

In Chapter 7 we discussed brand equity and the importance of reaching the top of the pyramid whereby the brand has resonance for the consumer. The relationships of brands to good causes and humanitarianism, as discussed here, can help to provide the resonance required. In the wake of the financial crisis, there is clearly a movement amongst consumers and indeed a demand that more is required from companies than merely providing high profits for themselves and shareholders.

It is also a sign of the increasing importance of brands in our lives that contemporary consumers look to brands to help solve global problems and also to soothe our consciences. The gap between the public and private sector has been eroded to the extent that many areas that used to be funded by taxpayers are now being funded by commercial brands. Is this part of the 'collective consciousness', a term coined by the French sociologist Émile Durkheim (1893) to refer to the shared beliefs and moral attitudes which operate as a unifying force within society?

> **Consumers look to brands to help solve global problems.**

> **Many areas that used to be funded by taxpayers are now being funded by commercial brands.**

On the subject of solving global problems, 'One Water' would be another example of a new form of corporate brand. All profits from 'One' go to funding clean water, nutrition and sanitation solutions in Africa. This is interesting as bottled water is a product that is often criticised as being symptomatic of the excessive consumption of the western world. Despite having a clean source of tap water, consumption of bottled water in the west has risen enormously using vast amounts of natural resources to provide consumers with something they already have. The One Foundation has so far raised £5 million and provided over 600 water solutions in Africa that have benefited over 1 million people. As a charity brand 'One' also promise not to engage in some of the practices that have led to donor fatigue, such as rattling tins or asking for direct debit contributions. This is a good example of the new breed of corporate brands.

Viewpoint 8.2 provides an example of a commercial brand, Innocent, that was started by three young entrepreneurs who adopted a more socially aware approach to business than was experienced previously.

Viewpoint 8.2 Unorthodox yet Innocent

Innocent's history is rather delightful. It came to fruition (pun intended) when three close university friends, who have since been described as hippies with calculators, moved on from organising college events to selling smoothies at a weekend London music festival and asked customers to vote as to whether they thought the three should quit their jobs to make smoothies.

After a resounding 'yes' vote, they obtained funding for their business and now sell over two million smoothies per week. The sense of fun engendered by this most modern of brands is emphasised by their attempts to be different and non-corporate. Marketing communications are light-hearted and irreverent.

Innocent drinks focus strongly on the composition of their product, emphasising the basic equation that a good product is manufactured from simple, nutritious and wholesome ingredients. The company prides itself on natural drinks produced from exclusively natural ingredients. The word natural is critical to the company, since the products comprise only fruit and vegetables with no additives or refined ingredients. These facts are also inferred by the brand name, which conjures up images of a medley of healthy items. Their vision remains 'to be Europe's favourite little juice company' (Richard Reed), a realistic goal given Innocent's 75.4 per cent domination of the £169 million UK smoothie market and status as number 1 smoothie company in Europe, which cements its position as market leader with a high level of profitability.

Innocent, through its insistence upon natural ingredients (no chemicals, preservatives or stabilisers), have definitely tapped into the recent health boom of the 21st century (one smoothie accounts for two of

Exhibit 8.2	Innocent is a good example of the new breed of corporate brands. Seen here is one of their Dancing Grass Vans.
	Source: Innocent Ltd, with permission.

the five fruit and vegetable portions in the recommended daily quota). There remains a certain kudos attached to carrying an Innocent bottle, since it conveys the image of a person who is diligent about his/her food choice and is also environmentally friendly.

The company fervently believes in the principle that a contented workforce is more inclined to remain a motivated and enthusiastic part of their company. One idea that originated from a staff member surrounded by the entrepreneurial work environment promoted at Fruit Towers in Shepherds Bush was the 'Big Knit', the campaign that helps old people stay warm in winter by raising money through the sales of smoothie bottles wearing little woolly hats. Over the past 8 years, the Big Knit has raised hundreds of thousands of pounds for Age UK.

An employee benefit trust comprising 10 per cent of the company stock, shares profits with everyone who works at Innocent for longer than a year. They boast the market's first and only 100 per cent recyclable plastic bottle which composts within 6 weeks, a feat they are looking to emulate for the packaging of their veggie pot product.

Interestingly, the consistency of plastic has declined over the years, which has resulted in tinting some of the lighter smoothies and making them look less appetising. Consequently the company has temporarily reduced the plastic content to a more manageable 35 per cent. They are working with their suppliers to produce cleaner grades of plastic so that Innocent can increase the recycled content once again.

In terms of the corporation's CSR, Innocent set up the 'innocent foundation' which receives 10 per cent of its annual profits in order to invest money into worthwhile causes. These causes ordinarily consist of non-governmental organisations (NGOs) and overseas projects whence Innocent sources its fruits. Their website proclaims, 'We sure aren't perfect but we're trying to do the right thing.' Since 2006, Innocent's revenue has increased from £76 million to a projected £172 million for 2011, showing that a brand can be both non-corporate in nature yet financially successful.

Question

Coca-Cola recently bought a £30 million stake in Innocent. What might the impact of this move have on Innocent's reputation?

New types of corporate brand

The rise of the service industry and the explosion of the internet have emphasised the importance of corporate rather than product branding. New forms of corporate brand have been introduced by the availability of new channels. The lesson here concerns the speed with which a brand can be built. Twenty-five years ago branding experts would have said that there was only one way to build a successful brand: through advertising, and particularly television advertising. Now a brand can be built through word-of-mouth. With one click we can pass on information to our entire address book via email or to all our friends on Facebook. Less than 10 years ago it didn't exist but Facebook has risen to become one of the great brands of the internet age (see Viewpoint 8.3).

> New forms of corporate brand have been introduced.

Viewpoint 8.3 | Face-to-face through Facebook

Facebook has arguably made the greatest impact of all in terms of virtual communication. It is a social networking site where users can add friends, send them messages, store and exchange photos, log posts and update their personal profile. Users can join and create groups that adhere to their own areas of interest. They can also update friends on their movements and activities. Facebook now claims over 600 million users worldwide, a staggering figure considering the site was only launched in 2004. Anyone aged 13 or over is eligible to join up.

The original idea for Facebook came from founder Mark Zuckerberg's school (Exeter College), which produced the Exeter facebook, a book of profiles of students, to allow new pupils to, quickly, become familiar with their peers. The website was initially launched for students at Harvard University, half of all Harvard students joining within a month of the launch, then taking in other universities in the vicinity before expanding to high schools and then rapidly to what we have today – the premier social networking site in the world.

Zuckerberg has already declined several substantial takeover bids from contemporary online giants such as Yahoo! (who bid $1 billion in 2006) and Google, as well as fending off keen interest from Microsoft. Zuckerberg fervently maintains that social networks cannot be monetised in the same way as search engines. He cites his original ideal, specifically to create a network that could unite people the world over, as his prime motive for retaining Facebook, with money a subsidiary factor. This is not to say the site is averse to generating revenue. It is in partnership with Microsoft, which provides banner advertising, Facebook's main source of revenue. There is much debate amongst media insiders about the effectiveness of advertising on Facebook, as it has a much lower click-through rate than other sites, e.g. Google.

The staggering exponential rise of online brands is underscored by the statistic that, during the autumn of 2007, 200,000 new subscribers per day were signing up for Facebook. The brand is not restricted to a single demographic; it has been adopted by consumers of all ages and nationalities. As a result, Facebook has developed well beyond the parameters of a conventional social network. It has also attracted businesses, which use the site to communicate on a more informal basis with consumers of their own brands. This is achieved when individuals sign up as fans of a particular brand, and receive information from the company direct to their own page; the site also acts as a tool/forum to advertise a multitude of matters, including jobs and events.

Facebook employs nearly 2,000 people in 12 countries and is estimated to have generated $2 billion in revenues in 2010. It is a 21st-century corporate brand par excellence.

Question

What difficulties may online brands face that are not encountered by traditional corporate brands?

New types of brand – celebrity brands

A newer area encompassed by the framework of corporate branding is celebrity branding and reputation management. The first decade of the 21st century saw the unprecedented rise of celebrity culture. The preponderance of modern-day luminaries insist on owning their own image rights, fully aware of the potential financial gain to be had. Many public personalities also establish independent websites, using them as a forum to afford direct contact with their fans. This also allows them to comment on information that may have been published about them in the media.

Footballers used to be, first and foremost, representatives of their club, with the club remaining the overriding priority. But with dramatically inflated wages and unprecedented global exposure, the players themselves have rapidly become the focal points of football clubs, entities in their own right. It can be no surprise, then, that modern-day contract negotiation revolves primarily around the likes of image rights and shirt sales.

If you are a household name, then your image and name have a value, in the same way that a brand name like Coca-Cola or Nike has value. The idea of image rights is that household names have control over how their image is used and exploited commercially. The image of the sports star no longer belongs to their club but to the individual sportsperson. This is in recognition of the fact that the individual has now also become a brand. Arguably, the king of celebrity brands is David Beckham, and Minicase 2.1 at the end of this chapter (p. 204), explores the dynamics and path taken by the lad from East London to global brand status (see also Viewpoint 8.4 on the 'athlete corporation' that is basketball star LeBron James).

The individual has now also become a brand.

A development of this idea of celebrity brands is the concept of Athlete Corporations.

Viewpoint 8.4 — Basket case or just an excellent reputation?

US basketball star LeBron James was the first pick in the 2003 NBA draft, aged only 18, joining the Cleveland Cavaliers. Prior to making his professional basketball debut, he had already signed a $90 million 7-year contract with Nike. Such is the competitive nature of the sports endorsement industry that brands such as Nike are prepared to gamble huge amounts on the potential of future stars.

James petitioned the NBA in an attempt to join the draft (the method by which the professional clubs select players) in 2002 despite its eligibility rules, which at the time required prospective players to have at least completed high school, and preferably university. The bid was unsuccessful; however, the resulting national publicity got the James brand well under way. Several of James' high school games were shown live on national television in the US.

James is a star member of a new breed of sportsmen and women labelled 'athlete corporations'. He was named by *Businessweek* magazine (October 2008) as the 17th most important person in the global sports business; in a list that predominantly comprises club owners, administrators and media moguls, he is the foremost enumerated athlete after Tiger Woods. *Forbes* signals that his endorsements (a host of multi-million-dollar deals with Nike, Coca-Cola, State Farm and MSN) comfortably outstrip his on-court earnings, even taking into account his $60 million 4-year playing deal with the Cleveland Cavaliers.

Fred Nance, LeBron's legal representative, conveys the distinct impression that James's brand image is a carefully crafted entity. He consciously selects products to endorse that befit his own personality traits and strengths in order that the vision of both corporation and athlete are synchronised. Every year James holds a marketing summit that assembles all his endorsement clients, allowing him to maintain a solid rapport with his commercial partners. Nevertheless, corporations are aware that sporting success and impeccable reputations are not necessarily linked. Hence, even with shining lights like James, sponsors

Exhibit 8.3 LeBron James, right, is one of a new breed of 'athlete corporations'.
Source: © 2011 NBAE; photo by Joe Murphy/NBAE via Getty Images.

aim to protect their investment by incorporating disincentive clauses into contracts that centre on sub-standard sporting performance or off-court misdemeanours.

Nance provides an insight into the key attributes that James represents: 'Cool, hip, hard-working – LeBron puts a positive spin on the hip-hop generation, away from the bad-boy scene.' These are the essential qualities embodied by James, the qualities in which corporations willingly and enthusiastically invest.

James has also enhanced his reputation in other ways: by donating $20,000 to Barack Obama's election campaign, actively encouraging young people to take an interest in politics; by hiring his childhood friends to represent his brand; and by establishing a foundation for single parents and inner-city children (The LeBron James Family Foundation) to which each of James's endorsement partners contribute.

However, there is a reputational lesson here. His contract with Cleveland expired in 2010 and a live television programme was scheduled during which James announced which team he would join next. Considered by many to be egotistical and narcissistic, the resulting bad feeling has led to a drop in James's position in the rankings of sports stars from number 2 (behind Tiger Woods) to number 11 in 2011.

Question

How do the reputations of playing stars and their clubs interlink with each other?

Source: Various, including *Businessweek* magazine.

Celebrities are a commonly used and often powerful means of promoting products. According to social anthropologist Grant McCracken's (1989) 'meaning transfer model', celebrity endorsers effectively imbue products with the personality and lifestyle meanings that the celebrities have cultivated during

> Celebrity endorsers imbue products with personality and lifestyle meanings.

their careers. However, celebrities are humans and humans are fallible, and this straightforward equation signifies that celebrity endorsers are not without risk. Keller (2008) notes five potential problems:

- The celebrity package (i.e. reputation and lifestyle) may not resonate with the product's personality and image.
- Celebrities may endorse an abundance of products, reducing their worth as an endorser.
- The celebrity may outshine (in performance and/or stature) the product, with the celebrity being more memorable than the product.
- Consumers may be cynical as to the celebrity's ulterior motives for endorsing a brand.
- Celebrities are only human and are thus liable to lapses in judgment. Allegations of impropriety, whether proven or not, can embarrass the brands associated with them.

Celebrity endorsements are an ever-growing industry, but there is an uncontrollable element that the brand manager needs to be both aware of and prepared for – it is unlikely, for example, that mangers of brands that have endorsement contracts with Wayne Rooney have been happy with much on his on- and off-field behaviour during 2011.

There should be a strong connection between the celebrity and the brand.

Critics complain that the use of celebrity endorsers is sheer laziness on the part of brands. Certainly, we feel that there should be a strong connection between the celebrity and the brand that is being endorsed in order to have the most positive effect.

Authenticity and the brand

The power of the reputation of a brand can be demonstrated by its longevity. A brand may even disappear but leave behind a repository of goodwill that allows it to be revived at some future date. Brands from yesteryear are sometimes reintroduced into the market in a modern guise that is tailored to accommodate contemporary requirements or preferences. Retro brands possess a symbolic permanence, and perhaps most significantly from a marketing perspective, retro products have an important provenance – they help to perpetuate the stories that have contributed to the brand's reputation. This is the essence of strong branding. The brand has a meaningful story to tell and a resonance in the mind of the stakeholder. Viewpoint 4.2 on page 84 about Adidas provides some insight into this concept.

Retro brands possess a symbolic permanence.

The brand has a meaningful story to tell and a resonance in the mind of the stakeholder.

It is difficult to put a finger on why there is such a demand for retro brands. Clearly there are many middle-aged people now in influential positions who like the idea of reliving their childhoods. Aligned to this is perhaps the security that old brands bring, harking back to a more stable time (which in reality may never have existed) in this current age of economic and social uncertainty. This phenomenon is visible across the cultural landscape. It is one of the reasons, for example, behind the recent plethora of films about comic-book heroes such as *Iron Man*, *The Fantastic Four* and *Captain America*.

The retro brand is often updated to modern standards, e.g. in terms of the manufacturing materials. This results in a brand with the classic appeal of yesteryear but featuring contemporary characteristics that seek to satisfy the more demanding present-day consumer. Naturally the internet provides opportunities for ideas to circulate and for brand communities to form, which can culminate in demanding the re-introduction of favourite brands from the past. Brown *et al.* (2003) provide the four As of retro branding: allegory (brand story), aura (brand essence), arcadia (idealised community) and antinomy (brand paradox) (see Figure 8.2).

| **Figure 8.2** | Dimensions of a retro brand. |
| | Source: Brown et al. (2003). |

These authors reinforce the idea that a retro brand includes an update of the product to contemporary standards of performance. This updating of performance distinguishes the retro brand from the 'nostalgia brand'.

Related to this is the concept of authenticity, an area in which brand managers need to demonstrate competence and transparency. Occupying a clear position within the life of its users and within an appropriate subculture is often the difference between a successful brand and ephemeral brand success. Invariably, authenticity is a prominent factor among strong brands and its values resonate with consumers of different generations.

> **Authenticity is a prominent factor among strong brands.**

The paradox is that the brand's sense of authenticity does not actually have to be based upon reality. As long as the brand resonates as authentic with its stakeholders then it can succeed. Still, in an overcrowded marketplace consumers are looking for a clear meaning and sincerity from their brands. Linked to the clear need for a strong value system, authenticity is about the brand practising what it preaches. Elements of originality are important here. For example, Levi's manufactured the first pair of jeans in 1873 and this heritage is very important to the continued success of the brand. Consider the idea of brand personality that was discussed in Chapter 7, i.e. the 'brand as person'.

> **Consumers are looking for a clear meaning and sincerity from their brands.**

We all know people who we consider are not genuine or authentic; similarly there are brands that give themselves away and betray their lack of dependability. The shallow brand is the one that we do not trust; it lacks substance and, to be frank, lies to us. The brand may, of course, change and adapt over the years and this is necessary and desirable; however, the brand promise should really remain unblemished and central to the stakeholders' experience.

The authentic brand is one that we can safely give our vote to, as outlined in Chapter 5.

New types of brand - country brands

Another important development in the expansion of corporate branding into new areas is that of 'place branding', which involves the branding of towns, regions or cities, and even countries. The branding of places allows them to compete for tourists, investment, migrating citizens, visitors, government support and sports and cultural events such as the Olympic Games. Place branding is used to provide an advantage in a market that is competing for scarce resources, in the same way that other market sectors also compete for business.

Place branding can be used to alter the perceptions of a specific target group.

Place branding can be used to alter the perceptions of a specific target group. Northern Ireland, for example, has been making great efforts in recent years to be recognised as a tourist destination with beautiful rolling countryside rather than a place of violence and conflict as it has been portrayed in the world's media for decades. Other areas best known to the wider public for conflict and tragedy, such as Vietnam and Cambodia, are also making efforts to reinvent themselves. One of the great difficulties with place marketing is agreeing amongst some very diverse groups what the core brand values of a place are. Lack of agreement on this issue can lead to difficulty in implementing a consistent communications plan.

Although it is difficult to identify the original example of place branding, the iconic 'I love New York' campaign from the 1970s often comes to mind. It undoubtedly helped to turn around New York's fortunes at one of the city's lowest points, and the campaign has had many imitators since then.

The development of place branding as a managerial and academic subject area is demonstrated by the increasing literature on the subject and the launch of specialist journals such as the *Journal of Place Management and Development*. The work of Simon Anholt has been very important to the subject's development. He produces the Anholt-GfK Roper Nation Brands Index (NBI), which measures the opinions of 1,000 consumers in 20 core countries in order to determine how countries are perceived by others. Table 8.1 sets out the measures used.

Table 8.1	Measured used to determine country perceptions
Measure	**Explanation**
People	Measures the population's reputation for competence, education, openness and friendliness and other qualities, as well as perceived levels of potential hostility and discrimination
Governance	Measures public opinion regarding the level of national government competency and fairness and describes individuals' beliefs about each country's government, as well as its perceived commitment to global issues such as democracy, justice, poverty and the environment
Exports	Determines the public's image of products and services from each country and the extent to which consumers proactively seek or avoid products from each country-of-origin
Tourism	Captures the level of interest in visiting a country and the draw of natural and man-made tourist attractions
Culture and heritage	Reveals global perceptions of each nation's heritage and appreciation for its contemporary culture, including film, music, art, sport and literature
Investment and immigration	Determines the power to attract people to live, work or study in each country and reveals how people perceive a country's economic and social situation

The United States took over first place in the Nations Brand Index from Germany in 2009, following the election of President Obama. It retained this position in 2010 from Germany in second place, France in third and the UK in fourth.

Brand communities

Corporate brands that are engaged with their stakeholders recognise the importance of the position the brand occupies in their lives. Does the company directly try to bring the brand into the lives of customers and other stakeholders? What does the brand look like through the eyes of stakeholders? A brand community can be an example of a deeper level of association among users of a brand, their relationship with other users and the company itself.

> A brand community can be an example of a deeper level of association.

Muniz & O'Guinn (2001) introduced the term 'brand communities', using it to describe the specialised and non-geographically bounded set of relationships that develop amongst admirers of a brand. Many of the aspects of human communities are displayed by brand communities such as Apple Mac aficionados and Harley-Davidson riders. Members feel a sense of togetherness, a connection with each other, a difference from others and an opposition to competitor brands (Muniz & O'Guinn, 2005). Members revel in an element of marginalisation which maintains cachet by keeping the membership of the community small and restricted. Muniz & O'Guinn show how consumers of a brand can create rituals and traditions and how they celebrate the stories that surround a brand.

Community members also feel a duty to protect what they consider to be the brand's sacred heritage. A code of ethics is another characteristic of the brand community. Members will not tolerate disloyalty to their brand. Monitoring and engaging with such brand communities can help brands to hold the line and ensure they are not sidetracked or tempted into areas that would lead to their rejection by supporters and damage to their reputation.

Brands can make use of the wider brand community to pass on messages in the form of viral campaigns. Posting videos on YouTube is one way of harnessing the brand community and calling it to action on behalf of the brand; the photography website Flickr is another online medium used by brands and their communities. There is an inherent danger, however, in trying to manage the brand community in this way and the brand needs to be very careful that it is not perceived as infiltrating or unduly influencing the community. So while it is a great opportunity to encourage customer-to-customer interaction, it is important not to be seen as trying to sell products to the brand community.

The brand community is a significant move away from the firm-centric model of brand management and it recognises two additional authors for the brand – consumers and cultures (Fournier *et al.*, 2009). Solomon tells us that a variety of cultural arbiters 'craft, clarify and sort meanings for the brand . . . including brand communities and subcultures, lifestyle and interest groups, media pundits, journalists and social critics, Hollywood producers, information gatekeepers and more'.

> The brand community is a significant move away from the firm-centric model of brand management.

The brand communities theme has been developed by other writers who talk of very close-knit communities as 'consumer tribes' (Cova, 2007; see also Viewpoint 8.5). The message to be taken from the concept of brand communities is that strong brands matter a great deal to the people who use them. They are far more than just products and services. They help people to make sense of and live their lives (Fournier, 1998).

> Strong brands matter a great deal to the people who use them.

| **Viewpoint 8.5** | What's the personality: Gates or Jobs? |

Apple is a pioneer in the area of technological products, its most notable products being computers, iPods and mobile phones. As a company, it exemplifies the phenomenon of 'consumer tribes'. It is a prime illustration of a company that is elevated in the mind of the consumer, whereby the brand assumes an exaggerated level of importance and its consumers become devotees. This devotion manifests itself in various fanatical

Exhibit 8.4   Apple's flagship store in New York City.
Source: Alamy Images/Patrick Batchelder.

acts, such as prolonged queuing outside flagship stores in anticipation of newly introduced products. Similarly, the opening of stores at midnight for new product launches seems to persuade rather than dissuade customers. Many customers do not have just one Apple product, but a whole suite of them, all linked together seamlessly to satisfy their work, leisure and entertainment needs.

Mike Solomon, a distinguished consumer behaviour academic who mainly writes on the meanings that underpin consumption, postulates that this type of purchase is inspired more by the symbolic value of the product and what it proclaims about the consumer than by the actual product itself and usage thereof. Apple thus found itself in a very powerful position, and they managed to appropriate such dedication by opening up exclusive Apple stores (as opposed to selling solely through department stores that had less knowledge about the products and had resellers' prerogative to undercut Apple prices). This moved Apple's focal point away from the less personal space of department stores to their own premises and consequently guaranteed that aficionados of the brand had the opportunity to interact with both the products and trained experts. Take a look at some of the pictures of flagship Apple stores on the web, such as the New York City store. Apple is a brand that inspires devotion in its customers.

There is a sizeable personality gulf between the two biggest IT powers – Apple and Microsoft. As a vibrant, youthful and exciting company, Apple's reputation and image may be directly juxtaposed with those of its closest IT market rival, Microsoft. The latter, whilst it also excels in the area of innovation (specifically software equipment), has a more monotonous, characterless reputation, that of a company that has traditionally prided itself on the efficient functionality of its products. The quandary herein is that AppleMac is also deemed to be highly practical, and is viewed by many as more straightforward to use than its equivalent Microsoft Windows format, thus also reducing the impact of Microsoft's USP.

Although they are competing head-on with each other, these are two brands with quite different brand personalities. Microsoft, acutely aware of its rather drab reputation, have recently released fresh advertising messages that have primarily focused on readdressing the balance in terms of its demographic quota of users. Whilst openly embracing the fact that a considerable portion of Windows users are suited business-types, the 'Life without walls' campaign also vividly demonstrates that 'cool people' and iconic household names (such as hip-hop artist Pharrell Williams) use Windows-ready PCs too.

Question

Compare and contrast the brand personalities of Apple and Microsoft.

The anti-branding movement

The complexity of managing corporate brands is demonstrated by the rise of the anti-branding movement. For many consumers, corporations have become too big and they often act in an uncompetitive manner. There is evidence to back up this claim. Many corporations behind the world's biggest brands are wealthier than many of the world's countries. The BrandZ valuation of Google at $114 billion, as detailed in Chapter 7, is higher than the GDP of all but four of the 52 countries on the African continent. It's a sobering thought.

> The world's biggest brands are wealthier than many of the world's countries.

Critics argue that the scale of this financial power is unhealthy, that it is the brands that have the real power in society, rather than the governments that supposedly run them. Unelected large corporations are calling the shots and not elected politicians. Of course, it has never been easier to come to such a conclusion than it is at the current time. We have discussed the banking crisis. The excesses of the banking industry contributed significantly to the swingeing cuts in public sector funding made by governments in many western countries. Meanwhile, the taxpayer-owned banks in the UK, for example, still award themselves large bonuses. Is this an example of the tail wagging the dog?

It is not just individuals who are critical. Groups of activists have banded together to become centres of investigative journalism, such as the research and publishing group Corporate Watch. The aims of this organisation, according to its website, are to 'strive for a society that is ecologically sustainable, democratic, equitable and non-exploitative. Progress towards such a society may, in part, be achieved through dismantling the vast economic and political power of corporations and developing ecologically and socially just alternatives to the present economic system.'

There is a feeling amongst many consumers that they are over-controlled, manipulated by brands and exposed to a bewildering number of marketing communications messages each day. The anti-branding movement is a backlash against such exploitation, power and manipulation. Added to this is the blurring of boundaries between the public and private sector. Thirty years ago there was a clear distinction but, faced by funding cuts, many organisations that were once free of com-

> The anti-branding movement is a backlash against exploitation, power and manipulation.

mercial influence have looked to the commercial sector to fill the gap. Children in schools can play in sports kit and equipment that is sponsored by McDonald's and use computers provided by Tesco; today's children are well used to seeing brand names in their schools (Watts, 2004).

This fusion of the public and private sectors leads to a malleable and overtly brand-focused new generation of consumers who see no problem in having clear links to the commercial world in every aspect of their lives, argue the brand critics. There have been cases of bullying in schools of children who do not have the 'correct brands' of training shoes (Elliot & Leonard, 2004). Roper & La Niece (2009) report that such bullying behaviour has even been related to not having the 'correct' brands of lunch snacks.

Commercialisation has overtaken every form of life. When Arsenal moved from Highbury stadium to The Emirates stadium, no-one batted an eyelid over the fact that the name of the new ground was sold to the highest bidder. What else would we expect in the brand-saturated, money-oriented world of (Barclays) Premier League football? The anti-branding lobby seethes, however.

> Commercialisation has overtaken every form of life.

The classic book by Naomi Klein, *No Logo: Taking Aim at the Brand Bullies*, detailed the rise of the mega-brands. Certainly, as set out in this book, major FMCG branding companies such as Procter & Gamble and Unilever have rationalised their brand portfolios, vastly reducing their range of brands in order to concentrate their efforts on the domination of key market segments. The chances of small companies breaking into these markets are therefore further reduced. Branding critics complain of such domination and refer to companies like Wal-Mart,

Starbucks or Toys 'R' Us as 'category killers', eliminating competition as they go along so that it ends up being a private monopoly, having forced smaller rivals to leave the industry.

There are many anti-branding websites in existence that target specific brands, such as www.ihatestarbucks.com or Facebook pages criticising McDonald's, while more general complaints may be addressed to www.pissedconsumer.com. Anti-consumerist organisation Adbusters (www.adbusters.org) demonstrate their fiercely anti-brand credentials by going as far as producing spoof adverts subverting and mocking the genuine message that has been put forward by the brand.

> There are many anti-branding websites in existence.

Countering the anti-brand messages

It could be argued that many of the criticisms outlined in the previous section are valid and that many brands do deserve to be criticised. If there is a large gap between what the brand promises and what it delivers then this is particularly true. It is, of course, convenient to blame brands for the evils of the world, but we should remind ourselves at this point that the majority of new brands fail – it is not that easy to take over the world.

> Many brands do deserve to be criticised.

Certain brands overtly present themselves as anti-corporate, such as Body Shop and Rainforest Café. Brands may also present themselves and their communications in an irreverent, edgy and ironic fashion, often poking fun at themselves in order to be at one with the ordinary consumer. Avoiding mainstream advertising and communicating via viral campaigns is another strategy used by brands seeking to avoid the anti-branding lobby. Brown (2006) talks of 'ambi-brands'. Ambi brand culture refers to the ambiguities that are present within postmodern branding. Brown discusses ironic brands and Machiavellian 'straight to the point' brands to emphasise the complexities of brand culture. Ryanair (discussed in Viewpoint 1.1, p. 12) is a great example of this ambivalent, non-corporate approach to branding. Ironically, in this game of bluff and double bluff, some of the world's most successful brands are those that claim to reject branding as an acceptable managerial practice.

> Some of the world's most successful brands are those that claim to reject branding as an acceptable managerial practice.

The key message for brands looking to offset criticisms of the anti-branding lobby is not to over-promise to consumers. It is also clear that brands must now be looked at as having a social value and not just the economic value that has always been the goal of the brand manager. As stated in this chapter, brands need to ensure that they are giving something back to society and not merely exploiting it. This takes us back to the issue of values, dealt with in Chapter 6. The successful brand will be trusted and able to demonstrate a clear set of values that not only differentiate it but also provide a flag around which the employees and other stakeholders can rally. The brand must stand for something. Such brands can actually enhance people's lives and provide the social value that ensures companies avoid the scrutiny of the anti-branding movement.

> The brand must stand for something.

Do we need to love brands?

There is much discussion amongst branding experts about the progression of brands to 'lovemarks'. A lovemark, it is said, transcends a brand, delivering beyond consumers' levels of expectations. According to www.lovemarks.com, such brands reach the heart as well as the mind, creating an intimate emotional connection that consumers can't live without. Respect is at the core of the relationship with the lovemark; it is then infused with three intangible ingredients: mystery, sensuality and intimacy.

The lovemarks matrix comprises four quadrants based upon two axes, love and respect. The four quadrants are labelled as follows:

Products: In the bottom left corner feature low love and low respect. Commodity items may fall into this undesired quadrant such as milk or eggs. Farmers have consistently bemoaned the low prices they are able to command from the supermarkets for their milk. This is largely because it seen as an undifferentiated commodity by both the business and consumer markets.

Fads: Lie in the bottom right hand side and feature high love but low respect. A short if glorious life may await the fad. Perhaps the must-have children's toy each Christmas or the latest winner of the talent contests X Factor or American Idol.

Brands: Make up the top left hand side of the matrix and feature low love but high respect. Highly successful brands such as Microsoft may fall into this category. In fact the majority of brands could be said to do so. We may need them but we don't love them.

Lovemarks: Are at the top right hand side of the matrix and represent the pinnacle of the matrix and the matrix places lovemarks at a level above brands in the hierarchy. There is no question that certain brands are loved by consumers, such as Harley-Davidson and Apple. The lovemarks website's own list of brands reaching this exalted level is esoteric to say the least. In addition to well-known brand names, it also features people prominently. Celebrity brands and athlete corporations have already been discussed in this chapter; bizarrely, however, the lovemarks list also features people such as country singer John Denver and Pope John Paul II.

For the majority of corporate brands, we would not recommend going down the lovemark route. Is it realistic that people should love your brand? It is perhaps precisely this raising of expectations that has led to the problems outlined in the section on anti-branding. We would direct brands to consider and espouse an honest value system in order to maximise their prospects for success.

> Is it realistic that people should love your brand?

The future of branding

So, where does all this leave us? We are living in an age of brands and branding and it is inconceivable that this will change in the foreseeable future. The brand, and in particular the corporate brand, will be the central principle around which everything, internally and externally, revolves.

We have discussed not-for-profit brands and it is clear that such brands will play a much more central part in the future development of branding practice. This will include NGOs as the world's population searches for the solutions to problems that will impact upon us all. Bearing this in mind, purely financial measures of success will no longer be sufficient. Much broader social measures will be necessary, and this does not mean merely the filing of a CSR report as part of the annual financial statement.

> Financial measures of success will no longer be sufficient.

The anti-branding lobby is a challenge to organisations, but whilst brands are often attacked in the west, in developing countries they are seen as a great opportunity to develop businesses both at home and overseas. China Mobile is one of the world's most powerful brands, and it is a warning to western brands that it has reached this status whilst only trading in its home market. Similarly, customers in developing countries, such as the all-important BRIC economies (the fast-growing countries of Brazil, Russia, India and China), are ready to place their trust in established brands, and tailoring offerings for these economies is crucial to western corporate brands faced with ageing populations and stagnant population growth in their home markets.

The internet continues to expand and offer new possibilities for organisations. It is important to remember that it is only in its early stages and that, to a large extent, its development is being held back by telecommunications companies and their reluctance to provide us with a full fibre-optic network. The internet as a medium also demonstrates how quickly powerful global brands can be created. How many of us had heard of Google 10 years ago? Now it is one of the world's top brands – and notably it has achieved this feat without the traditional use of advertising and marketing communications.

Product parity means that it is fairly straightforward for even innovative products to be copied quickly. Consumers also expect products to perform at a level of functionality and quality that are appropriate. Brands must therefore continue to innovate to survive and it will more likely be the service aspects of their offering, the relationship and crucially the emotional appeal of the corporate brand that will make the difference between sustained success and failure. The trust engendered in the corporate brand will ensure that it is trusted in multiple categories.

Newer forms of corporate brand have been discussed in this chapter and it is expected that place branding and people brands will continue to be key areas. There are also clear opportunities to develop in areas such as health and lifestyle, entertainment (particularly experience-based entertainment) and services. The growth of the sports industry is an example of this. With issues such as climate change and global terrorism very much to the fore, security is also a key area for development. There is still too much emphasis on youth and youth culture in the western world despite a clearly ageing demographic profile. Surely there is a branding opportunity in filling this gap? The internet and, of course, information will be key areas, as will opportunities presented by biotechnology. Macro-issues such as sustainability and the move towards carbon-neutral production and retailing will have a clear effect upon brand management.

> Sustainability and the move towards carbon-neutral production and retailing will have a clear effect upon brand management.

Certainly the old established form of brand management, where consumers are considered to be passive individuals who can be manipulated by a brand manager, will not be prominent in the future. There is great power in participation and stakeholders will want to play a bigger role in the co-creation and development of brands. Harnessing this power can create a huge advantage. This is not limited to internet-based brands such as Twitter that have been rapidly built on customer participation. Consider the development of the AppStore by Apple: businesses large and small as well as individual users can contribute applications that enhance the use of the Apple iPhone brand. This surely is an example of a brand community in action.

Chapter summary

In order to consolidate your understanding of the future for brands, here are the key points summarised against each of the learning objectives.

1. Consider those brands that have succeeded in developing a positive all-round reputation

There are various criteria that can be used to judge the reputation of a brand. It is the objective of many organisations to obtain a strong overall reputation, although few companies achieve this. A strong overall reputation will mean a strong corporate brand. This overall reputation will allow the brand to move from one area of expertise to another.

2. Think about brands that do good for society as well as for themselves

It is no longer enough that brands do well for themselves. Their importance in modern society means that they are expected to do good as well. New forms of corporate brand like One Water ensure all their profits go to good causes. Major brands have made efforts to do work that helps to solve world problems. This is all part of consumers expecting more of their brands.

There is a collective consciousness being displayed here and an element of partnership that has previously not been present. This is forging a much closer link between brand, consumer and society in general.

3. Investigate wider definitions of corporate brands e.g. celebrity brands, country brands

It is no longer sufficient to think of brands in term of product manufacturers and traditional FMCGs. Newer forms of corporate brands include place branding – the branding of towns, regions, cities and even countries – which aims to provide an advantage in a market that is competing for scarce resources in the same way that other market sectors compete for business.

Another key area here is the development of celebrity brands and 'athlete corporations'. Celebrity culture and the cult of the individual combine to ensure that many sports stars now brand themselves as separate entities, rather than firstly members of the team for which they play.

The growth in the service industry and the internet continue to provide opportunities for newer forms of corporate brand to come to the fore.

4. Consider the crucial importance of authenticity for a brand

The importance of brand values has been covered in previous chapters. Aligned to this (and in a difficult environment for brands) it is crucial that a brand is considered authentic in order that it commands respect. This level of authenticity can allow old brands to be revived in the future. The authentic nature of the brand promise that underpins the offer allows this to happen.

5. Discuss the importance of brand communities

The importance of brands in society is reflected by the attention that is paid to stakeholders. It is no longer sufficient for the brand to have a one-directional approach towards its customers. Instead the brand is often co-created with its stakeholders, through the phenomenon of brand communities.

In brand communities, users of the brand feel a common bond that transcends national boundaries. Members feel a sense of togetherness, a connection with each other, a difference from others and an opposition to competitor brands. It is important that brands do not try to control such groups as this would mitigate the element of stakeholder co-creation of the brand.

6. To consider the anti-branding movement and difficulty of managing brands in the 21st century

It is a difficult time for brand management. Brands bear the brunt of much of the anti-corporate, anti-capitalist sentiment that is at the fore. A criticism of the size and power of corporations has helped lead us to this state. People consider the modern world to be over-commercialised, with commercial brands penetrating areas that were previously free of any form of branding activity, e.g. education and healthcare.

Many brands have not helped themselves in this area. Not over-promising to consumers and realising that brands have a social as well as an economic value can help to offset some of the criticisms of the anti-branding lobby.

7. Summarise thoughts on the future of branding

Branding will continue to be of key importance; in fact the corporate brand will be the central focus of business around which all other elements will revolve. Purely financial measures of success will no longer be sufficient and the social importance of brands will be crucial, in particular brands' responsibility to society.

It is the relationship and the emotional elements of brands that will prove difficult for rivals to imitate and these areas are where the competitive advantage for companies will lie.

Discussion questions

1. Provide examples of three brands that could be said to have a comprehensive reputation.

2. Why do consumers now expect brands to do good rather than simply make profits?

3. What are the reasons behind the comeback of the retro brand? Illustrate your answer by using examples.

4. A brand must possess authenticity. Make notes on the concept of authenticity in relation to brands.

5. Place branding has become a growth area. Provide examples of a town or regional place brand, a city brand and a country brand. Outline the branding strategies of these places in each case.

6. Should brand communities be managed by the brand or should they be left entirely to their own devices?

7. Why has the anti-branding movement come to prominence? Is it justified in its criticisms of brands?

8. Should brands aim to be lovemarks? Justify your perspective.

9. What is your own opinion on how brands will develop in the future?

10. Conduct some research into the Red brand and consider the impact it has had.

References

BBC (2011). Bono bets on Red to battle Aids. Online: http://news.bbc.co.uk/1/hi/business/4650024.stm. Accessed: 3 February 2011.

Brown, S. (2006). Ambi-brand culture: on a wing and a swear with Ryanair. In: Schroeder, J. & Salzer-Morling, M., eds. *Brand Culture*. Oxford: Routledge.

Brown, S., Kozinets, R.V. & Sherry, J.F. (2003). Teaching old brands new tricks: retro branding and the revival of brand meaning. *Journal of Marketing* 67 (July), 19–33.

Cova, B. (1997). Community and consumption: towards a definition of the 'linking value' of product and services. *European Journal of Marketing* 31(3), 297–316.

Durkheim, E. (1893). *The Division of Labor in Society* (translated by Lewis A. Coser). New York: Free Press, 1997.

Elliott, R. & Leonard, C. (2004). Peer pressure and poverty: exploring fashion brands and consumption symbolism among children of the 'British poor'. *Journal of Consumer Behaviour* 13(4), 347–359.

Fournier, S. (1998). Consumers and their brands: developing relationship theory in consumer research. *Journal of Consumer Research* 24 (March), 343–373.

Fournier, S.G., Solomon, M.R., & Englis, B.G. (2009). Brand resonance. In: Schmitt, B.H. & Rogers, D.L. eds. *Handbook on Brand and Experience Management*. Cheltenham, UK; Northampton, MA, USA: Edward Elgar.

Keller, K.L. (2008). *Strategic Brand Management: Building, Measuring, and Managing Brand Equity*, 3rd edn. New Jersey: Prentice Hall.

McCracken, G. (1989). Who is the celebrity endorser? Cultural foundations of the endorsement process. *Journal of Consumer Research* 16(3), 310–321.

Muniz, A.M. & O'Guinn, T.C. (2001). Brand community. *Journal of Consumer Research* 27 (March), 412–432.

Muniz, A.M. & O'Guinn, T.C. (2005). Marketing communications in a world of consumption and brand communities. In: Kimmel, A.J., ed. *Marketing Communication: New Approaches, Technologies and Styles*. Oxford: Oxford University Press.

Roper, S. & La Niece, C. (2009). The importance of brands in the lunch-box choices of low-income British school-children. *Journal of Consumer Behaviour* 8(2–3), 84–99.

Watts, L. (2004). The acceptable face of brands in schools. *Young Consumers* 6(1), 44–49.

Minicases for Part 2

The following minicases are designed to help readers consider some of the issues explored in this part of the book. The questions that follow each case should be attempted and outline answers can be found on the supporting website.

Minicase 2.1 — David Beckham – the individual as a corporate brand

Jonathan Shrager

Countless articles have been written on David Beckham's construction of his own brand. The subject even has a book devoted to it: '*Brand It Like Beckham: The Story of How Brand Beckham was Built*' (Milligan, 2010). His philanthropic endeavour in the construction of various soccer schools globally can only serve to enhance his reputation. The advent of Beckham mania (as it has been labelled by the English press) has engendered a clear awareness amongst celebrities that they themselves can become a brand name.

The signing of David Beckham by Real Madrid from Manchester United in 2003 was commonly perceived as a loss more in terms of his off-field financial benefit to United (in the form of shirt sales, attraction of worldwide support, general publicity) than in terms of his not inconsiderable on-field contribution and presence. The statistics support this verdict, as Beckham helped to facilitate Real Madrid's overtaking of Manchester United as the world's richest football club and leading brand in 2006 (a standing held for 3 years between 2006 and 2008). Manchester United reassumed the mantle in 2009 (*Forbes*, April 2009) following Beckham's transfer to the LA Galaxy in 2007, again accentuating the clout of Brand Beckham.

Indeed, Beckham's off-field earning power proved a decisive factor in his £24.5 million transfer to Real Madrid from Manchester United in 2003. The intense rivalry that exists between the two clubs to reign victorious in the Champions League is paralleled only by their endeavour to capitalise upon the commercial potential of the growing Asian football market. Real Madrid's policy of annually purchasing a 'galáctico' (literally translated as superstar) is as much a commercial as a football imperative.

Beckham's footballing ability has been exceptional yet it is still arguably eclipsed by his capacity to sell replica kit. His 'metrosexual' image is in vogue in Asia, a continent in which Beckham generates a quarter of his endorsement earnings. Beckham has built his own brand in several stages. First and foremost, his celebrity was dependent upon his success as a sportsman, establishing himself as a United and England regular and winning numerous trophies and personal accolades. Secondly, he dated then married a celebrity contemporary (Victoria Adams of the Spice Girls) which acted as a catalyst to cement his own fame, increase exposure and facilitate and accelerate his transition onto the celebrity scene by positioning him at the heady pinnacle of sport, music and fashion. Notably the media were kept away from the Beckhams' wedding so as not to contravene an exclusive agreement to sell pictures of the event to celebrity publication *OK!* magazine. Godparents for the couple's children include Elton John and Elizabeth Hurley. No occasion is spared the opportunity for publicity and brand reinforcement. Naturally the Beckhams were high-profile guests at the marriage of Prince William in April 2011.

With his dashing good looks, successful career and global exposure, Beckham became the obvious choice for a handful of top brands to endorse their products (including Gillette, Police, Brylcreem, Marks & Spencer, Armani, Vodafone, Pepsi and Adidas), rendering him the highest earner from endorsements in football. Beckham earned £40 million alone for a 3-year deal with Gillette.

The next phase in brand-building was for Beckham to launch his own products into the market, marking a clear progression from external to personal endorsements. Beckham has increasingly focused on his own ventures by attaching his name to products, having founded a soccer academy in his native East London (and later in Los Angeles) and introduced a Beckham line of male fragrances. He is currently working on his own line of underwear and grooming products, signalling his unstoppable conversion from footballer to brand name.

Posh (the epithet attached to wife Victoria) was acutely aware of the branding potential of her husband, having been part of the 'girl power' concept, the light-hearted post-feminist sentiment upon which the Spice Girls' success rested. Victoria's foresight has paid vast dividends, with David, even as a seasoned football veteran at the ripe age of 36, still the top earner in world football, earning £24 million in 2010 (of which approximately 80 per cent was accumulated from off-field ventures). Note that this easily out-earned Lionel Messi, currently regarded as the best footballer in the world.

Beckham has effectively imitated the achievements of Fred Perry and Jean-René Lacoste (although on a hugely different financial plane), the notable sports figures who successfully pioneered the transformation from the traditional European sports star into a global brand. Beckham's move to the United States with LA Galaxy has further developed and expanded the markets for his brand. This again reinforces the position of Beckham as a brand rather than a sportsman. The move to LA, whilst a downgrade in football terms, was, in branding terms, a foothold in a new (and wealthy) continent and therefore a clear case of market development. The move provided Beckham with the opportunity to consolidate his brand name in an unconquered territory. Of course, Beverly Hills was the natural place for the family to choose to live.

There is an entire media industry based around Beckham. As an example, the *Guardian* newspaper's website has a section devoted to Beckham-related stories in the same way that it has a section for each Premier League club. The CSR angle of the Beckham brand is dealt with via his work as a goodwill ambassador for UNICEF together with other charitable work. The true international exposure of the Beckham brand would please the brand valuation team at Interbrand. It is claimed that 'Beckham' is the second most recognised foreign word in Japan (next to Coca-Cola).

As famous for his hairstyles and tattoos as his football, the search engine Ask Jeeves announced that David Beckham was the third most popular online search for the first decade of the 21st century. David Beckham is an incredible story of present-day corporate branding and he represents a brand that analysts have estimated make him the 36th highest earning sportsperson on earth despite no longer playing in one of the most important leagues (forbes.com).

Questions

1. What does the rise of celebrity brands tell us about the development of branding?

2. Create a diagram that outlines the brand architecture of the Beckham brand.

Reference

Milligan, A. (2010) *Brand It Like Beckham: The Story of How Brand Beckham was Built*. Marshall Cavendish.

Minicase 2.2   Warburtons – a brand built on family values

Dr Chris Raddats, University of Liverpool

Warburtons is a family-owned bakery based in Bolton, England, whose origins stretch back to the 19th century when Thomas Warburton started selling bread from his grocery shop in 1876. Since this time the company has grown by opening new bakeries and buying smaller rivals to become the UK's largest branded baker. To this day the company is still run by the Warburton family, with the ethos of the 'family bakers' important both for running the business and for the company's brand identity. According to Nielsen Data, Warburtons is the UK's second biggest grocery brand (the largest independent baking business) and is the main choice for consumers when it comes to buying bread and other bakery products.

The Warburton brand has been built on the tenet of authenticity, since the company's products have always been branded with the family name. This strong link to the Warburton name means that the family members who run the company emphasise the quality of the ingredients they use and the products they produce, with this akin to a personal guarantee. Equally, Warburtons do not make own-label bread for retailers so this quality is only available through Warburtons' branded products. The Warburton brand has an unrivalled heritage in the industry, since the family has only ever been involved in baking, with this exclusive focus in contrast to the company's main rivals whose baking businesses form part of larger ▶

groups selling non-bakery foods and even non-food products.

The Warburtons brand has to appeal to different audiences, all of which play an important role in supporting the idea of 'family bakers'. Of these the three most important are customers, shoppers and consumers. Warburtons' customers are the retailers (e.g. supermarkets) that sell their products, with the brand appeal centred on a commitment to product quality based on the company's singular focus on baking. This is supported by exemplary customer service (e.g. reliable product deliveries) and strong interpersonal relationships between senior executives at Warburtons and the major supermarkets. Warburtons' products compete with competitors' branded bakery products as well as supermarket own-label alternatives, so providing customers with compelling reasons to stock their product lines is a critical part of the company's strategy, with Warburtons' strong brand identity a major reason why they do this.

Shoppers (who buy the products in the retailers) represent the second important audience, with brand appeal based on family values and the idea of doing what is best for one's family. Warburtons' brand appeal for consumers (people who consume the products) involves an appreciation of the taste and freshness of the bread and other bakery products. Innovation also helps to maintain consumers' belief that Warburtons' products are differentiated, with new products such as 'square(ish) wraps' developing a strong market position. New product development takes account of consumers' desire for a healthier lifestyle, with a range of 'Weightwatchers' and wholemeal loaves, and also addresses new markets such as consumers who are seeking gluten-free/wheat-free bakery products.

Warburtons' employees play a critical role in maintaining the idea of the 'family bakers', with the company preserving this notion through a set of five core values, the first of which is 'family values' whereby employees work together as one 'family' and learn from each other. Potential new recruits to the company are encouraged to 'join our family', the metaphor being used to provide an association with a corporate culture in which everyone is working towards the same goal of creating and supplying quality products. The leadership of the company by the Warburton family also provides a symbolic association with the company's heritage. By owning and managing the business, Warburton family members can demonstrate to employees that they are 'living the brand' by genuinely taking account of employee interests when making decisions about the company, something non-family-owned businesses with outside shareholders to satisfy may struggle to do.

The company's advertising supports the notion that employees are striving to live up to the ideals of product quality and the family and has played an important part in creating the company's strong brand image among shoppers and consumers. A number of other stakeholder groups are addressed under Warburtons' 'corporate responsibility' strategy, which aligns to the company's brand values by demonstrating that the company cares for the communities in which it works. As part of this strategy, Warburtons aims to become the UK's most sustainable bakery by minimising the environmental impact of its business through working with suppliers, reducing energy use, better managing waste and eliminating unnecessary packaging on its products. Supporting charitable causes that improve family life is also an important element of corporate responsibility with this emphasis linking back to the concept of the family within the corporate brand. Family is clearly takes first place in the brand's values, the others being ambition, responsibility, care and quality.

Warburtons use the strapline 'Britain's favourite bakers' to reinforce a brand that has grown from one historically associated with a small northern bakery to one which is the UK's brand of choice. The brand stands for authenticity, family values and a commitment to quality through a bread-making heritage unrivalled in the industry. In the future the Warburtons brand will be used to spearhead growth into new markets such as new product lines and possibly international expansion, although new developments will always need to be strongly linked to the idea of the family bakers.

Questions

1. Warburtons emphasises the authenticity and heritage of its corporate brand. How might companies that do not have this authenticity and heritage create corporate brands that can compete in this market?

2. What other family businesses can you think of that have successfully used their family name to create a strong brand? What are the advantages and disadvantages of using the family name as the corporate brand?

Part 3
Corporate communication

Chapters 9-12

The third and final part of the book is concerned with corporate communication, one of the core means by which all the building blocks of reputation are interlinked.

Chapter 9 introduces the nature and characteristics of corporate communication before discussing the characteristics, scope and reasons why organisations use corporate communication. Having explored some of the tasks and activities expected of corporate communication, the chapter closes with a discussion about integration and its potential to influence the centrality of organisational communication and its efficiency.

Chapter 10 starts with a consideration of the impact of corporate culture on corporate communication. This enables exploration of the issues concerning the communication of an organisation's positioning and objectives, including its vision and mission, and its communication climate. Perhaps the most important part of this chapter concerns the role and nature of the corporate identity mix. The chapter closes with a discussion about the ways in which organisations address ethical, corporate social responsibility and sustainability issues through their communications.

Chapter 11 commences with ideas about message framing. This enables readers to consider how organisations use visual identifiers to influence their reputation. This is followed by an examination of some of the key tools used in the name of corporate communication, namely corporate advertising, public relations and corporate sponsorship. The chapter closes with a view of the main media used in corporate communication.

Chapter 12 is the final chapter in Part 3 and the book. In it the principal methods used by organisations to communicate with specific corporate stakeholders are explored, i.e. investor relations, public affairs, employee relations, media relations, issues management and crisis communications. The chapter closes with an explanation of the principles of measuring the effectiveness of corporate communication.

Part 3 closes with two Minicases designed to help readers consider some of the issues about how branding and its management can be best understood.

Case 1   Marks & Spencer – 'Plan A' sustainability strategy

Case 2   Primark – defending a reputation with social media

Chapter 9
The dimensions of corporate communication

Interest in corporate communication has risen sharply in recent years. The reasons for this are varied and reflect a multitude of forces, some of which have already been explored in the context of the rise of reputation and corporate branding, in preceding parts of this book. However, it appears that through an understanding of the nature, role and dynamics of corporate communication, organisations open opportunities to develop their brands as well as their reputation.

Aims and learning objectives

The aim of this chapter is to consider the nature and characteristics of corporate communication and its role in developing corporate reputation.

The learning objectives of this chapter are to:

1. Examine the nature, role and strategic orientation of corporate communication
2. Discuss the characteristics and scope of corporate communication
3. Explore the reasons why organisations use corporate communication
4. Consider the different dimensions of corporate communication
5. Establish the tasks corporate communication is expected to accomplish
6. Consider the main activities associated with corporate communications in practice
7. Examine ideas associated with integrated corporate communication.

Introduction

The value of corporate communication, in terms of the management of corporate brands and corporate reputation, is well established (Rindova & Fombrun, 1999). Indeed, the core responsibility of corporate communication is to manage the way in which stakeholders perceive an organisation. To a large extent this is achieved by managing the identity cues used to deliver the brand and in doing so influence the way in which stakeholders perceive the organisation. However, the value of corporate communication should be seen not only in terms of the content conveyed, the responses stimulated or the frequency of communication, but also in terms of the assortment of issues that the organisation chooses to reveal about itself. The transparency with which an organisation communicates enables stakeholders to develop a deeper understanding of its operations, which in turn facilitates a better reputation (Fombrun & Rindova, 1998).

There is also a strong link with corporate strategy (Rumelt *et al.*, 1994). For example, we know that a strong reputation can lead to superior corporate performance, increasing share value by as much as 15 per cent. Also, as Wry *et al.* (2005) report, reputation is a major factor in organisations achieving their objectives (Hall, 1992; Kitchen & Laurence, 2003) as share valuations, market shares and ease of recruiting quality staff all improve as a result of a strong reputation. Of those who have investigated this area, some touch upon the role that corporate communication plays in developing information that is aligned with corporate strategy. For example, the use of corporate communication to generate interaction and dialogue with stakeholders in order to understand their interests is advocated by Varey & White (2000). This in turn can aid the development of long term relationships, itself an important aspect of corporate strategy.

> There is also a strong link between corporate communication and corporate strategy.

Yamauchi (2001) claims there is a close link because corporate communication involves determining, understanding and targeting stakeholders with particular forms of information and that stakeholder responses to communication activities can be used to help inform and develop management strategy. Burke (1998, p. 8) argues that as corporate communication can develop reputation, this in turn reduces an organisation's transaction costs, so assisting corporate strategy. It is well understood that employee communication is fundamentally important during periods of strategic change. Engaging employees and encouraging buy-in can be crucial when downsizing, during a merger, or following leadership or significant strategy change.

In order that corporate communication impacts positively on strategy, Forman & Argenti (2005) argue that it is important to align the corporate communication function with strategy implementation. This is to ensure that the CEO has overall responsibility through the reporting structure and because internal communications are of vital importance whilst focusing on brand and reputation. Finally, Rindova & Fombrun (1999) found that competitive advantage can be developed through corporate communication that influences the way stakeholders perceive the organisation. They also suggest that competitive advantage can be created by 'socialising its stakeholders to its own culture' and, through this, use communication strategy to form long-term relationships with the stakeholders who shape the organisation's image and reputation (see Viewpoint 9.1).

> It is important to align the corporate communication function with strategy implementation.

Viewpoint 9.1	**More than a Shell of corporate communication**

The multinational oil company Shell uses corporate communication to help manage its reputation. In the mid-1990s Shell was subjected to public and media criticism at two main levels. The first concerned suspicion about just how responsible and transparent Shell (and other multinational organisations) were with regard to their use of power and influence. The second concerned their attitude towards the environment, as demonstrated through their actions in relation to the dumping of Brent Spar and their reported behaviour

Exhibit 9.1	The evolution of Shell's logo over time.
	Source: Shell Brands International AG.

and attitudes towards the environment and local people in Nigeria with regard to the oil extraction and pumping facilities. As a result, and despite a strong financial performance, their reputation was weak in the later 1990s.

In order to correct these perceptions, Shell launched a corporate communication campaign. Initially targeted at opinion leaders who had global influence in each of the sectors in which Shell operated, the campaign was designed to demonstrate Shell's commitment to engage with audiences about a range of issues. Among these were statements about their responsibilities towards the environment, people and the principles and values which guided Shell's behaviour. This had never been done before and the communication served to change perceptions and open up the organisation in a way that had not been done before.

The campaign used stakeholder forums, direct contact, key staff workshops, direct marketing, media relations and corporate advertising. Key media included the main broadsheets, the *FT*, *The Economist*, *Time*, *Newsweek*, *National Geographic* and the *Harvard Business Review*. The press was supported by television advertising. A new publication was launched, *The Shell Report*. This charted Shell's progress and was sent to key influencers for comment. The www.shell.com website has been developed since then to provide information and act as a means of interaction with interested stakeholders. For example, *The Eureka* film available on YouTube, not only demonstrates through storytelling how innovative Shell are but also clarifies the values and principles that guide the firm, technically, environmentally and socially, as a good, responsible employer.

Question

To what extent should corporate communication be about providing information, changing perceptions and changing behaviour?

Source: Woods (2007); Kerr (2002); Oechsle & Henderson (2000); www.shell.com; www.communicatemagazine.co.uk/archive/78-october-2009/475-personal-ads; www.youtube.com/watch?v=Yq3CnqChrL4.

Reputation and strategy are interlinked and corporate communication has two primary roles. One of these is to influence the way stakeholders perceive an organisation and to shape the esteem in which the organisation is held, i.e. its reputation. The second is to use corporate communication to inform, influence and guide corporate strategy.

> **Reputation and strategy are interlinked and corporate communication has two primary roles.**

Establishing the scope of corporate communication

Exploring the scope of any subject can often be initiated by examining the definitions offered by scholars who have specialised in the topic. Several definitions are presented and considered here, spanning the period 1987–2007. Although there are several texts in which corporate communication makes a substantial contribution, the focus is often on reputation and branding activities. In these circumstances, corporate communication is not defined. The following definitions have been identified in corporate communication texts. These are not the only books and definitions on this subject but they are considered to be representative of some of the leading authors and researchers in this area.

> Corporate communication is the total communication activity generated by a company to achieve its planned objectives.
>
> (Jackson, 1987)

> The aggregate of sources, messages and media by which the corporation conveys its uniqueness or brand to its various audiences.
>
> (Gray, 1995, p. 254)

> Corporate communication is an instrument of management by means of which all consciously used forms of internal and external communication are harmonised as effectively and efficiently as possible, so as to create a favourable basis for relationships with groups upon which the company is dependent.
>
> (van Riel, 1995, p. 26).

> Corporate communication is the set of activities involved in managing and orchestrating all internal and external communications aimed at creating favourable starting points with stakeholders on which the company depends. Corporate communication consists of the dissemination of information by a variety of specialists and generalists in an organization, with the common goal of enhancing the organization's ability to retain its license to operate.
>
> (Riel van & Fombrun, 2007, p. 25).

In the two books in which van Riel offers his definitions, stress is given to the importance of using the singular form of communication, a position initiated by Jackson (1987). This, it is argued, emphasises the integrative function of communication rather than impling a proliferation of methods (p. 25). This stance is echoed by Cornelissen (2008):

> Corporate communication is a management function that offers a framework for the effective coordination of all internal and external communication with the overall purpose of establishing and maintaining favorable reputations with stakeholder groups upon which the organization is dependent.

Cornelissen acknowledges the complexity associated with corporate communication and he also stresses the importance of seeing corporate communication as an integrative function. Corporate communication is not the same as public relations and other specialised communication activities, such as branding, media relations and internal communications. Cornelissen regards corporate communication as a means of crossing over these specialist activities in order to 'harness the strategic interests of the organization at large' (2007, p. 6). This view is not shared with Lowensberg (2006, p. 253). He considers that the term corporate communication means the same as organisational public relations, and prefers the latter, as the word corporate can be misleading, and suggests an applicability to profit-only 'corporations'.

Apart from an increasing word count as definitions emerge, an examination reveals a gradual change in orientation. From what is essentially an inward perspective proposed by Jackson in 1987, Cornelissen's view 20 years later stresses the importance of the reputation with which the organisation is perceived by stakeholders. The organisation itself is perceived to be the self-serving focus for Jackson's perspective of corporate communication. For Cornelissen, the organisation conducts corporate communication in order to sustain a reputation and with a desire to remain subservient to the wishes of the key stakeholders.

> The reputation with which the organisation is perceived by stakeholders is important.

Reasons to use corporate communication

It could be argued that examining the reasons why organisations use corporate communication is a pointless activity. All organisations communicate something about who they are, so the issue is about why some organisations take more interest and assign more resources to corporate communication than others. Table 9.1 sets out some of the principal categories concerning the use of corporate communication. It can be seen that corporate communication should be considered a strategic stakeholder activity.

> Corporate communication should be considered a strategic stakeholder activity.

Corporate communication is used to influence the way stakeholders perceive an organisation. Their perception of an organisation's various formal and informal identity cues shapes the image they form of that organisation. Therefore, the image they form is based largely on the identity the organisation presents to them. Corporate communication is concerned with presenting an organisation, in ways that management determine, so that stakeholders recognise, understand, like and interact with it in ways that are important to them.

Table 9.1	Principal categories for the use of corporate communication
Strategic category	**Examples**
Strategic events	To stabilise after merger and acquisition Chronic underperformance Change of leadership Change of strategy Environment or industry upheaval Crisis and disaster
Strategic development	To build a corporate brand To develop the corporate reputation To influence stakeholder groups, e.g. the public, investors, government, competitors, customers To communicate corporate strategy To (re)position an organisation To provide co-ordination and integration
Strategic maintenance	To monitor the environment To manage stakeholder perceptions, attitudes and behaviour To keep stakeholders informed about and engaged with organisational activities, developments and policies To engage employees to improve stakeholder interactions To support products and services To build and sustain relationships with key stakeholders

Organisations use corporate communication strategically to reduce stakeholder uncertainty and to develop stakeholder relationships. Through the development of positive relationships where there is understanding, trust, reciprocity and collaboration, participant organisations are better placed to achieve their goals, whether they are normative (e.g. social contracts, environmental responsibilities, community acceptance) or instrumental (e.g. profit, sales, return on investment, performance). Where there are neutral or negative relationships, or a gulf between identity and image, corporate communication has to work harder to narrow the gap. Viewpoint 9.2 shows how SAS used corporate communication to help change the way staff engaged with the organisation following a period of significant strategic uncertainty.

> Organisations use corporate communication strategically to reduce stakeholder uncertainty and to develop stakeholder relationships.

Viewpoint 9.2   Using photographs to impel strategic change

Scandinavian Airline Systems (SAS) experienced a turbulent period as they tried to adjust to the competitive conditions associated with a deregulated market. The organisation had been restructured in each of the previous 4 years, acquired new companies, repeatedly introduced new working practices, open/closed new destinations, implemented two rounds of employee dismissals, introduced salary cuts and failed to communicate anything purposeful or constructive.

Against this background the Crew Planning and Control department (CPC) embarked on a process of strategic change. The goal was to improve morale by understanding the belief systems and so develop a set of values created and owned by the employees. To do this they used photography plus drawing, collage and pottery and postcard exercises to encourage employees to tell stories about the organisation from their perspective.

Through interpretation of the employees' creative work it was possible to appreciate how they saw the organisation, what was of value and what wasn't. This created a new context, a new positive environment in which employees were encouraged to own the values by which they undertook their task in the organisation. This is seen as a radically different approach to the more common management imposed values.

Exhibit 9.2   SAS came up with a creative strategy to help their change process.
Source: Courtesy of SAS.

Question

To what extent might individual blogging enable expression of corporate values? Under what circumstances might this approach be more appropriate?

Source: Based on Langer & Thorup (2006).

Corporate communication provides opportunities to create and sustain competitive advantage (Balmer & Gray, 1999). It provides a point of distinctiveness which when harnessed appropriately enables strong, sustainable positioning.

A study by Gabbioneta *et al.* (2007) reveals the potential strength of corporate communication. They examined the criteria used by security analysts when recommending share trading initiatives. Previous studies have found that analysts use four main dimensions of reputation when evaluating a company: financial performance, vision and leadership, financial disclosure and corporate governance. Analysts are considered to be rational decision-makers, whose evaluation of prospective risk and return is underpinned by elaborating a range of information from a variety of sources. This study found that, although these factors may be positive, analysts' decisions are more likely to be driven by emotion, their overall feelings towards a company rather than their formal, rational evaluation. In other words, the extent to which an analyst trusts, likes, admires and respects a company has a significant and direct impact on his or her recommendations.

> An analyst's decision is more likely to be driven by emotion.

The implications for an organisation's corporate communication, and its investor relations in particular, are that providing information about financial performance and corporate intentions alone is not sufficient. Messages concerning an organisation's involvement with indirect performance activities are just as important when investors consider buy/sell opportunities. Therefore corporate communication in all its forms should reflect the richness of an organisation and all of its activities and this requires the use of emotional as well as rational messages.

> Corporate communication in all its forms should reflect the richness of an organisation and all its activities.

Dimensions of corporate communication

Corporate communication is a collective expression that embraces a variety of communication methods. van Riel & Fombrun (2007) identify three different broad types of communication, all of which are task-related: management communications, marketing communications and organisational communications. However, the border between marketing and organisational communication has become increasing blurred in recent years. We believe corporate communication embraces all the different forms of communications intended to influence specific audiences who have a potential to strategically influence an organisation. The focus of corporate communication is the organisation itself, not its products, services or ancillary elements. However, its role is to engage stakeholder audiences, internally and externally, by providing a core linkage. This linkage enables the character of the organisation to be transformed into an identity, it shapes and defines the brand and helps frame the way the organisation is perceived by stakeholders, namely its image. Increasingly, corporate communication should enable stakeholders to interact with an organisation and provide the basis for dialogue and relationships to develop. We will now consider each of these three elements of corporate communication.

> The focus of corporate communication is the organisation itself.

Management communications

Managers communicate externally and internally. Their role in relation to external stakeholders is one of representation and negotiation and in doing so they seek to communicate the vision and values of the organisation. In addition to this, the CEO has a specific role, one of symbolic leadership. The CEO's views, actions and comments are often regarded by the media and financial markets as particularly significant. For example, Stuart Rose, the former CEO of Marks & Spencer, regularly appeared in the media for one of two main reasons. The first of these was to answer questions and provide contextual information about his company's performance; in doing so he fulfilled the role of strategic leader. The second reason was either to provide an expert commentary on events in the retail industry or to make an executive speech. In both these circumstances, it was intended that the CEO was perceived as an expert, providing objectivity and credibility, which would help to raise his status. These attributes may have enhanced the perception stakeholders' had of Stuart Rose in terms of his trustworthiness and reliability, which in turn may have been transferred to the company.

External management communications are not confined to senior managers, as all managers who have an external-facing element to their job communicate with stakeholders, who form images of the organisation as a result of what is said, how it is said and the impact it has on others.

Perhaps the greatest impact of management communications is with employees, the internal stakeholders. One of management's key tasks is to enable employees to accomplish the firm's corporate objectives. To do this, management needs to agree on and then use communications to reinforce corporate values in such a way that they have meaning for employees, who in turn are prepared to work to satisfy them. Communication is an instrumental skill for managers, not only to develop a shared vision but also to strengthen the level of engagement employees have with the organisation. Internal communication issues are explored in more detail in Chapter 12.

Apart from everyday company maintenance, management communications are important at critical points in an organisation's evolution. One of these critical points occurs when an organisation experiences substantial change. Management needs to communicate prior to, during and after a restructuring and downsizing exercise (Carbery & Garavan, 2005). Management communications can reduce levels of uncertainty during the change process, enable employees to take greater control over their personal circumstances (Bordia *et al.*, 2004) and speed the return to a new form of stability.

> Management needs to communicate prior to, during and after a restructuring and downsizing exercise.

Marketing communications

Marketing communications is an audience-centred activity whose role is to engage an organisation's customers with its products, services and brands (Fill, 2009). To accomplish this, organisations use the various tools, media and messages that constitute the marketing communications mix: advertising, sales promotion, direct marketing, personal selling and marketing public relations. The range of media is expanding, with increasing emphasis being given by organisations to digital and online media in particular. The messages used to influence audiences constitute a balance between the need to provide information and the need to develop brand values through the use of emotional messages. The way in which the mix is configured varies according to the nature of the prevailing customer relationship, the task to be achieved and other contextual issues.

Organisational communications

Organisational communications is the term given to embrace a range of public relations activities, including public affairs, investor relations, corporate advertising, environmental and sustainability communications and media relations. What is common to these communications activities is that they are targeted at corporate audiences rather than individual consumers. They centre on corporate issues not products and services and they are generally focused on seeking agreement, acceptance and the development of relationships.

> Organisational communications embrace a range of public relations activities.

In many companies organisational communications are managed through the external affairs department. Some activities may be outsourced to specialist organisations but there is some discussion about what, whether and how organisations can develop integrated communications. This, in turn, provokes debate about centralisation, restructuring, costs and investment, a topic that is explored in Chapter 10.

This particular typology needs to be considered in the light of work by Balmer & Gray (1999). They suggest that the corporate communication mix consists of the following:

- **Primary communications** are derived from a composite of the effects or experience of consuming products and services, management, employee and corporate behaviour.
- **Secondary communications** emerge through the use of planned communications, essentially marketing communications, corporate advertising, sponsorship and promotion.
- **Tertiary communications** relate to the communication activity present among stakeholders and relevant networks. Here word of mouth, media commentary and community-based communications prevail.

What this interpretation recognises is the potentially rich communication generated through word of mouth and third-party channels, about the organisation. Media commentary and observations, industry and stakeholder references to the organisation in reports and market and investment analyses, and customer-to-customer comment all reflect the complexity of corporate communication. Viewpoint 9.3 considers the rebranding undertaken by RSA using different aspects of corporate communication.

Viewpoint 9.3	Rebranding the Royal & Sun Alliance

The Royal & Sun Alliance operates in 28 countries and provides insurance services in 130, using 48 brands. The company was formed by a merger in the 1990s and by stringing the two company names together a corporate name was produced that was too hard to pronounce, understand or place on a business card (Barda, 2009). The decision to rebrand was kick-started with events called 'world cafés'. These were intended to enable all employees across the globe to comment on the company as it was then. From this the brand proposition 'Keeping you moving' emerged. This was intended to reflect what the company does for its customers and to differentiate it from major competitors.

At the same time a strategic decision was being taken regarding the brand strategy. The decision was to present Royal & Sun Alliance in one of three main ways. The first option was to use a branded house strategy, using the Royal & Sun Alliance as the core brand and subsuming the product brands and giving them little, if any, individual identity (as is the case with General Electric). The second was to go in the opposite direction and create a 'house of brands'. Here the product brands stand on their own feet, have strong individual identities, and communications are not used to create ties with the parent company (as is the case with Royal Bank of Scotland). The third option, the one that was selected, was to use the company as an endorsement for its brands, in much the same way as Santander supported Abbey, the Alliance & Leicester and the Bradford & Bingley UK brands when it first acquired them, although it has subsequently reverted to a branded house strategy.

The company name was shortened to a punchy RSA and the company colours were changed to magenta and purple. The new brand identity was shared with the top 100 leaders in the RSA business before being disseminated to all employees through 256 presentations in 21 different languages across the world on the same day. A film demonstrating the meaning behind the slogan 'Keeping you moving' was shown at the presentations.

RSA explained the reasons for the change, what the business was to stand for and how it was intended to be positioned as a premium brand, and demonstrated how employees were to behave in support of the rebranding.

All websites and communication materials were updated with the new visual cues and staff members were given handbooks and workshops to help them understand the brand values and how they were to be delivered.

Question

What is the main focus of RSA's communications and how does it equate with both van Riel's and Balmer & Gray's typologies of corporate communication?

Source: Based on Barda (2008).

The roles and tasks of corporate communication

At a broad level the role of corporate communication is to engage stakeholders in order that they develop an overall positive disposition towards the organisation. Through time, consistency of

The role of corporate communication is to engage stakeholders.

communication, and the repetition of favourable images, stakeholders attribute a reputation to the organisation.

Dowling (2006, p. 83) refers to three particular roles of corporate communication, but in essence these are tasks. The first refers to 'externally directed communication which is designed to raise awareness and generate understanding and appreciation of the organization among key stakeholder groups'. This is distinctly reminiscent of a previous UK definition of public relations, until it was changed to focus on relationships. The second task is 'to defend or explain a company's (potentially controversial) actions'. The third task concerns internal communication and its involvement in explaining, reinforcing and refreshing the mission, values and beliefs of the organisation. This expression of the tasks of corporate communication is helpful because it highlights the external and internal dimensions and also signals the different outcomes that can be expected. However, these tasks might be deemed too broad and a more focused interpretation is required.

The activities or tasks that corporate communications are expected to accomplish can be considered at different levels. At one level these might be the functional, practical tasks that management implements to achieve particular skill-related outcomes, such as an improved understanding and image. At another level the tasks facing corporate communication can be considered in terms of transitional communication effects rather than functional outcomes. These two levels are considered in turn and are depicted in Figure 9.1.

Level 1 - functional outcomes

From an outcomes perspective, corporate communication can be considered to deliver linkages, profiling, positioning and communication outcomes.

Corporate communication can be considered to deliver linkages, profiling, positioning and communication outcomes.

Linkages

Corporate communication fulfils a general role of enabling corporate brands and facilitating the development of a positive corporate reputation. In essence, the task is to provide a linkage

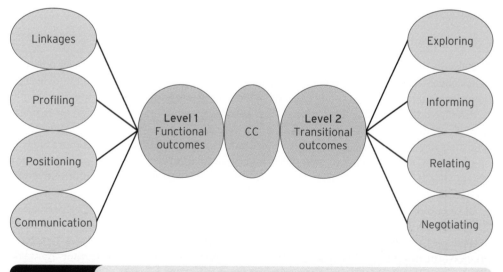

Figure 9.1   Functional and transitional levels of corporate communication.

between the corporate entity itself, the identity (or brand), and the images formed by stakeholders. As considered earlier (and to be discussed again later), the task of communicating the identity can be complex. This is because part of the delivery is through visual identity-based communications and the other part is strategic. Both of these constitute elements of corporate communication.

These linkages have focused on external stakeholders. However, there is an important internal linkage which serves to connect employees with one another, with management and with external groups as a branding element. Through effective delivery of corporate communications, linkages with a wide array of stakeholders can help to develop corporate reputation.

Profiling

The tasks necessary to fulfil this role can be considered to involve 'fleshing out the profile of the company behind the (corporate) brand' (van Riel & Fombrun, 2007, p. 23). As we shall see later, this is not an inconsiderable task as there are many activities that need to be undertaken. For example, at one extreme this can involve a variety of public relations activities, such as the issue of press releases, arranging conferences or other media-related events, whilst at another extreme it can involve communicating with employees so that they understand changes in strategy and identify strongly with the organisation.

A second related task concerns the organisation's attempt to minimise gaps that develop between the desired positioning, established through the identity mix, and the perceptions stakeholders have of the organisation and its positioning (see Viewpoint 9.4).

Positioning

Corporate communication is an integral part of corporate positioning.

Corporate communication is also involved with the management of the development and implementation of corporate strategy. Corporate communication is an integral part of corporate positioning and we know that there is a strong positive relationship between positioning strategy and corporate performance (Blankson *et al.*, 2008). From a planning and development perspective, corporate communication provides management with one of the few opportunities to a take a holistic, stakeholder perspective. Decisions concerning the positioning and direction of the organisation can be made more confidently in this context. However, this element is invariably misunderstood and excluded from the management activities of many organisations, especially where a short-term financial orientation prevails.

Corporate brands need to be positioned and sometimes repositioned as the environment changes. This is to enable stakeholders to comprehend what the organisation is and how they should relate to it and to appreciate how it is different from other organisations.

Communications

The use of corporate communication, both internally and externally, can be crucial if there is to be coherence, consistency and purpose to informing and persuading stakeholders, delivering on promises and behaving (and being seen to behave) in a responsible manner.

Associated with this idea of coherence is the centrality of communications within an organisation. If communications are organised around a central structure with relevant processes and reporting structures, many believe that an integrated communication system is more likely to be achieved. One of the goals of integration and co-ordination is to develop a communication system that is both efficient and effective in delivering messages that are informative and persuasive.

In essence all of these outcome-based tasks can be construed as informing or persuading stakeholders to think, feel or behave in particular ways. Whilst there is considerable merit in these perspectives, these interpretations of what corporate communications seek to achieve provide little insight (van Woerkum & Aarts, 2008). As these authors indicate, most messages that are intended to inform invariably contain an attempt to persuade.

| Viewpoint 9.4 | RWE uses corporate communication in a merger |

Corporate culture, an essential aspect of maintaining a good reputation, is a particularly important element during merger and acquisition activity. RWE Solutions, a wholly owned subsidiary of the multinational German multi-utility enterprise offering electricity, gas, water and waste water disposal and utility services, used corporate communications to establish a new culture when it was formed and to position itself as 'RWE: One Group – multi-utilities'.

RWE set up a new company in 1999. This consisted of 100+ medium-sized companies that had operated independently but under the RWE Group banner. This integration was necessary due to the liberalisation of the energy market and the necessity to provide substantial financial support if smaller companies were to survive. This company was established in 1999 as TESSAG but was renamed as RWE Solutions in 2001. One of the goals of TESSAG was to establish a robust culture and identity, and from there develop a communication strategy to disseminate the mission, values and goals to relevant stakeholders.

Phase one of the programme was directed to announcing the birth of TESSAG and positioning the organisation as a technical energy services company. This necessitated communication internally about the company orientation, strategy, markets and culture, and externally with key publics such as the media, financial and corporate analysts. A final task was to bond employees in order that not only did they identify with the value of RWE Solutions, but that they also acted as brand ambassadors and spread good word-of-mouth communication.

Phase two required the establishment of a strong corporate identity. Part of this phase was spent strengthening the bonds between the employees and the company. To this end dialogue sessions were held with employees. An intranet was set up to provide a source of key commercial information and also to link employees globally. A new customer periodical was launched, in-house trade fairs were established and customer events all promoted interaction and dialogue.

The third and final phase focused on communicating the changed name of the company with the media and customers as well as the business strategy and developing the familiarity of the company. The company used the name change to rebrand, and changed the name, style and colour of the corporate design in all its publicity materials. The mission statement was revised and new corporate advertising was launched.

| Exhibit 9.3 | Energy company RWE used corporate communications to establish a new culture when it was formed. |

Source: Pearson Online Database (POD)/Pearson Education Ltd/Photodisc.

Question

To what extent is a phased approach to corporate communication advisable?

Source: Based on Durig & Sriamesh (2004).

Exploring	Informing	Relating	Negotiating

Aim to stabilise the environment	Aim to inform stakeholders through formal and informal networks	Aim to create stronger bonds with stakeholders	Aim to reach solutions that reflect levels of mutual dependencies

Figure 9.2 Four tasks of corporate communication.
Source: Adapted from van Woerkum & Aarts (2008).

Level 2 – transitional

Researchers identify four primary tasks of corporate communication: exploring, informing, relating and negotiating.

In an attempt to provide a deeper insight van Woerkum & Aarts (2008) consider intentions linked with the intermediate effects of the communication process. They frame the term 'modalities' to examine the tasks of corporate communication. Their work draws on various authors and identifies four primary tasks: exploring, informing, relating and negotiating (see Figure 9.2).

Exploring

Many organisations attempt to understand the environments in which they operate, with a view to stabilising them. This enables them to improve levels of predictability and so reduce the occurrence of unexpected events that can interrupt operations, increase the use of resources and cause under-performance.

To achieve some level of stability, organisations undertake various research activities. These can be formalised through market research activities or be informal through word-of-mouth communication, media reports and government opinion. Information-gathering through environmental scanning is an essential aspect of crisis communication management. In the context of corporate reputation, exploring the views and perceptions held by stakeholders about an organisation or a brand is an act of exploration. Implicit in this exercise is the necessity to see one's own organisation as a part of a stakeholder network. Orton & Weick (1990) cited by van Woerkum & Aarts (2008) propose the interesting idea that the level of coupling between organisations in these stakeholder networks indicates the degree to which an organisation can detect what is going on in the environment. So, a tightly coupled network is thought to be less able than a loose network to sense what is happening.

Informing

Corporate communication is often associated with informing stakeholders of news and developments or influencing the way they perceive the organisation, e.g. through corporate advertising campaigns. This form of communication is often regarded as linear communication in which the organisation is active and the stakeholders are relatively passive. There is a view that individuals construct meaning by interpreting the signals, cues and information they perceive and make associations based on the meaning they ascribe to the information they receive. This, it is argued by van Woerkum & Aarts (2008), indicates that senders and receivers

Both senders and receivers are active in the communication process.

are both active in the communication process. This is necessary if stakeholders are to form an active understanding of what the organisation is and how they position it relative to competing or comparable organisations.

In addition to this formalised approach to the way organisations deliver information to stakeholders, there is another, more informal, approach. This occurs through networks populated by employees who comment on events to others, perhaps through blogs, or by email, during leisure activities and other social events (dinner parties) when a positive or negative twist is applied. In addition to the involvement of employees, journalists' comments may be fed by reactions to email messages sent about products, services and issues to do with corporate responsibility. Other rich informal sources of information include discussion boards, virtual communities and websites set up to attack an organisation deliberately and provide a forum for dissent.

Relating

Relating refers to a range of activities necessary to interact with individuals and organisations. Communications designed to develop relationships are often characterised by their intensity and frequency of interaction. This can result in the behaviour of external parties being more predictable and may also establish new levels of trust, which is seen as a critical aspect of managing stakeholder relationships. Indeed, the way in which an organisation relates to its stakeholders can impact on transaction costs as, according to Nooteboom (2002), trust enables relationships to be organised efficiently.

Perhaps the fundamental importance of the relating task concerns the quality and vibrancy of the bonds an organisation makes with other groups. Corporate communication is about interaction with a range of stakeholders and the closer the bonds, the greater the mutual understanding and the more likely it is that a suitable image will be formed and ultimately the reputation of the organisation will develop.

> The closer the bonds between stakeholders, the greater the mutual understanding.

Negotiating

The final modality to be considered is negotiation. Individuals and organisations negotiate constantly. The differing interests and moves to compromise reflect varying levels of mutual dependencies that exist within stakeholder networks. Negotiation, according to van Woerkum & Aarts (2008), can involve simple bargaining, whereby parties with opposing claims move to a compromise position somewhere in the middle; this is referred to as distributive negotiation. Another form is referred to as integrative negotiation, which occurs when the interests of all participants are at stake. In these situations the parties need to reframe the problem and any preconceived solutions. Successful outcomes require a new but common perspective through which the interests of all stakeholders are recognised.

From a communication perspective, organisations enter into formalised negotiations led by professionally trained individuals. However, many employees are required to negotiate with a variety of stakeholders, such as local retailers, interest groups, suppliers or customers, including complaint handling. All of these activities require management and consideration within the corporate communication remit.

Of course these four different communication modes do not exist in isolation. Indeed, van Woerkum & Aarts (2008) set out ideas about how these can be mixed together and they identify six intermediate combinations, outlined in Table 9.2 (also see an example in Viewpoint 9.5).

At a more practical level it is widely understood that many organisations use corporate communication to support their products and services. So this means that corporate communication is used primarily to influence consumers and, to some extent, channel intermediaries.

Consumers are considered to make two different kinds of corporate associations (Brown & Dacin, 1997): corporate ability associations and corporate social responsibility (CSR) associations.

Viewpoint 9.5 | MDA communicate change

The Magen David Adom (MDA) Society is the Israeli equivalent of the Red Cross. It supplies instruction in first-aid, pre-hospital emergency medicine, maintains a volunteer infrastructure and trains them in the provision of first-aid and basic and advanced life support. It also transports patients and women in labour, evacuates people injured in accidents and transports doctors, nurses and medical auxiliary forces.

For a long time, communications aimed to present the organisation as a 'hero'. The emphasis was on the organisation as an important life-saver. MDA attempted to build an image that would help it to recruit volunteers, mainly from among high school students, and to raise blood donations and funds. However, the rise in terrorist acts changed the context in which MDA operated. Whereas peace and relative calm prevailed previously, the new context served to disconnect the firm from the community and show it to be unreliable. This was because the organisation was forced to decrease its ongoing community-related activities, and reduce its contact with volunteers and potential blood donors in order to attend to terrorist incidents. The high frequency of terrorist attacks and the difficulty in adapting to new work routines led the organisation to operate under difficult and unfamiliar conditions. This led to operational difficulties and the provision of some inaccurate reports. When this was exposed, some perceived the MDA to be unprofessional and not doing its job properly. MDA needed to communicate more effectively with its stakeholders, and its management team made a strategic decision to change and strengthen the organisation's identity. Management realised that people identify more easily with the service providers and their personal stories than with the organisation as a whole. It was therefore decided to shift the focus from 'the organisation as a hero' to 'service providers as heroes'. It was decided to adopt a an integrated communication strategy to deliver its new 'service profiles as heroes' corporate identity to its internal audiences (workers and volunteers) and to its external audiences (the general public, health funds, governmental agencies and the media) based on the characteristics of terrorist events.

New procedures, workshops and newsletters constituted the formal internal communications used to inform all personnel of the organisation's conceptual change and new values. Informal internal communications were encouraged as well. Private employee parties and the celebration of birthdays, marriages and

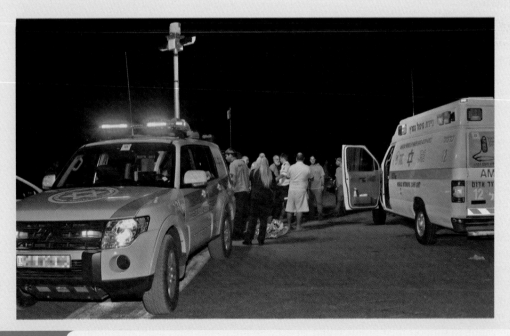

Exhibit 9.4 | Magin David Adom, the Israeli equivalent of the Red Cross.
Source: Courtesy of Magen David Adom.

births of children now enhance employees' pride as members of a team and enable them to connect to the personal life stories of their colleagues, imparting a sense of family. The informal information communicated at these events has helped the MDA to build its reputation as a fair and sensitive employer.

Formal external communications are used in two main ways. The internet allows the organisation to present to the general public its values and the uniqueness of the service provided by each of its personnel, while a television campaign focuses on the importance of contributing funds/money to the organisation. This increases awareness of both present and potential donors and focuses on MDA's personnel as heroes. It depicts personal stories of employees and volunteers in several areas throughout the country, in order to form a connection between local citizens and the organisation.

PR activities are crucial for MDA's attempts to communicate their values and image. For example, press conferences are held at which the director-general and the spokesperson present journalists with the main findings of the investigations they have conducted and information on actions that were taken in order to better prepare for future terrorist attacks. In addition, immediately after each terrorist event, managers meet representatives of the army, police, fire brigade and heads of local government to share their experience and improve communication and co-operation between the various authorities.

The main forms of informal external communications are feedback and word-of-mouth communications from citizens. In addition, there is an Israeli TV drama series based on the personal stories of MDA employees before, during and after a terrorist event, with an emphasis on the lives and experiences of the organisation's employees and volunteers. This conveys the essence of the organisation to the general public better than extensive communication campaigns have done in the past.

Question

Which of van Woerkum & Aarts' (2008) 'mixed communication modalities', depicted in Table 9.2, can you identify?

Source: Based on Herstein *et al.* (2008).

Table 9.2	Mixed communication modalities

Mixed mode	Explanation
Exploring-informing	The action of adapting messages and media in order to inform requires that there is an understanding, an exploration, of the receiver's current attitudes, preferred media and communication context.
Exploring-relating	In order to determine which relationships need to be even started, developed or terminated, it is necessary to explore the environment. In return, relationships themselves provide information about the environment.
Exploring-negotiating	This pairing can be seen to be a function of simultaneous interaction. Making arrangements to interview someone, exploring, in order that they impart information, is often negotiated in terms of what is to be asked, revealed and disclosed.
Informing-relating	Relationships can only develop if the parties reveal information about themselves. Corporate communication is often used to prompt responses, a sign that the relationship is of value.
Informing-negotiating	The act of negotiation requires that information be provided if progress is to be made. Corporate documents provide information and also serve to frame realistic expectations.
Relating-negotiating	To sustain suitable relationships when there is conflict requires negotiation that is fair and free of misrepresentation and threats.

Source: Adapted from van Woerkum & Aarts (2008).

Table 9.3	Corporate communication strategies
Communication strategies	**Explanation**
Corporate ability strategies	Stresses the objectives of building publics' cognitive associations related to an organisation's expertise and ability in terms of their products and services
Corporate social responsibility strategies	Used to create corporate associations regarding an organisation's social responsibility
Hybrid strategies	Refers to the existence of both ability and CSR strategies, where neither dominates

Ability-based associations refer to associations that a consumer makes regarding an organisation's marketplace expertise.

Ability-based associations refer to associations that a consumer makes regarding an organisation's marketplace expertise, essentially in product and service quality. CSR associations are founded on consumers' perceptions about a company's social obligations as a member of society.

Arising from this, Sora & Radar (2010) propose that there are three different corporate communication strategies that are based on the objectives of the organisation: corporate ability strategies, CSR strategies and hybrid strategies (these are explained in Table 9.3).

Sora & Radar (2010) investigated the extent to which these strategies are used and examined the websites of the Fortune 500 companies. They found that all three strategies are used but the overriding emphasis is placed on the corporate ability strategy. However, analysis of their results revealed that the top 100 companies in this list emphasised a CSR approach. Sora & Radar suggest this might be due to increased public interest as organisations get larger. It might also be a function of the way organisations use websites and the fact that other corporate communication methods are used to address other issues. However, the change in usage and emphasis is interesting.

Corporate communication activities

Having identified that corporate communication impacts on reputation and corporate strategy, it is helpful to establish the key activities undertaken by corporate communication to deliver these strategic outputs. Following research into the communication practices at three organisations, van Bekkum & van Ruler (2008) identify three common communication activities: consistent messaging; demonstrating the importance of communication to internal audiences; and the co-ordination of communication-related work and associated activities.

Consistent messaging

The importance of being clear about what an organisation is and what stakeholders will experience through interaction is well established. In effect these represent the principles of positioning and the delivery of the brand promise. Therefore, it is important to be consistent

It is important to be consistent in the way messages are conveyed.

in the way these messages are conveyed as this will help avoid confusion and misunderstanding and promote clarity, interaction and the development of suitable relationships.

This can be achieved through the use of guidelines, regulations and identity manuals, a form of control; alternatively this can be achieved through the use of online facilities, a form of consultation. Of course, there may be no mechanisms simply because the flexibility and laissez-faire corporate culture require that there be no mechanism.

Demonstrating the importance of communication internally

In many organisations, communication is regarded as a relatively lightweight activity that adds little to the prosperity or development of the organisation. Indeed, research by Holm (2006) into the curricula of Swedish communication and management schools found that ideas concerning communication and strategy are often taught at a tactical level, have not always been well articulated and have not been taught in a balanced format. The curricula at two leading Swedish communication schools contained 90 per cent communication-related material and just 10 per cent on leadership matters. In contrast, the strategic education courses at Sweden's leading management school devoted just 3 per cent of the time to communication issues.

With this background, many communication professionals see it as a key task to demonstrate internally the added value communications bring to an organisation. If completed successfully, it is more likely that corporate communication will have an increased strategic role and participation within the strategic decision-making process (van Bekkum & van Ruler, 2008).

Co-ordinating work and activities

The co-ordination of communication activities is an important, if overlooked, activity. Communication professionals need to ensure they and their departments are able to make their designated contribution and deliver their added value. We have seen that corporate culture can have a substantial and wide influence on the way in which work is performed in organisations. Corporate communication is no exception and the co-ordination mechanisms used occur within the cultural framework. For example, in organisations where the culture is formal and highly structured, it is likely that co-ordination is achieved through regimented work processes involving standardised procedures and frequent reporting, as at Philips for example. Alternatively co-ordination in an informal, unstructured culture can only be achieved through frequent yet informal liaison, as at Nokia. In other words, the co-ordinating mechanisms are to a large extent put in position by the culture and have to be used by communication professionals in order to deliver corporate communication outputs.

> The co-ordination mechanisms used occur within the cultural framework.

Integrated corporate communication

Integrated corporate communication is concerned with the communication of messages with targeted stakeholders that are coherent and consistent and that reinforce the prevailing corporate strategy and agreed messaging themes. Some believe that integration is enabled by bringing together the different elements of an organisation's communication activities so that they reside within the control of a single or central part of an organisation. This may or may not be true, and is probably dependent on contingency issues.

> Integration is enabled by bringing together the different elements of an organisation's communication activities.

In reality it is quite common for an organisation to disperse its advertising, internal communications, design, media relations, public affairs, sponsorship, direct marketing and other communication disciplines to a variety of geographic locations. What is more there is often an absence of processes and systems designed to connect these various functions. One of the results of this isolationism, or 'functional silos' as Schultz *et al.* (1993) call this practice, is that they tend to function as individual and independent centres of expertise. Consequently they interact with external and internal parties without co-ordination or common purpose.

The ideal associated with integrated corporate communication concerns two key issues. The first is that by establishing a central department, run by a communication chief, communication moves up the corporate agenda and reports directly into the CEO via the board. It moves from being a tactical to a strategic agenda item. The second is the attraction of lower costs, increased efficiency and greater clarity, principally internally but often claimed by advocates on behalf of stakeholders.

Any discussion about the management of corporate communication cannot be complete without reference to vertical and horizontal communication. Traditionally, organisations determine a series of primary communication disciplines, break them into pieces, assign priorities and designate managers to be responsible for them. These individuals are responsible for particular parts of the communication process, and work within a formalised reporting structure; hence the vertical format. Within each of these vertical arenas are various secondary tasks, or subtasks, within which specialist activities are performed. Cross-functional communication is necessary to connect these specialist activities, subtasks and departments (Cornelissen *et al.*, 2006).

Organisations use a variety of mechanisms to co-ordinate the different horizontal communications.

In practice, organisations use a variety of mechanisms to co-ordinate the different horizontal communications. These include project teams, standardised work processes, matrix structures and the use of mini-czars. The latter are communication professionals who co-ordinate and integrate activities between departments. In addition to the formal communications that occur through both the vertical and horizontal communication processes, there are different informal communication processes, which provide richness, speed and political slant to corporate communication. These aspects of vertical and horizontal communication are revisited later in this chapter.

An integrated approach should provide audiences with uniform or consistent sets of messages. These should be relatively easy for recipients to interpret and to assign meaning. For target audiences such integration might promote better understanding of and access to brands, enable them to perceive brands in a more positive and perhaps more open and honest context and in doing so encourage desired behaviours. For organisations this might lower costs, improve clarity and enhance the brand and its reputation. If this is followed through then organisational performance is likely to improve.

The literature on marketing communications provides an insight into the issues and tensions concerning integration.

Ideas concerning the formal integration of communication activities have been a prominent discussion topic within both the corporate and marketing communications literature for the past two decades. Of these the literature concerning marketing communications has been the most prominent. Consideration of this material provides an insight into the issues and tensions concerning integration and is considered first.

Integrated marketing communications (IMC)

Initial ideas about IMC were developed around the proposition that integration concerned the promotional tools and media. Much of the academic IMC activity was led by Schultz *et al.* (1993), Kitchen (1993) and Duncan & Everett (1993). Many organisations were equally enthusiastic about the new ideas that were emerging, particularly as the context was largely one of an economic downturn that was beginning to ease. The primary drivers were a desire to restructure internally, reduce costs and deliver consistent messages. Kitchen *et al.* (2004) refer to this perspective as the 'inside-out' IMC approach.

The primary drivers were a desire to restructure internally, reduce costs and deliver consistent messages.

Following this initial phase there was a period characterised by the examination of issues concerning the nature, direction and content of IMC practices. This was typified by definitions that introduced management, strategy and brand development into the IMC process. Shimp (2000), amongst others, supported the explicit introduction of these aspects to IMC. Perhaps the current phase is characterised by interpretations of IMC as an audience or customer-driven process, one that incorporates ideas concerning relationship marketing. To follow up Kitchen's earlier expression, this perspective is very much 'outside-in'.

However, IMC is not a universally accepted concept. Scholars such as Cornelissen & Lock (2000), Percy *et al.* (2001), and Spotts *et al.* (1998), for example, have voiced criticism of the concept pointing to the lack of empirical data and any theory to support the concept. Authors refer to the difficulties encountered by organisations when trying to implement IMC. Impediments cited include the prevailing technology, culture, operations, processes, the organisational structure and the seemingly perpetual resistance many employees demonstrate towards any type of change.

As part of his critique Cornelissen (2003) distinguishes two different themes running through the IMC literature. The first is that IMC is regarded as a predominantly content-oriented concept. This refers to the harmonisation of tools, media and messages in order to deliver a single consistent message each time a customer 'touches' the brand. The second theme identified refers to a process orientation whereby organisations, in addition to the delivery of a single message, restructure, redesign systems and create processes in order to help deliver IMC. The process perspective requires that organisations restructure and introduce processes, procedures and systems in order to enable integrated communications.

What this snapshot of the literature reveals is that not everyone believes that IMC is a valid concept. Even though there may be a dearth of empirical evidence to support the notion of what exactly IMC might be (Cornelissen, 2003), both practitioners and academics acknowledge the good practice inherent in the integration of content and processes that convey a single brand message. Apart from conceptual problems, IMC is challenged by issues concerning organisational structure and systems. Readers interested in a fuller appraisal of IMC are referred to Kitchen *et al.* (2004) and Cornelissen (2003).

> **IMC is challenged by issues concerning organisational structure and systems.**

Integrated corporate communication

Although IMC has been beset by conceptual and structural issues, these dwarf the attempts to integrate corporate communication. Integrated communication concerns the 'alignment of symbols, messages, procedures, and behaviours' (Christensen *et al.*, 2008, p. 424) that enable an organisation to communicate across and within the organisation's formal boundaries clearly, consistently and with continuity. In comparison with IMC, integrated communication incorporates a range of issues, messages and sources and deals with multiple stakeholder groups, internal as well as external, to the organisation.

According to Christensen *et al.* (2008) organisations centralise their communications in an attempt to integrate and in doing so implement tight control systems. Their view is that by being more aware and sensitive to the organisational context, in particular the internal dimensions of integration, integrated communication can become a more realistic goal for many organisations.

Pickton (2004) suggests that there are several features associated with what he refers to as integrated corporate communication. These are set out in Table 9.4, which provides an understanding of the range of features that need to be considered when developing and sustaining an integrated corporate communication programme. However, this list of features assumes an organisational infrastructure that is not only in place but also operational. In order that integration occurs, lessons learned from IMC experiences suggest that the structure should facilitate open communication flows both horizontally for informal communications and hierarchically for the more formal communications.

The range of issues that potentially impede the development of integrated corporate communications are many and varied but they revolve around three core elements – individuals, the organisation and skills – although the issues often overlap one another.

Individuals present difficulties in terms of the way many think, feel and often seek to defend their worlds rather than embrace change, adapt and move forward. The potential loss of control over what they do at work concerns many people, not just those involved in the communication business. Change has for a long time been regarded with hostility and fear, and as such

Table 9.4	Features of integrated corporate communication

ICC feature	Explanation
Objectives	The establishment and use of corporate communication objectives that are both consistent with and integral to the organisational goals
Planned	By adopting a planned approach the full range of corporate communications activities can be incorporated in a coherent and synergistic manner
Range of stakeholders	Integrated corporate communications needs to embrace a range of targeted stakeholders
Contact management	The establishment of suitable services to manage all forms of contact resulting through corporate communication
Activity management	The management of people and communication activities
Reciprocal impact	Understanding about how product/brand communications might impact on corporate communication
Communication tools	The full utilisation of formal, informal, personal and non-personal communication instruments
Message congruity	The need to use a range of product and corporate brand messages yet incorporate them within an agreed strategy
Media	The use of a full range of media to deliver corporate communication messages to targeted stakeholders

Source: Adapted from Pickton (2004).

is normally resisted. Any move towards corporate communication, therefore, represents a significantly different approach to work, as not only are the expectations of employees changed but so are the working practices and the associated roles, with a variety of internal staff and those providing communication-related outsourcing facilities.

By nature individuals have a pronounced tendency to associate with tribes. At work these tribes might be based on departments, types of skill, levels of management or job function. For example, the advertising department might see themselves as superior to those in direct marketing, finance or human relations. Those in sales might see themselves as superior to everyone, as they see themselves as indispensable. These tribes provide a number of benefits, including security and self-identity. Integration threatens the existence of tribes and the social and psychological benefits of membership.

Traditional hierarchical structures and systems are inflexible and slow.

From an *organisational* perspective there are several issues that need to be addressed. Part of the reluctance to move to corporate communication is linked with the structure and systems inherent in many organisations. Traditional hierarchical structures and systems are inflexible and slow to cope with developments in their fast-adapting environments. These structures can stifle the use of individual initiative, slow the decision-making process and encourage inertia. However, not all organisations are hierarchical and many have adopted lean structures enabling flexibility and adaptation to changing environments. Even in these organisations the development of their communication functions is partly based on specialisation, a reflection of the industry roots. The result is that, internally, organisations have created communication silos, departments and units that specialise in particular aspects of communications. Most typical of this silo approach is the physical distance that can exist between the public relations and marketing departments.

Resistance can also be experienced by senior managers who may not understand the benefits likely to accrue through integration. This might be manifested through political manoeuvring with or without the assistance of financial levers. Communication is often perceived to be tactical not strategic and the result of this is that not only are strategic actions difficult to initiate but they are often relegated or rejected on financial grounds. All too often communications are perceived as a cost rather than an investment, and the thought of making substantial structural and systems changes necessary to facilitate integrated corporate communication is perceived negatively. The advent of digital technologies and associated contemporary databases has proved to be an enabler and has helped the cause of integrated corporate communication.

The final element to be considered concerns the *skills* of individuals and the organisation. At an individual level, integration of this magnitude demands a different disposition from that normally expected of communication experts. Individuals are expected to find different ways of approaching communication problems and finding solutions that work across an organisation as well. Organisationally the huge range and levels of tasks associated with the integration of corporate communication pose difficulties in terms of the levels of implementation as well as the co-ordination, sequencing and timing of solutions.

Associated with the breadth and level of tasks is the issue of perceived complexity. The high levels of skill associated with integrating any combination of activities is often cited as a reason for delaying or postponing action. There can be substantial difficulties associated with co-ordinating actions across departments and geographic boundaries. Corporate communication requires the co-operation and co-ordination of internal and external stakeholder groups. Each group has an agenda that contains goals that may well differ from or conflict with those of other participants.

> Associated with the breadth and level of tasks is the issue of perceived complexity.

Finding the right person to fit the person specification necessary to run this high-profile, politically charged and dynamic aspect of internal and external communication is in itself a difficult task, especially when there are so few people with the necessary experience.

Many authors and organisations have argued the validity of a centralised unit or single department in order to manage the processes associated with integrated communications (Cornelissen *et al.*, 2001; Christensen *et al.*, 2009). Apart from the difficulties associated with establishing the right systems and processes necessary to facilitate vertical and horizontal communication, the main problem concerns the inherent contradiction presented by the centralised concept. Centralisation is about control, rigidity and standardisation. Through centralisation it is argued that improved formal and informal horizontal communications would flow, so overcoming one of the main hurdles to establishing integrated corporate communication. However, the demise of bureaucracies is a rejection of that particular organisational model. The rise of networks as a replacement for hierarchies, foreseen by Achrol (1991), represents flexibility as a means of responding and adapting quickly to an environment increasingly characterised by volatility, frequent change and unpredictability. Networks encourage flexibility through dispersed autonomy, characterised by improved horizontal communications. So, the idea that integrated corporate communication is best achieved through structural centrality, which should provide the necessary flexibility, is a contradiction and one that appears to be doomed. If the organisational structure needs to be more flexible then it seems that a change in the corporate culture is also required, even though the latter will take considerably longer to establish.

Christensen *et al.* (2008) put forward the view that integrated communication can only be achieved realistically through what they refer to as the 'flexible integration' approach. While conventional approaches to integration are concerned with a single message, i.e. one uniform message delivered through employees who conform to a predetermined pattern of message formulation, delivery and understanding, the essence of the flexible integration perspective is that what is really required is a process that enables local autonomy and responsiveness around a theme or set of communication values (see Viewpoint 9.6). Such flexibility enables ownership of communication activities across an organisation's boundaries and encourages what the authors refer to as 'sensitivity to the many different voices and types of wisdom in the organizational setting' (p. 443). In their view, integrated communication should be about responsiveness to changes in the environment and management should not attempt 'controlled' integration as this will exacerbate vertical communication and not assist horizontal communications. Readers interested in this topic should read the paper by Christensen *et al.* (2008).

| **Viewpoint 9.6** | **Integrating Microsoft's communication** |

Microsoft is a very large and complex international organisation. It is structured on matrix principles where horizontally organised international divisions sit next to vertical divisions of product groups. The result is that 'internal and external communicators each have geographical, functional and product area responsibilities' (Love, 2006). This can lead to myopia and a loss of the bigger Microsoft picture as communicators revert to silos and local or independent communications.

In order to control the flow of messages and to sort out those that will work from those that won't, all stories need to be passed through an integration group. Their task is to prioritise the best stories, target the appropriate journalists and make sure the stories do not clash, duplicate one another or bombard particular individuals in the media. Love refers to this as 'avoiding mid-air collisions'.

Communication directors and managers are also physically brought together on a regular basis to clear communication plans and campaigns to launch products as well as consider corporate communication activities and their potential impact on the organisation.

Question

Is Microsoft practising integrated corporate communication or just minimising duplication, reducing waste and being efficient?

Source: Based on Love (2006).

> **What is needed is a process that enables local autonomy and responsiveness around a theme or set of communication values.**

To end this chapter, a few words about how integration might be reasonably understood, implemented and researched may be useful. Integration is a compelling notion yet, as Christensen *et al.* (2009) suggest, it may be difficult to attain. This is because of the amount of resources and flexibility required to converse effectively with diverse stakeholders, whose entrance into conversations may be difficult to know and whose understanding of the dialogue's progression problematical.

Integration within both marketing and corporate communication contexts is manifest in the skill of storytelling. Telling a story about a brand in which the values, credentials and promises are embedded provides unification, a consistency and flexibility that stakeholders can understand and take away whenever they interact with the organisation. They might not know that it is an integrated message whose content is themed through the story context, but then they do not care. Corporate storytelling is examined in greater detail in Chapter 10 but perhaps it is the means through which corporate communication can be successfully integrated.

Chapter summary

In order to help consolidate your understanding of the dimensions of corporate communication, here are the key points summarised against each of the learning objectives.

1. Examine the nature, role and strategic orientation of corporate communication

Corporate communication involves determining, understanding, delivering and responding to messages targeted at an organisation's stakeholders. Interaction with stakeholders can be used to help inform and develop management strategy.

Corporate communication can develop an organisation's reputation, reduce transaction costs and assist corporate strategy through the development of competitive advantage. Corporate communication can influence the way stakeholders perceive an organisation and shape their thoughts regarding buying, recruiting, investing and supplying. Competitive advantage can also be created through the formation of long-term relationships with the stakeholders, fostered through corporate communication.

2. Discuss the characteristics and scope of corporate communication

Corporate communication is an integrative function that crosses over specialist activities such as branding, public relations, media relations and internal communications, in order to form a strategic perspective of an organisation. Corporate communication is used to deliver an organisation's identity, sustain a reputation and a desire to remain subservient to the wishes of the key stakeholders.

3. Explore the reasons why organisations use corporate communications

Organisations use corporate communication to influence stakeholders and to shape the way in which they perceive an organisation. This can be particularly helpful during strategic events, such as merger, change of strategy or leadership, during periods of strategic development and to maintain strategic positions and stakeholder relationships. In addition, organisations use corporate communication to promote visibility, recognition and acceptance and to drive competitive advantage.

4. Consider the different dimensions of corporate communication

Three different broad dimensions of communication have been identified: management communications, marketing communications and organisational communications. An alternative perspective suggests that there are primary, secondary and tertiary dimensions of corporate communication.

5. Establish the tasks corporate communication are expected to accomplish

Three particular tasks of corporate communication can be identified. The first two involve externally directed communication designed to raise awareness of, inform or educate key stakeholders, and to defend or explain a company's actions. The third task concerns internal communication designed to explain, reinforce and refresh the mission, values and beliefs of the organisation.

Alternatively corporate communication can be regarded at a functional level and provide linkages, profiling, positioning and communication outcomes. At a transitional level corporate communication can be used to explore, inform, relate and negotiate.

6. Consider the main activities associated with corporate communications in practice

Three common communication activities are consistent messaging, demonstrating the importance of communication to internal audiences and the co-ordination of communication-related work and associated activities. In reality many organisations use corporate communication to support products and service offerings and to recruit high-calibre staff.

7. Examine ideas associated with integrated corporate communication

Integrated corporate communication is concerned with bringing together different elements of an organisation's communication activities so that they reside within the control of a single or central part of an organisation. This control then enables the delivery of messages to targeted stakeholders that are consistent with and reinforce the prevailing corporate strategy and agreed messaging themes.

Discussion questions

1. What are the two primary roles that corporate communication can play in the interlinking between reputation and strategy?

2. How have definitions of corporate communication evolved, and what was Cornelissen's primary view of corporate communication in 2007?

3. What are the main ways in which corporate communication can be used strategically?

4. Identify the three main types of communication used by organisations.

5. Using an organisation with which you are familiar, try to identify the main ways in which management communication is used. Do you think this form of communication is being used effectively in the organisation?

6. Balmer & Gray (1999) suggest that the corporate communication mix consists of primary, secondary and tertiary communication. Discuss ways in which this may be a useful means of planning corporate communication activities.

7. Identify three corporate communication tasks undertaken at each of the functional and transitional levels.

8. What do exploring, informing, relating and negotiating mean in the context of communication activities?

9. What are considered to be the three common corporate communication activities?

10. Make brief notes referring to three arguments supporting and three rejecting the notion that integrated communications can only be generated from a centralised department.

References

Achrol, R.S. (1991). Evolution of the marketing organization: new forms of turbulent environments. *Journal of Marketing* 55 (October), 77–93.

Balmer, J.M.T. & Gray, E.R. (1999). Corporate identity and corporate communications: creating a competitive advantage. *Corporate Communications: an International Journal* 4(4), 171–176.

Barda, T. (2009). Resetting the Sun. *The Marketer*, December/January, 20–23.

van Bekkum, T. & van Ruler, B. (2008). Corporate communications and corporate reputation. In: Melewar, T.C. (ed.) *Facets of Corporate Identity, Communication and Reputation.* London: Routledge, pp. 83–95.

Blankson, C., Kalafatis, P., Chreng, J.M.-S. and Hadjicharalambous, C. (2008). Impact of positioning strategies on corporate performance. *Journal of Advertising Research* 48(1), 106–122.

Bordia, P., Hunt, E., Paulsen, N., Tourish, D. & Difonzo, N. (2004). Uncertainty during organizational change; is it all about control? *European Journal of Work and Organizational Psychology* 13(3), 345–365.

Brown, T.J. & Dacin, P.A. (1997). The company and the product: corporate associations and consumer product responses. *Journal of Marketing* 61 (January), 68–84.

Burke, T. (1998). Risks and reputations: The economics of transaction costs. *Corporate Communications* 3(1), 5–10.

Carbery, R. & Garavan, T. (2005). Organizational restructuring and downsizing: issues related to learning, training and employability of survivors. *Journal of European Industrial Training* 29(6), 488–508.

Christensen, L.T., Firat, A.F. & Torp, S. (2008). The organization of integrated communications: toward flexible integration. *European Journal of Marketing* 42(3/4), 423–452.

Christensen, L.T., Firat, A.F. & Cornelissen, J. (2009). New tensions and challenges in integrated communications. *Corporate Communications: an International Journal* 14(2), 207–219.

Cornelissen, J. (2008). *Corporate Communication: Theory and Practice*, 2nd edn. London: Sage.

Cornelissen, J., Lock, A.R. & Gardner, H. (2001). The organization of external communication disciplines: an integrative framework of dimensions and determinants. *International Journal of Advertising* 20(1), 67–88.

Cornelissen, J., van Bekkum, T. & van Ruler, B. (2006). Corporate communications: a practice-based theoretical conceptualization. *Corporate Reputation Review* 9(2), 114–133.

Cornelissen, J.P. (2003). Change, continuity and progress: the concept of integrated marketing communications and marketing communications practice. *Journal of Strategic Marketing*, 11 (December), 217–234.

Cornelissen, J.P. & Lock, A.R. (2000). Theoretical concept or management fashion? Examining the significance of IMC, *Journal of Advertising Research*, 50, 5, 7–15.

Dowling, G. (2006). Communicating corporate reputation through stories. *California Management Review* 49(1), 82–100.

Duncan, T. & Everett, S. (1993). Client perceptions of integrated marketing communications, *Journal of Advertising Research* 3(3), 30–39.

Durig, U.-M. & Sriamesh, K. (2004). Public relations and change management: the case of a multinational company. *Journal of Communication Management* 8(4), 372–383.

Fill, C. (2009). *Marketing Communications: Interactivity, Communities and Content*, 5th edn. Harlow: Financial Times/Prentice Hall.

Fombrun, C.J. & Rindova, V.P. (1998). Reputation management in global 1000 firms; a benchmarking study. *Corporate Reputation Review* 1(3), 205–214.

Forman, J. & Argenti, P.A. (2005). How corporate communication influences strategy implementation, reputation and the corporate brand: an exploratory qualitative study. *Corporate Reputation Review* 8(3), 245–264.

Gabbioneta, C., Ravasi, D. & Mazzola, P. (2007). Exploring the drivers of corporate reputation: a study of Italian securities analysts. *Corporate Reputation Review* 10(2), 99–123.

Gray, E. (1995). Corporate Image as a strategic concept. In: *Proceedings of the 13th Annual Conference of the Association of Management*, Vancouver, pp. 250–257.

Hall, R. (1992). The strategic analysis of intangible resources. *Strategic Management Journal*, 13(2), 135–144.

Herstein, R., Mitki, Y. & Jaffe (2008). Corporate image reinforcement in an era of terrorism through integrated marketing communication. *Corporate Reputation Review* 11(4), 360–370.

Holm, O. (2006). Integrated marketing communication: from tactics to strategy. *Corporate Communications: An International Journal* 11(1), 23–33.

Jackson, P. (1987). *Corporate Communication for Managers*. London: Pitman.

Kerr, D. (2002). Shell corporate image; opening a dialogue with opinion leaders. *Institute of Practitioners in Advertising*. Online: from www.warc.com. Accessed: 30 August 2009.

Kitchen, P.J. (1993). Towards the integration of marketing and public relations. *Marketing Intelligence & Planning* 11(11), 15–21.

Kitchen, P.J. & Laurence, A. (2003). Corporate reputation: an eight-country analysis. *Corporate Reputation Review* 6(2), 103–117.

Kitchen, P., Brignell, J., Li, T. & Spickett-Jones, G. (2004). The emergence of IMC: a theoretical perspective. *Journal of Advertising Research* 44 (March), 19–30.

Langer, R. & Thorup, S. (2006). Building trust in times of crisis. *Corporate Communications: An International Journal* 11(4), 371–390.

Love, M. (2006). Cutting through the clutter at Microsoft. Online: www.melcrum.com/articles/clutter_at_microsoft.shtml. Accessed: 23 August 2009.

Lowensberg, D. (2006). Corporate image, reputation and identity. In: Tench, R. & Yeomans, L., eds. *Exploring Public Relations*. Harlow: Financial Times/Prentice Hall, pp. 250–264.

Melewar, T.C., Bassett, K. & Simões, C. (2006). The role of communication and visual identity in modern organizations, *Corporate Communications: An International Journal* 11(2), 138–147.

Nooteboom, B. (2002). *Trust: Forms, Foundations, Functions, Failures and Figures.* Cheltenham: Edward Elgar.

Oechsle, S. & Henderson, T. (2000). Identity: an exploration into purpose and principles at Shell. *Corporate Reputation Review* 3(1), 75–77.

Orton, J.D. & Weick, K.E. (1990). Loosely coupled systems: a reconceptualization. *Academy of Management Review* 15(2), 203–223.

Percy, L., Rossiter, J.R. & Elliot, R. (2001). *Strategic Advertising Management.* New York: Oxford University Press.

Pickton, D. (2004). Assessing integrated corporate communication. In: Oliver, S.M. ed. *Handbook of Corporate Communication and Public Relations.* London: Routledge, pp. 227–242.

van Riel, C.B.M. (1995). *Principles of Corporate Communication.* Hemel Hempstead: Prentice Hall.

van Riel, C.B.M. & Fombrun, C.J. (2007). *Essentials of Corporate Communication.* London: Routledge.

Rindova, V.P. & Fombrun, C.J. (1999). 'Constructing competitive advantage: the role of firm-constituent interaction. *Strategic Management Journal* 20(8), 691–710.

Rumelt, R.P., Schendel, D.E. & Teece, D.J. (1994). 'Fundamental issues in strategy'. In: Rumelt, R.P., Schendel, D.E. & Teece, D.J. eds. *Fundamental Issues in Strategy: A Research Agenda.* Boston, MA: Harvard Business School Press, pp. 9–47.

Schultz, D., Tannenbaum, S.T. & Lauterborn, R.F. (1993). *Integrated Marketing Communications: Putting It Together & Making It Work.* Maidenhead: McGraw-Hill.

Shimp, T.A. (2000). *Advertising Promotion: Supplemental Aspects of Integrated Marketing Communications*, 5th edn. Fort Worth, TX: Dryden Press, Harcourt College Publishers.

Sora, K. & Rader, S. (2010). What they can do versus how much they care: assessing corporate communication strategies on Fortune 500 web sites. *Journal of Communication Management* 14(1), 59–80.

Spotts, H.E., Lambert, D.R. & Joyce, M.L. (1998). Marketing déjà vu: the discovery of integrated marketing communications. *Journal of Marketing Education* 20(3), 210–218.

Tench, R. & Yeomans, L. (2006). *Exploring Public Relations.* Horlow: Financial Times/Prentice Hall.

Varey, R.J. & White, J. (2000). The corporate communication system of managing. *Corporate Communications* 5(1), 5–11.

van Woerkum, C. & Aarts, N. (2008). Staying connected: the communication between organizations and their environment. *Corporate Communications: An International Journal* 13(2), 197–211.

Woods, S. (2007). Shell launches first new retail identify for more than a decade. *Design Week*, 18 January. Online: www.designweek.co.uk/news/. Accessed: 13 January 2011.

Wry, T., Deephouse, D.L. & McNamara, G. (2005). Substantive and evaluative media reputations among and within cognitive strategic groups. *Corporate Reputation Review* 9(4), 225–242.

Yamauchi, K. (2001). Corporate communications: a powerful tool for stating corporate mission. *Corporate Communications* 6(3), 131–136.

Chapter 10

Contexts for corporate communication

Corporate communication is partly a reflection of management's aspirations and partly a manifestation of the personality or character of the organisation. If messages conveyed in the name of corporate communication are to be successful, it is necessary to understand an organisation's characteristics and context, among other elements.

Aims and learning objectives

The aim of this chapter is to examine the way in which the culture and strategy of an organisation shape its communications.

The learning objectives of this chapter are to:

1. Determine the impact of corporate culture on corporate communication

2. Explain the characteristics and importance of communication climate

3. Consider the issues associated with communicating an organisation's objectives, including its vision and mission

4. Explore how time and circumstance can influence the impact of corporate communication

5. Examine the identity mix and its use in corporate branding

6. Examine how corporate communication can impact on an organisation's positioning

7. Discuss ways in which organisations address ethical, corporate social responsibility (CSR) and sustainability issues through their communications.

Introduction

The range of messages conveyed through corporate communication is immense. Not only are the target audiences different in nature, location and need, but their relationships and communication requirements can also differ considerably. The message issue is complicated further because corporate culture, a key foundation upon which communications are developed, can both impede and accelerate the impact of corporate communication messaging. Schein (1991, p. 15) comments that corporate cultures 'provide group members with a way of giving meaning to their daily lives, setting guidelines and rules for how to behave, and, most important, reducing and containing the anxiety of dealing with an unpredictable, and uncertain environment'. Understanding the context in which corporate communication occurs is therefore critical.

This chapter opens by examining organisational culture and its influence on corporate communication. From there it considers the nature and impact of mission statements. The timing and reasons for the use of corporate communication are considered before examining the identity mix and exploring the important issue of positioning. The chapter concludes with a review of the way organisations communicate corporate responsibility, ethics and sustainability issues.

The influence of culture on corporate communication

Culture is concerned with the beliefs, norms and values that guide the behaviour of groups of people. Culture refers to ideas about routine, unspoken patterns of behaviour and the actions that people take when faced with particular issues. Schein's (1992) definition of corporate culture, referred to earlier in Chapter 3, is one of the most often quoted. He says it is 'the basic assumptions and beliefs that are shared by members of an organization, that operate unconsciously and define in a basic taken-for-granted fashion an organization's view of itself and its environment'.

> Culture refers to ideas about routine, unspoken patterns of behaviour and the actions that people take when faced with particular issues.

Organisational culture is therefore concerned with the way in which employees and managers behave towards each other and those stakeholders external to the organisation. Their behaviour reflects the prevailing culture or ideology and is used by external stakeholders as a means of understanding the organisation and predicting how it will behave and respond to events in the future. Corporate culture defines acceptable behaviour which serves to provide a certain consistency of behaviour within an organisation. Therefore establishing and maintaining acceptable behaviour provides a mechanism for social control (O'Reilly & Chatman, 1996).

> Schein believes that culture exists at three levels.

Schein believes that culture exists at three levels: artefacts, beliefs and values, and the underlying assumptions. Artefacts refer to a range of items that non-members can see, hear, smell and touch when engaging with an organisation. Understanding what they mean or represent can be difficult, but the architecture, colour scheme, rituals and written statements provide initial signposts about an organisation.

At a deeper level, Schein refers to the beliefs and values held by members of an organisation. Through time, members develop a shared system of beliefs and values about what works, what is right and how tasks are to be accomplished. Social reinforcement encourages consensus so that the beliefs and values used to solve problems become strongly held assumptions about what is the correct attitude, value and behaviour. Through time these assumptions are used to shape and guide what is regarded as the correct behaviour, thus perpetuating the values and beliefs shared by the members in an informal or semi-formal manner. However, readers should note that not only are there various subcultures, but the idea of shared values suggests uniformity and consistency, whereas in reality conflict, factions and disharmony are more regularly observed (Martin, 2002; Martin & Siehl, 1983).

Corporate culture can be considered as a context through which the values and behaviour of the members can be interpreted and understood. Culture precedes behaviour and management's task is to influence the organisational identity through the corporate identity. The latter, of course, is enabled through corporate communication, and internal communications in particular. Management's goal is to influence behaviour, and that is achieved through corporate communication.

Tellis *et al.* (2009) claim that in addition to shared values and beliefs, employees can also share common goals. Those who do are more likely to assist corporate performance in a positive way. They claim that it is generally agreed that organisations with strong cultures outperform those with weak cultures. Sørensen (2002) cites various authors who demonstrate that above-average performance stems from improved internal co-ordination, control and goal alignment between an organisation and its members (Kotter & Heskett, 1992; Gordon & DiTomaso, 1992; Burt *et al.*, 1994). Some organisations have a distinct cultural attitude and associated practices, e.g. Apple. As Tellis & Golder (2001) commented, Apple stand out in terms of their radical approach to innovation. They cite *Businessweek* (2005), who claim that neither sales nor design awards are the best way to measure Apple's success. Their greatest innovation is their culture of innovation and the fact that it works as 'an incubator of the best designers and engineers' in order to fund long-term impact (see also Viewpoint 10.1 in which three examples of corporate culture are explored).

> **Some organisations have a distinct cultural attitude and associated practices.**

Viewpoint 10.1 Global growth through corporate culture

HCL Technologies, a Delhi-based IT services provider, was growing at around 30 per cent in 2005. Unfortunately the market was growing at 40 to 50 per cent so a new president was recruited to transform the company. This required moving away from being an undifferentiated service provider that simply provided transactional or discrete deals. What customers wanted were long-term partners, companies that could provide end-to-end services on a collaborative basis. The problem that faced the new president was how to create a culture that would enable the new business model.

One significant development occurred when analysis of customer feedback revealed that it was not HCL's products, services, or technologies that were valued, but HCL's employees. It was the interface between frontline employees and customers that presented HCL with value opportunities. This led to thinking about the structure of the organisation, and how to invert the traditional triangle. The process of change was characterised by an opening period of honesty and openness, followed by one of trust and transparency, to a point where executives and support functions are now accountable to frontline employees. This culture is called 'Employees First, Customers Second' (EFCS) and now underpins HCL. When the recession struck in 2008 employees were asked for their views on what should be done, with the majority suggesting ways in which revenue could be increased. Indeed, in 2008 orders doubled when competitor companies were losing 20 per cent. By 2009, HCL revenue had tripled and its market value doubled.

Ikea is a distinctly Swedish company and has three distinct features; function, quality, and low price. These are used to develop product ranges that are said to reflect its Swedish heritage and which inform IKEA values and the IKEA culture. Part of its culture is grounded in doing things differently. For example, it started as a catalogue marketing company which was combined with a showroom so that customers could see and touch IKEA products. A huge retail store was opened in Stockholm in the 1960s so that customers could pick the products they wanted, directly from the shelves themselves. In doing so IKEA switched a problem of capacity into a new way of delivering products to their customers, the warehouse principle.

Ikea has an informal, unassuming culture, where cost consciousness, and responsibility are paramount. Ikea's corporate strategy is influenced by its culture.

▶

Exhibit 10.1	IKEA's growth has been achieved partly on the Swedishness of the product range, its Swedish heritage.

Source: © Inter IKEA Systems BV 2011, with permission.

Samsung's rise from a low-cost original equipment manufacturer to world leader and a brand worth more than Pepsi, American Express or Nike, has required a change in corporate culture. So, in order to embark on a growth strategy in the 1990s, the company needed to become agile, innovative and creative. To do this it needed to break with its then inward facing culture and cautious business strategy. So, Samsung utilised some Western best practices concerning strategy formulation, financing, market dynamics (pricing) and compensation. These were integrated into Samsung's existing business model. For example, rather than perpetuate the current compensation system where the more senior got paid the most, differential pay was introduced, dependent on performance, as used on schemes run at Hewlett Packard and General Electric.

Global growth required Samsung to break away from the status quo and start to use non-Koreans in non-Korean contexts. Selected South Korean staff were sent abroad to learn a language, become immersed in the country and to learn about their practices and culture. This has led to long standing relationships and networks upon which business was later established. Non-Koreans were also recruited, bringing with them new styles and methods of working.

Question

To what extent should a country culture, or any other regional culture, be successfully 'copied and pasted' into organisations in different countries?

Source: Based on Kling and Goteman (2003); Nayar (2010); Khanna *et al.* (2011).

The characteristics or traits that form an integral part of corporate culture shape the way in which members behave and communicate. These traits provide stability, continuity and a means through which an organisation can change and evolve. Previously we have referred to the corporate personality of an organisation. This, it is argued, constitutes the core of an organisation and is characterised by the prevailing strategic processes and culture. Some researchers refer to this as organisational identity rather than personality.

> Traits provide stability, continuity and a means through which an organisation can change and evolve.

Organisational identity is concerned with how members perceive themselves and how they think and feel about their organisation. In contrast, corporate identity is about how an organisation expresses itself in terms of its strategy, values and aspirations (see Viewpoint 10.2).

Viewpoint 10.2   Are these oily corporate values?

Shell's stated corporate values

As a global energy company we set high standards of performance and ethical behaviours. We are judged by how we act – our reputation is upheld by how we live up to our core values of honesty, integrity and respect for people. The Shell General Business Principles, Code of Conduct and Code of Ethics help everyone at Shell act in line with these values and comply with all relevant legislation and regulations.

BP's stated corporate values

BP wants to be recognised as a great company – competitively successful and a force for progress. We have a fundamental belief that we can make a difference in the world.

We help the world meet its growing need for heat, light and mobility. We strive to do that by producing energy that is affordable, secure and doesn't damage the environment.

BP is progressive, responsible, innovative and performance driven.

Chevron's stated corporate values

Our company's foundation is built on our values, which distinguish us and guide our actions. We conduct our business in a socially responsible and ethical manner. We respect the law, support universal human rights, protect the environment and benefit the communities where we work.

Question

What are the key differences in these sets of values?

Source: www.shell.com; www.bp.com; www.chevron.com.

Albert & Whetten (1985) refer to three particular characteristics or traits that help define an individual. They propose that these traits apply equally well to organisations. These characteristics provide a point of distinctiveness, are central or core to the organisation and provide continuity or endure through time. Organisational identity enables members to relate to one another and to their organisation. This last point refers to the level of identification and affinity, or strength of affiliation, individuals feel towards the organisation. This affiliation is a measure of the degree to which individuals believe they share the same characteristics that are used to describe their organisation. In principle, therefore, the closer the degree to which the norms, beliefs and values are shared, the stronger the affiliation. Organisational identity precedes affiliation, which in turn is an antecedent to behaviour that is expressed through corporate identity.

Organisational performance

Why is there such interest in corporate culture? Apart from the intrinsic interest and desire to improve organisational life and experiences for individuals, culture is important because, as O'Reilly & Chatman (1996) point out, strongly held and widely shared norms and values enhance organisational performance. Sørensen (2002) examined the impact of corporate culture on organisations and found that strong cultures create competitive advantage and can also enhance the reliability of an organisation's performance under the right environmental conditions.

> Strong cultures create competitive advantage.

Kotter & Heskett (1992) found that organisations said to have strong cultures generally had higher performance outcomes, as measured by return on investment, net income growth and share value growth. They suggest there are three interrelated reasons that help explain this observation: social control, a reduction in uncertainty and improved motivation.

Strong cultures are characterised by wide support for organisational values and norms (Sørensen, 2002). So, when any violation of behavioural norms is detected, employees act quickly to redress the balance. Employees provide an informal means of social control, one which is more effective than formal controls, from both a cost and a communication perspective (O'Reilly, 1989). In addition, informal social control reinforces the acceptance of the prevailing cultural values. Second, a strong corporate culture reduces uncertainty for employees, especially when they are faced with unusual or unexpected situations. Clarity about corporate goals and practices enables employees to co-ordinate their actions and to decide what the right behaviours are, as there is less room for parties to debate what they should do (Hermalin, 2001). Finally, strong cultures enable employees to feel motivated and involved with the organisation. This is due in part to believing that their actions are not constrained and are chosen freely (O'Reilly & Chatman, 1996). The result of this is that organisational performance improves.

Clarity about corporate goals and practices enables employees to co-ordinate their actions.

Communication climate

The corporate culture plays a significant role in the nature and form of the prevailing corporate communication within an organisation. At a general level this is referred to as the communication climate. The term communication climate refers to the internal atmosphere concerning the way in which information is exchanged by managers and employees. These exchanges can occur through two main processes. One is the formalised exchange that occurs through predetermined or official communication channels, and the other embraces the informal channels through which information is exchanged unofficially, as gossip or 'on the grapevine'. These two communication modes exist in all organisations but in different proportions and configurations.

Communication climate refers to the internal atmosphere concerning the way in which information is exchanged.

The communication climate can be designated as closed or open. An open climate means that information is exchanged freely and without constraint. Participants do not hide or conceal information and their suggestions, ideas and opinions are offered in the knowledge that they will be accepted and acted upon because it is perceived to be of value. In an open climate information suffers little degradation and minimal distortion, regardless of whether it is exchanged upwards, downwards or horizontally. Employee trust in management is high and identification with the organisation's values is also high, which in turn leads to productivity increases (Rosenberg & Rosenstein, 1980).

On the other hand, closed climates reflect information blockages. In closed climates, information moves through established formalised processes, very often hierarchies. This top-down exchange is based on a need-to-know principle which in turn promotes little reciprocal information, resulting in managers missing potentially useful information. In much the same way, closed climates can also be termed silent. This occurs when no one speaks up, offers an opinion or makes suggestions because they believe that whatever they say will not be acted upon as it is not valued by others, most notably managers. In closed climates, trust in management is low and productivity moderate as employee identification with the organisational values and systems is also low.

Understanding the communication climate is important because it not only provides insight into the core character of the organisation and the identity but can also be of assistance when managing change. Communicating change issues in a top-down organisation requires the use of particular tools, media and messages that reflect a generally formalised approach. In an open climate employees are actively involved in the change process, and the informal tools, media and message processes dominate. See Chapter 12 for a deeper consideration of internal communication issues.

It is possible to develop the notion of a communication climate into a more significant and deeper level of analysis and understanding. van Bekkum & van Ruler (2008) propose some interesting ideas based on research examining what Gratton & Ghoshal (2005) refer to as 'signature practices'. These are the unique, company-specific practices and processes that represent an organisation's character. They evolve through an organisation's history and development so they signify what is important, the core values of the organisation.

At Philips, for example, the culture is based on the company's engineering and technocratic origins. At Nokia the culture is one of improvisation and innovation which extols a 'can do' mentality. This reflects the rapid growth of the organisation and it also suggests that the flexibility trait of the Finnish people has been incorporated as well. van Bekkum & van Ruler (2008) propose that the signature practice at Philips is based on the use of tools to deliver processes and undertake surveys within their communication activities. This approach is derived from the engineering and precision mentality that the engineering background has fostered (see Viewpoint 10.3). At Nokia the signature practice is informal co-ordination, again reflecting the flexibility and inno- vative culture of the organisation. The researchers conclude that

> **At Nokia the signature practice is informal co-ordination.**

the way in which an organisation uses corporate communication and branding is a function of the culture, size, structure and history of an organisation. In other words, the unique contex- tual elements frame the way in which corporate communication is managed and delivered.

Viewpoint 10.3 Philips - simply making sense out of tradition

The current slogan used by Philips proclaims 'sense and simplicity' and this constitutes the brand's key promise. This pledge is not an accident of design, more an insight into the organisation's history and origins. Indeed, the slogan appears to be an accurate reflection of the company's core values.

Philips was originally an engineering organisation. Engineers attend to detail, always measure and docu- ment their work and prefer to standardise work-based methods and processes, often through the use of formalised templates and uniform working routines. Standardisation and measurement are ingrained into the work practices of the entire organisation, not just communications. For example, the appraisal process requires that individuals demonstrate how they have helped the company realise and align themselves with the business goals and these measurements are used as the basis of the reward system.

The company believe that 'sense and simplicity' is a combination of two unique capabilities, understand- ing people and their ability to integrate technology and product design. This last capability reflects the company's roots, its history and engineering tradition. The Philips identity therefore demonstrates the way the character of the organisation is reflected in how it chooses to be seen.

PHILIPS
sense and simplicity

Exhibit 10.2	Philips' slogan 'Sense and simplicity' constitutes the brand's key promise.
	Source: Courtesy of Philips Consumer Electronics.

Question

Visit the Philips website (www.philips.com) and review the history of the brand pages to find out how the company has used advertising and symbolism to communicate with stakeholders.

Source: Based on van Bekkum & van Ruler (2008).

Communicating corporate objectives: vision and mission

The communication and reinforcement of an organisation's values are important for several reasons. First, there is the need to provide stability and continuity, yet continuity requires change. Secondly, organisational performance can be improved through a strong culture. Thirdly, it enables the development of a strong reputation, which in turn helps attract good staff and managers, as well as suppliers and other resources.

Management aspirations for the organisation are often expressed in a number of ways. This is only natural as the needs of the target stakeholders are many and varied. One of the more common and enduring ways of communicating the values, beliefs and goals of the organisation are through mission and vision statements. Such proclamations have been subject to public vilification, especially in cases of company collapse following inappropriate strategies or dubious trading or financial arrangements. However, as research by Williams (2008) demonstrates, the use of mission statements continues unabated and unhindered by scandal, scepticism or spin.

The vision and mission statements presented by organisations should be explicit managerial statements of their intentions, aspirations and values (Yamauchi, 2001). As Falsey (1989, p. 3) puts it, in simple terms, a mission statement 'tells two things about a company: who it is and what it does'. Bartkus *et al.* (2000) regard these statements merely as communication tools to define the company's business and goals. However, many statements are neither brief nor succinct and are used to convey messages about purpose, direction, plans, values, beliefs, distinctiveness and, increasingly, how the organisation contributes value to society and the communities in which it operates. Table 10.1 provides some examples of mission statements. See also www.missionstatements.com/fortune_500_mission_statements.html.

The most common reason for creating a mission statement is that it informs stakeholders, primarily employees, of the organisation's direction and goals. As Klemm *et al.* (1991) suggest, one reason to use a mission statement is to provide leadership but in addition there are intentions to motivate employees, provide a means of unification and control (Bart, 1998) and to frame the expectations and stimulate enthusiasm for the organisation (Bartkus *et al.*, 2000). This applies not only to employees but also to various external stakeholders such as analysts, suppliers and customers.

In addition to these more direct benefits, mission statements also provide a number of indirect benefits. These include the assumption that if an organisation can produce a coherent

Mission statements provide a number of indirect benefits.

mission statement, the implication, according to Williams (2008), is that it can 'think reflectively, plan carefully, work collaboratively, and make informed decisions'. Extending this thought suggests that if the organisation can do this (produce a coherent mission statement) then it should have the necessary strategic and operational expertise and skills to be successful.

Mission statements are fashioned by management and are a form of planned corporate communication as they are designed to influence a range of stakeholders. Mission statements are a construct of corporate identity and therefore it is important that the content is both relevant and effective. Several studies have been undertaken to examine the content of mission statements and to see if there is any inter-relationship with organisational financial performance. Both Bart (1997) and Pearce & David (1987) found that four components were particularly significant and appeared more often in mission statements of high-performance organisations: purpose, values, self-concept and desired public image. Concern for public image and employees was clearly apparent in the statements of high-performing organisations and confirmed by a recent study by Williams (2008).

Mission statements articulate the business philosophy and signal to employees what is appropriate behaviour and their role in passing on the right business messages (Simoes *et al.*, 2005, p. 162). Mission statements should be seen as a critical element of corporate identity, developed through corporate communication.

| Table 10.1 | Sample mission statements (as per websites) |

Organisation	Mission statement
The Oberoi Group - operates 28 hotels and three cruisers in five countries under the luxury 'Oberoi' and five-star 'Trident' brands	**Our guests** We are committed to meeting and exceeding the expectations of our guests through our unremitting dedication to every aspect of service. **Our people** We are committed to the growth, development and welfare of our people upon whom we rely to make this happen. **Our distinctiveness** Together, we shall continue the Oberoi tradition of pioneering in the hospitality industry, striving for unsurpassed excellence in high-potential locations all the way from the Middle East to Asia-Pacific. **Our shareholders** As a result, we will create extraordinary value for our stakeholders.
Lion Nathan - a leading alcoholic beverages business with operations in Australia and New Zealand	Our core purpose is bringing more sociability and well-being to our world. It's more than a vision statement - it's a driver of how our business and people behave each and every day.
China Haisum Engineering Co. - provides engineering consultation, design, supervision and EPC, including procurement, construction, training and trial run	Benefiting mankind with science and technology and winning respect with achievements.
Tata - an Indian-based global company operating in communications and information technology, engineering, materials, services, energy, consumer products and chemicals	We are committed to improving the quality of life of the communities we serve. We do this by striving for leadership and global competitiveness in the business sectors in which we operate. Our practice of returning to society what we earn evokes trust among consumers, employees, shareholders and the community. We are committed to protecting this heritage of leadership with trust through the manner in which we conduct our business.
EDF Group - a leading energy player, active in all major electricity businesses	Our mission is to bring sustainable energy solutions home to everyone.
Petrobras - a Brazilian-based, global energy company	To operate in a safe and profitable manner in Brazil and abroad, with social and environmental responsibility, providing products and services that meet clients' needs and that contribute to the development of Brazil and the countries in which it operates.
Transnet - a South African government-owned integrated freight transport company, formed around a core of five operating divisions	Our vision and mission is to be a focused freight transport company, delivering integrated, efficient, safe, reliable and cost-effective services to promote economic growth in South Africa. We aim to achieve this goal by increasing our market share, improving productivity and profitability and by providing appropriate capacity to our customers ahead of demand.

Corporate identity is an expression of what is distinctive, central and continuous about the organisation.

Referring back to the ideas offered by Albert & Whetten (1985), corporate identity is an expression of what is distinctive, central and continuous about the organisation. It is a reflection of what the organisation is and what it hopes to be in the future, ideas that should be shared, understood and encapsulated in mission and vision statements.

Criteria for effective corporate communication

The rationale for using corporate communication has been established, but a key question now is what determines the successful or effective use of corporate communication? A number of criteria need to be considered when answering this question as there is no single prerequisite that is going to be suitable. Figure 10.1 sets out some of the criteria that need to be considered.

Form

The form of the communication will have a direct bearing on the outcome. If the communication is not suited to the task or the expectations of the audiences then the event is unlikely to be successful. The form of a communication can be considered to involve three dimensions. These are inter-related and concern the style, timing and tone of the communication.

Style

The style of the communication refers to the direction and inherent truth of the communication. Using Grunig & Hunt's (1984) 2×2 model of communication it is possible to distinguish four types of communication. These can be seen in Figure 10.2. Grunig & Hunt (1984) attempted to capture the diversity of public relations activities through a framework. They set out four models to reflect the different ways in which communication – or as they approached it, public relations – is, in their opinion, considered to work. These models, based on their experiences as public relations practitioners, constitute a useful approach to understanding the complexity of this form of communication.

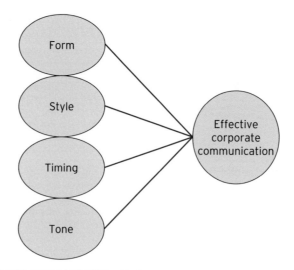

Figure 10.1   Criteria for effective corporate communication.

Characteristic	Model			
	Press agentry/publicity	**Public information**	**Two-way asymmetric**	**Two-way symmetric**
Purpose	Propaganda	Dissemination of information	Scientific persuasion	Mutual understanding
Nature of communication	One way; complete truth not essential	One way; truth important	Two way; imbalanced effects	Two way; balanced effects
Communication model	Source →Rec.*	Source →Rec.*	Source ⇌ Rec.* Feedback	Group ⇌ Group
Nature of research	Little; 'counting house'	Little; readability, readership	Formative; evaluative of attitudes	Formative; evaluative of understanding
Leading historical figures	P.T. Barnum	Ivy Lee	Edward L. Bernays	Bernays, educators, professional leaders
Where practised today	Sports, theatre, product promotion	Government, not-for-profit associations, business	Competitive business, agencies	Regulated business, agencies
Estimated percentage of organisations practising today	15%	50%	20%	15%

* Receiver.

Figure 10.2 Models of communication.
Source: Grunig & Hunt (1984).

The press agentry/publicity model

The essence of this approach is that communication is used as a form of propaganda. That is, the communication flow is essentially one way, and the content is not bound to be strictly truthful as the objective is to convince the receiver of a new idea or offering. This can be observed in the growing proliferation of media events and press releases.

The public information model

Unlike the first model, this approach seeks to disseminate truthful information. While the flow is again one way, there is little focus on persuasion, more on the provision of information. This can best be seen through public health campaigns and government advice communications in respect of crime, education and health. There is little focus on persuasion, and more on the provision of information.

The two-way asymmetric model

Two-way communication is a major element of this model. Feedback from receivers is important, but as power is not equally distributed between the various stakeholders and the organisation, the relationship has to be regarded as asymmetric. The purpose remains to influence attitude and behaviour through persuasion.

The two-way symmetric model

This represents the most acceptable and mutually rewarding form of communication. Power is seen to be dispersed equally between the organisation and its stakeholders, and the intent of the communication flow is considered to be reciprocal. The organisation and its respective publics are prepared to adjust their positions (attitudes and behaviours) in the light of the information flow. A true dialogue emerges through this interpretation, unlike any of the other three models, which see an unbalanced flow of information and expectations.

The model has attracted a great deal of attention and has been reviewed and appraised by a number of commentators (Miller, 1989). As a result of this and a search for excellence in public relations, Grunig (1992) revised the model to reflect the dominance of the 'craft' and the 'professional' approaches to public relations practices. That is, those practitioners who utilise public relations merely as a tool to achieve media visibility can be regarded as 'craft'-oriented. Those organisations whose managers seek to utilise public relations as a means of mediating their relationships with their various stakeholders are seen as 'professional' practitioners. They are considered to be using public relations as a longer-term and proactive form of planned communication. The former see public relations as an instrument, the latter as a means of conducting a dialogue.

The use and interpretation of these models depend upon the circumstances that prevail at any one time. Organisations use a number of these different approaches to manage the communication issues that exist between them and the variety of different stakeholder audiences. However, there is plenty of evidence to suggest that the press/agentry model is the one most used by practitioners and that the two-way symmetrical model is harder to observe in practice.

Timing

The timing of any communication can be critical. Too early and audiences can be caught off guard, too late and the informal communication channels have already delivered an inaccurate version and have confused, upset or diminished the impact of the message.

The timing of any communication can be critical.

Tone

The tone of the message refers to the level of formality. Broadly, organisations can express themselves in a formal and business manner, or be informal, friendly and approachable. For most organisations an entirely formal or informal style is not acceptable; a blend is usually required.

Managers may adopt a style internally that is not necessarily reflected in the externally orientated communications. This can lead to confusion and misunderstanding. However, adopting a more informal style can help to build teams, and the tactical use of the first person and the collective term 'we' can help to embrace and help build internal identity.

Reason for change

Corporate communication contributes to a range of activities, some of which occur regularly as a form of maintenance communication, reinforcing the identity, e.g. the use of internal communication and press releases. The publication of statutory reports and reporting documentation occurs frequently, the intention being to provide information in order to maintain stakeholders' interest, involvement and relationship with the organisation. However, corporate communication is often associated with one-off or unexpected events. Typically these involve crises and disasters, but in an environment characterised by sudden change and unexpected stakeholder actions, communication needs to be adaptive and capable of being used flexibly. Whilst corporate communication plays an important role preventing and ameliorating any damage caused by crises, the depth of damage and speed of recovery can be a function of the strength of the prevailing reputation prior to the crisis.

Corporate communication can be used to herald, prepare, inform, advise, direct and reconcile issues associated with the change process.

Corporate communication is particularly important during periods of organisational change. It can be used to herald, prepare, inform, advise, direct and reconcile issues associated with the change process.

Table 10.2	Key reasons for corporate rebranding
Core reason for change	**Form and explanation**
Structural and ownership	Merger, acquisition and divestiture activity often means that the previous positioning and names, logos and slogans are no longer relevant.
Marketplace realignments	Previous poor performance, ethical issues or severe media comment require that the organisation distance itself and starts again.
	Competitors reposition and effectively sideline the organisation.
	The value (or esteem) of the organisation has fallen.
Changed internal dynamics	The current image has become outdated or stakeholders misunderstand what the organisation is or what it is trying to achieve.
	A new corporate structure and/or vision and values have been established.
	A new leader has been appointed who wishes to imprint themselves on the organisation.

Type of change

The reasons for using corporate communication were examined in Chapter 9. Many of these involve some form of organisational change, often concerning some form of corporate rebranding. Stuart & Muzellec (2004) argue that corporate rebranding requires stakeholders to be informed of change and that this should only be undertaken when there has been genuine transformation. The key reasons for rebranding range from changes in the organisational structure and ownership through to competitive and image related issues. These are set out in Table 10.2.

Corporate credibility

Messages are perceived in many different ways but a critical determinant concerns the credibility that is attributed to the source of the message itself. Kelman (1961) believes that the source of a message has three particular characteristics: the level of perceived credibility as seen in terms of perceived objectivity and expertise; the degree to which the source is regarded as attractive and message recipients are motivated to develop a similar association or position; and the degree of power that the source is believed to possess. This is manifest in the ability of the source to reward or punish message recipients.

From this construct of source characteristics, three key components of source credibility can be distinguished:

> Three key components of source credibility can be distinguished.

- What is the level of perceived expertise (how much relevant knowledge is the source thought to hold)?
- What are the personal motives the source is believed to possess (what is the reason for the source to be involved)?
- What degree of trust can be placed in what the source says or does on behalf of the endorsement?

Stakeholders trade off the validity of claims made by brands against the perceived trustworthiness and expertise of the organisation, about whom the message refers. The result is that a claim may have reduced impact if either of these two components is doubtful or not capable of verification, but if repeated enough times it may enable audiences to accept that the organisation and its products are very effective and of sufficiently high performance to try them.

Table 10.3	Elements of corporate credibility
Element of corporate credibility	**Explanation**
Expertise	The degree to which a corporate brand is perceived to possess relevant knowledge and skills
Trustworthiness	The degree to which a corporate brand is perceived to be an honest source of products
Likeableness	The degree to which a corporate brand is valued by stakeholders in terms of sympathetic behaviour, perseverance and smartness

Source: Based on Li *et al.* (2011).

Using these constructs, corporate credibility refers to the extent to which stakeholders believe that the company is trustworthy, has sufficient expertise, and, as Yi *et al.* (2011) indicate, is likeable. These terms are set out in Table 10.3.

Corporate image is partly construed from perceived credibility.

Corporate image is therefore partly construed from perceived credibility. In much the same way that product related credibility is important, so corporate credibility plays an important role in influencing stakeholder perceptions and customer purchase intentions (Lafferty *et al.*, 2002).

Fombrun (1996) suggests that corporate-brand credibility can be used to evaluate an organisation's products/services, which in turn affects purchase intention. From this position, Aaker & Joachimsthaler (2000) believe that a strong and positive corporate-brand credibility can enhance overall brand image. This influences brand equity, which results in higher purchase intentions, and, as Winters (1988) and Davis (1994) found, is positively related to sales.

The corporate identity mix

Corporate communication expresses the corporate personality.

Corporate communication expresses the corporate personality. It is used to convey the corporate identity, influence the perception stakeholders have of the organisation and ultimately enhance corporate reputation. Corporate identity was originally deemed to be about the visual aspects of communication. Corporate communication was rooted in graphic design and the use of logos, colour, letterheads, brand design and workwear were seen as a means of creating a positive first impression when a stakeholder contacted an organisation.

van Riel & Fombrun (2007) cite Birkigt & Stadler (1986) as the researchers who extended the original idea that corporate identity was a purely visual activity to one that encompassed other expressions of the personality. Although the role of symbolism and design is still recognised as an important facet of an organisation's expression, other elements, such as behaviour and planned communication, are now considered to play complementary roles. Birkigt & Stadler identified two further elements that contribute to the corporate identity: behaviour and communication. They referred to this combination of elements as the corporate identity mix, as set out in Figure 10.3. Each is considered in turn.

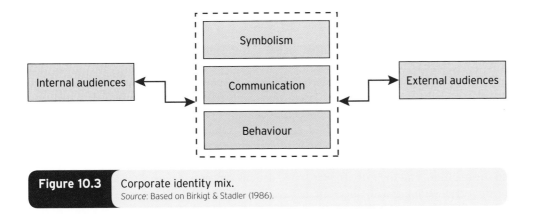

Figure 10.3	Corporate identity mix.
	Source: Based on Birkigt & Stadler (1986).

Symbolism

There are many graphic elements that can be used to communicate the identity of an organisation. In addition to those mentioned above, an organisation's architecture and office design, the style and layout of the reception area, signage, the website and its navigability, labelling and depth and range of content all communicate something about the values, beliefs and direction of the organisation.

Visual artefacts trigger associations.

However, out of all the many elements used to communicate symbolically, three stand out as central to an organisation's visual appearance: the company name, the logo and the slogan or strapline. These visual artefacts trigger associations and enable stakeholders to help them recognise an organisation, attribute meaning and understand what it stands for and the values it represents. Think of the shell used by Shell, the whoosh of Nike and arches of McDonald's. All are instantly recognised, understood and assigned meaning. Think of the names BBC, Samsung and National Trust and consider the meaning each conveys. Chapter 11 explores issues associated with these three types of symbol.

Planned communications

Organisations use a range of premeditated communication activities in an attempt to influence particular stakeholders. In addition to the use of mission and vision statements discussed earlier, these planned communications can be seen in terms of corporate advertising, sponsorships, public relations, brochures, company reports, web pages and more contemporary activities such as corporate blogs, podcasts and white papers.

These planned communications provide an opportunity for management to consider what messages they want to convey to their stakeholders and how they should achieve this. This requires internal co-ordination and a systematic planning process. Agencies and other external stakeholders need to be incorporated into the process. When there is an organisational structure coupled with a system and processes that encourage integration, these decisions can be made with a greater sense of purpose and confidence. However, in the absence of an integrative framework, the emphasis on managers is to drive for consistency in what is said and how it is conveyed.

Chapter 11 explores issues related to specific forms of planned communication, including corporate advertising, public relations, websites and the use of corporate blogs.

Behaviour

The behaviour exhibited by an organisation has a strong influence on the way it is perceived by stakeholders. Behaviour is manifested in various ways. At one level the behaviour of employees provides cues about the extent to which individuals support and understand the organisation.

Behaviour is manifested in various ways.

Their interactions with stakeholders reveal levels of endorsement, engagement and empathy with audience needs plus their depth of support and association with their organisation.

Management behaviour is expressed through their actions and decisions. A third form of behaviour concerns the way CEOs communicate. CEOs represent the public face of an organisation, and their deeds, words and actions can provide insight into the true values of the organisation. Finally there are behaviours exhibited by the organisation as a whole, not attributable to particular individuals. These may concern the organisation's level of disclosure in relation to financial issues or its position regarding environmental and sustainability issues.

Another way of considering means to build corporate reputation is to consider two main approaches, both identifiable in the identity mix. These are symbolic management and behavioural management (Grunig & Grunig, 1998). The former involves the use of resources to create impressions through positive symbolic signals. This involves creating media visibility and favourability. The latter concerns the use of resources to develop positive behavioural signals relevant to the needs of stakeholders; e.g. the development of corporate policy controls and codes of conduct which can lead to improved business performance. Research by Kim *et al.* (2007) found that organisations should direct resources to build corporate performance

Symbolic attempts to improve reputation are important because they can complement the behavioural strategies.

through operational processes and innovation as this leads to enhanced performance reputation and financial results. Symbolic attempts to improve reputation are important because they can complement the behavioural strategies, but in isolation their impact may be limited.

Messages and organisational positioning

As corporate communication expresses the organisation's values and beliefs through the corporate identity, it has a central role in developing the images stakeholders have of an organisation. These images are framed by the key messages they receive and the context in which communications are exchanged.

It follows that the core messages employed by an organisation are of paramount importance as these are used by stakeholders to position the organisation in their minds. Corporate communication strategy should be developed thematically and consistently around an agreed core theme, or a 'reputational platform' according to van Riel & Fombrun (2007). If stakeholders do not discern any core messages then the organisation will not be positioned clearly and the resultant diffused or confused positioning might lead to under-performance.

The core positioning theme should be authentic, transparent, consistent and credible.

The core positioning theme should be authentic, transparent, consistent and, of course, credible. There are five main core themes that can be developed. These are set out in Table 10.4.

When selecting a root position, van Riel & Fombrun (2007) refer to the need for the reputational platform to reflect the organisation's history, identity, values and reputation accurately and authentically. Selection should be based around a test of three criteria. Is the platform relevant, realistic and appealing?

Once a core theme is agreed, it should be used as a central tenet for all communications (see Viewpoint 10.4 on Hewlett Packard).

Table 10.4	Core positioning themes	
Core positioning theme	**Explanation**	**Examples**
Functional	Functional positioning uses rational information and should be based on a claim not yet used by competitors. This strategy is founded on being superior about its products, customers served, achievements or contribution to society or the industry. This is informational content claimed through the use of justified information.	Lucent Technologies BMW
Expressive	This form of positioning attempts to differentiate the organisation through the use of symbols and values. By repeated use of the symbols that represent a particular set of values, the organisation can become associated with those values. This is transformational content claimed through association.	Kingfisher, AstraZeneca
Emotional	Positioning through an emotional theme aims to draw stakeholders to an organisation by provoking positive responses and involvement. This is emotional content claimed through involvement and affiliation.	Orange
General	This positioning strategy can be made by any organisation in an industry and attempts to raise overall industry demand rather than set out a point of differentiation or superiority. Often used by organisations who have a substantial market share. This is informational content claimed through an industry-wide issue without reference to industry leadership.	Campbell's Soup
First strike	This positioning is similar to the generic strategy but under this strategy the organisation claims superiority, and hence differentiation, on the basis of being the first and only organisation to make the claim. This is informational content claimed through an industry-wide issue with reference to industry leadership.	Philips, BP

Source: Based on Cornelissen (2008) and van Riel & Fombrun (2007).

Viewpoint 10.4	Far from being saucy, the HP story

When Carly Fiorina became CEO at Hewlett Packard she inherited a company whose origins and values lay with computer manufacturing and a reinforcing culture, known as 'the HP way'. It was her belief that the culture was restricting innovation and was the main reason preventing the company from moving forward. Her strategy was to develop a new corporate story, one that either acknowledged the strength of the past in terms of the company's origins and roots with the founders, or one that looked to a new future. She chose to use the heritage of Hewlett Packard to frame the future. William Hewlett and David Packard had founded the company in a garage and so the new story was based around the 'rules of the garage' to drive innovation.

The identity mix included corporate advertising which was used to convey the mission, values and appropriate behaviour. The story was that the company was reinventing itself as an information technology player and featured selected 'star' employees in the communications, to suggest that the current employees were

Exhibit 10.3 Hewlett Packard's advertising shows the garage in which the founders started the company.
Source: Alamy Images/SiliconValleyStock.

purveyors of the company's mission and were spiritually descended from the founders. The corporate slogan was changed to 'invent' and advertising showed the garage where the founders started the company.

Question

The garage has evolved into a firm storyline and has become a cultural element. Is the garage an asset or liability? Justify your response.

Source: Based on Dowling (2006).

Storytelling

Once the core theme is established and the desired positioning agreed, corporate communication messages can be developed. There are numerous ways in which this can be accomplished, but van Riel & Fombrun (2007) use corporate storytelling as a central and critical foundation.

In the last chapter an exploration of the principles of integrated corporate communication finished with the idea that integration may be best understood, and practised, through storytelling. Building corporate stories brings an emotional dimension to an organisation and can help people to learn, understand and share information and ideas. Stories can help people to understand an organisation, they enable people to make a personal connection and they can demonstrate, across the organisation, how others are contributing to it. For example, Honest Tea, a company that sells loose and bagged teas have a page on their website called 'Our Story', recalling how the idea for the company was shaped and how the business was started. This approach is quite common.

> **Stories can help people understand an organisation.**

Market research indicates that many people are interested in more than just the product or service. They want to know the behind-the-scenes stories of organisations. Meeting this need helps provide organisations with a strong point of differentiation, something that cannot be copied. Whilst these and other stories are often about accomplishment and success, they are considered to be ways in which improved working practices can help advance performance by reducing levels of absenteeism and staff turnover, and enhancing efficiency, productivity and engagement.

> **Stories about corporate successes and failures are remembered.**

Unlike facts, text and figures, stories about corporate successes and failures are remembered. Stories enable stakeholders to understand the organisation and develop relationships and they serve to convey aspirations and purpose. For example, 3M uses stories as part of its business planning to outline the challenges the company is facing and its future. Stories help to enrich the process and, if necessary, give drama in order for the messages to be recalled. Stories can be communicated through press releases, websites, intranets, speeches and even the annual report, which in itself is an attempt to tell a financial story.

Stories can be understood in terms of four main categories:

- **Myths and origins** are used to recall how a company started and what its principles are, but very often the focus is on how it overcame early difficulties and achieved success. The current values can often be seen embedded in these stories.

- **Corporate prophecies** are predictions about an organisation's future, which are often based on past stories or stories about other organisations.

- **Hero stories** recall people from the organisation who confronted and overcame a dilemma. The story provides a set of behaviours and values to be copied by others, especially during periods of crisis. These stories help people to establish priorities and make decisions.

- **Archived narratives** are an organisation's collection of stories which trace its history and development. With organisations changing names, being merged, bought out and reconstituted there is an increasing need to access key stories from the past in order to provide a sense of history.

Microsoft has developed a 'storytelling framework' to generate focused relevant communications. The framework acts as a filter so that key messages are constantly reinforced. Using a 'master narrative', which sets out the three key elements that all Microsoft stories must contain, the framework provides a means of simplifying stories and communications emerging from a complex environment. Rather than promote this approach as a communication device Microsoft has stressed the business significance of the storytelling framework (Love, 2006).

Picking up the idea floated at the beginning of this section, namely that storytelling provides a strong point of integration, Douglas (2009, p. 23) explains that stories help Mindshare, the global media network, 'pull together the rational pieces of a picture into a more emotional, meaningful whole'. He also refers to the ability of stories to be a 'coherent, cohesive force that pulls people together and moves them forward'. In other words, the writing of stories (the process), storytelling (the delivery) and the reading of stories (the consumption) provide integration opportunities, from both an internal and an external perspective.

Communicating corporate responsibility

Corporate responsibility refers to the ethical and moral issues related to the social, environmental and economic impact of organisations' decisions and behaviour. The importance of organisations behaving in a responsible manner and communicating with stakeholders how responsible they are has grown considerably in the last 10–15 years. One of the reasons for this is the increasing consumer demand for improved corporate transparency following a series of high-profile corporate failures, such as Enron and Lehman Brothers, and near failures, such as AIG, RBS and Lloyds. In addition, organisations have started to address their corporate responsibilities in increasing numbers because it makes business sense. Also, some organisations hold strong values and beliefs regarding the way they conduct business from both a moral and an ethical perspective, e.g. The Body Shop and The Co-operative Society. Other organisations have sensed the shift in culture and values, particularly as the debate on climate and environmental change has become more prominent and more widely reported. Marks & Spencer has developed an environmental strategy called Plan A (see Viewpoint 10.5) in response to these changes and in the belief that it makes business sense in the long run.

> Some organisations hold strong values and beliefs regarding the way they conduct business.

Viewpoint 10.5 | M&S take full responsibility

(See also Minicase 3.1, p. 319)

Plan A, launched in January 2007, involves working with customers and suppliers to combat climate change, reduce waste, use sustainable raw materials, trade ethically, and help M&S's customers to lead healthier lifestyles. These are regarded as the five pillars of the plan, within which there are 100 commitments.

M&S call it Plan A because it's now the only way to do business. There is no Plan B. For example, M&S aim to make all their UK and Irish operations carbon-neutral by 2012, by maximising their use of renewable energy. They are already reducing the number of carrier bags and packaging and are looking for new ways to recycle. The goal is that by 2012 none of their clothing or packaging should be sent to landfill.

With over a quarter of million workers worldwide, M&S aim to set new trading standards that improve the lives and communities of those whose work is associated with the firm. They have identified 20 ways to improve the sustainability of their key raw materials. With regard to health, they have expanded their range of healthier options and introduced a clearer 'traffic light' labelling system on packaging to help customers make informed food choices.

Finally, in support of Plan A, M&S have set up the Clothes Exchange campaign. Referred to as their Wardrobe Intervention scheme, M&S cheekily invites people to nominate a friend or relative with a 'questionable taste in fashion' and sends them an e-card informing them how they can update their wardrobe with the M&S/Oxfam Clothes Exchange. Should they decide to take their redundant M&S clothes to a local Oxfam, they are given a £5 M&S voucher for each visit. This not only helps Oxfam but also helps to reduce the amount of clothing going to landfill.

Exhibit 10.4 | Marks & Spencer's Plan A involves aims to combat climate change, reduce waste, use sustainable raw materials, trade ethically and help its customers to lead healthier lifestyles.
Source: Marks and Spencer plc (company), with permission.

Question

To what extent is Plan A the act of an organisation demonstrating responsibility and leadership rather than a cynical exploitation of fashionable rhetoric?

Source: Based on www.plana.marksandspencer.com/about.

During this 10- to 15-year period various terms have been used to express the activities associated with the moral, social, environmental and ethical issues faced by organisations. These range from 'corporate social responsibility' (CSR) and 'corporate ethics' to 'corporate citizenship', 'business ethics' and 'corporate environmental and sustainability management'. These umbrella terms have been used to describe organisational initiatives concerning their approach to corporate philanthropy, compliance, regulation, social justice, and environmental and sustainability issues. Of these, the term corporate responsibility has emerged as the dominant terminology and is the one used here.

> Various terms have been used to express the activities associated with the moral, social, environmental and ethical issues faced by organisations.

The role of organisations in society can be considered in terms of a spectrum. At one end, organisations seek to maximise profits for their shareholders and simply comply, at a minimal level, with the prevailing regulations and legal requirements. At the other end of the spectrum, organisations assume a wide role in society, one that extends to all stakeholders and reaches far beyond the minimal legal and regulatory requirements to encompass the 'non-financial expectations of stakeholders' (Doorley & Garcia, 2007, p. 359). Most organisations lie somewhere on this scale and most make compromises as they seek to find a comfortable balance between the need for profit and the need for altruism and responsibility.

A discussion about the nature, characteristics and issues associated with corporate responsibility is beyond the brief for this book. What is important here is to examine why the communication of a firm's actions regarding their corporate responsibilities is important and to consider how organisations can use communication to convey their corporate responsibility.

What should be communicated as corporate responsibility?

There is some agreement that corporate reputation communication should provide information that legitimates an organisation's behaviour by trying to influence stakeholders' and society's image of the company (Birth and Illia, 2008). Various researchers provide evidence to suggest that corporate and product ads that are claim specific are more effective than ads that make general or open-ended, unspecific claims. For example, ads that specify the number of trees an organisation plants each year are deemed to have a positive impact on corporate reputation rather than ads that state that the organisation plants trees (Holbrook, 1978; Winters, 1988; Darley & Smith, 1993).

Berens & van Rekom (2008) extend these ideas and consider ways in which messages about CSR are communicated by organisations. They adopt ideas about the degree to which a message might be deemed factual. A factual message is capable of verification, perhaps on a scale (e.g. 'We planted 375,000 trees last year'). The converse is an impressionistic claim, which is characterised by claims that require individual interpretation ('We planted a lot of trees last year') and hence are capable of being widely misinterpreted. Berens & van Rekom (2008) found that not only does factualness positively influence corporate reputation for CSR but it can also have a positive impact on the credibility of the message. This has the capability to enhance the reputation of the organisation in terms of its overall corporate ability and hence achieve its core performance goals.

> A factual message is capable of verification.

Finally, Berens & van Rekom (2008) refer to work by Semin *et al.* (2005), which suggests that concrete (factual) messages are more effective when the focus is on harm prevention, while abstract (impressionistic) messages are more effective when the focus is on promoting benefits. This is because details are important to those trying to prevent harm whereas the desired outcomes need to be central when supporting a benefit campaign. Therefore, CSR messages about an organisation caring for the environment are likely to be successful.

> Abstract messages are more effective when the focus is on promoting benefits.

How to communicate corporate responsibility activities

The delivery of an organisation's corporate responsibility is often undertaken through corporate advertising, public affairs, issues management and website facilities. Details about how these are used are examined in Chapters 11 and 12.

A CSR Europe (2000) report claimed that CSR is communicated through a variety of tools and media, including 'social reports, thematic reports, codes of conduct, web sites, stakeholder consultations, internal channels, prizes, events, cause related marketing, product packaging, interventions, in the press and on TV, and points of sale' (p. 185). Birth & Illia (2008) researched the CSR communication strategies of the top 300 companies in Switzerland, and found that internal channels, websites and stakeholder consultations are the most commonly used. Doorley & Garcia (2007) identify four particular tools which deliver messages about corporate responsibility: codes of conduct, monitoring and certification initiatives, training and education programmes and corporate responsibility reporting.

Codes of conduct

The purpose of a code of conduct is to communicate to suppliers and employees the minimal standards expected within their relationship. Codes can be formatted as:

- **compliance codes** – these statements specify conduct that is not permitted and is intended to provide guidance
- **corporate credos** – these are intended to inform stakeholders about corporate commitments, values and objectives
- **management philosophy statements** – these are formal announcements about the way the company or CEO wants the business to develop and the approach that will be taken (ILO, 2009).

The code of conduct, often voluntary, serves to provide a performance benchmark.

The code, often voluntary, serves to provide a performance benchmark and can act as a compliance mechanism. However, codes of conduct can be double-edged to the extent that, should an organisation fail to meet the standards it has set, then it is open to criticism and its reputation may be tarnished.

Monitoring and certification initiatives

Through the use of independent research, audits, surveys and inspections, organisations attempt to keep stakeholders informed about how well they are progressing towards the achievement of code compliance goals. Certification provided by an independent body is another means by which compliance with a code can be communicated.

Training and education programmes

Training and education programmes targeted at employees are critical if they are to understand and support the codes of conduct that have been agreed, and behave responsibly towards others and the environment. However, all members of an organisation's value chain need to be involved in order that they not only appreciate the business benefits of acting in a socially and environmentally responsible manner but they also perform above the minimum standards.

Corporate responsibility reporting

Whilst there is a legal and regulatory requirement to report financial performance data, organisations are increasingly choosing to report non-financial information. In particular, organisations are reporting their actions towards improving their performance with regard to best practice and their responsibilities towards other stakeholders and the environment. Some organisations even convene committees of independent experts to publicly comment on their reports. One of the main reasons for publishing these reports is to provide a source of information that stakeholders can use to make judgments about the organisation and so inform their decision-making with regard to investments they might choose to make.

In addition to these methods, some organisations use corporate advertising to disclose information about their activities related to corporate responsibility. These are considered in Chapter 11.

> Some organisations use corporate advertising to disclose information about their CSR activities.

Dimensions of corporate responsibility messages

However, just as using the right tools is important, so is the communication of the right corporate message concerning an organisation's responsibilities. There are four important dimensions to communicating corporate responsibility; the communications must be accurate, timely, transparent and credible.

Accuracy

Providing accurate information, either voluntarily or in response to stakeholder observations, is the act of a responsible organisation. Whether this information relates to financial performance, strategy, operational issues concerning working conditions at home or abroad, environmental practices, matters of disclosure or breaches of code of conduct, accuracy is paramount. For example, Wolfson Microelectronics were fined £200,000 for delaying the announcement (to disclose news) about the loss of a significant customer's business. This was deemed by the FSA to be inside information, and it was stated that the action created a false investors' market (Pinsent Masons, 2011).

Timely

Some messages can be regarded as fulfilling a maintenance function in that they keep stakeholders informed and up-to-date about corporate developments, changes in policies, codes of conduct and position on various relevant issues. These need to be communicated at the first appropriate opportunity. Other messages might be required as a response to externally generated issues and concerns. It is critical that responses are timed to meet the needs of the media as well as stakeholders, in order to appear both concerned and involved. Delays can be interpreted as stalling, hesitancy and not distanced from the issue.

Transparency

The information provided should be complete, relevant and meaningful or, in other words, transparent. Transparent information is necessary as not only does it allow recipients to assess

> The information provided should be complete, relevant and meaningful.

issues based on full information but it also conveys openness and willingness to engage with stakeholders on issues that are important to them.

Credibility

Transparency also aids credibility which is an important foundation when building reputation. The views of independent experts and stakeholders are perceived as objective and credible, in contrast to an organisation's self-proclamation. The use of voluntary codes of conduct and reviews of business practice in the light of adverse media comment are perceived to be stronger and more effective if reviewed by independent organisations and individuals. For example, Doorley & Garcia (2007) suggest that credibility can be earned through acknowledging the existence of a problem, by adopting global or widely held standards or by working with stakeholders in a partnership, either formally or informally.

Using corporate responsibility for positioning

Although the use of corporate responsibility as a means of positioning an organisation is intuitively appealing, it does not appear to be well established in the literature. Maignan & Farrell (2001) report that negative/positive CSR associations might have a harmful/supportive impact on product evaluations but argue that further research is required. Jones *et al.* (2008) looked at the use of CSR by retailers in store. They found considerable disparity concerning the communication of these issues across the top 10 major grocery retailers. Even though some make considerable efforts to communicate these issues through their websites, the volume of their related in-store communications was noticeably weak. They report that the main themes communicated in store are organic and Fairtrade products, healthy and locally produced foods and community issues. CSR information is printed on packaging and labels, shelf edges, leaflets, banners and posters. What is clear from their relatively limited sample is that these national retailers were not incorporating corporate responsibility as a positioning strategy.

Anselmsson & Johansson (2007) found that the perception consumers have of the different aspects of corporate responsibility revolved around three main dimensions: human responsibility, product responsibility and environmental responsibility (see Table 10.5). The study was based on retailer, producer and me-too brands in the Swedish grocery market. The study measured consumer attitudes, at the point of purchase, towards frozen food products and their perceived level of CSR. One of the findings supports the point made originally by Kolk (2005), that manufacturers or producers are often distanced from consumers relative to retail brands. These multinational organisations are often criticised for their perceived lack of responsibility, especially in the countries that supply them. On the other hand, retailer brands are often closer to the markets in which they operate and are perceived to be more responsible.

Although the link between corporate responsibility and intention to purchase was weak, possibly a function of the methodology, there is sufficient evidence that consumers do consider an organisation's corporate responsibility when making purchase decisions. The study by Anselmsson & Johansson (2007) found that there are opportunities for brands to use corporate responsibility as a point of differentiation and positioning. Indeed, Cornelissen (2007) highlights the Co-operative Bank as a supreme example of a financial services brand positioning itself successfully on a CSR platform. The parent company, the Co-operative (Society), was founded on moral and egalitarian principles, so the positioning of the bank in the same way is a natural development, utilising the goodwill and understanding already embedded in the name.

> There is evidence that consumers consider an organisation's corporate responsibility when making purchase decisions.

Table 10.5	Three key consumer perceptions of CSR responsibility
CSR area of responsibility	**Explanation**
Human responsibility	A perception that the company's suppliers uphold natural, good farming principles and provide good working conditions for their employees
Product responsibility	A perception that the company has clear environmental policies, uses recyclable packaging, and produces environmentally friendly, ecologically sound, non-harmful products
Environmental responsibility	A perception that the company lists the full contents of products, the country of origin and accepts liability for the performance and functionality of its products

Source: Based on Anselmsson & Johansson (2007).

Chapter summary

In order to help consolidate your understanding of the messaging issues associated with corporate communication, here are the key points summarised against each of the learning objectives.

1. Determine the impact of corporate culture on corporate communication

The characteristics or traits that form an integral part of corporate culture provide stability, continuity and a means through which an organisation can change and evolve. Corporate culture shapes the way in which members behave and communicate with one another and with external stakeholders.

2. Explain the characteristics and importance of communication climate

The term communication climate refers to the internal atmosphere concerning the way in which information is exchanged by managers and employees. These exchanges can be formal or informal and both modes exist in all organisations, but in different proportions and configurations. Understanding the communication climate is important not only because it provides an insight into the core character of the organisation and its identity but also because it can also be of assistance when managing change.

3. Consider the issues associated with communicating an organisation's objectives, including its vision and mission

Vision and mission statements are a critical element of corporate identity, developed through corporate communication. They articulate the business philosophy and inform stakeholders, primarily employees, of the organisation's direction and goals, and signal what is appropriate behaviour and what is their role in passing on the right business messages.

4. Explore how time and circumstance can influence the impact of corporate communication

A number of criteria are involved in understanding the circumstances in which corporate communications are used. These include the form of the messages, the timing, type and reason for the change and issues associated with the credibility of the messages themselves.

5. Examine the identity mix and its use in corporate branding

The corporate identity mix consists of three main elements: symbolism, planned communications and behaviour. These elements are used, in varying degrees, by all organisations to communicate how they want to be seen.

6. Examine how corporate communication can impact on an organisation's positioning

Corporate communication strategy should be developed thematically and consistently around an agreed core theme, or a 'reputational platform'. The core messages developed by an organisation are used by stakeholders to position the organisation in their minds. When the core theme is established and the desired positioning agreed, corporate communication messages can be developed. Corporate storytelling can be used as a central and critical foundation upon which the position is developed. Stories can be understood in terms of four main categories: myths and origins, corporate prophecies, hero stories and archived narratives.

7. Discuss ways in which organisations address ethical, CSR and sustainability issues through their communications

Corporate responsibility refers to the ethical and moral issues related to the social, environmental and economic impact of organisations' decisions and behaviour. Corporate reputation communication should provide information that legitimates an organisation's behaviour by trying to influence stakeholders' and society's image of the company.

Discussion questions

1. Write brief notes explaining the nature of culture in organisations.

2. Identify the three core characteristics or traits that Albert & Whetten (1985) highlighted as present in individuals and organisations.

3. Explain why strong corporate cultures are beneficial to organisations.

4. Prepare notes for a PowerPoint presentation outlining the key characteristics of a communication climate.

5. Write a brief report arguing the case for and against the use of mission statements. How do they assist corporate communication?

6. Grunig & Hunt (1984) identified four types of communication (publics). What are they and how do they differ from one another?

7. Identify the elements of the corporate identity mix. Select one of them and find four ways in which an organisation of your choice uses it.

8. Set out the four features that distinguish an organisation's core positioning theme. Now find examples for each of the five core positioning themes.

9. Organisations use a variety of channels and tools to deliver messages about their corporate responsibility. Name seven.

10. Consumers are thought to consider corporate responsibility in one of three ways, according to Anselmsson & Johansson (2007). What are they and how might they impact on a brand's communications?

References

Aaker, D. & Joachimsthaler, E. (2000). *Brand leadership*. New York, NY: The Free Press.

Albert, S. & Whetten, D.A. (1985). Organisational identity. In: Cummings, L.L. & Straw, B.M., eds. *Research in Organizational Behavior*. Greenwich, CT: JT Press, pp. 239–295.

Anselmsson, J. & Johansson, U. (2007). Corporate responsibility and the positioning of grocery brands. *International Journal of Retail and Distribution Management* 35(10), 835–856.

Bart, C.K. (1997). Industrial firms and the power of mission. *Industrial Marketing Management* 26, 371–383.

Bartkus, B. Glassman, M. & McAfee, R.B. (2000). Mission statements: are they smoke and mirrors? *Business Horizons* 43(6), 23–29.

van Bekkum, T. & van Ruler, B. (2008). Corporate communications and corporate reputation. In: Melewar, T.C. ed. *Facets of Corporate Identity, Communication and Reputation*. London: Routledge, pp. 83–95.

Berens, G. & van Rekom, J. (2008). How specific should corporate communication be? In: Melewar, T.C. ed. *Facets of Corporate Identity, Communication and Reputation*. Routledge: London, pp. 96–119.

Birkigt, K. & Stadler, M.M. (1986). *Corporate Identity, Grundlagen, Funktionen, Fallspielen*. Landsberg am Lech: Verlag Moderne Industrie.

Birth, G. & Illia, L. (2008). Communicating CSR: practices among Switzerland's top 300 companies. *Corporate Communications, an International Journal* 13(2), 182–196.

Burt, R.S., Gabbay, S.M., Holt, G. & Moran, P. (1994). Contingent organization as a network theory: the culture performance contingency function. *Acta Sociologica* 37: 345–370.

Businessweek (2005). Apple's other legacy: top designers. (September 6). Online: http://www.businessweek.com/technology/content/sep2005/tc2005096_1655_tc210.htm. Accessed: 11 February 2009.

Cornelissen, J. (2008). *Corporate Communication: Theory and Practice*, 2nd edn. London: Sage.

CSR Europe (2000). *Communicating Corporate Social Responsibility*. Brussels: CS Europe Publications.

Darley, W.K. & Smith, R.E. (1993). Advertising claim objectivity: antecedents and effects. *Journal of Marketing* 57, 100–113.

Davis, J.J. (1994). Consumer response to corporate environmental advertising. *Journal of Consumer Marketing* 11(2), 25–47.

Doorley, J. & Garcia, H.F. (2007). *Reputation Management*. New York: Routledge.

Douglas, K. (2009). Integration essays: the power of the story. *Campaign*, 4 December, 23.

Dowling, G. (1996). Corporate identity traps, *Australian Graduate School of Management, Working Paper Series*. Sydney, Australia: University of New South Wales.

Dowling, G. (2006). Communicating corporate reputation through stories, *California Management Review* 49(1), 82–100.

Falsey, T.A. (1989). *Corporate Philosophies and Mission Statements: a Survey and Guide for Corporate Communicators and Management*. Westport, CT: Greenwood.

Fombrun, C.J. (1996). *Reputation: Realizing Value from the Corporate Image*. Boston, MA: Harvard Business School Press.

Gordon, G.G. & DiTomaso, N. (1992). Predicting corporate performance from organizational culture. *Journal of Management Studies* 29, 783–799.

Gratton, L. & Ghoshal, S. (2005). Beyond best practice. *MIT Sloan Management Review* 6(3), 49–57.

Grunig, J. (1992). Models of public relations and communication. In: Grunig, J.E., Dozier, D.M., Ehling, P., Grunig, L.A., Repper, F.C. & Whits, J. eds. *Excellence in Public Relations and Communications Management*. Hillsdale, NJ: Lawrence Erlbaum, pp. 285–325.

Grunig, J.E. & Grunig, L.A. (1998). The relationship between public relations and marketing in excellent organization: evidence from the IBC study. *Journal of Marketing Communications* 4, 141–162.

Grunig, J. & Hunt, T. (1984). *Managing Public Relations*. New York: Holt, Rinehart & Winston.

Hermalin, B.E. (2001). Economics and corporate culture. In: Cartwright, S., Cooper, C.L. & Earley, P.C., eds. *Handbook of Organizational Culture and Climate*. New York: Wiley, pp. 217–261.

Holbrook, M.B. (1978). Beyond attitude structure, toward the informational determinants of attitude. *Journal of Marketing Research* 15(6), 545–556.

ILO (2009). *Corporate Codes of Conduct, International Labour Organization*. Online: http://actrav.itcilo.org/actrav-english/telearn/global/ilo/code/. Accessed: 8 March 2009.

Jones, P., Comfort, D. & Hillier, D. (2008). Corporate responsibility and marketing communications within stores: a case study of UK food retailers. *Journal of Food Products Marketing* 14(4), 109–119.

Kellaway, L. (2002). Beyond parody: PwC's rebranding exercise is demoralizing for employees and satirists alike. *Financial Times*, 17 June, 12.

Kelman, H. (1961). Processes of opinion change. *Public Opinion Quarterly* 25 (Spring), 57–78.

Khanna, T., Song, J. and Lee, K. (2011). The paradox of Samsung's rise. *Harvard Business Review*, July–August, 142–147.

Kim, J-N., Bach, S.B. & Clelland, I.J. (2007). Symbolic or behavioural management? Corporate reputation for high emission industries. *Corporate Reputation Review* 10(2), 77–98.

Klemm, M., Sanderson, S. & Luffman, G. (1991). Mission statements: selling corporate values to employees. *Long Range Planning* 24(3), 73–78.

Kling, K. & Goteman, I. (2003). IKEA CEO Anders Dahlvig on international growth and IKEA's unique corporate culture and brand identity. *Academy of Management Executive* 17(1), 31–37.

Kolk, A. (2005). Corporate responsibility in the coffee sector: the dynamics of MNC responses and code development. *European Management Journal* 23(2), 228–236.

Kotter, J.P. & Heskett, J.L. (1992). *Corporate Culture and Performance*. New York: Free Press.

Lafferty, B.A., Goldsmith, R.E., & Newell, S.J. (2002). The dual credibility model: The influence of corporate and endorser credibility on attitudes and purchase intentions. *Journal of Marketing Theory and Practice* 10(3), 1–12.

Li, Y., Wang, X. & Yang, Z. (2011). The effects of corporate-brand credibility, perceived corporate-brand origin, and self-image congruence on purchase intention: evidence from China's auto industry. *Journal of Global Marketing* 24, 58–68.

Love, M. (2006). Cutting through the clutter at Microsoft, *Strategic Communication Management*. Online: www.melcrum.com/articles/clutter_at_microsoft.shtml. Accessed: 24 August 2009.

Maignan, I. & Farrell, O.C. (2001). Corporate responsibility and marketing: an integrative framework. *European Journal of Marketing* 35(3/4), 457–484.

Martin, J. (1992). *Cultures in Organizations: Three Perspectives*. New York: Oxford University Press.

Martin, J. & Siehl, C. (1983). Organizational culture and counterculture: an uneasy symbiosis. *Organizational Dynamics* 12(2), 52–64.

Melewar, T.C., Bassett, K. & Simoes, C. (2006). The role of communication and visual identity in modern organizations. *Corporate Communications: An International Journal* 11(2), 138–147.

Miller, G.R. (1989). Persuasion and public relations: two 'Ps' in a pod. In: Botan, C.H. & Hazleton, V., Jr, eds. *Public Relations Theory*. Hillsdale, NJ: Lawrence Erlbaum Associates, pp. 45–66.

Nayar, V. (2010). A maverick CEO explains how he persuaded his team to leap into the future. *Harvard Business Review*, June, 110–113.

O'Reilly, C.A. (1989). Corporations, culture and commitment: motivation and social control in organizations. *California Management Review* 31(4), 9–25.

O'Reilly, C.A. & Chatman, J.A. (1996). Culture as social control: corporations, culture and commitment. In: Staw B.M. & Cummings, L.L. eds. *Research in Organizational Behavior*. Greenwich: CT JAI Press, pp. 157–200.

Pearce, J.A. & David, F. (1987). Corporate mission statements: the bottom line. *Academy of Management Executive* 1(2), 15–24.

Pinsent Masons (2011). Cases on disclosure of price-sensitive in formation. Online: www.out-law.com/page-8302. Accessed: August 2011.

van Riel, C.B.M. & Fombrun, C.J. (2007). *Essentials of Corporate Communication*. London: Routledge.

Rosenbuerg, R.D. & Rosenstein, E. (1980). Participation and productivity: an empirical study. *Industrial and Labour Relations Review* 33(3), 355–367.

Schein, E.H. (1992). *Organizational Culture and Leadership*, 2nd edn. San Francisco: Jossey-Bass.

Schein, E.H. (1991). The role of the founder in the creation of organizational culture. In: Frost, P.J., Moore, L.F., Louis, M.R., Lundberg, C.C. & Martin, J., eds. *Reframing Organizational Culture*. Beverly Hills, CA: Sage, pp. 14–25.

Semin, G.R., Higgins, E.T., Gil de Montes, L., Estourget, Y. & Valencia, J.F. (2005). Linguistic signatures of regulatory focus: how abstraction fits promotion more than prevention. *Journal of Personality and Social Psychology* 89, 63–74.

Simoes, C., Dibb, S. & Fisk, R.P. (2005). Managing corporate identity: an internal perspective. *Journal of the Academy of Marketing Science* 33(2), 153–168.

Sørensen, J.B. (2002). The strength of corporate culture and the reliability of firm performance. *Administrative Science Quarterly* 47(1), 70–91.

Stuart, H. & Muzellec, L. (2004). Corporate makeovers: can a hyena be rebranded? *Brand Management* 11(6), 472–482.

Tellis, G.J. & Golder, P. (2001). *Will and Vision: How Latecomers Grow to Dominate Markets*. New York: McGraw-Hill.

Tellis, G.J., Prabhu, J.C. & Chandy, R.K. (2009). Radical innovation across nations: the preeminence of corporate culture. *Journal of Marketing* 73(1), 3–23.

Williams, L.S. (2008). The mission statement. *Journal of Business Communication* 45(2), 94–119.

Winters, L.C. (1988). Does it pay to advertise to hostile audiences with corporate advertising? *Journal of Advertising Research* 28(3), 11–18.

Yamauchi, K. (2001). Corporate communication: a powerful tool for stating corporate missions. *Corporate Communications: An International Journal* 6(3), 131–136.

Chapter 11
Symbols, tools and the media

Organisations frame their messages to focus on particular issues and to direct the way in which stakeholders understand an organisation, its practices and behaviour. In order that key audiences assign meaning to corporate messages, organisations use various symbols, such as the company name, logo and slogans. In addition to this however, organisations use the key communication tools and increasingly, a range of offline and digital media in order to encourage corporate recognition, understanding and the development of relationships.

Aims and learning objectives

The aim of this chapter is to explore the use of corporate symbols, tools and media in order to communicate effectively with key stakeholder audiences.

The learning objectives of this chapter are to:

1. Evaluate ideas associated with message framing
2. Appraise the use of symbols in developing corporate reputation
3. Examine the characteristics of corporate advertising
4. Explore the methods and approaches associated with public relations
5. Evaluate ideas associated with corporate sponsorship activities
6. Consider the characteristics of the main media used in corporate communication.

Introduction

Understanding the different ways in which corporate communication can be used to reach various stakeholder groups requires an appreciation of the tools, media and approaches used to influence different stakeholder groups. Before considering these, however, two aspects of corporate communication need to be examined. The first concerns message framing, as this can assist understanding of the way in which tools, and media are used to present messages and promote interaction with stakeholders. The second involves visual identity, in particular the use of symbols to express the identity of an organisation.

Message framing

Messages are used to influence audiences, and the degree of change is thought to be enhanced if these messages are constructed in particular ways. By emphasising specific issues and drawing an audience's attention to positive rather than negative elements, messages can be become more influential. This approach is referred to as 'message framing' and works on the hedonic principles of our motivation to seek happiness and avoid pain. Messages can be framed either to focus a recipient's attention on positive outcomes (happiness) or to shift them away from possible negative outcomes (pain). Framing enables selected materials, perhaps facts, values or beliefs, to become the salient factors used by stakeholders in their decision-making. For example, a positively framed message might be a set of financial results which are presented as 'excellent, a reward for our hard work' or the government referring to the latest crime figures as 'a triumph for their policies'. Conversely these messages could be presented as 'excellent in times of difficult trading conditions' and 'contrary to popular expectations', respectively, but these are regarded as negatively framed messages.

> **Framing enables selected materials to become the salient factors used by stakeholders in their decision-making.**

Watkins *et al.* (2001) state that, 'Framing is the use of argument, analogy and metaphor to create a favourable definition of the problem to be solved and the set of acceptable solutions.' Framing therefore involves the use of langauage, not only to present a problem in a particular way but also to shape the desired solution.

> **Many practitioners work on the basis that positive messages are better than negative messages.**

Although Tsai (2007) indicates it is controversial and an empirically unproven strategy, many practitioners work on the basis that positive messages are better than negative messages. It can be argued that negative framing promotes deeper thinking and consideration. Coombs (2007) observes that frames are used in two main ways, first, as a form of outward communication, the message-sending aspect, and secondly, as a means of interpreting and understanding messages received. So, citing Cooper (2002), Coombs believes that the way in which a message is framed for outward communication shapes the way in which recipients define issues or problems, what they understand the cause of a problem to be, who might be responsible for the problem and the possible solutions that might be implemented.

Framing is also used extensively in the news industry and by political organisations. The application to corporate communication in order to convey a certain identity and hence enhance reputation should also be apparent. Framing is therefore an interesting and important concept through which corporate communication can be interpreted and understood. However, particular reference to framing will be made later in this chapter and in Chapter 12 when examining public affairs, issues management and crisis communication. Viewpoint 11.1 provides an example of the way framing was used by Kraft Foods.

| Viewpoint 11.1 | Obesity – you've been framed |

The worldwide obesity crisis has posed challenges for many sections of society, including individuals, governments and food manufacturers. Various reports issued since the turn of the century have proclaimed that the fast food industry is a major culprit and condemned if for its poor nutritional values and unsafe levels of saturated and trans fats.

Kraft Foods were aware of the need to take action early and to be one of the first food manufacturers to treat the obesity problem as an issue that directly concerns them and thus prevent it from becoming a crisis. The company's reaction was to undertake a series of initiatives and then communicate their actions through predetermined media. The aim was to present Kraft as the first packaged food manufacturer to address the obesity issue and to use it as part of their positioning strategy.

The first initiative was to present an overarching message about Kraft's efforts to tackle the obesity issue globally. This was supported by various other frames such as those concerning product nutrition, marketing practices, consumer information and advocacy and dialogue. Each of these contained subframes concerning the particular actions that Kraft were taking.

Reseach by Darmon et al. (2008) shows that the way in which Kraft presented its messages influenced the way the media reported Kraft's actions. The main frame was covered by the print media most frequently. This was attributed to Kraft leading with this frame in their news release and to the fact that it was embedded in the title of the news release. It was noted that journalists were probably drawn to frames because of the saliency and the timely and controversial nature of the content. The frame regarding product nutrition was covered most by broadcast media and the messages framed around marketing practices were most visible in the print media.

Darmon et al. (2008) suggest that the optimal number of frames in any one campaign is three and that the placement of frames within an active document, a news release, in this case may have been a significant contributor to the success of Kraft's campaign.

Question

To what extent is framing merely a matter of presenting a limited amount of information in the best way possible?

Source: Based on Darmon et al. (2008).

The use of symbols in developing corporate reputation

In Chapter 10 the corporate identity mix was introduced. One part of this mix concerns the way in which organisations use symbols to communicate with stakeholders. They use visual identifiers to influence the reputation of the organisation. Fombrun & van Riel (2004) suggest that reputation is developed and established around five key dimensions: visibility, distinctiveness, transparency, authenticity and consistency. Van den Bosch et al. (2005) consider how corporate visual identity impacts upon each of these dimensions.

Visibility. Visual identity supports the presence, or visibility, of an organisation. Indeed, there is a strong connection between visibility, recognition and reputation, which can be either negative or positive. The use of logos, signage and names not only signifies the existence of an organisation but can also serve to reinforce reputational status and the meaning a stakeholder attributes to the symbols.

Distinctiveness. There can be little doubt that visual identity provides a powerful platform upon which to create organisational distinctiveness. The McDonald's golden arches are instantly

> Visual identity provides a powerful platform upon which to create organisational distinctiveness.

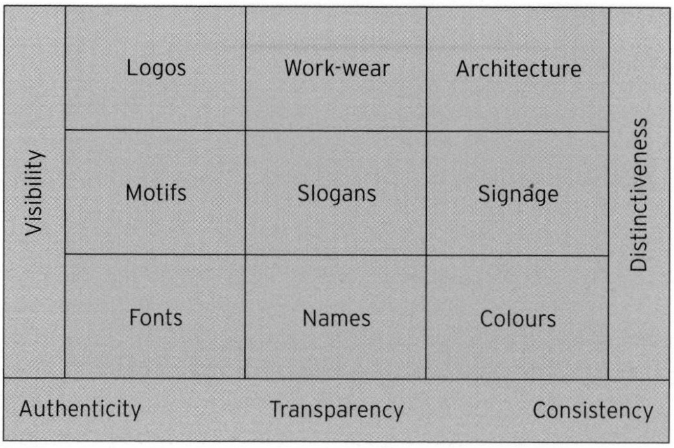

	Logos	Work-wear	Architecture
Visibility	Motifs	Slogans	Signage
	Fonts	Names	Colours
	Authenticity	Transparency	Consistency

(Distinctiveness on right axis)

Figure 11.1 Visual identifiers used to support reputation.

recognisable and understood globally, as are Nike's swoosh and the slogan used by Philips, 'Sense and simplicity', to reflect their mission, values and relatively recent change in corporate strategy.

Authenticity is a little harder to identify through visual means, but some organisations attempt to establish this by referencing their roots. By using symbols to represent a significant historical factor or founders, organisations call on experience and substance as the basis of their identity. For example, the use of heraldic motifs by universities is an attempt to demonstrate age, a sense of permanence and, hence, legitimacy to act as an authentic learning institution.

Transparency serves to reduce uncertainty and increase trust. Visual identity can be used to help customers identify who owns a brand. For example, a corporation that operates a house of brands architecture can remain hidden from the view of customers and other stakeholders. However, where the product brand is the same as the corporate brand, transparency is not only high but research indicates that reputation tends to be higher (Clifton & Maughan, 2000). Transparency can also be enhanced through the use of certification and quality trade marks.

Consistency of visual communication can enhance identity and reputation. Consistency in the way a brand is presented, through time, facilitates recognition and understanding. Well-known identity cues include the Coca-Cola bottle, Orange's use of the colour orange, and the three crowns used by Swedish shipping companies, e.g. the Swedish Orient Line and other brands.

Consider the case of British Airways, in Viewpoint 11.2, and determine the extent to which each of the five dimensions of visual identity was affected by the change of tail fin design.

Viewpoint 11.2 British Airways in a tailspin

Research undertaken by British Airways in the mid-1990s suggested that travellers wanted the airline to be more global and more caring. In response to this, Rob Ayling, the then CEO, embarked on a £60 million rebranding exercise. The goal was to provide a strong point of differentiation through high-quality service levels. So, apart from the new identity the rebranding required encouraging its 58,000 employees to adopt new values such as honesty and teamwork. This alone was not an easy task as morale was low and there was even the threat of strike action.

The rebranding exercise contained both a visual and a behavioural dimension. The change of visual identity, it was felt, had to reflect the internationalism of their customers, so the airline introduced a new identity for its aircraft based on approximately 50 different designs from artists around the world. This was intended to reflect the global nature of their passengers and their destinations and their position as 'the undisputed leader in world travel'.

Exhibit 11.1 Some of the radical new tail fin designs introduced but soon rejected by British Airways.
Source: Press Association Images.

The most prominent placement for the designs was the tail fins and these replaced the Union Flag which had been the key identifier up until then. In addition, however, the plan had been to repaint these multicultural images on ground vehicles, baggage tags and stationery such as ticket envelopes.

The exercise proved to be a disaster. By replacing the Union Flag with these new multicultural designs, the implication was that being British was bad for business (Lloyd, 1999). The new designs made BA stand out but it wasn't an identity that matched BA's personality. As Lloyd put it, BA was not the brave and lively organisation represented in the multicultural liveries. By dropping the flag it effectively threw away the one element that international passengers wanted to be associated with, not to mention alienating the home market and offering its arch rival, Virgin Atlantic, an opportunity to use the Union Flag. The most visible disapproval occurred when the ex-Prime Minister, Margaret Thatcher, attended the 1997 Conservative Party conference. When presented with a model BA aircraft with the new design, she covered the tail fin with her handkerchief. Referring to the design she said, 'We should fly the British flag, not these awful things, as they make us look like a third world airline.'

The designs were withdrawn and the flag was reinstated.

Question

To what extent did the changes to the visual identity sanctioned by the BA CEO represent a strategic approach to corporate branding?

Source: Bryant (1997), Lloyd (1999) and Balmer *et al.* (2009).

Rebranding for strategic change

Most corporate brands experience some form of transition or change at some point in their history. Sometimes this transition can be sudden, dramatic and cause considerable upheaval, e.g. a merger (Lloyds and HBOS) or crisis (BP or BlackBerry) resulting in the loss of or change in leader. At other times these transitions can be slow, relatively quiet and have little impact, such as a self-imposed restructuring (Ford in Germany) or repositioning (the hotel group, Best Western). In many cases, rebranding is required in order to re-establish the brand competitively.

Stuart & Muzellec (2004) consider the visual issues associated with corporate rebranding. They rightly acknowledge that some organisations attempt a revolutionary rebrand which involves changing the name, logo and slogan of the corporate identity. However, some changes can be classified merely as evolutionary and these involve changes to just the logo or just the slogan. There are several other combinations involving changes to just two of the logo, slogan or name cues.

> Some organisations attempt a revolutionary rebrand which involves changing the name, logo and slogan of the corporate identity.

Name changes

Changing the name of an organisation is both risky and potentially expensive. As Kellaway (2002) put it, 'a new name is never going to suit an existing company', simply because the personality should be reflected in the name. If a new name is required then there are several opportunities. Following a merger or acquisition it is possible to include the names of all the existing parties but this can result in a long and rather unexciting list. Politically this may be feasible in the short and medium term, but eventually the dominant party will see that the other names are dropped.

New names can be derived through a range of techniques. An employee of Andersen Consulting proposed the new name, Accenture, which means ascent or an emphasis on the future. Computers can also be used to generate lists of names, or the use of Latin and Greek words can add a feeling of permanence and distinction. For example, Altria (formerly Philip Morris Companies) means 'high performance and constant improvement' and may have been chosen to disguise the tobacco business that was at the root of the group's interests in 1985 when the restructuring and renaming occurred. Novartis is Latin for 'new skills' and was the name adopted for the healthcare company formed from the merger of the Swiss-based life sciences companies, Ciba-Geigy and Sandoz.

Another approach is to shorten the name of the existing organisation to its initials. For example, Royal & Sun Alliance, featured in Viewpoint 9.3, contracted its name to RSA when it embarked on a rebranding exercise.

Slogan changes

> One of the strongest mechanisms used to position brands is the slogan.

One of the strongest mechanisms used to position brands is the slogan. Slogans should complement the strategy and the other visual cues used to position the organisation. For example, 'blue ocean' refers to the creation of new markets where previously there was nothing. Nintendo adopted the term internally as it complemented its business strategy. Rather than following its competitors and adding faster processors and more violent games, its strategy was to attract new users in different demographic groups, people who hadn't played games before. By using innovative touch-screens, voice activation and motion-sensing technology, the games were less gimmicky, more accessible, easier to play and yet equally addictive, and resulted in increased numbers of women and middle-aged people becoming regular gamers. Nintendo now outsells Microsoft and Sony, and in 2008 its market capitalisation outstripped that of Sony.

However, the use of a slogan that fails to reinforce or, worse, contradicts the other messages conveyed by the organisation can lead to either a confused positioning, or under-positioning.

For example, Stuart & Muzellec (2004) refer to Griffith University in Australia which used the slogan 'Get smarter' in an advertising campaign. However, they used celebrities such as Bob Geldof and Ray Charles to associate themselves with the core values of social justice and equity. Ultimately the slogan and the values did not complement each other, something that can lead to brand obscurity or unknown positioning.

Slogans are contentious issues and perhaps the only guideline to developing effective slogans is to make them memorable. *Forbes* magazine (2008) reports on an issue of the *Strategy & Innovation* newsletter which suggested that the most effective corporate catchphrases should be 'sticky'. To put it another way, slogans should 'be understandable, memorable and effective in changing thought or behavior'.

Slogans are contentious issues.

Logo changes

The use of logos to encapsulate the values and personality of an organisation and to promote recognition and recall among stakeholders is both common and well practised. One of the more common problems arises when the designer has a crystal-clear understanding of what the logo represents but the meaning is obscure to stakeholders. The use of abstract logos, in particular, can exacerbate this problem.

The logo is an important brand identifier. When Peugeot and Citroën merged in 1976, the change was not marked by a new logo, or by dropping one of the two. Both organisations retained their marques and their identities for several years. Melewar *et al.* (2006) also cite the takeover of Midland Bank by HSBC. The Midland's Griffin logo was retained for several years enabling stakeholders to transfer their trust to the new company gradually.

The logo is an important brand identifier.

Many universities have dropped their official heraldic logos and have developed modern abstract identities in an attempt to be perceived as contemporary, commercially oriented organisations. This realignment might be said to reflect the changing financial structures, as these institutions are required by government to seek a higher proportion of their income from private rather than public sources. Once again the personality of the organisation is reflected in the visual identity.

Some universities adopt dual logos. The abstract, often contemporary logos are for everyday use on letterheads, web pages and signage, while the original, heraldic devices are used for public events such as graduation ceremonies and the installation of chancellors and vice-chancellors. On the one hand, this might be seen as a clever way of meeting the needs of their students without throwing away the credibility, heritage and intellectual associations attached to heraldic devices; on the other, however, it could be interpreted as uncertainty about how the organisation wishes to be seen or, worse, neglect or poor strategic management on behalf of the owners, namely the government.

Dowling (1996) warns against changing logos when there is no apparent reason for the change. He refers to this as 'the corporate identity trap' which can occur when no one notices the change in logo or, if it is noticed, it is regarded with suspicion. In other words, the whole reason for presenting a new identity is lost, along with the associated costs incurred in making the change.

The tools for corporate communication

Delivering effective corporate communication requires the use of several communication tools in order that key messages reach target stakeholders. The mainstream tools are corporate advertising, public relations and sponsorship, and these are discussed in turn in the following sections.

The mainstream tools are corporate advertising, public relations and sponsorship.

Corporate advertising

Defining corporate advertising is more difficult than it might first appear (Kitchen, 1997; White, 2008). This is partly because this form of communication does not necessarily always provide a clear divide between product and non-product advertising. In addition, corporate advertising is regarded by some as a form of public relations and they refer to this form of communication as 'public relations advertising', other terms include issues advertising, image advertising and institutional advertising. However, in recent years a wide range of organisations (including commercial, media and creative agencies, charity, government, social enterprise, trade unions and associations and political parties) have increasingly adopted the term corporate advertising.

Whether the roots of the topic lie in the softly influential discipline of public relations or the more overtly influential advertising arena, the intention of non-product advertising is to inform and build awareness, define a position or defend an organisation's activities and reputation. The focus is on managing organisational reputation and trust (White, 2008) amongst a wide array of stakeholders, rather than selling products and services to customers.

Just as other forms of corporate communication need to be founded on an organisation's mission and values, so does corporate advertising. Indeed, the messages conveyed should provide direction and positioning by building on the reputational platform, continue and build the corporate story and articulate the corporate promise clearly and unequivocally. According to Helgesen (1994), successful corporate advertising campaigns are characterised by two dimensions, professionalism and creativity:

> **Successful corporate advertising campaigns are characterised by two dimensions: professionalism and creativity.**

- Professional campaigns are distinctive, unique and credible, target particular audiences, offer a clear promise, and appeal to the organisation's own employees.

- Creativity based campaigns are striking, authentic, original, surprising, humorous and contemporary.

van Riel & van Bruggen (2003) add a third dimension, consistency, reflecting the need for coherence and the long-term focus of corporate advertising. These three dimensions can impact the success of a campaign, which can be measured in terms of changes in knowledge, attitude and behaviour. van Riel & van Bruggen (2003) found that if the goal of a corporate advertising campaign is to improve knowledge, the key dimension is professionalism. If attitude change is required then creativity should be stressed, whilst changes in behaviour are more likely to be stimulated through an emphasis on professionalism and consistency.

Perhaps of greater significance was the finding that there was no difference between the judgments offered by internal and external stakeholders. This suggests that internal audiences can be used with reasonable confidence to measure the effectiveness of corporate advertising campaigns on a pre-test basis. This can increase the speed of analysis and reduce costs as it obviates the need for external post-campaign testing.

White (2008) suggests that corporate advertising messages can be considered in terms of four main forms, as set out in Table 11.1. Corporate advertising is used for a wide range of corporate communication tasks, as set out in Table 11.2.

> **Most corporate advertising is for recruitment of quality staff and support of product and services.**

The majority of corporate advertising is used for two main reasons: recruitment of quality staff and supporting product and services. In addition, however, corporate advertising is used to support sponsorship arrangements, improving community and customer relations, influencing investor relations and increasingly as a means of informing stakeholders about activities and issues related to corporate responsibility. For a classic example of this, see the case of Reckitt Benckiser in Viewpoint 11.3.

Farache & Perks (2010) examined the way corporate print advertising is used to disclose information about an organisation's corporate responsibility activities. Referred to as CSR

Table 11.1	Forms of corporate advertising
Message form	**Explanation**
What we have done	A story about the company's achievements
What we do	A description of the scope of the company's activities
What we are going to do	A statement of intent
This is how we want to be seen	This is who we are, how we are different and how we want to be perceived – our positioning

Source: White (2008).

Table 11.2	Tasks for corporate advertising	
Primary stakeholder group	**Communication task to . . .**	**For example**
All stakeholders	Manage the overall reputation of an organisation	Cisco, RBS, Tata, BA
	(Re)position an organisation	Santander following its takeover of Abbey and the Alliance & Leicester
	Support a corporate responsibility initiative	Marks & Spencer – Plan A, Co-op
	Support or advocate a position on an issue	Greenpeace, MDA
	Create awareness or announce the identity of a new organisation	BNP Paribas to reach a younger audience ViiV Healthcare created by GlaxoSmithKline and Pfizer Bitfenix (computer hardware and peripherals) launched in 2010
Financial	Support or defend against a takeover bid	Portugal Telecom vs Sonaecom; Mouchel vs VT Group; Cadbury vs Kraft
	Communicate financial and performance outcomes	IBM, Rolls-Royce, Deloitte, Rio Tinto
	Raise capital, support company valuation	Twitter, Petrobras, Genworth UK
Internal	Inform and motivate employees and distributors	GEC, Volkswagen, Serco, American Express
	Recruit employees	London Fire Brigade, Lloyds Bank
	Signal and manage a change in strategy/structure	Apple, ExxonMobil, NatWest, Carrefour
Customers	Inform or reassure customers	Toyota, London Toursit Authority,
	Support products and services	Procter & Gamble, Reckitt Benckiser

advertisements, they are considered important because they act as an identity cue and demonstrate how organisations want to be seen and understood. Using legitimacy theory to underpin their research, they consider the congruence between a society's value system and the actions and activities undertaken by an organisation. When these two systems are congruent, legitimacy is said to be established and an organisation's existence is continued. When there is a

Viewpoint 11.3 The flexibility of corporate advertising

In 2009 Reckitt Benckiser, a 200-year-old company operating in the household cleaning, health and personal care markets, launched the first corporate advertising campaign in its history. The campaign sought to achieve two key objectives: to boost awareness among young people of the owner of its well-known product brands, such as Nurofen, Vanish and Clearasil; and to reinforce the new name of the company, RB. The original name emerged following a merger in 1999. The global public affairs director is reported to have said that the company had decided to raise its corporate profile as there was reduced competition, particularly from the finance sector, in the battle to attract the best potential graduate employees.

Sony have used corporate advertising extensively since the mid-1990s. The initiative came when research showed that Panasonic was perceived as similar to Sony. The new campaign marked a significant shift in Sony's communication strategy. Rather than use advertising to support products and services, this campaign sought to reposition Sony as a world-leading brand and dominant player in the emerging audiovisual/information technology market. It was to do this by capturing the entertainment values at the heart of the company.

Exhibit 11.2 Sony used corporate advertising to reposition itself as a world-leading brand and dominant player in the emerging audiovisual/information technology world.
Source: Image courtesy of The Advertising Archives.

Question

If corporate advertising assists reputation, why do companies cut back on this type of communication when economic conditions deteriorate?

Source: Clews (2009); Sampson & Linz (2000).

Organisations disclose information about their corporate responsibility activities so that their behaviour can be legitimised by their stakeholders.

lack of congruency, the organisation's legitimacy, and its ability to fulfil its objectives, is said to be threatened (Mathews, 1993).

Therefore, organisations disclose information about their corporate responsibility activities so that their behaviour can be legitimised by their stakeholders. Four different communication strategies can be identified which organisations can use to develop legitimisation. These are set out in Table 11.3.

The media classes used to deliver corporate advertising messages are predominantly print and digital. The most frequently used types of print media are newspapers, magazines and journals. The choice of media vehicle should, of course, reflect the status and positioning of the organisation. For digital media, corporate web pages are the most popular, supported increasingly by corporate blogs and video. The other media format used for this form of communication is television advertising, supported increasingly by arts, sports and programme

Table 11.3	Legitimacy strategies
Legitimacy strategy	**Explanation**
Improvement	Inform stakeholders of an intention to improve performance
Manipulate	An attempt to change stakeholder perceptions of events without changing behaviour
Distraction	Divert attention by focusing on a different (unlinked) positive activity
Practical	An attempt to change stakeholder expectations regarding organisational performance
Announce	Straightforward declaration of performance activities, confident of stakeholder approval
Perceived complexity	By providing complex data, an audience's rationality concludes that the organisation is responsible
Visual impact	By using minimal text and high-impact visuals, acceptance is developed through an audience's emotions

Source: Based on Lindblom (1994).

sponsorship. However, these latter activities are the preserve of organisations with substantial financial resources and are usually out of the reach of smaller organisations.

Public relations

Public relations are used by organisations to identify their policies with the interests of their stakeholders. To do this an organisation formulates and executes a programme of action to develop mutual goodwill and understanding and, in turn, develop relationships that are in the long-run interests of all parties. Public relations provides some of the cues that enable stakeholders to develop images and shape perceptions. These cues are used to recognise, understand, select and converse with particular organisations.

> Cues are used to recognise, understand, select and converse with particular organisations.

It is helpful at this point to consider the term public relations, rather than stakeholder relations. The word 'publics' is traditionally used to refer to the various organisations and groups with which an organisation interacts. So far, this text has referred to these types of organisation as stakeholders. 'Stakeholders' is a term used in the field of strategic management, and as public relations is essentially concerned with strategic issues, the word stakeholders is perhaps more appropriate. However, the industry has continued to use the term publics in this context and it will therefore be used here.

Traditionally, public relations has been perceived as a tool that dealt with the manner and style in which an organisation interacted with its major publics. It sought to influence other organisations and individuals using public relations, projecting an identity that would affect the image that different publics held of the organisation. By spreading information and improving the levels of knowledge that people held about particular issues, the organisation sought ways to advance itself in the eyes of those it saw as influential. However, this view has been extended to the point that public relations is now seen as the management of relationships between organisations and their stakeholders (Bruning & Ledingham, 2000).

This shift to a relationship management perspective effectively alters the way public relations is perceived and practised by organisations. Instead of trying to manipulate audience opinion through spin, so that the organisation is of primary importance, the challenge is to use symbolic visual communication messages, with behaviour, such that the organisation–audience relationship improves for all parties (Ehling, 1992). Kent & Taylor (2002) argue that it is the ability of organisations to encourage and practise dialogue that really enables truly symmetrical relationships to develop. This has evolved further with the recession and the storm surrounding the banking profession. Not only do relationships need to be symmetrical but the information exchange needs to be founded on transparency and honesty.

In order to use communication to develop the full potential within relationships, many argue that dialogic interaction should be encouraged. Kent & Taylor (2002) argue that organisations should place email, web addresses, 0800 telephone numbers and organisational addresses prominently in all forms of external communication, most notably in advertisements and on websites, to enable dialogue. What follows from this is a change in evaluation, from measuring the decimation of messages to measuring audience influence and behavioural and attitudinal change and, of course, relationship dynamics. Bruning & Ledingham (2000) phrase this as a change from measuring outputs to measuring outcomes.

> Dialogue produces a change from measuring outputs to measuring outcomes.

In considering the role of public relations, namely to build relationships that are of mutual value, Bruning *et al.* (2008) conclude that input, interaction and participation of key public members in the organisation–public dynamic is critically important. In other words, dialogue, arising through interaction, and the personalisation of communications are important for relationship development.

Public relations methods

The range of public relations cues or methods available to organisations is immense. Different organisations use different permutations in order that they can communicate effectively with their various stakeholder audiences. While there is general agreement on a definition, there is a lower degree of consensus over what constitutes public relations. This is partly because the range of activities is diverse and categorisation is problematic. Public relations consists of a range of communication activities, including sponsorship, media relations, cause-related marketing, publicity and event management. In addition there are a range of specialist activities developed to reach specific stakeholders. These include investor relations, internal communications, public affairs and issue/crisis management, all of which are explored in the following chapter.

Cues can be considered to influence stakeholders in one of two main ways: to improve the visibility of the organisation, to make it salient and differentiate it sufficiently to provide stand-out; and to improve its credibility in the eyes of stakeholders (see Exhibit 11.3). The cues used to achieve these two outcomes are presented in Table 11.4.

> Cues influence stakeholders in one of two main ways.

Table 11.4	Cues used by PR to project corporate identity	
Cues to build credibility	**Cues to signal visibility**
Product quality	Website, sales literature and company publications, editorials
Customer relations	Publicity and media relations
Community involvement	Speeches and presentations
Strategic performance	Event management
Employee relations	Marketing communications messages
Crisis management skills	Media mix and behaviour
Third-party endorsement	Symbolism through design (signage, logo, slogan and letterhead)
Perceived ethics and environmental awareness	Dress codes
Architecture and furnishing	Exhibitions/seminars and sponsorships

Exhibit 11.3   Virgin's support for music festivals is an event cue that boosts its corporate visibility.
Source: Alamy Images/Photogenix.

The characteristics of public relations

There are a number of elements that characterise this particular tool and differentiate it from the others in the identity mix. Unlike corporate advertising, the use of public relations does not require the purchase of air time or space in media vehicles, such as television or magazines. The decision about whether an organisation's public relations messages are transmitted or not rests with those charged with managing the media resource, not the message sponsor. Those messages that are selected are perceived to be endorsements or the views of parties other than management. The outcome is that these messages usually carry greater perceived credibility than those messages transmitted through paid media, such as advertising.

The degree of trust and confidence generated by public relations singles out this tool from the others as an important means of reducing stakeholder perceived risk. However, while credibility may be high, the amount of control that management is able to bring to the transmission of the public relations message is very low. For example, a press release may have been carefully prepared in-house extolling the organisation's recycling activities, but as soon as it is passed to the editor of a magazine or newspaper, a possible opinion former, all control is lost. The release may be destroyed (highly probable), printed as it stands (highly unlikely) or changed to fit the available space in the media vehicle (almost certain, if it is decided to use the material). This means that any changes will not have been agreed by management, so the context and style of the original message may be lost or corrupted.

The costs associated with public relations also make this an important tool in the identity mix. The absolute costs are minimal, except for those organisations that retain an agency, but even then their costs are low compared with those of advertising. The relative costs (the costs associated with reaching each member of a target audience) are also very low. The main costs associated with public relations are the time and opportunity costs associated with the

> **The costs associated with public relations make it an important tool.**

preparation of press releases and associated literature. If these types of activity are organised properly, many small organisations could develop and shape their visibility much more effectively and in a relatively inexpensive way.

A further characteristic of this tool is that it can be used to reach specific stakeholders in a way that paid media cannot. With increasing media fragmentation and finer segmentation (customisation) of markets, the use of public relations represents a cost-effective way of reaching such markets and audiences.

New technology has played a key role in the development and practice of public relations. Gregory (2004) refers to the internet and electronic communication as 'transforming public relations'. With regard to the use of the internet by public relations practitioners, she identifies two main schools: one comprises those who use the internet as an extension to traditional or pre-internet forms of communication, while the second concerns those who see opportunities through the internet to develop two-way, enhanced communication. There can be little doubt that new technology has assisted communication management in terms of improving the transparency, speed and reach of public relations messages and at the same time has enabled interactive communication between an organisation and specific audiences.

The main characteristics of public relations are that it represents a very cost-effective means of carrying messages with a high degree of credibility. However, the degree of control that management is able to exert over the transmission of messages can be limited.

Sponsorship

Organisations use sponsorship in a variety of ways to generate awareness, develop brand associations and to cut through the clutter of commercial messages. Sponsorship can also be used to build relationships. The following represent key opportunities for the sponsoring organisation:

1. **Build awareness** – sponsorship is used to build exposure to particular stakeholders that each event attracts, in order to convey simple awareness-based company or brand messages.

2. **Image transfer** – sponsorship is used to suggest to stakeholders that there is an association between the sponsor and the event being sponsored and that by implication this association may be of interest and/or value.

3. **Indirect communication** – sponsorship allows stakeholders to perceive the sponsor indirectly through a third party and, in doing so, diffuse any negative effects associated with traditional mass media and direct persuasion-based communications.

4. **Integration** – sponsorship alone is not always very effective, but when used integratively with other tools and media, sponsorship-based communication can be considerably more effective and efficient.

Sponsorship is a commercial activity, whereby one party permits another an opportunity to exploit an association with a target audience in return for funds, services or resources (Fill, 2009). Normally sponsorship involves two parties, a sponsor and a sponsored party, although many sponsors may be assigned to a single sponsored party. The degree of fit between these parties can help to determine the relative effectiveness of the relationship (Poon & Prendergast, 2006). The degree of fit, or product relevance as proposed by McDonald (1991), can be considered in terms of two main dimensions. Function-based similarity occurs when the product is used in the event being sponsored, e.g. the piano manufacturer Bösendorfer sponsoring a Viennese piano recital. The second dimension concerns image-based similarities, which reflects the image of the sponsor in the event, e.g. Airbus's sponsorship of a major technical or even artistic exhibition serving to bestow prestige on all parties. Poon *et al.* (2010) suggest that, rather than treat these as mutually exclusive elements, there can be four interconnected dimensions (see Figure 11.2).

Function-based similarity occurs when the product is used in the event being sponsored.

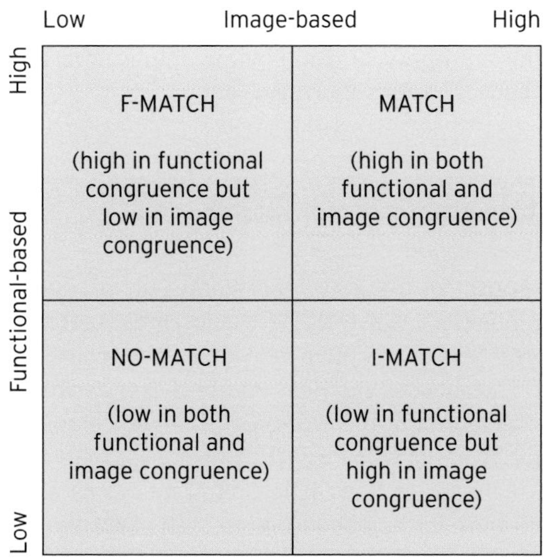

	Image-based	
Low		High

F-MATCH (high in functional congruence but low in image congruence)	**MATCH** (high in both functional and image congruence)
NO-MATCH (low in both functional and image congruence)	**I-MATCH** (low in functional congruence but high in image congruence)

High — Functional-based — Low

Figure 11.2 Dimensions of sponsorship interaction.
Source: Poon & Prendergast (2010). WARC, with permission.

Sponsorship is a form of communication which, unlike advertising, attempts to influence stakeholders indirectly. The relatively relaxed disposition experienced by stakeholders when consuming sponsorship messages contrasts vividly with an evasive or defensive posture assumed when consuming advertising. Such differences in message reception suggest there are opportunities for organisations to reach stakeholders more effectively through the use of sponsorship than through advertising alone.

Sponsorship objectives

There are both primary and secondary objectives associated with the use of corporate sponsorship. The primary reasons are to build awareness and improve the perception (image) held of an organisation. Secondary reasons are more contentious, but generally they are to attract and retain new stakeholders, very often customers, to support dealers and other intermediaries and to act as a form of staff motivation and morale-building (Reed, 1994). LG uses sponsorship to humanise its products and provide a means of connecting consumers with the brand. Sponsorship ties with Fulham and Arsenal football clubs, the 2008 New Year celebrations in London and London Freeze, a snowboarding and music event, have all served to engage consumers with LG (Barda, 2009).

Sponsorship is normally regarded as a communications tool to reach external stakeholders. However, if chosen appropriately, it can also be used effectively to reach internal audiences. Care is required because different audiences transfer diverse values (Grimes & Meenaghan, 1998). According to Harverson (1998), one of the main reasons IT companies sponsor sports events is that this form of involvement provides opportunities to 'showcase' their products and technologies, in context. Through application in an appropriate working environment, the efficacy of a sponsor's products can be demonstrated. The relationship between sports organisers and IT companies becomes reciprocal as the organisers of sports events need technology to run the events. Corporate hospitality opportunities are often taken in addition to the brand exposure that the media coverage provides. EDS claims that it uses sponsorship to reach two main audiences, customers (and potential customers) and potential employees. The message it uses is that the EDS involvement in sport is sexy and exciting.

A further important characteristic concerns the impact of repeat attendance on brand image. Work by Lacey *et al.* (2007) found that a car manufacturer's image improved modestly,

> Care is required because different audiences transfer diverse values.

by sponsoring a sporting event. However, through repeat visitor attendance positive opinion scores towards the sponsor improved. The obvious implication for marketing is that it is important to attract attendees back to sporting events.

Viewpoint 11.4 Oily support for corporate sponsorships

Castrol, the motor oil company, was a sponsor of the 2010 FIFA World Cup in South Africa. To help draw attention to their sponsorships and the company, Castrol use brand ambassadors. Traditionally Castrol have sought to involve themselves with the best competitive individuals and teams in motorsport.

In order to support the football event, Castrol used the Real Madrid striker Cristiano Ronaldo as a brand ambassador to support the Edge and Power1 brands in a World Cup-themed campaign. The company also used the Arsenal manager, Arsène Wenger, to assist with business-to-business marketing, and Alan Shearer, the former England striker and, briefly, manager of Newcastle United, to act as a brand ambassador for Castrol at UK events and in doing so contribute to their sponsorship of the FIFA World Cup in South Africa.

Question

Why does Samsung feel it is important to sponsor the Olympic Games?

Source: Based on Parsons (2009).

Corporate sponsorships, according to Thwaites (1994), are intended to focus upon developing community involvement, public awareness, image, goodwill and staff relations. This needs to be seen in contrast to product- or brand-based sponsorship activity, which is aimed at developing media coverage, sales leads, sales/market share, target market awareness and guest hospitality. What is important is that sponsorship is not a tool that can be effective in a stand-alone capacity. The full potential of this tool is only realised when it is integrated with some (or all) of the other elements of the identity mix. As Tripodi (2001) comments, the implementation of integrated marketing communications is further encouraged and supported when sponsorship is an integral part of the mix in order to maximise the full impact of this communication tool.

Sponsorship represents a form of collaborative communication, in the sense that two (or more) parties work together in order that one is enabled to reach the other's audience. Issues regarding the relationship between the parties concerned will impact on the success of a sponsorship arrangement and any successive arrangements. This reflects a relational perspective, one that is concerned with the concept of mutual value rather than the mere provision of goods and services (Gummesson, 1996).

Olkkonen (2001) adopts a similar approach as he considered sponsorship within interactional relationships and ultimately a network approach. The network approach considers the range of relationships that impact on organisations within markets and therefore considers non-buyers and other organisations, indeed all who are indirectly related to the exchange process. This approach moves beyond the simple dyadic process adopted by the interaction interpretation. Some scholars have advanced a broad conceptual model within which to consider inter-organisational networks (Hakansson & Snehota, 1995). These are actors, activities and resources (see Table 11.5).

A relationship consists of activity links based on organisations working together. Some of the activities will use particular resources in different configurations and differing levels of intensity. These activities will impact on other organisations and affect the way they use resources. In addition, organisations try to develop their attractiveness to other organisations in order to access other resources and networks. This is referred to as network identity and is a basis for determining an organisation's value as a network partner. Sponsorship, therefore,

Table 11.5	Layers within networks

Network layer	Explanation
Actors	These can be organisations, smaller groups within organisations or just single individuals. These actors are interconnected through bonds: economic, social, procedural, legal, etc. These bonds influence perception and behaviour and shape both identities and image.
Activities	Transformation activities concern the generation of new resources from pre-existing resources. Transfer activities refer to the change of direct control of activities from one actor to another. A relationship comprises the linking of different types of activities.
Resources	Resources include time, money, image, raw materials, skills, knowledge and intellectual property which underpin activities and are controlled by one or more actors.

Source: Based on Hakansson & Snehota (1995).

can be seen as a function of an organisation's value to others in a network. The sponsor and the sponsored party are key actors in sponsorship networks, but agencies, event organisers, media networks and consultancies are also actors, each of whom will be connected (networked) with the two lead organisations.

Sponsorship has traditionally lacked a strong theoretical base, relying on managerial cause-and-effect explanations and loose interpretations of marketing communications mix. The network approach may not be the main answer but it does advance our thoughts, knowledge and research opportunities in relation to this subject.

One concept that has been established in the literature is emotional intensity. This concerns the audience's attention (and associated cognitive orientation) towards the stimulus that is provoking the emotion (Bal *et al.*, 2007). So, if the event

> If an event is highly engaging, attention may be diverted from the sponsors.

becomes dramatic and highly engaging then it is probable that attention will be diverted from the sponsors and any information they might provide (e.g. ads). What this means is that a strongly emotional event (sport, exhibition, programme, film) is likely to reduce the awareness scores associated with the sponsor.

Finally, one of the fastest-growing areas is the use of naming rights, whereby organisations buy the right to have buildings, often sports stadia, named after them. In the UK, the airline Emirates bought the 15-year rights to name Arsenal's new stadium for £100 million in 2006. Before that Reebok had bought the rights to Bolton Wanderers' stadium. However, this stadium or property-naming strategy is not always successful. For example, it was announced in 2009 that the Sears Tower in Chicago was going to be renamed the Willis Tower, following its purchase by the Willis Group (Klora, 2009). But it is generally believed that it will continue to be referred to by the public as the Sears building. This might not be in Willis' best interests, suggesting that the use of naming rights only works if the organisation buying the rights is the first to do so for that property or building.

Clark *et al.* (2002) refer to a number of practitioner reports and articles that claim the practice does not lead to profitable returns. However, Quester (1997) found that acquiring the naming rights 'fostered better recognition', while Clark *et al.* (2002), in their detailed study, found that the announcement of new naming rights can have a positive effect on a company's share price.

Corporate entertainment

Closely allied with sponsorship is corporate entertainment or hospitality. This aspect of corporate communication may be an integral part of a sponsorship contract or it may be a series of

> Corporate entertainment or hospitality is closely allied with sponsorship.

separate, stand-alone activities, designed to reward, motivate and build on relationships. Corporate entertainment provides an opportunity for face-to-face contact, and in an environment where relationships are often sustained through electronic communication, these moments of personal interaction can help to enhance relationships.

Before the recession these events were very popular and tended to be overly indulgent. The backbone entertainment activities were theatre, music or cultural/sporting events, often accompanied by a three-course meal. These are largely passive, spectator events. The recession saw the corporate entertainment market shrink and it is anticipated that corporate entertainment will in the future be more understated, and experiential, with attendance expected out of hours, i.e. in an executive's own time. This then puts pressure on the entertainer to provide an event that is worth giving up personal time for (Wallace, 2010).

Cause-related marketing

One major reason for the development of public relations and the associated corporate reputation activities has been the rise in use and importance of cause-related marketing activities. This has partly been due to the increased awareness of the need to be perceived as credible, responsible and ethically sound. Developing a strong and socially oriented reputation has become a major form of differentiation for organisations operating in various markets, especially where price, quality and tangible attributes are relatively similar. Being able to present corporate brands as contributors to the wider social framework, a role beyond that of simple profit generators, has enabled many organisations to achieve stronger, more positive market positions.

Cause-related marketing is a commercial activity through which profit-oriented and not-for-profit organisations form partnerships to exploit, for mutual benefit, their association in the name of a particular cause.

Cause-related activities help to improve corporate reputation.

The benefits from a properly planned and constructed cause-related campaign can accrue to all participants. Cause-related activities help to improve corporate reputation, enable product differentiation and appear to contribute to improved customer retention through enhanced sales. In essence, cause-related marketing is a means by which relationships with stakeholders can be developed. As organisations outsource an increasingly larger part of their business activities and as the stakeholder networks become more complex, so the need to be perceived as (and to be) socially responsible becomes a critically important dimension of an organisation's image (see Viewpoint 11.5).

Viewpoint 11.5   **Cause it's the right thing to do**

An increasing number of organisations are working on projects enabling cash, attention and resources to be raised for the benefit of designated third parties. For example, Marks & Spencer worked with Breakthrough Breast Cancer, and Yell ran the Yellow Woods Challenge in partnership with the Woodland Trust to encourage the recycling of old Yellow Pages directories and to help children learn about the importance of conservation. Blockbuster Entertainment partnered the Starlight Children's Foundation with the goal of entertaining acutely and terminally ill children while they were in hospital.

The Supergran Campaign, run by Innocent drinks in association with Age Concern, Sainsbury's and Eat Cafés, provides an interesting example of a cause-related campaign involving a number of parties. The campaign was an attempt to address the problems faced by many older people in winter. Cold-related illnesses emerge when many people have to choose between warmth and eating, often resulting in a huge number of deaths. For each smoothie sold through Sainsbury's stores and Eat Cafés nationwide, Innocent gave 50p to Age Concern. This money was used to provide hot meals, warm blankets and advice on how to

Exhibit 11.4	Innocent's advertisement to promote the Supergran cause-related campaign.
	Source: Innocent Ltd, with permission.

manage energy costs in their homes. However, the smoothies had to have a woolly hat on them, each knitted by local Age Concern users, Sainsbury's employees, Innocent staff and the general public.

Innocent organised knitting events for partners and consumers, and wool specialists, Rowan, provided all the wool for the knitting kits and in-store knitting activities. A total or 230,000 hats were produced for the campaign, raising £115,000 for Age Concern. Sainsbury's also witnessed the largest number of Innocent smoothie sales in a week.

Apart from these tangible outcomes, the campaign also generated £300,000 worth of publicity, enhanced team-building and improved interaction and engagement with consumers. The knitting groups that were established to meet the demand for hats also encouraged older people to get involved and take advantage of support at Age Concern centres, and boosted the numbers of younger Age Concern's campaigners.

Question

Is cause-related communications a misguided attempt to win stakeholder approval?

Source: Business in the Community (2007).

Media for corporate communication

Before examining the impact of digital media on corporate communication, it is worth noting the array of traditional, offline media that have been used to support corporate communication initiatives. Television provides a visually entertaining though

Outdoor and print have been used more often than TV but the message is still predominantly one-way.

relatively expensive opportunity to reach target stakeholders. Outdoor and print have been used more often but the message is still predominantly one-way and provides little or no opportunity for feedback or interaction with interested parties.

Eurostar launched a monthly magazine following the disastrous breakdowns over the Christmas period in 2009. Having had to pay out £10 million in compensation to stranded passengers, as well as coping with the negativity arising from an independent report that found Eurostar had handled the crisis and its customers poorly, and facing competition on the Channel Tunnel route, the company needed to re-establish itself. The magazine, distributed through its trains, is seen as a way of adding value to a customer's experience. Amongst other

things, the content emphasises Eurostar's green and environmental credentials as it reposi-
tions itself (Clark, 2010).

Digital media has transformed the way in which organisations communicate with their
stakeholders. It has also challenged the way in which they organise and structure themselves
in order to deliver messages (Hearn *et al.*, 2009). Although some of the principles associated
with the way traditional media works still apply, digital media demands a different approach
and offers new opportunities for organisations. Those organisations that attempted to super-
impose their former approach to public relations onto the digital media landscape have
invariably had to adapt and change.

This is not intended to suggest that there is no role for traditional media in contemporary
communications. The premise that offline and online media work better together rather than
independently is still valid. However, digital media, particularly in the era of Web 2.0, enable
interaction through knowledge and information-sharing. The way in which this facility is
incorporated into organisations varies considerably, especially as collaborative software and
associated applications continue to evolve quickly. Viewpoint 11.6 highlights an example of
the way in which a variety of media can be configured not only to provide a point of differentiation but also to improve perceptions of an organisation.

Viewpoint 11.6	Using media to differentiate and grow

Because Desjardins is a co-operative financial group and shares its profits rather than rewarding shareholders, its mission and values are different from those of commercial banks. In 2003 the Canadian group
ran a humourous ad campaign entitled 'This is not a bank'. The goal was to emphasise its difference, as the
group attempted to gain a foothold in Montreal and the ethnocultural communities. In 2005 the marketing
strategy was based on targeting affluent segments but its closest competitor launched a similar humourous
campaign that served to dilute the differences created by Desjardins.

In 2006 a new campaign was developed that sought to change the strength of perception that Desjardin
added value for individuals. The strategy behind the campaign was based on the insight that Desjardin is
more than a bank, because it puts money at the service of people, not the other way round. As a result
Desjardin embarked on a campaign that was led by a corporate image programme and followed up by a
series of specific product campaigns. All were positioned around demonstrating how their customers have
had their needs met by Desjardin, using an aspirational tone.

The corporate camapign started with a 2-week teaser campaign using outdoor media in Montreal and Quebec.
This was followed by TV ads, based around four executions that depicted Desjardin's co-operative status.
Newspapers, radio and web banners, search and further outdoor work were then used to support particular
products and services, starting with insurance and concluding with car insurance in spring 2008. The overall
media spend was not increased in the 2-year period, just refocused for more efficient resource allocation.

The results were outstanding and all attributed to the advertising work rather than changes to products
and services. The sales performance in each product/service category improved significantly. From a corporate perspective net goodwill reached its highest level since 2001, member perceptions of Dersjardin's
co-operative distinctiveness rose 3 per cent, the company's perceived expertise reached 85 per cent and
the campaign proved to be successful amongst the target audiences in Montreal and internally as a sense
of pride and identification with Desjardin was established with employees.

Question

If Desjardin were to launch a similar campaign this year, how and why might they change their media mix?

Source: Based on Canadian Congress of Advertising, retrieved 30 August 2008 from www.warc.com.

Web logs, or blogs, are a typical Web 2.0 or social media application and are used to communicate and develop interaction. Lee *et al.* (2006) identify a top-down blog strategy designed

primarily to enable management to reach external audiences in order to enhance the identity and to promote the exchange of product, market and industry-related ideas. The bottom-up strategy features blogs written by employees, for sharing with either colleagues internally or with the media and interested parties externally; these often focus on product development or customer service issues.

Bottom-up strategy features blogs written by employees, wikis and podcasts.

'Wikis' provide opportunities to enhance users' control over the streams of information they receive. From an organisational persepctive, knowledge that was previously fragmented can be gathered according to user needs and so streamline the flow of information and impact on productivity.

Storytelling, as examined in the previous chapter, can be a powerful means of communication. Digital media incorporating text and audio, but increasingly photos and video through podcasts and TV, provide a variety of powerful means of delivering corporate stories to audiences.

The use of blogs, wikis and podcasts, plus the influence of online communities and user-generated content, presents a series of new issues for the management of public relations. These tools have facilitated a steep rise in word-of-mouth communication and the promotion of citizen journalism. People are now much more able than they used to be, and more willing, to comment on brands, organisations and events that affect their lives. One of the implications of this is the way in which brands are perceived (see Chapter 12). Another is the way in which organisations use public relations. Gray (2007) claims that organisations need to provide training and guidelines or policies for employees who blog.

Organisations also need to ensure that blog sites provide transparency, full disclosure and are honest. Some companies have tried to create artificial blogs and deceive readers. These 'floggs' risk damaging the very entity they are trying to promote and endorse. One-way communications enabled organisations a degree of control over what was said about a brand. Social media empowers interaction and that means reduced control over communications and an increased need to be prepared to deal with controversy and even digitally enabled, brand-related crises. However, Kent (2008) claims that the role of blogs within public relations is not as extensive as suggested by many commentators.

Internet-based communications have radically altered the way in which previous communication processes were deemed to operate (Springston, 2001). Now anyone with internet access can post and compare information whilst remaining anonymous if they wish. Whilst the internet has provided a valuable new form of external communication, users are also more open, more exposed and more vulnerable to a range of stakeholders. The internet provides for crisis potential as critical information about them, whether true or false, can erupt at any time and spread rapidly around the globe.

Although measures to manage internet crises should include managing stakeholders, preparing an internet crisis communication plan and regularly monitoring the online environment, Conway *et al.* (2007) found that 77 per cent of organisations do not manage their internet crisis potential.

Chapter summary

In order to help consolidate your understanding of the symbols, tools and media used in corporate communication, here are the key points summarised against each of the learning objectives.

1. Evaluate ideas associated with message framing

Framing involves the development of messages that emphasise specific issues and draws an audience's attention to positive rather than negative elements. Messages can be framed to either focus a recipient's attention on to positive outcomes (happiness) or shift them away from the possible negative outcomes (pain). Framing enables selected materials, perhaps facts, values or beliefs, to become the salient factors used by stakeholders in their decision-making.

2. Appraise the use of symbols in developing corporate reputation

Organisations use symbols and visual identifiers to influence the way they are perceived, to aid recognition and, in the long term, to develop positive associations and the reputation of the organisation. Fombrun & van Riel (2004) suggest that reputation is developed and established around five key dimensions: visibility, distinctiveness, transparency, authenticity and consistency. The principal symbols are the corporate name, slogan and logo and some or all of these are often changed during rebranding and strategy changes.

3. Examine the characterisitics of corporate advertising

Corporate advertising campaigns are characterised by consistency, professionalism and creativity. The messages conveyed through corporate advertising should provide direction and positioning by building on the reputational platform; continue and build the corporate story; and articulate the corporate promise clearly and unequivocally.

The majority of corporate advertising is used for two main reasons: recruitment of quality staff and supporting product and services. In addition, however, corporate advertising is used to support sponsorship arrangements, improve community and customer relations, influence investor relations and, increasingly, inform stakeholders about activities and issues related to corporate responsibility.

4. Explore the methods and approaches associated with public relations

Public relations provides some of the cues that enable stakeholders to develop images and shape perceptions of an organisation. These cues are used to recognise, understand, select and converse with particular organisations. Public relations is used by organisations to develop mutual goodwill and understanding and, in turn, develop relationships that are in the long-run interests of all parties. The main characteristic of public relations is that it is a very cost-effective means of carrying messages with a high degree of credibility. However, the degree of control that management is able to exert over the transmission of messages can be limited.

5. Evaluate ideas associated with corporate sponsorship activities

Sponsorship is unlike advertising, because it attempts to influence stakeholders indirectly. The primary reasons to use sponsorship are to build awareness and improve the perception (image) held of an organisation. Secondary reasons are to attract and retain new stakeholders, very often customers, to support dealers and other intermediaries and to act as a form of staff motivation and morale-building.

Sponsorship represents a form of collaborative communication, in the sense that two (or more) parties work together in order that one is enabled to reach the other's audience. Issues regarding the relationship between the parties concerned will impact on the success of a sponsorship arrangement and any successive arrangements.

6. Consider the characteristics of the main media used in corporate communication

A range of media are used in corporate communication. With print traditionally an important element for corporate advertising to support recruitment and product and services messages, it is digital media that has transformed the way in which corporate communication works, especially public relations. The use of blogs, wikis and podcasts, plus the influence of online communities and user-generated content, presents a series of new issues for the management of corporate communication. These tools have facilitated a steep rise in word-of-mouth communication and citizen journalism.

Discussion questions

1. Discuss the view that message framing is necessary in order to convey particular points.
2. List the five dimensions of corporate reputation and show how corporate visual identity might impact upon each of them.
3. Prioritise three aspects of visual design and consider the way each influences corporate branding.
4. Helgesen (1994) suggests that successful corporate advertising campaigns are characterised by two dimensions: professionalism and creativity. Find examples that, in your opinion, support this view.
5. What is a cue and how are they used in a public relations context?
6. Find two examples of corporate sponsorship and try to discover the objectives for the campaign.
7. To what extent should organisations secure the naming rights to properties they do not own?
8. Compare and contrast two different cause-related campaigns.
9. Use an organisation of your choice and show how the use of conventional and digital media working together can assist corporate communication.
10. Make a list of the different ways an organisation might be vulnerable to an internet-based crisis.

References

Bal, C., Quester, P.G. & Boucher, S. (2007). Emotions and sponsorship marketing. *Admap* 486, September, 51–52.

Balmer, J.M.T., Stuart, H. & Greyser, S.A. (2009). Aligning identity and strategy: corporate branding at British Airways in the late 20th century. *California Management Review* 51(3), 6–23.

Barda, T. (2009). The science of appliances. *The Marketer*, May, 25–27.

van den Bosch, A.L.M., De Jong, M.D.T. & Elving, W.J.L. (2005). How corporate visual identity supports reputation. *Corporate Communications: An International Journal* 10(2), 108–116.

Bruning, S.D. & Ledingham, J.A. (2000). Perceptions of relationships and evaluations of satisfaction: an exploration of interaction. *Public Relations Review* 26(1), 85–95.

Bruning, S.D., Dials, M. & Shirka, A. (2008). Using dialogue to build organization-public relationships, engage publics, and positively affect organizational outcomes. *Public Relations Review* 34, 25–31.

Bryant, A. (1997). A new look for British air: tail fins in 50 designs. *New York Times*, 11 June. Online: http://www.nytimes.com/1997/06/11/business/a-new-look-for-british-air-tail-fins-in-50-designs.html. Accessed: 11 July 2009.

Business in the Community (2007). Innocent Drinks – Supergran Campaign. Online: http://www.bitc.org.uk/resources/case_studies/afe1311_innocent.html. Accessed: August 2009.

Clark, N. (2010). Eurostar plots mag to boost customer loyalty. *Marketing*, 17 February, 4.

Clark, J.M., Cornwell, T.B. & Pruitt, S.W. (2002). Corporate stadium sponsorships, signaling theory, agency conflicts, and shareholder wealth. *Journal of Advertising Research* 42(6), 16–32.

Clews, M.-L. (2009). Reckitt Benckiser readies corporate campaign. *Marketing Week*, 14 July. Online: www.marketingweek.co.uk/news/reckitt-benckiser-readies-corporate-campaign/3002362.article. Accessed: 1 August 2009.

Clifton, R. & Maughan, E. (2000). *The Future of Brands*. Basingstoke: Macmillan Business.

Conway, T., Ward, M., Lewis, G. & Bernhardt, A. (2007). Internet crisis potential: the importance of a strategic approach to marketing communications. *Journal of Marketing Communications* 13(3), 213–228.

Coombs, W.T. (2007). Protecting organization reputations during a crisis: the development and application of situational crisis communication theory. *Corporate Reputation Review*, 10(3), 163–176.

Cooper, A.H. (2002). Media framing and social movement mobilization: German peace protest against INF missiles, the Gulf War, and NATO peace enforcement in Bosnia. *European Journal of Political Research* 41, 37–80.

Cornelissen, J. (2008). *Corporate Communication: Theory and Practice*, 2nd edn. London: Sage.

Darmon, K., Fitzpatrick, K. & Bronstein, C. (2008). Krafting the obesity message: a case study in framing and issues management. *Public Relations Review* 34(4), 373–379.

Dowling, G.R. (1996). Corporate identity traps. *Working Paper 96–002*, February. Australian Graduate School of Management.

Ehling, W.P. (1992). Estimating the value of public relations and communication to an organization. In: Grunig, J.E., Dozier, D.M., Ehling, P., Grunig, L.A., Repper, F.C. & Whits, J. *Excellence in Public Relations and Communication Management*. Hillsdale, NJ: Lawrence Erlbaum, pp. 617–638.

Farache, F. & Perks, K.J. (2010). CSR advertisements: a legitimacy tool? *Corporate Communications: an International Journal* 15(3), 235–248.

Fill, C. (2009). *Marketing Communications: Interactivity, Communities and Content*, 5th edn. Harlow: Financial Times/Prentice Hall.

Fombrun, C.J. & van Riel, C.B.M. (2004). *Fame and Fortune: How Successful Companies Build Winning Reputations*. New York: Prentice Hall/Financial Times.

Forbes Staff (2008). Slogans that work. *Forbes Magazine*, 7 January. Online: http://www.forbes.com/forbes/2008/0107/099.html. Accessed: 23 March 2011.

Gray, R. (2007) Rapid response. *Marketing* 7, November, 48–49.

Gregory, A. (2004). Scope and structure of public relations: a technology driven view. *Public Relations Review* 30(3), 245–254.

Grimes, E. & Meenaghan, T. (1998). Focusing commercial sponsorship on the internal corporate audience. *International Journal of Advertising* 17(1), 51–74.

Gummesson, E. (1996). Relationship marketing and imaginary organizations: a synthesis. *European Journal of Marketing* 30(2), 31–45.

Hakansson, H. & Snehota, I., eds (1995). *Developing Relationships in Business Networks*. London: Routledge.

Harverson, P. (1998). Why IT companies take the risk. *Financial Times*, 2 June, 12.

Hearn, G., Foth, M. & Gray, H. (2009). Applications and implementations of new media in corporate communications. *Corporate Communications: an International Journal* 14(1), 49–61.

Helgesen, T. (1994). Advertising awards and advertising agency performance criteria. *Journal of Advertising Research* 34, July/August, 43–53.

Kellaway, L. (2002). Beyond parody: PwC's rebranding exercise is demoralising for employees and satirists alike. *Financial Times*, 17 June, 12.

Kent, M. (2008). Critical analysis of blogging in public relations. *Public Relations Review* 34, 32–40.

Kent, M.L. & Taylor, M. (2002). Toward a dialogic theory of public relations. *Public Relations Review* 28(1), 21–37.

Kitchen, P.J. (1997). *Public Relations: Principles and Practice*. London: International Thomson Business Press.

Klara, R. (2009). A tower by any other name is . . . still a tower. *Brandweek* 50(13), 34.

Lacey, R., Sneath, J.Z., Finney, R.Z. & Close, A.G. (2007). The impact of repeat attendance on event sponsorship effects. *Journal of Marketing Communications* 13(4), 243–255.

Lee, S., Hwang, T. & Lee, H-H. (2006). Corporate blogging strategies of the Fortune 500 companies. *Management Decision* 44(3), 316–334.

Lloyd, P.R. (1999). Britain rebranded. Online: http://paulrobertlloyd.com/articles/britain_rebranded/. Accessed: 11 July 2009.

Mathews, M.R. (1993). *Socially Responsible Accounting.* UK: Chapman & Hall.

McGrath, C. (2007). Framing lobbying messages: defining and communicating political issues persuasively. *Journal of Public Affairs* 7, August, 269–280.

Melewar, T.C., Bassett, K. & Simoes, C. (2006). The role of communication and visual identity in modern organizations. *Corporate Communications: An International Journal* 11(2), 138–147.

McDonald, C. (1991). Sponsorship and the image of the sponsor. *European Journal of Marketing* 25(11), 31–38.

Olkkonen, R. (2001). Case study: the network approach to international sport sponsorship arrangement. *The Journal of Business and Industrial Marketing* 16(4), 309–329.

Parsons, R. (2009). Castrol readies Ronaldo campaign, *Marketing Week*, Wednesday, 29 July. Online: http://www.marketingweek.co.uk/castrol-readies-ronaldo-campaign/3002852.article. Accessed: 1 August 2009.

Poon, D.T.Y. & Prendergast, G. (2006). A new framework for evaluating sponsorship opportunities. *International Journal of Advertising* 25(4), 471–487.

Poon, P.T.Y., Prendergast, G. & West, D.C. (2010). Match game: linking sponsorship congruence with communication outcomes. *Journal of Advertising Research*, June, 214–226.

Quester, P. (1997). Sponsorship returns: the value of naming rights. *Corporate Communications: An International Journal* 2(3), 101–108.

Reed, D. (1994). Sponsorship. *Campaign*, 20 May, 37–38.

van Riel, C.B.M. & van Bruggen, G.H. (2003). IMPACT: a management judgment tool to predict the effectiveness of corporate advertising campaigns. *Journal of Brand Management* 11(1), 22–33.

Sampson, I. & Linz, A. (2000). Sony; the great campaign only got bigger and better. *Advertising Effectiveness Awards.* Online: www.warc.com. Accessed: 20 October 2008.

Springston, J. (2001). Public relations abd new media technology: the impact of the internet, in Heath, R.L. ed. *Handbook of Public Relations.* London: Sage Publications, pp. 603–614.

Stuart, H. & Muzellec, L. (2004). Corporate makeovers: can a hyena be rebranded? *Brand Management* 11(6), 472–482.

Taylor, M. & Kent, M.L. (2007). Taxonomy of mediated crisis responses. *Public Relations Review* 33(2), 140–146.

Thwaites, D. (1994). Corporate sponsorship by the financial services industry. *Journal of Marketing Management*, 10, 743–63.

Tripodi, J.A. (2001). Sponsorship: a confirmed weapon in the promotional armoury. *International Journal of Sports Marketing and Sponsorship* 3(1), 1–20.

Tsai, S.-P. (2007). Message framing strategy for brand communication. *Journal of Advertising Research* 47(3), 364–377.

Wallace, C. (2010). Hospitality gets personal. *PRWeek*, 22 January, 21–23.

Watkins, M., Edwards, M. & Thakrar, R. (2001). *Winning the Influence Game: What Every Business Leader Should Know about Government.* New York: John Wiley.

White, R. (2008). Corporate advertising. *WARC Best Practise.* Online: www.warc.com. Accessed: 23 March 2008.

Chapter 12
Methods of corporate communication

Organisations use different methods of corporate communication to influence specific stakeholders. Key audiences are the government, the public, employees, customers, investors and the financial community, and each requires a specific form of communication. Consideration also needs to be given to the issues associated with the way organisations use communication to defend their reputations. The chapter closes with a consideration of the ways in which corporate communication activities can be measured.

Aims and learning objectives

The aim of this chapter is to examine the core characteristics of the individual methods of corporate communication.

The learning objectives of this chapter are to:

1. Examine ways of building reputation with financial stakeholders - investor relations
2. Consider methods to manage government, officials and regulators - public affairs
3. Appraise ways of building reputation through employees - internal communications
4. Evaluate the use of communications with customers - media relations
5. Explore communications arising in the environment - issues management
6. Assess ideas associated with defending reputation - crisis communications
7. Explain the principles of measuring the effectiveness of corporate communication.

Introduction

Understanding the different ways in which organisations can reach specific stakeholders is an important aspect of managing corporate communication. Financial services organisations not only need information that is different from the information required by customers or employees but will need it delivered in different ways, in different frequencies and at different speeds. This diversity requires different managerial skill sets and can work against the principles of integrated communications. It is important therefore to ensure that these seemingly separate functions work within a planned framework, a core theme that continually reinforces the organisation's positioning strategy.

This chapter is concerned with an exploration of each of the main methods of corporate communication: investor relations, public affairs, internal communications, media relations, issues management and crisis communications. Attention is drawn to the purpose, role and issues associated with each of these forms of corporate communication.

Investor relations

The changing dynamics associated with the recent economic recession have highlighted failures in financial regulations and the guidelines used to regulate the flow of investment funds. However, ensuring that investors have the necessary, accurate information and confidence in potential funds and organisations has always been a critical factor and is not a post-recession knee-jerk reaction. Indeed, many researchers, such as Day & Fahey (1990) and Higgins & Bannister (1992), have found that communications received by the stock market that are related to an organisation's corporate strategy can have a significant impact on the value of shares.

The financial public relations function, now referred to as investor relations, has grown in importance following the deregulation of the financial markets in the late 1980s. Deregulation opened up markets, reduced the influence of government and the volume of constraining legislation, and placed responsibility for the management of financial markets with the financial services industry and the constituent organisations.

Partly as a result of deregulation, the number of target audiences for financial services and related communications has grown. On the one hand, there are large institutional investors such as the government, multinational organisations and agencies such as stock exchanges, all of which require financially related information. On the other hand, there are increasing numbers of individual investors who wish to invest part of their savings in various funds, equities and savings plans. In addition to these, there are the financial press, shareholders, investment analysts, financial advisers and fund managers. This means that communication, and the provision of timely, transparent and accurate information should have become significant factors in the marketplace. Public relations experts were expected to work with financial experts in order to understand and operate within the increasingly complex market as new products and services flooded the industry.

Public relations experts were expected to work with financial experts.

Cutlip *et al.* (1999) define investor relations as 'a specialized part of corporate public relations that builds and maintains mutually beneficial relationships with shareholders and others in the financial community to maximize shareholder value'. The UK Investor Relations Society (2009) considers investor relations to be the 'communication of relevant and necessary information by which the investment community can consistently make an informed judgment about the fair value of a company's shares and securities'. Interestingly the former stresses the maximisation of shareholder value and relationships, whilst the latter emphasises fair value rather than maximisation, and implicitly stresses the significance of one-way communication, which is not suitable for relationship development. In practice the core activity of investor relations is to react to requests for information, although the development and use of websites has helped to make the discipline more proactive.

One of the first investor relations programmes was started in 1953 by General Electric. Since then the discipline has been used intensively by major organisations, but has assumed a background role, attracting little attention or public visibility. Indeed, academic interest has also been quiet. All of this changed through two events. The first was the Enron scandal. This case is notorious for the fact that the directors urged investors to keep investing knowing that the business model had failed and that the company was failing. They even withdrew their investments as fast as they were encouraging others to invest. The second event has been the worldwide collapse of financial markets, triggered by the colossal sub-prime mortgage debacle. At the root of these events was a form of trust and financial culture that overrode any perceived need or sense of moral responsibility to check out claims, statements and financial projections.

The role of investor relations is of strategic importance.

Investor relations were previously regarded as a financial function of organisations (Petersen & Martin, 1996), and although sometimes loosely attached to public relations, it was more often conducted by the department of financial affairs (Hong & Ki, 2007). Today, the role of investor relations is seen to be of strategic importance and one which requires clarity and transparency, with communication and not finance as its central tenet (Laskin, 2009). Co-ordination with other aspects of an organisation's communications becomes essential and, as Silver (2004) puts it, 'the convergence of IR [investor relations] with PR [public relations] has become so important that not combining these functions could have negative consequences for a public company's share price' (p. 60). By developing the communication dimension, the traditionally reactive stance of investor relations could be changed and new opportunities for competitive advantage achieved. Unfortunately, Laskin's research later in the decade has revealed that investor relations is still regarded by CEOs as a financial rather than a communication function.

What, then, is the role of investor relations in a corporate environment that sees it as a financial instrument yet clearly has huge potential as a communication tool? At a general level the role of investor relations is to provide potential investors with the necessary financial and non-financial information to enable them to make appropriate investment decisions. This might be regarded as attracting attention, providing information, reducing risk and creating a desire to be associated with an organisation and, through that, a positive demand for its shares. At a corporate level, investor relations seek to protect the interests of the organisation by providing accurate, timely and truthful information to the marketplace. In doing so it seeks compliance with various financial and regulatory bodies and the maintenance of a suitable trading environment. At an individual corporate level, investor relations involves the development and maintenance of relationships with senior management (Hong & Ki, 2007) and investors, which inevitably involves trust and commitment, through which there is co-operation to buy and sell shares. Relationships with top management are important partly because of the CEO's desire to increase the value of the organisation. To achieve this, the reputation of the organisation needs to be maintained. However, it is interesting that the communication element of this function is so under-rated.

If investor relations are to have an enhanced communication focus, a variety of public relations strategies are necessary to reach different target audiences (see Viewpoint 12.1 for an example of how SingTel use investor relations). Hanrahan (1997) highlights four particular strategies: expansive, defensive, creative and adaptive.

Viewpoint 12.1   In-House and personal investor relations at SingTel

Investor relations (IR) at Singapore Telecommunications (SingTel) is a critical activity. While the company's operations are focused on the Asian region, it has investors from around the world. It might be reasonably expected that communications over this geographically dispersed audience would be best managed through technology. Well, some of it is, but face-to-face communication is still perceived to be important. This is used in order to generate interaction with investors, so that the company can listen to them and answer their questions. For example, different teams of SingTel senior managers spend over 4 weeks every year travelling to the United States and Europe to meet with investors.

SingTel's IR department consists of seven professionals. They manage shareholder questions, advise senior management on material disclosure and monitor the press and investment communities to make sure messages are clearly received and understood. From this information, it is possible to brief senior managers on what the market doesn't know or misunderstands.

Exhibit 12.1   SingTel website page.
Source: SingTel, with permission.

Some of the technical aspects of the IR operations are outsourced to service providers in the IR industry, e.g. services such as shareholder analysis and webcast transcription.

In addition to the international meetings, IR activities include events, conferences, presentations and business luncheons, which are organised in-house. For example, SingTel organises annual investor days that bring together investors and analysts from both the buy and sell sides. Senior management from the Singapore and Australian operations, as well as from the regional associates, are present to provide brief presentations on each of the different business divisions. Ample time is allocated for questions and answers, as well as informal interaction.

Although SingTel does not use social media, it does use some technology. The company sends out substantial market analysis and material information, in addition to communications mandated by the Singapore Exchange. Investor presentations, annual reports, webcasts of earnings presentations, announcements to SGX and ASX are also available on the IR website. Conference calls with investors and analysts are transcribed and posted on the IR website, as are PowerPoint presentations that explain the company's business, prospects and market overviews. The website also hosts other relevant information, including the investor calendar, shareholder meetings, shares and dividend information, factsheets and financial summaries.

Question

How might use of social media assist investor relations at SingTel?

Source: Based on Pisik (2010) and SingTel Investor Relations.

Expansive strategies are followed during periods of growth, when the size of product portfolios increases. In this context competition can be aggressive so it is critical that awareness, recognition and trust are developed. This can be achieved through serving on committees and public interest groups, publishing white papers, speaking at conferences, writing articles and other activities that serve to raise the profile and credibility of the organisation. Sponsorship can also be used to make associations with an event. This can also be used as a way of establishing networks and leveraging goodwill.

Defensive strategies are needed in times of crisis, such as a recession, very poor trading performance, when accused of malpractice or irregular reporting or when faced by a hostile takeover bid. In these situations the timely provision of the correct information, perhaps as a separate report, is important.

Creative strategies involve the use of digital technologies to deliver the corporate identity in novel and interesting ways. This might be through the use of interviews which can be beamed across the television world instantly, if necessary, across the internet and through Reuters and world services. With information and analysis instantly available, 24/7, the primary role of the press has shifted to one focused on the provision of comment and interpretation.

> The primary role of the press has shifted to one focused on the provision of comment and interpretation.

Adaptive strategies are used when an organisation experiences considerable change. Moving into new financial product and/or geographic markets, merging with another organisation or simply developing key services all warrant strategies that are flexible and can adapt to local press and media needs. Corporate advertising, adapted for local use, has been a significant tool. Today, one of the roles of the website is to provide fast, localised information that can be targeted at particular opinion leaders and formers.

Finally, research by Geppert & Lawrence (2008) provides an interesting link with the use of storytelling, examined in Chapter 10, and an element of investor relations, namely, the CEO's letter to shareholders. These letters, included in the annual report, are a potentially powerful and influential means of shaping attitudes towards the organisation. The language, linguistic style and clarity of these letters can be instrumental in the effectiveness of the message. Geppert

& Lawrence's (2008) research, based on content analysis, found a relationship between the style of writing and content in these letters and the reputation of the organisations. Organisations with a high reputation were found to write these letters using short sentences and 'concrete' words, avoiding puffery and complexity. This, they argue, builds credibility and trust, unlike organisations with a low reputation whose letters were complex, and used words that were far from concrete. Geppert & Lawrence refer to Zhou *et al.* (2002), who found that greater word variety increases perceived deception. Firms with a low reputation used a narrative containing a greater number of filler words, presumably in an attempt to suggest that the content was more meaningful than might actually have been the case.

> Greater word variety increases perceived deception.

Public affairs

The term public affairs has been used to describe a number of communication activities. For some it represents the interface between an organisation and its external social stakeholders (Meznar *et al.*, 2006). This could embrace a whole range of public relations activities and does not really help us understand its key role and tasks. For others, public affairs is concerned with communications that are focused on those who regulate markets and industries, legislators, elected officials and appointed representatives. In short these are government-focused communications which seek to influence the regulations and legislation associated with the markets in which an organisation operates. Oberman (2008) believes that public affairs is a tool that is used strategically to exploit public opinion, influence and policy in order to develop market power and use resources to develop competitive advantage.

> Public affairs is a tool that is used strategically to exploit public opinion, influence and policy.

Hillman & Hitt (1999) identify three main forms of corporate political communication strategies – the provision of information, financial support and the building of constituencies:

- By providing information, knowledge and expertise, it becomes possible to influence the models and criteria used by decision-makers when making public policy choices.

- The provision of financial support, e.g. the support given by organisations to people running for election to public positions, can result in a sympathetic consideration of the organisation's requests when attempting to influence decisions. This approach is restricted in European countries and is more common in the USA (Tamianau & Wilts, 2006).

- Constituency-building concerns the creation of local support for specific public policy solutions and then creating and applying pressure to government agencies to favour these solutions.

Tamianau & Wilts (2006) suggest that organisations follow different strategies simultaneously and do not rely on a single approach. Two other strategic responses, borrowed from issues management, refer to the broad responses made by organisations. In situations where the organisation decides to adapt to the external expectations, it is said to be following a 'bridging strategy'. In those situations where an organisation wishes to adapt the expectations and practices of external stakeholders, without any internal adjustments, a 'buffering strategy' is said to be in place.

It might be expected that buffering strategies (changing the expectations of stakeholders) will attract more press coverage and hence bring greater visibility to an organisation. So, in order to avoid extensive media coverage, it might be reasonable to expect a bridging strategy (internal adaption) to be a better solution as it will bring less media attention. Research by Meznar *et al.* (2006), however, found that whilst buffering does lead to increased media attention, bridging strategies have no impact on media coverage. Indeed, organisations that adopt a bridging public affairs strategy appear to be 'most satisfied with

> Buffering strategies attract more press coverage and hence bring greater visibility to an organisation.

their public affairs performance' (p. 65). Their findings suggest that the perception of public affairs among officers/managers is that those who tend to bridge and accommodate are more satisfied with the public relations performance than those who buffer and resist. As Meznar *et al.* (2006) suggest, tongue in-cheek, 'no news is good news'.

Lobbying

Collectively these three strategies, the provision of information and financial support and the building of constituencies, constitute the public affairs practice of 'corporate lobbying'. While legislation is being prepared, lobbyists provide a flow of information and expertise into their organisations to keep them informed about events as a means of scanning the environment. They also ensure that the views of the organisation are heard by public decision-makers, in order that legislation and regulations can be shaped appropriately, limiting any potential damage or restrictions to the organisation in their attempt to achieve their own objectives.

Lobbying is concerned with persuasive communication designed to influence policymakers.

Lobbying is concerned with persuasive communication designed to influence policymakers. To achieve their goals, lobbyists present their messages carefully, framing them using language to focus the attention of their audience on a particular perspective of an issue. By crafting a specific angle, the media are encouraged to take up the cause using the same perspective, similar stories and the same language. When the USA imposed tariffs on steel imports, for example, rather than refer to tariffs (a negative story) the media were fed stories about the need to punish foreign steel producers for their illegal behaviour. In doing so the story became one of support for US jobs and pro-American sentiment. The message was framed around preventing foreign producers dumping subsidised steel in the US and preserving American jobs (McGrath, 2007; see also Viewpoint 12.2).

Viewpoint 12.2   Try Google for lobbying

Google is now involved in many different industries, and as a result it has significantly increased its lobbying activities (Harvey, 2010). Google has increased its lobbying so that it is now active in advertising, energy, trade, telecoms and anti-trust matters. According to statistics released by the US Senate, Google spent $4.03 (£2.58) million in 2009, making it one of the top five internet and technology lobbyists. However, these activities are not confined to the US as Google has teams in most European capitals.

The most popular reason for this increase in lobbying is that the company is responding to increasing controls applied by the state. As the company has grown, so Google has been subjected to increasing inspection and regulation. Google seeks to protect its stakeholders' interests and has actively campaigned to protect their various business interests. In 2008 regulations stopped a deal with Yahoo and it took 2 years for Google to get permission to buy Admob, a mobile advertising platform, for $750 million, in May 2011.

Google's lobbying is founded on the idea of a 'free and open internet'. This is evident in their attempt to get the digital rights to millions of out-of-print books, and their threat to pull out of China due to several cyber-attacks.

Question

To what extent might Google's entry and possible exit from China be viewed as hypocritical in the light of its quest for a 'free and open internet'?

Task

Make notes detailing ways in which Google might have spent $4.03 million on lobbying.

Source: Based on Harvey (2010).

Exhibit 12.2 Google is not involved in many different industries and has intensified its lobbying activity.
Source: Photo courtesy of Google UK.

Moloney (1997, p. 173) suggests that lobbying is 'inside public relations' as it focuses on the members of an organisation who seek to persuade and negotiate with its stakeholders in government, on matters of opportunity and/or threat. He refers to in-house lobbyists (those members of the organisation who try to influence non-members) and hired lobbyists contracted to complete specific tasks. Koeppl (2001), a little more succinctly, defines lobbying as 'a communication instrument especially targeted to political decision making authorities'.

Moloney's view of lobbying is that it is 'monitoring public policy-making for a group interest; building a case in favour of that interest; and putting it privately with varying degrees of pressure to public decision makers for their acceptance and support through favourable political intervention'. Where local authorities interpret legislation and frame the activities of their citizens and constituent organisations, the government determines legislation and controls the activities of people and organisations across markets.

This control may be direct or indirect, but the power and influence of government are such that large organisations and trade associations seek to influence the direction and strength of legislation, because any adverse laws or regulations may affect the profitability and the value of the organisation. Recent initiatives by the UK government to reduce the length of time that new drugs are protected by patent were severely contested by representatives of drug manufacturers and their trade association, the Association of British Pharmaceutical Industries. Despite a great deal of lobbying, the action was lost, and now manufacturers have only 8 years to recover their investment before other manufacturers can replicate the drug. The pharmaceutical industry has also been actively lobbying the EU with respect to legislation on new patent regulations and the information that must be carried in any marketing communications message. The tobacco industry is well known for its lobbying activities, as are chemical, transport and many other industries.

Internal communications

The role that employees play in supporting a brand, in order that the gap between image and identity is minimised, can be crucial (Vallaster & de Chernatony, 2006). To achieve this desirable outcome, internal brand-building is necessary. This involves aligning internal behaviour with a corporate brand's identity. There are many approaches to achieving this, but these are beyond the scope of this chapter. However, corporate brand structures, leadership and change management are cited by Vallaster & de Chernatony (2006) as key.

The role of the employee is changing. Previously considered to be an element of production capable of achieving increasing levels of efficiency, their role has been expanded to embrace that of a brand ambassador (Freeman & Liedtka, 1997; Hemsley, 1998). This is particularly important in service environments where employees represent the interface between an organisation's internal and external environments and where their actions can have a powerful effect in creating images among customers (Schneider & Bowen, 1985; Balmer & Wilkinson, 1991). It is evident that many now recognise the increasing importance of internal communications (Storey, 2001; Punjaisri, *et al.*, 2009).

Many now recognise the increasing importance of internal communications.

Internal marketing (communications) serves several important roles, including encouraging efficient communication, by reducing duplication, promoting clarity and establishing control. Further roles concern connectivity within the organisation and within sub-networks or work-related networks, the generation of shared meaning among employees and groups of employees, enhancing organisational identity and reinforcing corporate values through managerial interaction with employees.

Research by Foreman & Money (1995) indicates that managers see the main components of internal marketing as falling into three broad areas, namely development, reward and vision for employees. These will inevitably vary in intensity on a situational basis. All three components have communication as a common linkage. Employees and management (members) need to communicate with one another and with a variety of non-members, and do so through an assortment of methods.

Aggerholm *et al.* (2010) refer to managerial interaction with employees that embraces issues related to planning, organising, commanding, co-ordinating, controlling and persuading employees about the desirability of striving towards corporate goals. In essence, this approach to internal communication is about 'control and information management' (p. 265). However, they extend this perspective by exploring the nature and potential for managerial conversations to communicate corporate strategies and values.

The four types of corporate communication are recruitment conversations, job appraisal interviews, sickness leave and dismissal-focused conversations.

They identify four types of conversation that can be considered from a corporate communication perspective: recruitment conversations, job appraisal interviews, sickness leave and dismissal-focused conversations. Their research found that in recruitment and job appraisal conversations, a wide range of issues are often explored. In the latter two, sickness and dismissal conversations, the focus was invariably on the role of the employee.

What this indicates is that the communication of corporate values is very evident in the sickness and dismissal conversations. However, it is often absent in the recruitment and appraisal conversations, due primarily to the breadth of issues considered. The researchers conclude that there is considerable potential for organisations to develop the communication of corporate strategies and values through management conversations. They also recognise the challenges associated with integrating values into these conversations and ensuring consistency.

The values transmitted to customers, suppliers and distributors through external communications need to be reinforced by the values expressed by employees, especially those who interact with these external groups. Internal marketing communications are necessary in order

Table 12.1	Internal communication matrix			
Dimension	Level	Direction	Participants	Content
1. Internal line management communication	Line managers/ supervisors	Predominantly two-way	Line managers–employees	Employees' roles Personal impact, e.g. appraisal discussions, team briefings
2. Internal team peer communication	Team colleagues	Two-way	Employee–employee	Team information, e.g. team task discussions
3. Internal project peer communication	Project group colleagues	Two-way	Employee–employee	Project information, e.g. project issues
4. Internal corporate communication	Strategic managers/top management	Predominantly one-way	Strategic managers–all employees	Organisational/corporate issues, e.g. goals, objectives, new developments, activities and achievements

that internal members are motivated and involved with the corporate brand such that they are able to present a consistent and uniform message to external stakeholders.

If there is a set of shared values then internal communications are said to blend and balance the external communications. This process, whereby employees are encouraged to communicate with non-members so that organisations ensure that what is promised is realised by customers, is referred to as 'living the brand'. Hiscock (2002) claims that employees can be segmented according to the degree and type of support they give to a brand. He claims that, in the UK, 30 per cent of employees are brand-neutral, 22 per cent are brand saboteurs and 48 per cent are brand champions, of whom 33 per cent would talk about the brand positively if asked, and 15 per cent spontaneously.

Welch & Jackson (2007) provide an interesting and helpful insight into some of the issues associated with understanding internal communication. They assume a stakeholder approach and suggest that internal communication should be considered in terms of four dimensions: internal line management communication, internal peer communication, internal project communication and internal corporate communication. These are intended to provide a typology of internal communication and are set out in Table 12.1.

Attention is given to the fourth dimension, internal corporate communication. Welch & Jackson (2007) believe that this refers to communication between an organisation's strategic managers and its internal stakeholders, with the purpose of promoting commitment to the organisation, a sense of belonging (to the organisation), awareness of its changing environment and understanding of its evolving goals (p. 186), as depicted in Figure 12.1.

These four goals serve to engage employees not only with their roles, tasks and jobs but also with the organisation. It is recognised that the internal environment incorporates the organisation's structure, culture, subcultures, processes, behaviour and leadership style and that this interacts with the external environment and provides context for the internal communication.

> The internal environment incorporates the organisation's structure, culture, subcultures, processes, behaviour and leadership style.

Intellectual and emotional engagement

Employees are required to deliver both the functional aspects of an organisation's offering and the emotional dimensions, particularly in service environments. By attending to these twin elements, it is possible that long-term relationships between sellers and buyers can develop

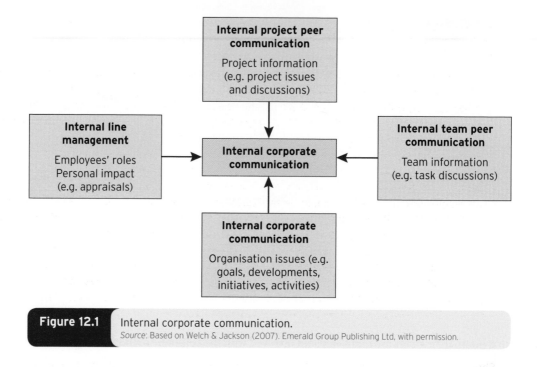

| Figure 12.1 | Internal corporate communication. |

Source: Based on Welch & Jackson (2007). Emerald Group Publishing Ltd, with permission.

effectively. Hardaker & Fill (2005) explore the notion that employees need to buy in to organisational vision, goals and strategy (Thomson & Hecker, 2000). This buy-in, or engagement, consists of two main components, an intellectual one and an emotional one (Figure 12.2). The intellectual element is concerned with employees buying into and aligning themselves with the organisation's strategy, issues and overall direction. The emotional element is concerned with employees taking ownership of their contribution and becoming committed to the achievement of stated goals. Communication strategies should be based on the information-processing styles of employees and access to preferred media. Communications should reflect a suitable balance between the need for rational information to meet intellectual needs and expressive types of communication to meet the emotional needs of the workforce. It follows that the better the communication, the higher the level of engagement.

The development of internal brands based around employees can be accomplished effectively and quickly by simply considering the preferred information-processing style of an internal audience. By developing messages that reflect the natural processing style and using a diversity of media that best complements the type of message and the needs of each substantial internal target audience, the communication strategy is more likely to be successful (see Viewpoint 12.3 on Microsoft).

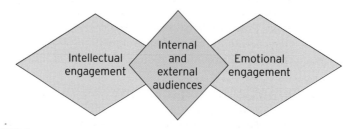

| Figure 12.2 | Brand engagement. |

Viewpoint 12.3	**Microsoft look through yet more windows**

In large, divisionalised and geographically dispersed organisations, the management of internal communications can pose challenges, especially with regard to the consistent delivery of strategic messages. Microsoft has addressed this by bringing together all those with a responsibility for internal communication, from across the organisation, to share best practice and exchange ideas. Microsoft have established an 'internal communicator community' which runs training workshops, establishes work groups and drives cross-functional projects.

In an attempt to manage the vast amount of information Microsoft employees exchange with one another, up to 13 million emails every day and 52,000 My Sites (a Microsoft tool for sharing information via an intranet), they have established a process designed to self-regulate the flow by focusing on the relevance of messages. Communication should be professional, unambiguous, respectful and essential, or, to put it another way, PURE. By encouraging staff to consider whether a message meets the PURE standards before transmitting, it is hoped to reduce the volume of messages and focus on business needs.

Communication should be audience-centred and Microsoft demonstrates this in two ways. First, all internal audiences are asked how they would prefer to receive internal communications, what makes them delete messages and what gets their attention. Secondly, senior managers are encouraged to use the communication tools and media that are most appropriate to them personally in order to effect leadership communication. Some use podcasts, while others prefer road shows, email or even internal radio or webcasts.

Question

Should all organisations apply this type of scheme and should it be extended to the management of corporate blogs?

Source: Based on Love (2006).

The effectiveness of internal communication is shaped by several characteristics – the structure, flow, content and climate (van Riel & Fombrun, 2007) – which together provide the context in which employee relations operate. The key dimensions of these characteristics are set out in Table 12.2.

Table 12.2	**The characteristics of internal communications**

Dimension	Explanation
Structure	Information can be disseminated and shared in three main ways: • through a formal organisational structure (e.g. hierarchical) • through supporting media endorsed by the organisation (newsletters, internal magazines, intranets, etc.) • through informal networks, word-of-mouth and what some refer to as 'water cooler' chats or the grapevine.
Flow	This refers to the direction of the communication. Typically communications flow vertically and downwards, especially through formalised organisational channels, e.g. decisions, assignments and requests. Flows from employees upwards towards senior management often involve reports and information.
Content	Employees prefer content that is easily understood, timely, sufficient and readable. Interestingly, information that serves to clarify the role of an employee and the relative standing is often well received and has been shown to improve levels of self-confidence.
Climate	Sometimes referred to as the 'communication atmosphere', the climate reflects how conducive or receptive the culture is to positive and negative information. A positive climate has been shown to improve productivity and, in doing so, improve employee identification with the organisation through a sense of participation.

Source: Based on van Riel & Fombrun (2007).

Managing customers - media relations

Customers represent a major stakeholder audience and are often the target of public relations activities. This is because, although members of the public may not be current customers, the potential they represent is important. If their attitude towards the organisation and its products is unfavourable, it is unlikely that they will purchase its products or speak positively about it. By creating awareness and trust, it is possible to create goodwill and interest, which may translate into purchase activity or favourable word-of-mouth communications. This is achieved through media relations. The relationships that organisations develop with the media are extremely important in order that their messages reach current and potential customers.

> **Media relations is not a public relations activity designed merely to capture the attention of customers.**

It should be emphasised that media relations is not a public relations activity designed merely to capture the attention of customers. A whole range of stakeholders are targeted and, as Hallahan (2001) explains, 'the strategic value of media coverage rests with its potential to create broad public awareness or a generalised knowledge, of organizations, causes, products and services'.

Of all the media, the press is the most crucial, as it is always interested in newsworthy items and depends to a large extent on information being fed to it by a variety of corporate press officers. Consequently, publicity can be generated for a range of organisational events, activities and developments.

Media relations consist of a range of activities designed to provide bloggers, journalists, editors and other influential media-related people with information. The intention is that they relay the information, through their media, for consumption by their audiences. Of course, the original message may be changed and subject to information deviance, but audiences perceive much of this information as highly credible simply because opinion-formers have bestowed their judgment on the item.

Of the various forms of media relations, press releases, interviews, press kits and press conferences are the most frequently used. Media relations used to work on the basis that the media were perceived to be highly credible purveyors of information. In other words, news stories were believed because the media was perceived to be credible. However, this is no longer the case, as in conjunction with media fragmentation, the news media are no longer regarded to be highly credible (Geary, 2005) (but see Viewpoint 12.4 for an example of authority in the media).

Viewpoint 12.4 Authoritative Greenpeace

All organisations strive to achieve positive media attention, if only to capture the attention of large and widely dispersed audiences (Cutlip et al., 2000). Not-for-profit organisations, in particular, use media reporting to circulate knowledge, influence public opinion and raise awareness about issues that are important to them and their cause. In 2003, for example, Greenpeace New Zealand delivered a campaign against the lifting of a national suspension on the release of genetically modified organisms (GMOs).

Greenpeace were initially faced with the difficulty that the media believed the GM issue had already been extensively covered 3 years earlier during the Royal Commission that led to the suspension of commercial GM activity. Their strategy became one of creating consumer pressure in order to influence government and commercial decision-makers and so minimise the release of GMOs. To achieve this, Greenpeace attracted the attention of the national and regional media though media commentaries, and press releases. In addition to this they used direct action events, lobbying, scientific reports, the internet and sponsored international expert comments and opinions.

The media's position on GMOs was reasonably positive at the outset of the campaign but became more investigative and critical once the government issued the BERL report on the issue, which failed to provide an economic case for the use of GMOs. Greenpeace used a single media spokesperson who was perceived to be an expert adviser to journalists. Not only did he build a strong relationship with journalists, but he also ensured that the Greenpeace story and associated facts were understood, used and disseminated. Through the spokesperson and other activities, Greenpeace was seen as an expert news source, was able to set the media agenda, was perceived to be entirely credible and assumed overall authority on the issue.

Question

To what extent do organisations need a single expert to convey their position on an issue?

Source: Based on Motion & Weaver (2005).

Press releases

The press release is a common form of media relations activity. A written report concerning a change or development in the organisation is made available to media houses, inviting them to include it as a news item. Traditionally this was sent to the journalists, but these days they are likely to receive an email notifying them that a press release has been posted on the website. The media house may cover a national area, but very often a local house will suffice. These written statements concern developments in the organisation, such as staff promotions, new products, awards, prizes, new contracts and customers. The statement is deliberately short and written so as to attract the attention of the editor. Further information can be obtained if it is to be included within the next issue of the publication or news broadcast.

The press release is a common form of media relations activity.

Press conferences

Press conferences are used when a major event has occurred and where a press release cannot convey the appropriate tone or detail required by the organisation (see Exhibit 12.3). Press

Exhibit 12.3   Toyota holds a press conference on a brake system problem in one of its models.
Source: Getty Images.

conferences are mainly used by politicians, but organisations in crisis (e.g. major accidents, product recalls and mergers) and individuals appealing for help (e.g. police requesting assistance from the public) can use this form of communication. Press kits containing a full reproduction of any statements, photographs and relevant background information should always be available.

Interviews

Interviews with representatives of an organisation enable news and the organisation's view of an issue or event to be conveyed. Other forms of media relations concern bylined articles (articles written by a member of an organisation about an issue related to the company and offered for publication), speeches, letters to the editor, plus photographs and captions.

Media relations allow organisations to try to convey information concerning strategic issues.

Media relations can be planned and controlled to the extent of what is sent to the media and when it is released. While there is no control over what is actually used, media relations allow organisations to try to convey information concerning strategic issues and to reach particular stakeholders.

The quality of the relationship between an organisation and the media will dramatically affect the impact and dissemination of news and stories released by that organisation. The relationships referred to are those between an organisation's public relations manager and the editors and journalists of the press and the broadcast media.

Publicity and events

Control over public relations events is not as strong as that for media relations. Indeed, negative publicity can be generated by other parties, which can impact badly on an organisation by raising doubts about its financial status or perhaps the quality of its products. Events can be used to promote products and are normally focused on increasing sales. Community-based events contribute to the life of the local community, e.g. sponsoring local fun runs and children's play areas, making contributions to local community centres and disability charities. The organisation attempts to become more involved with the local community as a good employer and a good member of the community. This helps to develop goodwill and awareness in the community. Corporate events are designed to develop corporate awareness and reputation. Entertainment-infused events can generate a lot of local media coverage, which in turn facilitates awareness, goodwill and interest. Events such as open days, factory visits and donations of products to local events are also often used.

There is evidence to suggest that the relationship between some journalists and corporate communication practitioners is not as strong or as positive as it should be (Pang, 2010). Indeed it is claimed by Supa & Zoch (2009) that many practitioners do not understand journalism and the processes involved. The tension concerns a tendency for practitioners to see media relations simply as an information dissemination process. This contrasts with the journalists' need for material that is newsworthy, interesting, timely, of local interest, well-written and not perceived as self-serving.

Media relations is a form of storytelling.

Media relations is a form of storytelling. In order that a story be utilised and published, it needs to be newsworthy, i.e. of value to audiences. Among other characteristics, the item should contain elements of unpredictability and surprise, according to Galtung & Ruge (1965). Above all else the story should be framed. This enables audiences to understand the context in which the storyteller wants them to interpret the story. Thus media relations should be strategically oriented to encompass the reputational platform or core theme (Chapter 10). This in turn provides consistency, integration and reinforcement of the desired positioning.

Issues management

Before considering how corporate communication can be measured, the next section of this chapter concerns two distinct yet interlinked areas, issues and crisis management. Some issues, if not managed, can lead to a crisis for an organisation, but not all issues have the potential to be a crisis.

There have been many definitions of an issue, but one of the most cited is that offered by Chase (1984), who defined an issue as 'an unsettled matter which is ready for decision' (p. 38). He believes an issue involves a point of contention between a representative of a particular stakeholder group and the organisation. This point of contention needs decisive action in order that a resolution be formed and, in doing so, protect the organisation's reputation.

Many issues exist in the environment but most remain latent and docile. Those issues that receive media attention or action from a group of stakeholders move from latent to active status (for example, obesity has been a social problem for some time but it only became an issue for fast-food branded retailers as a result of media attention). Managing issues requires the organisation to scan the environment in order to detect shifts in public opinion that may lead stakeholders to form links with the industry, and, more pertinently, the organisation itself.

When the media and public opinion escalates to the point that the organisation is highlighted and perhaps required to resolve the issue, the status of the issue can be regarded as intense (see Viewpoint 12.5). The step from active to intense status can be regarded as the bridge to a crisis.

Viewpoint 12.5	Putting the squeeze on blackcurrant juice

Allowing an issue to turn into a crisis is not good practice, yet GlaxoSmithKline (GSK) appear to have been guilty of just that in a lapse in issue management. According to Jaques (2008), GSK were found guilty of misleading advertising when they claimed that Ribena ToothKind (a reduced sugar formulation) did not encourage decay in children's teeth. The UK Advertising Standards Authority thought otherwise as they found that the product was 'simply less harmful than other sugary drinks'. In 2004 two New Zealand teenagers tested Ribena to see if it contained four times the vitamin C found in oranges, as claimed by Ribena in their advertising. Their tests showed that it didn't and when Ribena failed to give a suitable response, they took their case to a consumer television programme and from there to Auckland District Court, who fined Ribena £81,750 for misrepresentation and faulty labelling. They were then required to publicly apologise through their advertising, which was then reported globally.

The case rests on two failures of corporate communication. The first was a failure of issues management, namely to recognise a problem early on, and the second was a failure to put in position a suitable response once the issue had been aired on television. Sales fell by up to 12 per cent according to Gregory (2007), and although they had started to recover in Australia, 4 months after the ruling and apologies sales of Ribena in New Zealand continued to struggle.

Question

To what extent did issues management fail to prevent this crisis?

Source: Based on Jaques (2008); Gregory (2007).

Issues management involves
scanning the environment
in order to detect potential issues.

Issues management involves scanning the environment in order to detect potential issues. It also involves monitoring identified latent issues to detect if they are likely to become a more serious threat. From this point, analysis is necessary in order to appreciate the intensity of the issue, identify and categorise the types of stakeholder involved and then formulate and implement issue-specific response strategies (Cornelissen, 2008).

Nutt & Blackoff (1992) identify four categories of stakeholder based on their level of importance and whether the stakeholder supports or opposes the organisation's position on the issue:

- **Problematic stakeholders** – oppose the organisation on the issue but have little power or influence and so represent little threat and are unimportant. Use educational programmes to change opinions and prepare defensive statements in case of coalition and attack.
- **Antagonistic stakeholders** – not only do they oppose the organisation on the issue but they are also important because they have power and are influential. Anticipate objections, develop counter-arguments and negotiate with selected stakeholders.
- **Low-priority stakeholders** – although they support the organisation on the issue, this group of stakeholders have little power and influence on the organisation. Use educational programmes and promote the organisation's involvement with these stakeholders.
- **Supporter stakeholders** – this group of stakeholders are important to the organisation because they have power and influence and support the organisation on the issue. Use information to reinforce the position and request that they influence indifferent stakeholders.

Strategic responses to issues

Four key response strategies can be
identified: silence, accommodation,
reasoning and advocacy.

Having understood the type and nature of the affected stakeholders it becomes possible to formulate effective response strategies. Drawn partly from Cornelissen (2008), four key strategies can be identified: silence, accommodation, reasoning and advocacy. Each is considered in turn.

Silence strategy

Some issues represent little perceived threat to the organisation and may invoke little public attention. Alternatively the issue may be real but the organisation is uncertain about how to respond. In these cases the organisation might seek to buy time, restrict the development of the issue and remain silent. By distancing the issue from the organisation, it is hoped that the operations and processes of the organisation can continue unimpeded. Sometimes referred to as a buffering strategy, the response might be to update the website and release some restricted media comment, all designed to reinforce the organisation's position on the issue.

Accommodation strategy

In some cases the issue may be so overwhelming that the only viable course of action is to conform to the changes in the environment and accommodate the issue through internal adaption. Sometimes referred to as a bridging strategy, corporate communications should be extensive, comprising not only website updates and internal communications to inform employees of the change but also corporate advertising to communicate the change of policy and, depending on the intensity of the issue, the repositioning that the issue has driven.

Reasoning strategy

In some situations the impact on the organisation might not be clear-cut and discussion with key stakeholders is necessary as part of the relationship development values. In this case the response strategy should be to encourage discussion, either online or through focus groups, and to engage opinion leaders and opinion formers. By openly driving two-way communication and establishing dialogue with key stakeholder groups, the organisation avoids making a hasty, ill-informed decision and can develop a reasoned response to the issue and, in doing so, enhance its reputation.

Advocacy strategy

There are certain issues that have the potential to threaten the organisation and thus prevent it from achieving its objectives. In these cases, rather than accommodate the issue and adapting internally, the strategy should be to change public opinion and the way stakeholders perceive the issue, an externally driven change. Communications should use messages that help stakeholders to perceive the issue differently, in this case from the organisation's perspective. This use of framing is quite common. Corporate communication needs to focus on lobbying key constituencies and persuading them to rethink. Corporate advertising can be used to link with the sponsorship of an issue related to the organisation. In addition, communications should be used to reach key opinion leaders and formers to help shape the way stakeholders perceive the issue and to establish the moral ground on which the organisation seeks change.

These strategies are not mutually exclusive and some will be used throughout the life of an issue as the intensity varies and the context evolves.

Defensive or crisis communications

Issues management and crisis management are both strategic communication issues. They do not lie at opposite ends of a spectrum; they are interlinked and both are concerned with managing corporate reputation. Just as corporate communication plays a significant role in the development of corporate reputation it also plays a critical role when defending an organisation's reputation in times of crisis and disaster. The event that triggers a crisis is not normally of major concern, other than the need to stop it recurring. The focus is on the uncertainty that exists as part of the aftermath of the crisis (Ho & Hallahan, 2003).

The drive to restore stability and order predominates over other motivations. It is generally assumed that those organisations that take the care to plan in anticipation of disaster will experience more favourable outcomes than those that fail to plan. Fink (2000) reports that crises involving organisations that do not plan last over twice as long as those involving organisations that do plan. However, Quarantelli (1988) reports that there is only a partial correlation between those that plan and those that experience successful outcomes. He attributes this to the fact that only some of the organisations that take care to prepare do so in a professional way. Poor planning can only deliver poor results. Crisis planning is about putting into position those elements that can affect speedy outcomes to the disaster sequence. When a crisis strikes, it is the application of contingency-based tactics by all those concerned with the event that will determine the strength of the outcome.

Crises are arising with greater frequency as a result of a number of factors. These range from economic and managerial to political, environmental and technological, with the increasing influence of new media and the emerging power associated with consumer groups.

Crises are arising with greater frequency.

When a crisis hits an organisation, damage to its reputational capital often occurs. Those organisations with a strong reputational capital are more likely to recover in a stronger position than those with a poor pre-crisis reputation. However, many different stakeholders are vulnerable to the repercussions of a crisis. Pearson & Mitroff (1993) suggest that stakeholders may perceive the focus organisation as adopting a particular role. This role may be as a rescuer, hero, victim, villain, protector, ally, or enemy. Table 12.3 explains these roles that stakeholders themselves might be cast in – roles that reflect the perception of the focus organisation. It is interesting to monitor the ascribed roles and to see whether stakeholders actually fulfil their designated role or perhaps another when crisis strikes. Perhaps a move from rescuer to enemy is not uncommon.

Table 12.3	Roles assumed by stakeholders during a crisis
Stakeholder 'crisis' role	**Explanation**
Rescuer	A stakeholder organisation that provides a solution or which saves the organisation by terminating or abating the crisis. This can be achieved directly through collaboration and skills, an injection of finance, by opening new markets, or perhaps alleviating pressures of regulation and legislation. Very often finance companies, tax authorities and management buy-outs are perceived to rescue organisations.
Hero	A stakeholder organisation that achieves fame or notoriety as a result of making claims or acting on behalf of the stricken organisation. Heroes might emerge as a result of speaking out on behalf of the crisis organisation, avoid compiling further pressure or buy a part of the crisis-torn business. Again the tax authorities can be in the hero role if they withdraw or postpone claims, enabling the crisis organisation to continue trading.
Victim	Victims are other organisations that suffer financially, lose customers or market share, or endure reputational loss as a result of the crisis that the victim did not instigate. Suppliers are often victims of their customer's crisis.
Protector	An organisation that shields the focus organisation, rallies support during the crisis and works with the media to present another side of an argument or issue. Legal and public relations practitioners have the potential to protect an organisation in crisis.
Ally	An organisation that provides support during the crisis and shares the views and opinions of, or acts in a similar way to the organisation in crisis. Alternatively, an ally might try to explain the reasoning for the actions taken originally that may have led to the crisis. Trade unions and employees can act as allies on behalf of the crisis organisation.
Enemy	An organisation that brings about the crisis or maintains hostile and aggressive actions, with a view to perpetuating the situation in order to ruin the crisis-ridden organisation.
Villain	A villain might be the organisation generally perceived to have caused the crisis (e.g. an oil company negligently causing an oil spill) or an organisation regarded as having engineered the situation that led to the crisis (e.g. a bank calling in a loan that leads a company to collapse and creates redundancies). In some cases the villain may be seen to be an individual, often the CEO, a negligent employee, or ruthless politician.

Source: Based on Pearson & Mitroff (1993).

The importance of this perspective is that crises do not just impact on a single organisation; they also affect the many other affiliated organisations. The organisation that has a crisis plan of value is one that has considered the impact upon its stakeholders.

Crisis phases

Most crises move through a number of phases.

Most crises move through a number of phases. Some believe that there are three main stages (Sturges *et al.*, 1991; Robinson, 2010) and others four (Coombs, 2007; Gonzalez-Herrero & Smith, 2008). Common to all of these discussions, three core phases can be identified: pre-impact, impact and readjustment phases. The duration of each phase can vary considerably, depending upon the nature of the crisis and the manner in which management deals with the events associated with it. Corporate communication needs to be used in different ways according to the characteristics of each phase.

The pre-impact phase consists of two main episodes: scanning and planning; and event identification and preparation. The objective is not to prevent the crisis but to understand and defuse it as much as possible, to inform significant stakeholders of its proximity and possible effects, and finally to manage the crisis process.

The impact phase is the period when the 'crisis breaks out' (Sturges *et al.*, 1991). If a plan has been developed it is implemented with the expectation of ameliorating the damage inflicted by the crisis. One method of reducing the impact is to contain or localise the crisis. By neutralising and constraining the event it can be prevented from contaminating other parts of the organisation or stakeholders. Pearson & Mitroff (1993) suggest that the containment of oil spills and the evacuation of buildings and aircraft are examples of containment and neutralisation. Through the necessity to communicate with all stakeholders, management at this point will inevitably reveal its attitude towards the crisis event. Is its attitude one of genuine concern for the victims and stakeholders? Is the attitude consistent with the expectations stakeholders have of the management team? Alternatively, is there a perception that management is making lame excuses and distancing itself from the event, and is this consistent with expectations?

The readjustment phase concerns the recovery and realignment of the organisation and its stakeholders to the new environment, once the deepest part of the crisis event has passed. The essential tasks are to ensure that the needs of key stakeholders can still be met and, if they cannot, to determine what must be done to ensure that they can be. For example, continuity of product supply is critically important. This may be achieved by servicing customers from other locations. Common characteristics of this phase are the investigations, police inquiries, public demonstrations, court cases and media probing that inevitably follow major crises and disasters. The manner in which an organisation handles this fallout and tries to appear reasonable and consistent in its approach can have a big impact on the perception that other stakeholders have of the organisation.

The rate at which organisations readjust is partly dependent upon the strength of the image held by stakeholders prior to the crisis occurring. If the organisation had a strong reputation then the source credibility attributed to it will be high. This means that messages transmitted by the organisation would be received favourably and trusted. However, if the reputation is poor, the effectiveness of any corporate communication is also going to be poor. The level of source credibility held by the organisation will influence the speed with which stakeholders allow it to readjust and recover after a crisis.

> If the organisation's reputation is poor, the effectiveness of any corporate communication is also going to be poor.

Managing stakeholders' images

Benoit (1997) developed a theory concerning image restoration following an organisational crisis, which states that there are five general approaches: denial, evasion of responsibility, reduced offensiveness, corrective action and mortification (see Table 12.4). Benoit has used these approaches to evaluate the responses given by a variety of organisations when faced by different disasters and crises.

Table 12.4	Image restoration approaches
Damage retrieval	**Explanation**
Simple denial	Outright rejection that the act was caused by them or even occurred in the first place, or shifting the blame by asserting that another organisation (person) was responsible for the act
Evasion (of responsibility)	Provocation – a reasonable response to a prior act Defeasibility – the act occurred because of a lack of time or information Accident – the act was not committed deliberately Good intentions – the wrongful act occurred despite trying to do well
Reducing offensiveness	This involves demonstrating that the act was of minor significance or by responding so as to reduce the impact of the accuser
Corrective action	This may involve putting right what was damaged and taking steps to avoid a repeat occurrence
Mortification	An apology or statement of regret for causing the act that gave offence

Source: Benoit (1997).

Organisations that have not planned their management of crisis events and have survived a disaster may decide to instigate a more positive approach so as to mitigate the impact of future crisis events. This is not uncommon and crisis management planning may occur at the end of this cycle.

Framing for crisis communication

As noted in the previous chapter, the use of framing can serve to shape the way stakeholders perceive the organisation and the associated crisis. Crises can be categorised by type (Coombs, 2007) and the type provides the frame through which stakeholders pick up clues about how to interpret the event. Coombs identifies three main types: the extent to which the event was caused by an uncontrollable external force or agent; whether it was the result of an intentional or accidental action by the organisation; or if it was caused by human or technical error. The frame therefore enables stakeholders to determine the extent to which the organisation was responsible for the crisis occurring in the first place. From these, three clusters of types of crisis can be identified: victim, accident and preventable clusters (see Table 12.5).

> The frame enables stakeholders to determine the extent to which the organisation was responsible for the crisis occurring in the first place.

Table 12.5	Crisis types by crisis clusters
Crisis clusters	**Explanation**
Victim cluster	The organisation is seen as a victim of the crisis. Stakeholders attribute little responsibility to the organisation so there is only a mild reputational threat. Common events include natural disasters, rumours, workplace violence and product tampering.
Accident cluster	The actions of the organisation leading to the crisis were minimal and the threat to reputational status is moderate. Typical events include stakeholder challenges to the operations, technical error accidents and technical errors resulting in product defect and subsequent recall.
Preventable cluster	The organisation deliberately placed people at risk, took inappropriate actions or violated regulations and, in doing so, caused a strong threat to the reputation. Typical events include human-error accidents and product harm/defects, deception, misconduct and actions that lead to injury.

Source: Based on Coombs (2007).

Coombs (1995) claims that in order to repair reputation, crisis response strategies are necessary to shape perceptions of those responsible, change perceptions of the organisation and reduce the negative effects of the crisis event. He identifies three main forms of response based on the perceptions of those responsible for the crisis. The first are denial strategies which attempt to remove connections between the organisation and the crisis. The second are diminish strategies, which argue that the organisation did not lack control over the crisis and that it is not as bad as is claimed by others. The third are rebuild strategies which involve offering compensation or an apology to victims (Coombs, 2006). Coombs developed a 'situational crisis communication theory' which anticipates how stakeholders will perceive a crisis and how they will react to various response strategies. He argues that his approach bridges deficiencies in the 'image restoration' theory offered by Benoit, which offers 'no conceptual links between the crisis response strategies and elements of the crisis situation' (p. 171).

For an example of how an organisation attempted to frame its response to a crisis in the pharmaceutical industry, see Viewpoint 12.6.

Viewpoint 12.6   Communicating the withdrawal of Vioxx

Merck, once the world's largest pharmaceutical company, developed and marketed a drug for the treatment of pain, inflammation and stiffness caused by arthritis. The drug, called Vioxx, was launched in 1999 and was withdrawn in 2004. It was estimated that sales of Vioxx contributed $1.2 billion, or 18 per cent, to Merck's $6.59 billion net income in 2003.

Following various tests, studies and clinical trials, the overwhelming results showed that taking Vioxx increased the risk of heart attacks and strokes. A decision to pull the drug from the market was made on Monday, 27 September, to be announced 3 days later. As more than 100 million prescriptions had been written for the drug since its approval in 1999, the withdrawal was framed as the responsible thing to do. Merck had 3 days to prepare the withdrawal communications.

One of the first tasks of the 25-strong, specially assembled communications team was to identify who had to be notified, how this was to be achieved and what resources would be available. This was partly achieved through the preparation of audience/channel grids. The team developed more than 65 documents to notify investigators who were conducting the clinical trials, patients who were participating in the trials, physicians and patients worldwide, and numerous regulatory agencies. In addition Merck's worldwide sales representatives had to be contacted.

The communication team spent nearly 60 hours writing releases for the media, statements for doctors and patients worldwide, preparing a special website (www.vioxx.com), and making a free telephone number available for medical professionals and the general public to call.

On 29 September, a day before the announcement, an outside public relations crisis management firm reviewed the documents, examined the team's procedures, and offered advice based on their experience with similar withdrawal announcements.

At 8.00am, on 30 September, Merck issued a press release announcing the worldwide voluntary withdrawal of Vioxx. At 9.00am, a press conference was held in New York at which the CEO repeated the announcement and took questions from news media. The company also conducted an investor relations teleconference at 10.00am that morning to explain the news to Wall Street and the financial community. An email was sent to all Merck employees worldwide, at the same time as the press release was issued. A second email sent each employee a link to view the webcast of the press conference in New York.

On 2 October, Merck ran full-page advertisements in 25 major newspapers throughout the country, explaining the research findings and the company's decision to withdraw Vioxx. The advertisement was in the form of a letter to patients letting them know where they could find more information about the drug and the reason for the withdrawal. The campaign incorporated a wide range of communication vehicles: press releases, corporate statements, teleconferences, webcasts, paid advertising, and letters to editors in response to misleading or inaccurate articles, frequent communication with employees, along with the development of internal and external websites dedicated to Vioxx issues.

Merck's public affairs efforts generated more than four billion media impressions on the topic. The company's Vioxx website traffic grew from about 4,000 daily visits on 29 September to 234,000 on 1 October. By early December, the vioxx.com website had attracted more than two million visitors, while the company's merck.com website had experienced an additional one million visitors. The free telephone number received more than 120,000 calls in the first 6 days following the announcement. Additionally, the company reported issuing more than half-a-million refunds for Vioxx prescriptions worldwide.

A number of important lessons in communication strategy emerged. First, a crisis communication plan was important. The plan allowed Merck to identify the key individuals who needed to be involved, their roles and responsibilities. It also helped to establish a mechanism to enable them to start working together. A second important lesson concerns persistence and a long-term view. The more Merck communicated, the better their positions were understood.

Question

Why do you think a professional and sophisticated company such as Merck, did not have a crisis communication plan in position?

Source: Based on O'Rourke (2006).

Best-practice crisis communications

Advice on how organisations should respond to crises has been offered by many associations (e.g. Swiss Association for Crisis Communication, the Swedish Association of Health Professionals), academics (Coombs, 2006) and practitioners (agencies such as Luther Pendragon). In general, the advice is consistent, with the emphasis placed on different areas or activities. Taylor & Kent (2007) undertook a 7-year longitudinal study into how organisations use the internet within their crisis communication. They identify six areas of best practice and show how these integrate traditional offline practices into the digital format.

1. Upload traditional tactics to the website. Traditional communication tactics include news conferences, fact sheets, news releases, Q&As, open letters to specific audiences and transcripts of interviews with key personnel. All of these can be easily transferred to the website to provide the media, the public and other specific interest groups with access to reliable, up-to-date and pertinent information about the progress and issues concerning the crisis.

2. Integrating innovative tactics. The internet enables interactivity and Taylor & Kent identify four applications. The first is two-way communication, which can be used to obtain feedback, promoting dialogue, understanding and ultimately improved management of the crisis. The second is connecting links, which enable visitors to reach other websites that can provide valuable information. The third is real-time monitoring which enables organisations to provide timely updates on the crisis and reduce response delays, and the final interactive element concerns the provision of video/audio materials. The use of satellite images, video, digital photography and audio effects helps journalists as they can use actual files rather than textual transcripts.

> A key internet application is connecting links, which enable visitors to reach other websites that can provide valuable information.

3. Reducing uncertainty during product recalls. Information can be posted on websites to answer consumer questions and so reduce uncertainty. This approach also helps to divert traffic away from the telephone and the consequent call-centre blockages and associated frustrations that can occur through overload. When Toyota had to recall over eight million cars early in 2010, at an estimated cost of $2 billion, the company president was considered to be very late in publicly acknowledging and apologising for the problems. It was reported that he was prompted to make the apology by the Japanese Prime Minister, because of the adverse impact of the worldwide recall on the reputation of Japanese products.

4. Informing of the organisation's side of the crisis. Through the use of an organisation's website it is possible to provide direct communication with targeted stakeholder audiences. The advantage is that the information is not prone to filtering or editing by journalists or news editors. Organisations thus remain in control and can present as much information as they like, when they want to and at a depth which enables them to present their side of any dispute, accident or disruption.

5. Communicating with different stakeholder groups. In many crises, different stakeholders groups require different types of information. Investors requiring information about the financial consequences of crises, suppliers concerned about production continuity and customers interested in part-completed orders can be directed to separate web pages providing information about their specific issues. Different cultures require different approaches. Further to the Toyota recall referred to earlier, Japanese culture requires that a bow be made to signal the degree of apology being offered. When the president of Toyota made a 45° bow, he indicated that he was 'quite sorry'. The expected 90° bow would have said he was 'deeply remorseful' (Lewis & Lea, 2010). See Exhibit 12.4 for a depiction of the different bows.

6. Work with the government throughout a crisis. Wherever possible, work with the appropriate government department or ministry and provide links to government sites. This promotes credibility and demonstrates concern and a proactive approach to resolving the crisis in a transparent manner.

Scarcely bothered
25-degree bend, no hold.
Connotes "Sorry, that was clumsy of me"

Quite sorry
45-degree bend, 1 to 3-second hold depending on extent of inconvenience.
Connotes "Yes, we messed up, won't happen again"

Actually or officially sorry
90-degrees, held for 3-7 seconds depending on total loss of money/life/reputation. Connotes "We have done something pretty awful. We need you to forgive us"

Really spectacularly sorry
the *dogeza* (rare) kneeling, head on floor, could last for up to 30 seconds.
Connotes "The law may punish me, but that does not cover how sorry I am"

Exhibit 12.4	The Japanese bows of apology.
	Source: The Times. Courtesy of nisyndication.com.

Gonzalez-Herrero & Smith (2008) agree that the internet plays a significant role in the way organisations manage crisis communication. However, not all organisations are increasing their usage as might be expected. Perry *et al.* (2003) found that it is financial, high-tech organisations and consumer groups that use the internet most when a crisis strikes but it is probable that this scope of companies and markets has expanded in recent years.

> The internet plays a significant role in the way organisations manage crisis communication.

Measuring corporate communication

The measurement of corporate communication can be considered at a number of levels. At one level, it is possible to attribute the success of a communication strategy to a measure or assessment of an organisation's reputation. Whilst this enables a strategic perspective, this association can ignore the many mediating variables that can affect a stakeholder's perception of an organisation.

At another level, corporate communication can be considered in terms of the degree to which the goals set out at the beginning of a communication programme have been achieved. This equates to the objective-and-task approach used in marketing communications and is perhaps the most rigorous and managerially orientated approach of all. However, the breadth of activities associated with these programmes makes a collective understanding problematic.

At a more detailed level, measurement can be undertaken of the success achieved through each individual corporate communication activity. For example, the effectiveness of a particular media relations campaign, the speed and sensitivity of handling an issue, or the value of shares or investor sentiment following an investor relations programme all provide valuable insight into the investment activity. The trouble, of course, is that the impact on reputation is hard to determine and hence a measure of the strategic orientation of corporate communication can be missed. If measurement is undertaken against the degree to which each activity helps meet the organisation's strategic objectives, then it becomes a more relevant measure of achievement.

van Riel & Fombrun (2007) consider the measurement of corporate communication in two, interconnected ways. The first involves an assessment of the effectiveness of corporate communication in creating strategic alignment internally, and the second concerns the effectiveness of corporate communication in building reputation.

Developing strategic alignment is critical.

Developing strategic alignment is critical, because it is only through employees that the strategic objectives can be accomplished consistently. When employees engage with the strategic objectives then, as Gagon & Michael (2003) find, so their decision-making becomes supportive of the objectives and this can lead to improved corporate performance. Corporate communication is a significant activity in achieving this alignment.

The measurement of corporate reputation has been examined in depth in Chapter 4 and does not need to be repeated here. What these different research methods involve is an assessment of the perceptions external stakeholders have of the organisation, and these are founded on the effectiveness of corporate communication and the stakeholders' propensity to share and process information.

Corporate communication is a manifestation of an organisation's stakeholder relationships. These can vary from communication that is open, transparent, and hence perceived to be credible and trustworthy, to communication content and practices that are closed, minimal in terms of information depth and richness, and which leave many questions unanswered or avoided. The former is characteristic of communication with stakeholders where the relationship is supportive and co-operative; the latter where the relationship is distant, functional and tenuous.

So, reputation is a function of the way in which an organisation chooses to express itself and the relationship it has with stakeholders. It is also a reflection of the way stakeholders process the cues and attribute meaning. Although the measurement of reputation can be complex, it is important because it enables managers to build a holistic, and hence strategic, view of the organisation and its progress.

Chapter summary

In order to help consolidate your understanding of the methods of corporate communication, here are the key points summarised against each of the learning objectives.

1. Examine ways of building reputation with financial stakeholders – investor relations

The role of investor relations is to provide potential investors with the necessary financial and non-financial information to enable them to make appropriate investment decisions. This might be regarded as attracting attention, providing information, reducing risk and creating a desire to be associated with an organisation and, through that, a positive demand for its shares. At a corporate level, investor relations seek to protect the interests of the organisation by providing accurate, timely and truthful information to the marketplace.

2. Consider methods to manage government, officials and regulators – public affairs

Public affairs is concerned with communications that are focused on those who regulate markets and industries, legislators, elected officials and appointed representatives. In short these are government-focused communications which seek to influence the regulations and legislation associated with the markets in which an organisation operates.

3. Appraise ways of building reputation through employees – internal communications

The role of internal marketing (communications) includes encouraging efficient communication, by reducing duplication, promoting clarity and establishing control. Further roles concern connectivity within the organisation and within sub-networks or work-related networks, the generation of shared meaning among employees and groups of employees, enhancing organisational identity, and reinforcing corporate values through managerial interaction with employees.

4. Evaluate the use of communications with customers – media relations

Media relations consist of a range of activities designed to provide bloggers, journalists, editors and other influential media-related people with information. Press releases, interviews, press kits and press conferences are the most frequently used forms of media relations. The intention is that they relay information received, through their media, for consumption by their audiences. Of course, the original message may be changed and subject to information deviance, but audiences perceive much of this information as highly credible simply because opinion-formers have bestowed their judgment on the item.

5. Explore communications arising in the environment – issues management

An issue involves a point of contention between a representative of a particular stakeholder group and the organisation. Issues management therefore involves scanning the environment in order to detect potential points of contention, and then taking decisive action in order that a resolution is formed in order to protect the organisation's reputation.

6. Assess ideas associated with defending reputation – crisis communications

Issues management and crisis management are interlinked and both are concerned with managing corporate reputation. Just as corporate communication plays a significant role in the development of corporate reputation, it also plays a critical role when defending an organisation's reputation in times of crisis and disaster.

Most crises move through a number of phases, such as the pre-impact, impact and readjustment phases. The duration of each phase can vary considerably, depending upon the nature of the crisis and the manner in which management deals with the associated events. Corporate communication needs to be used in different ways according to the characteristics of each phase.

7. Explain the principles of measuring the effectiveness of corporate communication

Measurement of corporate communication should be considered at two interconnected levels. The first concerns the degree to which employees are aligned with, and hence supportive of, the organisation's strategic objectives. The second concerns the perceptions held by external stakeholders of the organisation. The degree to which an organisation chooses to express itself is reflected in its corporate communication and these cues help stakeholders to shape the way they view the organisation and its reputation.

Discussion questions

1. Discuss the extent to which investor relations should be about providing financial information rather than general information about the organisation.
2. Explain the differences between bridging and buffering strategies in public relations.
3. Make notes outlining reasons to use lobbying.
4. Identify and explain the different types of managerial conversation suggested by Aggerholm *et al.* (2010).
5. Discuss the view that the communication climate dictates effectiveness of an organisation's corporate communication.

6. How might media relations contribute to corporate communication?

7. Identify the four categories of stakeholder identified by Nutt & Blackoff (1992), based on their level of importance and whether a stakeholder supports or opposes the organisation's position on the issue.

8. Find two examples of crisis communication and compare and contrast the effectiveness of the communications used through each of the events.

9. Benoit (1997) suggested five ways in which an image might be restored. Find examples to illustrate each of the techniques.

10. What is strategic alignment and how might it assist the development of corporate reputation?

References

Aggerholm, H.K., Andersen, M.A., Asmuß, B. & Thomsen, C. (2010). Management conversations in Danish companies. *Corporate Communication: an International Journal* 14(3), 264–279.

Balmer, J.M.T. & Wilkinson, A. (1991). Building societies: change, strategy and corporate Identity. *Journal of General Management* 17(2), 20–34.

Benoit, W.L. (1997). Image repair discourse and crisis communication. *Public Relations Review* 23, 177–186.

Chase, W.H. (1984). *Issue Management: Origins of the Future*. Stanford, CT: Issue Action Publications.

Coombs, W.T. (1995). Choosing the right words: the development of guidelines for the selection of appropriate crisis response strategies. *Management Communication Quarterly* 8, 447–476.

Coombs, W.T. (2006). The protective powers of crisis response strategies: managing reputational assets during a crisis. *Journal of Promotion Management* 12, 241–259.

Coombs, W.T. (2007). Protecting organization reputations during a crisis: the development and application of situational crisis communication theory. *Corporate Reputation Review* 10(3), 163–176.

Cornelissen, J. (2008). *Corporate Communication: Theory and Practice*, 2nd edn. London: Sage.

Cutlip, S.M., Center, A.H. & Broom, G.M. (1999). *Effective Public Relations*, 8th edn. Englewood Cliffs, NJ: Prentice-Hall.

Day, G.S. & Fahey, L. (1990). Putting strategy into shareholder value analysis. *Harvard Business Review* 68(2), 156–162.

Fink, S. (2000). *Crisis Management Planning for the Inevitable*. New York: AMACON.

Foreman, S.K. & Money, A.H. (1995). Internal marketing: concepts, measurements and application. *Journal of Marketing Management* 11, 755–768.

Freeman, E. & Liedtka, J. (1997). Stakeholder capitalism and the value chain. *European Management Journal* 15(3), 286–296.

Gagon, M. & Michael, J. (2003). Employee strategic alignment at a wood manufacturer: an exploratory analysis using lean manufacturing. *Forest Products Journal* 53(10), 24–29.

Galtung, J. & Ruge, M. (1965). The structure of foreign news: the presentation of the Congo, Cuba and Cyprus crises in four foreign newspapers. *Journal of International Peace Research* 1, 64–90.

Geary, D.L. (2005). The decline of media credibility and its impact on public relations. *Public Relations Quarterly* 50(3), 8–12.

Geppert, J. & Lawrence, J.E. (2008). Predicting firm reputation through content analysis of shareholders' letter. *Corporate Reputation Review* 11(4), 285–307.

Gonzalez-Herrero, A. & Smith, S. (2008). Crisis communications management: how Internet based technologies are changing the way public relations professionals handle business crises. *Journal of Contingencies and Crisis Management* 16(3), 143–153.

Gregory, A. (2007). Ribena sales down after vitamin C revelation. *NZ Herald*, 2 April.

Hallahan, K. (2001). Strategic media planning: towards an integrated public relations media model. In: Heath, R., ed. *Handbook of Public Relations*. Thousand Oaks, CA: Sage Publications.

Hanrahan, G. (1997). Financial and investor relations. In: Kitchen, P., ed. *Public Relations Principles and Practice*. London: Thomson.

Hardaker, S. & Fill, C. (2005). Corporate service brands: the intellectual and emotional engagement of employees. *Corporate Reputation Review: an International Journal* 8(1), 365–76.

Harvey, M. (2010). 'Google steps up fight for hearts and minds'. *The Times*, 13 February, p. 64.

Hemsley, S. (1998). Internal affairs. *Marketing Week* 21(5), 49–51.

Higgins, R.B. & Bannister, B.D. (1992). How corporate communication of strategy affects share price. *Long Range Planning* 25(3), 27–35.

Hillman, A. & Hitt, M. (1999). Corporate political strategy formulation: a model of approach, participation and strategy decisions. *Academy of Management Review* 24(4), 825–842.

Hiscock, J. (2002). The brand insiders. *Marketing*, 23 May, 24–25.

Ho, F.-W. & Hallahan, K. (2003). Post-earthquake crisis communications in Taiwan: an examination of corporate advertising and strategy motives. *Journal of Communication Management* 8(3), 291–306.

Hong, Y. & Ki, E.-J. (2007). How do public relations practitioners perceive investor relations? An exploratory study. *Corporate Communications: An International Journal* 12(2), 199–213.

Jaques, T. (2008). When an icon stumbles: the Ribena issue mismanaged. *Corporate Communications: An International Journal* 13(4), 394–406.

Koeppl, P. (2001). The acceptance, relevance and dominance of lobbying the EU Commission – a first time survey of the EU Commission's civil servants. *Journal of Public Affairs* 1(1), 69–80.

Laskin, A.V. (2009). A descriptive account of the investor relations profession. *Journal of Business Communication* 46(2), 208–233.

Lewis, L. & Lea, R. (2010). 'Toyota chief bows to pressure for apology over pedal defect'. *The Times*, 6 February, p. 13.

Love, M. (2006). Cutting through the clutter at Microsoft online: www.melcrum.com/articles/clutter_at_microsoft.shtml. Accessed: 23 August 2009.

McGrath, C. (2007). Framing lobbying messages: defining and communicating political issues persuasively. *Journal of Public Affairs* 7, 269–280.

Meznar, M.B., Johnson, J.H. & Mizzi, P.J. (2006). No news is good news? Press coverage and corporate public affairs management. *Journal of Public Affairs* 6, 58–68.

Moloney, K. (1997). Government and lobbying activities, In: Kitchen, P.J., ed. *Public Relations: Principles and Practice*. London: International Thomson Press.

Motion, J. & Weaver, C.K. (2005). The epistemic struggle for credibility: rethinking media relations. *Journal of Communication Management* 9(3), 246–255.

Nutt, P.C. & Blackoff, R.W. (1992). *Strategic Management of Public and Third Sector Organizations: A Handbook for Leaders*. San Francisco: Jossey Bass Publishers.

Oberman, W.D. (2008). A conceptual look at the strategic resource dynamics of public affairs. *Journal of Public Affairs* 8, 249–260.

O'Rourke, IV, J.S. (2006). Merck & Co. Inc.: communication lessons from the withdrawal of Vioxx. *Journal of Business Strategy* 27(4), 11–22.

Pang, A. (2010). Mediating the media: a journalist-centric media relations model. *Corporate Communications: An International Journal* 15(2), 192–204.

Pearson, C.M. & Mitroff, I. (1993). From crisis prone to crisis prepared: a framework for crisis management. *Academy of Management Executive* 7(1), 48–59.

Perry, D.C., Taylor, M. & Doerfel, M.L. (2003). Internet based communication in crisis management. *Management Communication Quarterly* 17(2), 206–232.

Petersen, B.K. & Martin, H.J. (1996). CEO perception of investor relations as a public relations function: an exploratory study. *Journal of Public Relations Research* 8(3), 173–209.

Pisik, B. (2010). How they do investor relations at SingTel. *Inside Investor Relations*, 9 September. Online: www.insideinvestorrelations.com/articles/16368/how-they-do-investor-relations-singtel/. Accessed: 10 December 2010.

Punjaisri, K., Evanschitzky, H. & Wilson, A. (2009). Internal branding: an enabler of employees' brand-supporting behaviours. *Journal of Service Management* 20(2), 209–226.

Quarantelli, E.L. (1988). Disaster crisis management: a summary of research findings. *Journal of Management Studies* 25(4), 373–385.

van Riel, C.B.M. & Fombrun, C.J. (2007). *Essentials of Corporate Communication*. London: Routledge.

Robinson, H. (2010). The evolution of reputation management. *Communication World*, March-April, 40–41.

Schneider, B. & Bowen, D.E. (1985). Employee and customer perceptions of service in banks: replication and extension. *Journal of Applied Psychology* 70(3), 423–433.

Silver, D. (2004). The IR-PR nexus. In: Cole, B.F., ed. *The new investor relations: expert perspectives on the state of the art*. Princeton, NJ: Bloomberg Press, pp. 59–88.

Storey, J. (2001). Internal marketing comes to the surface. *Marketing Week*, 19 July, 22.

Sturges, D.L., Carell, B.J., Newsom, D.A. & Barrera, M. (1991). Crisis communication management: the public opinion node and its relationship to environmental nimbus. *SAM Advanced Management Journal*, Summer, 22–27.

Supa, D.W. & Zoch, L.M. (2009). Maximising media relations through a better understanding of the public relations-journalist relationship: a quantitative analysis of changes over 23 years. Paper presented at the International Public Relations Research Conference, Miami, Florida.

Tamianau, Y. & Wilts, A. (2006). Corporate lobbying in Europe, managing knowledge and information strategies. *Journal of Public Affairs* 6, May, 122–130.

Taylor, M. & Kent, M.L. (2007). Taxonomy of mediated crisis responses. *Public Relations Review* 33(2), 140–146.

Thomson, K. & Hecker, L.A. (2000). The business value of buy-in. In: Varey, R.J. & Lewis, B.R., eds. *Internal Marketing: Directions for Management*. London: Routledge, pp. 160–172.

UK Investor Relations Society (2009). Online: www.ir-soc.org.uk/. Accessed: 23 March 2011.

Vallaster, C. & de Chernatony, L. (2006). Internal brand building and saturation: the role of leadership. *European Journal of Marketing* 40(7/8), 761–784.

Welch, M. & Jackson, P.R. (2007). Rethinking internal communication: a stakeholder approach. *Corporate Communications: an International Journal* 12(2), 177–198.

Zhou, L., Twitchell, D., Qin, T., Burgoon, J. & Nunamaker Jr., J. (2002). An exploratory study into deception detection in text-based computer-mediated communication. *Proceedings of the 36th Hawaii International Conference on System Sciences*.

Minicases for Part 3

The following minicases are designed to help readers consider some of the issues explored in this part of the book. The questions that follow each case should be attempted and outline answers can be found on the supporting website.

Minicase 3.1   Marks & Spencer – 'Plan A' sustainability strategy

Marks & Spencer (M&S) is a bastion brand of British retailing. Its advertising is regularly honoured with awards and prizes and, for many consumers, it provides memorable images and, of course, strong brand triggers. However, its communications took a different path in 2006 when the company unveiled its 'Look behind the label' campaign. This focused on the initiatives the organisation was taking with regard to incorporating Fairtrade products, using environmentally friendly dyes and other responsible actions. However, as with most corporate responsibility (CSR) programmes much of this was about the company and its own internal practices and behaviours and was not something most stakeholders could become involved with. For M&S and others the scope of these campaigns was limited, to the extent that for many the term 'corporate social responsibility' was no longer a viable strategy. Indeed, many brands, such as Nike, Unilever and Google, have recognised the demise of CSR (Barry & Calver, 2009). The emerging public concern about climate change had led some companies to start communicating the actions they are taking to respond to these challenges.

In 2007 M&S published its 'Plan A (because there is no Plan B)', which detailed a major programme of investments over the next 5 years. These were designed to reduce the impact of M&S's business on the natural environment. As the company's website puts it:

> Plan A is our five-year, 100-point 'eco' plan to tackle some of the biggest challenges facing our business and our world. It will see us working with our customers and our suppliers to combat climate change, reduce waste, safeguard natural resources, trade ethically and build a healthier nation.
>
> We're doing this because it's what you want us to do. It's also the right thing to do. We're calling it Plan A because we believe it's now the only way to do business. There is no Plan B.

By working systemically to make the M&S business more sustainable and by addressing the social and environmental issues on which it had an impact, the company changed the orientation and dynamics of its business. Plan A was a scheme for changing the nature and dynamics of the relationships the company held with its various stakeholders. The goal was to embrace their various supply chains, which involve thousands of factories and farms, their own operations, which span hundreds of stores, warehouses and lorries, and the use of millions of products that they sell each year. They also needed to involve their customers, encourage employees and reach other stakeholders by improving processes and practices under an umbrella of sustainability.

The achievements have been considerable. M&S reported a 10,000 tonne reduction in packaging, a 40,000 tonne reduction in CO_2 emissions, a change in employee awareness, plus £15 million for charities. What Plan A had not achieved was a change in the attitudes and behaviours of its customers. So, in 2009 the company launched the third part of its campaign, 'Doing the right thing'. The name says it all and is reflected in the 417 million fewer carrier bags that have been sold. Another initiative was called the Oxfam Clothes Exchange. Consumers were rewarded with a £5 voucher when they donated their old M&S clothes to Oxfam. This scheme alone raised over £2 million for the charity.

Plan A allowed M&S to demonstrate to all of its stakeholders, including the 10 per cent of their customers who are 'green crusaders', that M&S was committed to playing a leading role on sustainability. However, Plan A did not enable a bond with customers which is why the change to 'Doing the right thing' provided a simple tag that helped consumers to become involved with sustainability. By becoming engaged in the change, and not simply being informed about it, the programme was perceived to be something that people wanted to be associated with. The Clothes Exchange scheme with Oxfam demonstrates this point. Indeed, changing consumer attitudes and behaviour might be easier when there is a critical mass, or, as Barry & Calver (2009) put it, when consumers feel that they are part of a 'tribe for change'. The success of these types of programmes can often stem from making people aware that they are one of millions who are all making small changes, and that they are not a single lone voice.

▶

Tribes are recognised within the academic buyer behaviour literature (see Cova, 1997). There are two schools of thought (Cooper *et al.*, 2005). The northern school recognises individual consumption as means of self-expression and identity, and is an end in itself. The southern school believes that individuals only value products in as far as they provide a link to multiple communities. One of the essential characteristics of tribes is that there is a common sense of community around which the members can gather and share meaning. Tribes manifest themselves through, for example, religion, football, local hobby groups, music and, of course, brands, which in this context have enormous potential to inspire more sustainable living habits and behaviours.

M&S recently anounced that the majority of its commitments are on track to be achieved by the deadline. It has said that 62 of its original commitments have been achieved, 30 are on plan to be achieved, and seven were behind plan. It said that one of the seven commitments, the use of bio-diesel, was on hold until a sustainable supplier was found. Thomas (2010) reports results that included:

- 33 per cent less waste sent to landfill year on year
- 40 per cent of electricity sourced from 'green' tariff renewable supplies
- 18 per cent reduction in refrigeration emissions (compared with 2006/07)
- 1.8 million garments recycled through the Oxfam Clothing Exchange
- packaging reduced by 36 per cent on general merchandise products
- 84 per cent of pet food plastic packaging made using recycled materials
- 72 per cent of wood used is Forest Stewardship Council, recycled or from sources which otherwise protect forests and communities
- healthier food now makes up 38 per cent of food products ranges
- 91 per cent of food products now meet FSA salt reduction targets
- more than £13.2 million invested last year in community projects.

Not content with these achievements, M&S announced in 2010 that it was to become the world's most sustainable national retailer. This requires building customer commitment with the sustainability strategy and this was to be supported with 80 new commitments. One of these was that by 2015 at least 50 per cent of its products will have at least one sustainable or ethical quality standard. For example, these might include a Fairtrade or Marine Stewardship Council certification. By 2020,

this is to be extended to 100 per cent (Kimberley, 2010). M&S stated that it was to become the first major retailer to ensure that the raw materials it uses, such as palm oil, soya, beef, cocoa, coffee and leather, will come from sustainable sources that do not contribute to deforestation. It is also intends to ensure full traceability of all key raw materials used in its home and clothing products.

At this point it was noticeable that communications had become more dialogic. For example, customers were incentivised to join a competition, called 'Your green idea'. This required consumers to submit ideas for green actions which M&S could adopt. The winning idea received £100,000 which was to be spent 'greening' an organisation such as a school, charity or small business.

Questions

1. Review the M&S 'Plan A' web pages. Why, in your view, has M&S embarked upon this programme and what is the evidence for this conclusion?

2. Many companies still refer to corporate social responsibility while others use the term corporate responsibility. What does this name change signify and is it important?

3. How might M&S have communicated their ideas and intentions about sustainability? Which media might they have used and why?

4. To what extent does this sustainability strategy dominate M&S's corporate communication?

References

Barry, M. & Calver, L. (2009). Marks & Spencer describes its journey from corporate social responsibility to sustainability. *Marketingmagazine.co.uk*, 28 October.

Cooper, S., McLoughlin, D. & Keating, A. (2005). Individual and neo-tribal consumption: tales from the Simpsons of Springfield. *Journal of Consumer Behaviour* 4(5), 330–344.

Cova, B. (1997). Community and consumption: Towards a definition of the 'linking value' of product or services. *European Journal of Marketing* 31, 297–316.

Kimberley, S. (2010). M&S bids to be world's most sustainable retailer within five years. *Marketing*, 01 March. Online: www.brandrepublic.com/news/987067/M-S-bids-worlds-sustainable-retailer-within-five-years/. Accessed: 5 July 2011.

Thomas, J. (2010). Marks & Spencer announces achievements through Plan A. *Marketing*, 10 June. Online: www.brandrepublic.com/news/1009147/Marks&Spencer-announces-achievements-Plan. Accessed: 5 July 2011.

Minicase 3.2 | Primark – defending a reputation with social media

Brian Jones and John Temperley, Leeds Business School, Leeds Metropolitan University

This case study examines how Primark used social media to manage its reputation. Social media includes a range of communication methods, including blogs, podcasts and wikis, plus social networks such as Facebook, Twitter and LinkedIn. Businesses of all types and sizes are increasingly engaging with social media and this case highlights one example of how this can be done and the benefits to be gained from doing so.

Primark is a subsidiary company within the Associated British Foods (ABF) group. It is now an international business with a global supply chain and employs over 25,000 people. Primark offer good-quality fashion at low prices. Their business model is based on high volume, low mark-ups and minimal advertising. They claim to be a lean business and one that responds quickly to marketplace developments. There is a flat management hierarchy, strong buying skills and excellent distribution.

The first Penneys store opened in Mary Street, Dublin, in 1969 and within a year, four more stores in the Dublin area were added. By the end of 1971 there were 11 more stores in Ireland and one in Northern Ireland. Expansion into the UK followed with 18 stores in the next 10 years, and by 1994 there were a total of 66 stores, 32 in the UK and 34 in Ireland. Primark then acquired stores from the BHS One-Up discount chain, the Co-Op, including Reading, where they relocated their buying offices, C&A and Littlewoods.

In May 2006, Primark opened its first store in Spain, followed by stores in the Netherlands, Portugal, Germany and Belgium. Primark offers fashionable high street clothing at affordable prices. There can be no doubt that Primark is a hugely successful business, one that contributes significantly to ABF's overall results. Felsted & Thompson (2010, p. 22) write:

> Primark, one of the winners of the recession as thrifty shoppers snapped up its low-priced high fashion trends, delivered sales growth from stores open at least a year of 8 per cent in the first half in spite of the poor weather. 'It is more a story of the decade than the recession,' said John Bason, finance director. 'We are in the right place for the consumer at the moment, both in terms of the merchandise and the value for money.'

Whilst it might be in the right place for consumers Primark is regarded by many to have a long-term problem, one that Hall (2009, p. B4) refers to as their 'one weak link: its supply chain'. This problem relates to recurrent criticism about its suppliers' use of cheap factory labour.

Supply chain mismanagement

Primark has been hit by negative comments and much discussion around their ethical stances and claims. These appear on discussion sites, blogs and also on YouTube where there are many videos concerned with Primark's alleged abuses of human rights. Primark has been subject to criticism by activists and the media who have questioned the company's ethical approach to doing business. Such criticism has in large part been directed at the way in which the company has managed some of its supply chain activities. In recent years it has been subject to a number of high-profile investigative media reports.

According to research conducted by *Ethical Consumer* magazine (Whitehead, 2005), Primark was voted the most unethical retailer in the UK. In 2008 the BBC programme *Panorama* revealed some of Primark's business practices. The BBC reported on the treatment received by people working for Primark's suppliers, including the employment of illegal child labour. The *Panorama* programme 'triggered a barrage of negative publicity, with footage of child refugees in India making low-cost garments for Primark' (Magee, 2008, p. 3). Primark sought to defend its reputation using various tools and channels of communication and it also set about addressing the substantive concerns raised by the *Panorama* programme.

The BBC *Panorama* programme along with other investigative and media reports very much caught Primark doing something it ought not to have been and clearly something had to be done. Such investigations have in large part focused on the company's supply chain rather than on the retailer per se. Nevertheless, the resultant media storm found the company accused of failing to source some of its goods from ethical suppliers. Primark's claim to be a socially responsible ethical retailer was called into question. By associating with suppliers that operated unethical practices Primark was in danger of being perceived as corporately socially irresponsible (Jones *et al.*, 2009). The company was at risk of having its reputation irrevocably damaged.

Managing the story via social media

Whilst the allegations are serious enough, it is Primark's response that is the focus here. They undertook a damage limitation exercise to minimise harm, and to recover and repair the organisation's reputation. The question was, how should Primark respond and what should they do? With their reputation damaged and under continual media pressure, their response had to stem the flood of formal and informal media comments.

One of the first things they did was to announce that they had sacked three established suppliers in southern India for using child labour. The conventional approach to negative news management would have been to release statements and launch a public relations campaign to put their side of the issue. They would also have had the opportunity to appear on the *Panorama* programme to refute the allegations. Instead Primark made the decision to ignore the mass media route, and use the web to generate conversations with their customers. A good and positive company image can help realise long and lasting business value in terms of things like improving levels of customer loyalty and consequently companies seek to guard their reputation. Primark perceived its reputation was under attack from traditional media sources and responded using social media. Such an approach to corporate reputation management was undoubtedly innovative and signified the important role social media now plays in the world of corporate communications.

Primark constructed and launched a micro-site at the same time as the BBC programme went to air. Views for and against Primark were posted on the web. However, it was some of Primark's staff, together with some devotees of affordable fashion clothing, that rallied to defend their favourite fashion brand. Primark's management and press officers are noticeable by their absence on the website and other sites concerned with the issue, such as Let's Clean up Fashion (http://www. cleanupfashion.co.uk/).

Primark do use their corporate website to address the issues on an ongoing basis. They suggest that the problems of endemic non-compliances, control of working hours, unauthorised subcontracting, minimum wages and the definition of a living wage are all shared with their competitors. Primark has a four-fold strategy for supporting compliance with Primark's Ethical Trading Code of Conduct (http://www.primark.co.uk/ethical/in_practice) and living up to their own ethical standards, and these involve supplier selection, auditing, remediation and training.

It appears that there is more work to be done to improve Primark's commitment to an ethical supply chain. Whilst the company's reputation was, it might be argued, tarnished by the allegations, the actual damage to the business in terms of loss of sales is difficult to quantify or prove. Primark sales continue to do well despite the negative publicity caused by the supply chain investigative journalism exposé. Policing, monitoring and regulating supply chains are not easy to do, requiring continual vigilance and engagement. Businesses can always do more, but equally there is only so much they can do. Today, businesses have to negotiate the boundaries between competing commitments to an array of objectives that include profit, social, environmental and ethical issues, or what is commonly referred to as the triple bottom line of people, planet and profit. Part of the difficulty of supply chain management is that, by definition, it is built on relations of trust that are, at certain points, prone to breakage. Primark has had to learn to factor and build trust relations into the supply chain management process. It is apparent that there is a need for continuous involvement, investment, control and monitoring of Primark's supply chain processes and activities.

Primark's decision to use relational-based communications reflects the reciprocal relationship they enjoy with their customers. Many of their customers avidly support Primark in social networking sites, chatrooms, forums and blogs. They serve as Primark's social media brand ambassadors who are prepared and willing to defend, as appropriate, the company's image and reputation. The retailer has acquired something of a cult status amongst UK high street shoppers and amongst the value-shopping followers of the fashion fraternity; Primark remains the darling of the high street. The name 'Primani' is often used by brand advocates, suggesting that the retailer is perceived to deliver designer fashion (Armani) at highly competitive prices (Primark). Primark therefore works with its loyal customers to defend its reputation and even uses them as part of its identity mix. As Jones *et al.* (2009) suggest, Primark's approach encourages participation, co-ownership and reciprocity. Ballantyne (2004) argued communication should be 'with' rather than just 'to', especially with audiences who are knowledgeable, online 24/7, bloggers and brand activists all producing new content.

Findings

Some of the key lessons to be learned are that organisations can use social media to limit reputation damage and communicate directly with their stakeholders. An equally important finding is that companies can and do act on media reports to deliver real and effective change. Since the media storm first erupted, Primark has put in place a number of initiatives to better monitor and improve the ethical standards and practices of its suppliers. Clearly traditional methods of investigative journalism have an important role to play in helping companies identify problems so that they can then improve, for example, their standards of CSR.

Primark recognises customers as editors, citizen journalists and its strategy marks a shift from broadcasting to social-casting. This is not to suggest that broadcasting is redundant, far from it, as it remains an important and legitimate media for corporate communication.

Communication through social media allowed Primark greater control of the message and the means by which it was disseminated. Managing the news has rarely been more interesting or more challenging. The implications of social media for businesses are that they increasingly have to share ownership of reputation, messages and brand with their stakeholders. Messages, reputation and brand cannot be imposed, but are rather subject to negotiation and debate. Getting it wrong can bring catastrophe for a company but getting it right can deliver huge rewards, not just in terms of improved reputation but also in terms of the financial bottom line. Companies such as Primark use the online social media environment to communicate but also to monitor, measure and manage their reputation.

Conclusion

Managing corporate reputation requires skill and careful judgment and this is especially so with developments in social media. Communication has always been a two-way process but the new media has changed the way in which businesses communicate with their stakeholders. Increasingly consumers along with other stakeholders are using social media to air their grievances in relation to companies that have not always met or delivered on their promises, such as to operate in a fair and ethical way. Equally, some are using such media to extol the virtues of companies that are perceived to be behaving in a corporately responsible and ethical manner.

To the dedicated followers of high street fashion, it seems 'Primani' can do no wrong. Today Primark is committed to ethical trading as evidenced by its Supplier Code of Conduct (http://www.primark.co.uk/aboutus/supplier). It is clear that the company is keen to work with suppliers and other stakeholders to deliver improvements in supply chain practices. Moreover, Primark is keen not only to act on but also to communicate its commitment to this area of its work. This work, by its very nature, is ongoing and requires investment and the deployment of sophisticated management skills to carefully monitor, control and stamp out ethically questionable supplier practices. It is evident from recent reports in *Supply Management* that Primark has improved and is keen to continue to improve its work in this area:

> Dan Rees, director of ETI, said: 'Primark has made enormous strides over the past 12 months and, while there is still a great deal of work left to do, given the pace of improvement and the resources now committed, we are satisfied that Primark is committed to a robust and credible ethical trade strategy.' In a statement, Primark welcomed the findings and set out further ethical trade targets. The firm aims to increase its team of eight ethical trade managers to 15 this year and will launch a website for suppliers to provide them with training tools and guides. The retailer, . . . , spends around £700 million in developing countries and nearly doubled the number of vendor audits it conducted last year to 1,080.

Continuous vigilance of suppliers and supply chain activities alongside building and developing trust relations is likely to result in a better future for all. What can be asserted with a degree of certainty is that in the future social media will continue to play an increasingly important role in companies' communication strategies and practices. Consumers, publics, suppliers and other stakeholders also call for an increased input into shaping and determining company image, reputation and ultimately results both in terms of the financial bottom line but also in terms of real commitment to issues of corporate social responsibility.

(Note that the BBC subsequently issued an apology, through its website, regarding their failure to be able to authenticate parts of the footage used in the *Panorama* programme.)

Questions

1. To what extent is supply chain management the weakest link in reputation management?

2. Businesses can always do more, but equally there is only so much they can do. Discuss this statement with reference to:

▶

- corporate social responsibility
- reputation management
- Primark
- a business with which you are familiar.

3. Primark might be accused of putting profit before people and the planet. Under what circumstances might this view be supported?

4. Explain how social media can facilitate the co-creation of reputation.

References

Ballantyne, D. (2004). Dialogue and its role in the development of relationship specific knowledge. *Journal of Business and Industrial Marketing* 19(2), 114-123.

BBC (2011). BBC apology over *Primark: On the Rack*. Online: http://news.bbc.co.uk/panorama/hi/front-page/newsid_9519000/9519830.htm. Accessed: August 2011.

Felsted, A. & Thompson, J. (2010). 'Primark brightens up outlook at ABF'. *The Financial Times*, 23 February, p. 22.

Finch, J. (2008). 'Primark axes suppliers for using child labour'. *The Guardian*, 16 June. Online: www.guardian.co.uk/business/2008/jun/16/primark.child.labour. Accessed: 4 April 2011.

Hall, J. (2009). 'Quiet man who changed the face of retail'. *Daily Telegraph* (Business).

Jones, B., Bowd, R. & Tench, R. (2009). Corporate irresponsibility and corporate social responsibility: competing realities. *Social Responsibility Journal* 5(3), 300-310.

Jones, B., Temperley, J. & Lima, A. (2009). Corporate reputation in the era of Web 2.0: the case of Primark. *Journal of Marketing Management* 25(9-10), 927-939.

Magee, K. (2008). Primark uses web to counter BBC. *PRWeek*, 27 June, p. 3.

Primark (2011). Online: http://www.primark.co.uk/aboutus/supplier. Accessed: 10 April 2011.

Primark (2011). Online: http://www.primark.co.uk/ethical/in_practice. Accessed: 20 April 2011.

Supply Management (2011). Online: http://www.supplymanagement.com/news/2010/primark-praised-for-ethical-sourcing/. Accessed: 20 April 2011.

Whithead, J. (2005). Primark tops list of unethical clothes shops in poll that shames high street brands. Online: www.brandrepublic.com/News/532319/Primark-tops-list-unethical-clothes-shops-poll-shames-high-street-brands. Accessed: 4 April 2011.

Index

Note: Page numbers in *italics* denote a figure/table.

Aaker, D.A. 113, 137, 164, 250
Aaker, J. 172
Aarts, N. 222, 223
ability associations 223, 226
Abimbola, T. 119
Abratt, R. 34
Abu Dhabi investment fund 147–9
Ac²ID Test 34, *34*
Accenture 76, 270
accommodation strategy, and issues management 306
Achrol, R.S. 231
Action on Smoking and Health (Ash) 176–7
Adbusters 198
Adidas 84–5, 192
advertising, corporate *see* corporate advertising
advocacy strategy, and issues management 307
Aggerholm, H.K. 298
AIG 255
Albert, S. 32, 241, 246
Altria (formerly Philip Morris Companies) 270
Ambler, T. 68, 139
American Express 186–7
Amnesty International 160–1
Andersen Consulting 270
Anheuser-Busch Companies Inc 40
Anholt, S. 194
Anholt-GfK Roper Nation Brands Index (NBI) 194
Anselmsson, J. 260
Anthony N. 174–5
anti-branding movement 197–8, 199, 201
anti-globalisation movement 11
Apple 195–6, 199, 200, 239
archived narratives 255
Argenti, P.A. 6, 118, 119, 137, 211
Arthur Andersen 13, *14*, 82
Asda 66

Askegaard, S. 128, 129
association
    and measuring corporate brands 163
    reputational 14–17, 24
Aston Villa FC 120–1
AT&T 40, 76
athlete corporations 190, 199, 201
audit, reputational 76–7, *77*, 98
authenticity
    and brands/branding 192–3, 201
    use of symbols to impact 268
awareness, and measuring corporate brands 163
Ayling, R. 268

BA (British Airways)
    tail fin design 268–9
    and Terminal 5 79–80
Backhaus, K. 68
balanced scorecard 90
Ballantyne, D. 322
Balmer, J.M.T. 32, 34, 119, 128, 139, 143, 218
Balmer's Affinity Audit 81
banking crisis 18–20, 22, 38, 78
Bannister, B.D. 291
Barcelona Football Club 120–1
Barclays 79
Barrow, S. 68
Bart, C.K. 244
Batkus, B. 244
BAV (BrandAsset Valuator) 168–70, *169*
Beaverbrooks 97
Beckham, David 204–5
behaviour, and corporate identity mix 252
behavioural approach, and measuring corporate brands 162
Ben & Jerry's 14, 137
Bennett, R. 6
Benoit, W.L. 309, 310
Berens, G. 257
Bergvall, S. 128
Bernstein, D. 35, 36, 147
Best Companies to Work For list 96–7, *97*, 98

Birkigt, K. 250
Birth, G. 258
Black, E.L. 89
Blackoff, R.W. 306
Blockbuster Entertainment 282
blogs 284–5
BMW museum (Munich) 151
Body Shop 32–3, 110, 137, 198, 255
Boo.com 90
book-to-market value ratio 119
Boots 10
BP 9, 39, 78, 241
BrandAsset Valuator (BAV) 168–70, *169*
brand communities 195, 201
brand ecosystems 128
brand equity 5, 162–5, *163*, *164*, 187
    in third sector 175–6
brand equity pyramid 164, *164*
brand extensions 164
brand identity prism 116, *117*
brand loyalty, and third sector 176
brand as person *see* brand personality
brand personality 171–3
brand strength 166, *167*
brands/branding
    anti-branding movement 197–8, 199, 201
    and authenticity 192–3, 201
    background 107–8
    characteristics of 110–11
    citizen 124–5
    co-creation of 128, 130
    with a comprehensive reputation 184–6, 200
    definitions 108–10, 112, *112*, 129
    and 'doing good' for society 186–8, 201
    emotional power of 128–9, 130
    future of 199–200, 202
    importance of trust 113–16
    input and output features 112–13
    intangible nature of 109, *109*
    and internet 189, 200
    levels 110–11, *110*
    link between reputation and 6, 116–19, 129–30, 184

brands/branding (*continued*)
    progression of, to lovemarks 198–9
    retro 192–3, *193*
    stages of classic 113
    and stakeholders 195, 201
    top ten superbrands *114*
    types of 111
    see also corporate brands/branding
BrandZ 167–8, *168*, 171, 180
Branson, Richard 45, 70
BRIC economies 199
bridging strategies 295
'Britain's Most Admired Companies' 9,
    10, 85–8, *88*, 98
British Airways *see* BA
British Gas 108
Bromley, D.B. 5, 11, 13, 24, 81
Brown, M. 62, 70, 84, 86
Brown, S. 192, 198
Browne, J. 70
Bruning, S.D. 276
buffering strategies 295
Burberry 11, 15–16
Burke, T. 211

Cadbury's 29, 30, 31, 124
Calvin Klein 110
capitalism 20
Carnes, T.A. 89
Carrefour 129
Cartwright, C. 40
Caruana, A. 89
Castrol 280
cause-related marketing 282–3
Cebula, R.J. 81
celebrity brands 190–2, 199, 201
centralisation, and integrated
        communication 231
CEOs
    and corporate communication
        216–17
    letter to shareholders 294–5
    and quality of management 70
    responsibility for corporate
        reputation 53
    and trust issue 22
certification 258
Charity Brand Index 178–9, *179*
Chase, W.H. 305
Chatman, J.A. 241
Chester Zoo 153–4
Chevron 241
China Haisum Engineering Co. *245*
China Mobile 171, 199
Christensen, L.T. 231, 232
Chun, R. 81, 151
Churchill, W. 45

citizen brands 124–5
Clark, J.M. 281
closed communication climate 242
Co-operative Bank 126–7, 260
Co-operative Society 255
Coca-Cola 38, 119, 124
codes of conduct 258
Colvile, R. 38
Comcast Corporation 40
communal organisation 59, *60*
communication climate 242–3, 261
communication, corporate *see*
        corporate communication
community-based events 304
Competing Values Framework 61
competitive advantage
    and corporate communication 216,
        233
    and corporate reputation 9, 23
    and strong cultures 241
complexity, and corporate brands 137
compliance codes 258
Condon, P. 65
Cone non-profit top 100 178
Conrad, C. 13
consistency 268
Conway, T. 285
Coombs, W.T. 266, 310
Cooper, A.H. 266
core brand essence 68
core messages 252
core positioning themes 252, *253*
Corebrand's Brand Power 170–1
Cornelissen, J.P. 214, 229, 260
corporate advertising 272–5, *273*, 286,
        294
    choice of media vehicle 274–5
    and corporate social responsibility
        272–4
    dimensions of successful 272
    flexibility of 274
    forms *273*
    reasons for using 272, 286
    tasks for *273*
corporate brands/branding
    arguments for and against 152, 155
    celebrity brands 190–2, 199, 201
    core attributes of 137–8
    and corporate culture 65–7, 72,
        138–9
    and corporate identity 139
    country brands 193–4, *194*, 201
    defining 136–8, 141, 154
    differences between product brands
        and 142–4, *144*, 155
    and employees 28–9, 142, 143, 151,
        155, 298, 299

factors to be considered when
        implementing 152–3
    gaps in 149–51, 155
    and growth of service industry
        141–2, 154–5
    halo of 140–1, 154
    and internet 189, 200
    measuring of *see* measuring
        corporate brands
    mixing ingredient brands 145
    new types of 189, 201
    promise conveyed by 139–40, 149,
        154
    rise of and reasons 146–7, 154
    success and failure of 151–3
    three waves of 141
    and values 29, 66, 72, 110, 138, 175,
        186, 198
    vision-culture-image (VCI)
        alignment of *150*
Corporate Character Scale 93–6, *94*,
        98–9, 151, 172–3
corporate communication 32, 117
    activities 226–7, 233
    and advertising *see* corporate
        advertising
    co-ordination of activities 227
    communication climate 242–3, 261
    and competitive advantage 216, 233
    and consistent messaging 226
    and corporate culture 238–42, 261
    and corporate identity mix 250–2,
        261, 267
    and corporate responsibility 255–60,
        261–2
    and corporate strategy 211, 220
    and crisis *see* crisis communication
    criteria for effective 246–8, 246–50,
        261
        corporate credibility 249–50, *250*
        form 246–8
        and organisational change 248–9
        style 246–8, *247*
        timing 248
        tone 248
    definitions and nature of 36, 213–14,
        233
    and digital media 284–5
    dimensions of 216–18, 233
    establishing scope of 213–14
    forms of 36, *36*
    functional outcomes 219–20, 233
        communications 220
        linkages 219–20
        positioning 220
        profiling 220
    integrated 223–32, *230*, 233, 254

corporate communication (*continued*)
  internal 227, 298–301, *299*, *301*,
    314–15
  investor relations 291–5, 314
  issues management 305–7, 315
  legitimacy strategies 274, *275*
  management communications
    216–17
  marketing communications 217
  measuring 313–14, 315
  media for 283–5, *286*
  and media relations 302–4, 315
  message framing 266–7
  organisational communications 217
  and organisational positioning
    252–5, 261
  and public affairs 295–7, 314
  public relations *see* public relations
  reasons to use and value of 211,
    214–16, *214*, 233
  roles and tasks of 213, 219–26, *219*,
    233
  and sponsorship *see* sponsorship
  storytelling 254–5
  strategies 226, *226*
  tools for 271–81
  transitional outcomes 222–6, *222*,
    233
    exploring 222
    informing 222–3
    mixed communication modalities
      223, *225*
    negotiating 223
    relating 223
  types of 218
  vision and mission statements
    244–6, *245*, 261
corporate credibility *see* credibility
corporate credos 258
corporate culture 52–73
  artefacts and behaviours 56
  and assumptions 57, 71
  benefits of 58
  and corporate brands 65–7, 72, 138–9
  and corporate communication
    238–42, 261
  defining 56–8, 71, 238
  difficulties associated with changes
    63–5
  and employees 66–7, 242
  and employer branding 68–70, 72
  espoused values 56
  and Football Association 61–2
  functions 59
  and iceberg metaphor 56–7, 71
  levels of 57, *57*, 71, 238
  and Metropolitan Police 64–5

and organisational performance
    241–2
  and people management 70
  and quality of management 70
  strong and weak 58–9, 71–2
  types of 59–62, *63*, 72
corporate entertainment 281–2
corporate identity 7, *8*, 31–4, 48–9,
    240–1, 246
  and AC²ID Test 34, *34*
  academic perspectives 31–2
  and Body Shop 32–3
  and corporate brands 139
  and corporate image 32, 34, 149
  cues used by public relations to
    project *276*
  meaning 35–6
corporate identity mix 250–2, 261, 267
  and behaviour 252
  planned communications 251
  and symbolism 251, 267
corporate image 7, *8*, 48–9
  and corporate identity 32, 34, 149
  and corporate reputation 102–3
  meaning 36
corporate personality 35, 240–1, *see*
    also Corporate Character Scale
Corporate Personality Scale 82
corporate prophecies 255
corporate rebranding *see* rebranding
corporate reputation
  academic perspectives on 6–7
  aggregating of 12, 24
  and association 14–17, 24
  averaging principle of 12, 24
  broad indicators of 77–80
  building blocks of 34–7, *35*, 49
  criteria influencing 42–6, *42*, 49,
    184, *184*
  decline in 18–20
  definitions 6, 7, *7*, 23, 36
  difficulty in controlling of in 21st
    century 20–2, 24
  external forces 37–8, *37*, 49
  factors building good 7, *8*, 36
  as 'Gestalt' 23
  influences on 37–42
  internal forces 38, 49
  key dimensions of 267
  levels of 11–13, 24
  measuring of *see* measuring
    corporate reputation
  reasons for importance 9–11, 23
  relational forces 38–40, 49
  responsibility for 53–5, 71
  strategic use of 17–18
Corporate Reputation Chain 118, *118*

corporate responsibility
  and advertising 273–4
  consumer perceptions of 260, *260*
  use of for positioning 260
  see also CSR
corporate responsibility
    communication(s) 255–60,
    261–2
  codes of conduct 258
  content of 257
  dimensions of messages 259
  monitoring and certification
    initiatives 258
  reports/reporting 258–9
  training and education programmes
    258
corporate social responsibility *see* CSR
corporate social responsibility (CSR)
    associations 223, 226
corporate strategy, and corporate
    communication 211, 220
cost approach, and measuring
    corporate brands 162
country brands 193–4, *194*, 201
Cravens, K. 89, 90
credibility 42
  and corporate communication
    249–50, *250*
  and corporate reputation 12, 36
  and corporate responsibility
    messages 259
crisis communication 307–13, 315
  best-practice 312–13
  crisis types by crisis clusters *310*
  framing for 310
  managing stakeholders' images
    309–10, *309*
  phases of crisis 308–9
  response strategies 310
CSR (corporate social responsibility)
    11, 119–25, 130, 257
  and advertising 272–4
  and corporate reputation 45–6,
    122–4
  key consumer perceptions of 260,
    260
  and most admired companies
    surveys 124–5
  old and new perspectives and
    dilemmas 124
  reasons why companies engage in
    121–2, 122–3
  and Starbucks 123, 124
  and Tesco 124, 185–6
  tools for communicating 258
  use of for positioning 260
  see also corporate responsibility

culture, corporate *see* corporate culture
customer satisfaction, influence on
corporate reputation 43
customer service
definition 44
influence on corporate reputation 44
Cutlip, S.M. 291

Darmon, K. 267
David, F. 244
Davies, G. 66, 93, 117, 118, 150–1
Davis, J.J. 250
Day, G.S. 291
de Chernatony, L. 5, 29, 110, 111–12,
116, 117, 118, 138, 298
Deal, T.E. 59
Deephouse, D.I. 79
Dell 144
Denmark 22
Desjardins 284
digital media, and corporate
communication 284–5
Disney 77–8, 139, 140, 164
distinctiveness 267–8
Doorley, J. 258, 259
dot.com boom and fall 89–90
Douglas, K. 255
Dowling, G.R. 7, 76, 116, 219, 271
Druckenmiller, B. 118, 119, 137
Duncan, T. 228
Durkheim, Émile 187
Dyson 54–5, 66

ecological, impact of on corporate
reputation 37
economic, impact of on corporate
reputation 37
Edelman Trust Barometer 22, 179
EDF Group 245
EDS 279
education programmes 258
Elfenbein, H.A. 122
Elkington, John 125–6
Emirates airline 281
employees 35
and communication climate 242–3,
261
connecting of to the company 29–31
and corporate brands/branding 28–9,
142, 143, 151, 155, 298, 299
and corporate culture 66–7, 242
influence of satisfaction of on
corporate reputation 43
intellectual and emotional
engagement 299–300
and internal communication 298–9
and management communications
217

employer branding 68–70, 72
employment value proposition 68
Encyclopaedia Britannica 114–16
Enron 13, 82, 84, 255, 292
entertainment, corporate 281–2
EquiTrend 170
Ericsson 101–2
ethics 11, 18
European Social Research Council
(ESRC) 173
Eurostar 283–4
events 304
Everett, S. 228
Ewing, M.T. 13
expenses scandal 21
exploring, and corporate
communication 222
external forces, and corporate
reputation 37–8, 37, 49

Facebook 21, 189
Fahey, L. 291
Fair-trade initiative 125
Farache, F. 272
Farrell, O.C. 260
Fill, C. 300
financial performance
and measuring corporate brands
162, 166
and measuring corporate reputation
80–1, 98
Fink, S. 307
Fiorina, C. 253
First Direct Bank 44, 110–11, 144
five forces model 38, 39
flexible integration approach 231–2
Flickr 195
Fombrun, C.J. 5, 7, 23, 31, 32, 36, 42,
76, 77, 80, 82, 84, 90–1, 98, 118,
152, 211, 213, 216, 250, 252,
254, 267, 286, 313
Football Association (FA) 61–2
Forbes '100 Best Corporate Citizens'
125
Ford 84, 124, 152
Foreman, S.K. 298
Forman, J. 211
Fortune's 'Most Admired Companies'
82–5, 83, 89, 98, 124
fragmented organisation 59, 60
framing
for crisis communication 310
message 266–7, 285–6
Freedom of Information Act 21
Friedman, M. 9
Fryxell, G.E. 83
Fullerton, R.A. 107
Furnham, A. 59

Gabbioneta, C. 216
Gabriel, H. 6
Gagon, M. 314
Gaines-Ross, L. 17, 39, 53
gangster rap 16
Garcia, H.F. 258, 259
Gardner, B.B. 108–9
Gates, Bill 70
General Electric (GE) 84, 292
Geppert, J. 294, 295
Germany 11, 22
Ghoshal, S. 243
Gilbert, S. 175
Glaxo Wellcome 40
GlaxoSmithKline (GSK) 305
Goffee, R. 59, 61, 63, 72
Golder, P. 239
Goldman Sachs 89
Gonzalez-Herrero, A. 313
goodwill 160
Goodwin, F. 20
Goodyear, M. 111, 113, 117
Google 31, 171, 197, 200
and employer branding 69
lobbying activities 296, 297
Gore-Tex 145
Grand Metropolitan 162
Gratton, L. 243
Gray, E.R. 119, 139, 213, 218
Gray, R. 285
Greater Manchester congestion charge
22
Greenpeace 302–3
Greyser, S.A. 32
Griffin, A. 11, 21, 53, 122, 124
Gunter, B. 59

Haigh, D. 162, 175
Hallahan, K. 302
halo effect 17, 84, 98, 119
Hankinson, P. 173
Hanrahan, G. 292
Hardaker, S. 300
Harley-Davidson 37, 102–3, 199
Harris, F. 5, 116, 117, 118
Harris Interactive's EquiTrend 170
Hart, S. 29, 109, 137
Harverson, P. 279
Hatch, M.J. 28, 63, 92, 140, 141, 142,
149
Hayes, J. 187
HBOS 19
headquarters, company 66
Helgesen, T. 272
Herbig, P. 119
hero stories 255
Heskett, J.L. 67, 242
Hewlett-Packard 125, 253–4

Higgins, R.B. 291
Hillman, A. 295
Hiscock, J. 299
Hitt, M. 295
Holm, O. 227
Honest Tea 254
horizontal communication 228
Horrox, S. 177
hospitality *see* corporate entertainment
HSBC 79
Human Rights Act 21

IBM 84
identity, corporate *see* corporate
        identity
IKEA 239–40
Illia, L. 258
image, corporate *see* corporate image
image restoration 309, *309*, 310
Inbev Inc. 40
income approach, and measuring
        corporate brands 162
Ind, N. 29, 137, 138, 143
information processing, levels of
        11–12, 24
ingredient branding 145
Innocent 38, 128, 187–8
        Supergran Campaign 282–3
innovation, influence of on corporate
        reputation 44–5
intangibility, and corporate brands 137
integrated corporate communication
        223–32, *230*, 233, 254
integrated marketing communications
        (IMC) 228–9
Intel 145
interactivity, and internet 312
Interbrand's best global brands 166–7,
        166, *167*, 171, 176, 178
internal communications 227,
        298–301, *299*, 314–15
        characteristics of *301*
internal corporate communication
        299, *300*
internal forces, and corporate
        reputation 38, 49
internet 285
        and brands/branding 189, 200
        corporate reputation and
                information posted on 21, 24
        and crisis communication 313
        and interactivity 312
        and public relations 278
interviews 304
investor relations 291–5, 314
ISO 10688 standard 162
issues management 11, 305–7, 315
        accommodation strategy 306

advocacy strategy 307
        reasoning strategy 306–7
        silence strategy 306
        and stakeholders 306
        strategic responses to issues 306–7

Jackson, Michael 14
Jackson, P. 213, 214, 299
James, LeBron 190–1, *191*
Japan 11
        bows of apology *313*
        and corporate branding 137
        culture 312
Jaques, T. 305
Joachimsthaler, E. 250
Jobs, Steve 70
Johansson, U. 260
John Lewis Partnership 31, 43, 67
Johnson & Johnson 63
Jones, B. 322
Jones, G. 59, 61, 63, 72
Jones, P. 260
Judson, K.M. 139

Kapferer, J.N. 116, *117*
Kellaway, L. 270
Keller, K.L. 113
Kelman, H. 249
Kennedy, A.A. 59
Kent, M.L. 276, 285, 312
Kim, J-N. 252
Kim, P. 109
King, J. 21, 70
King, S. 136, 172
Kinsella, M. 97
Kitchen, P.J. 119, 228
Kitching, J. 40
Klein, N. 197
Klemm, M. 244
Knittel, C.R. 76
knowledge capital scorecard 90
Knox, S. 119
Kocak, A. 119
Koch, J.V. 81
Kochan, N. 110
Koeppl, P. 297
Kotler, P. 5, 110, 121, 129
Kotter, J.P. 242
Kowalczyk, S.J. 81, 89, 117, 118
Kraft Foods 267
Krakower, J.Y. 61
Kramer, M.R. 121

La Niece, C. 197
Lacey, R. 279–80
Laidler-Kylander, N. 176
Laskin, A.V. 292
Laurence, A. 119

Lawrence, J.E. 294, 295
Lawrence, S. 64
leadership, influence of on corporate
        reputation 45
Ledingham, J.A. 276
Lee, N. 121
Lee, S. 284–5
legal
        impact of on corporate reputation
                37
        and measuring corporate brands 162
legitimacy strategies 274, *275*
Lehman Brothers 19, 255
Lever Bros 124
Levi 193
Levy, S.J. 108–9
Lewis, S. 89
LG 279
licensing agreements 77
Lion Nathan *245*
Lloyd, S. 68
Lloyds 79, 255
lobbying 296–7
Lock, A.R. 229
logo 251
        rebranding and changes in 271
L'Oréal 33, 119
lovemarks 198–9
Low, G.S. 107
Lowensberg, D. 214
loyalty, and measuring corporate
        brands 163

McCracken, Grant 191
McDonald, M.H.D. 110, 136, 138, 142
McDonald's 43, 171, 251, 267–8
Macpherson, W. 64
McWilliams, A. 121
Magen David Adom (MDA) Society
        224–5
Maignan, I. 260
Maklan, S. 119
management communications 216–17
management philosophy statements
        258
Management Today 85
Manchester City 147–9
Margolis, J.D. 122
market approach, and measuring
        corporate brands 162
market position, influence on
        corporate reputation 46
marketing communications 217
Marks & Spencer 86, 144
        cause-related marketing 282
        corporate culture of *58*, 59
        and Plan A 255, 256, 319–20
Mars 88

Martineau, P. 117, 172
measuring corporate brands 159–81
 and Amnesty International 160–1
 BrandAsset Valuator (BAV) 168–70,
  169
 and brand equity 162–5, *163*, *164*,
  180
 and brand personality 171–3
 Corebrand's Brand Power 170–1
 difficulties 171, 180
 Harris Interactive's EquiTrend 170
 Interbrand's best global brands
  166–7, *166*, *167*, 171, 176, 178
 and ISO 10688 standard 162
 Millward Brown/WPP BrandZ
  167–8, *168*, 171, 180
 third sector 178–9, 181
measuring corporate communication
  313–14, 315
measuring corporate reputation
  75–99
 '100 Best Companies to Work For'
  list 96–7, *97*, 98
 broad indicators 77–80, 98
 Corporate Character Scale 93–6, *94*,
  98–9
 development of models 81–2
 and financial performance 80–1, 98
 limitation of 'most admired' scales
  88–9, 98
 and media comment 79, 98
 'Most Admired Companies' indices
  82–9, *88*, 98
 RepTrak Model 91–3, *93*, 98
 Reputation Quotient (RQ) 82, 90–1,
  92
 and reputational audit 76–7, *77*, 98
 return on investment (ROI) 78
 and shareholder value 78–9
 specific tools 82–9, 98
 tangible and intangible facets 89–90
Médecins Sans Frontières (Doctors
  Without Borders) 95–6
media comment, and measuring
  corporate reputation 79
media relations 302–4, 315
 interviews 304
 press conferences 303–4, *303*
 press releases 303
 publicity and events 304
media reputation index (MRI) 79
Meijer, M. 175
Melewar, T.C. 271
mercenary organisations 59, *60*
Merck 84, 311
mergers and acquisitions 39–41, 152
Merlin Entertainment 164–5

message framing 266–7, 285–6
messages
 dimensions of corporate
  responsibility 259
 and organisational positioning
  252–3
Metropolitan Police 64–5
Meznar, M.B. 295
Michael, J. 314
Microsoft 46, 140, 196
 and communication integration 232
 and internal communications 301
 storytelling framework 255
Midland Bank 271
Miles, L. 117
Milewicz, J. 119
Millward Brown 167–8
Mindshare 255
mini-czars 228
Mintzberg, H. 61
mission statements 244–6, *245*, 251
Mitchell, A. 147
Mitroff, I. 307–9
Moloney, K. 297
Money, A.H. 298
Moorthy, K.S. 119
Morgan, G. 71
'Most Admired Companies' indices
  82–9, *83*, 98, 124
MTV 44–5
Muniz, A.M. 195
Murphy, J. 29, 109, 137
Muzellec, L. 249, 270, 271
myths and origins 255

name of company 251
 rebranding and changes in 270
naming rights 281
National Childbirth Trust (NCT) 177
National Society for the Prevention of
  Cruelty to Children (NSPCC)
  176
Nationwide 66
negotiation, and corporate
  communication 223
Nestlé 108, 152
network approach, and sponsorship
  280–1, *281*
networked organisations 59, *60*
networks, and integrated
  communication 231
New York 194
Newman's Own 186
NHS (National Health Service) 146,
  173
Nike 138, 190, 251, 268
Nintendo 270

Nokia 227, 243
Nooteboom, B. 223
Northern Ireland 194
not-for-profit sector *see* third sector
Notorious B.I.G. 16
Novartis 270
Nutrasweet 145
Nutt, P.C. 306

Oberman, W.D. 295
Oberoi Group *245*
obesity 267
O'Guinn, T.C. 195
oil companies 38
O'Leary, Michael 12
Olins, W. 35, 146
Olkkonen, R. 280
One Water 187, 201
open communication climate 242,
  242–3
opinion polls 18
O'Reilly, C.A. 241
organisational communications 217
organisational culture *see* corporate
  culture
organisational identity *see* corporate
  identity
organisational performance, and
  corporate culture 241–2
Orton, J.D. 222
Oxfam 176

P&G *see* Procter & Gamble
P3 97
Pawlish, M.J. 117, 118
Pearce, J.A. 244
Pearson, C.M. 307–9
people management 70
Pepsi 14
perceived quality, and measuring
  corporate brands 163
Perks, K.J. 272
personality, corporate *see* corporate
  personality
PESTLE framework 37, *37*, 49
Peters, T. 9, 59
Petrobras *245*
pharmaceutical industry, and lobbying
  297
Philips 227, 243, 268
Pickton, D. 229
place branding 193–4, 200, 201
politics, impact of on corporate
  reputation *37*
Pooler, S. 13
Poon, D.T.Y. 278
Porter, M.E. 38, *39*, 121

positioning, organisational 220, 252, *253*, 260
Presley, Elvis 16
press agentry/publicity model of communication 247
press conferences 303–4, *303*
press releases 277, 303
Primark 9, 17, 321–4
primary communications 218
Pringle & Gordon 29
Procter & Gamble (P&G) 8, 70, 135, 197
product brands, differences between corporate brands and 142–4, *144*, 155
product recalls, reducing uncertainty during 312
product/service quality, influence of on corporate reputation 42–3
profiling 220
profitability, influence on corporate reputation 46
prophecies, corporate 255
psychological contract 68
public affairs 295–7, 314
public information model of communication 247
public relations 275–8, 285, 286
    characteristics 277–8, 286
    costs associated with 277–8
    cues used to project corporate identity *276*
    and internet 278
    and investor relations 292, 294
    methods 276
    see also media relations
Puente, E. 90
Pulp Juice Bars 17

quality of management 70
Quarantelli, E.L. 307
Quelch, J. 175, 179
Quester, P. 281
Quinn, J.B. 61

Rader, S. 226
Rainforest Café 198
Randall, G. 110, 111
Rank Hovis McDougall (RHD) 162
RBS (Royal Bank of Scotland) 19, 20, 78–9, 255
reasoning strategy, and issues management 306–7
rebranding, corporate 144, 249, *249*, 270–1
    logo changes 271
    name changes 270
    slogan changes 270–1

Reckitt Benckiser 274
Red Brand 186
Reebok 281
Rees, Dan 323
relational forces, and corporate reputation 38–40, 49
reliability 36, 42
reports/reporting 258–9
RepTrack 91–3, *93*
reputation, definitions of 5–6
reputation, corporate *see* corporate reputation
Reputation Institute 42, 79
Reputation Quotient (RQ) 82, 90–1, 92
reputational audit 76–7, *77*, 98
reputational damage 39
Reputational Index 90
responsibility, corporate *see* corporate responsibility
retro brands 192–3, *193*
return on investment (ROI) 78
Ribena 305
Richer Sounds 86–7, 88
Riley, F.D. 111–12
Rindova, V.P. 211
Roddick, Anita 32, 33
Roper, S. 150–1, 197
Rose, S. 70, 216–17
Rostand, A. 40
Rotterdam Organisational Identification Test (ROIT) 81
Royal & Sun Alliance (RSA) 218, 270
Royal Bank of Scotland *see* RBS
RWE Solutions 221
Ryanair 12–13, 17, 46, 53, 198

Sabate, J.M. 90
Sainsbury's 21
Sargeant, A. 176
Scandinavian Airline Systems (SAS) 215
Scarman Report 64–5
Schein, E. 56, 57, 63, 71, 238
Schoenberg, R. 40
Schultz, D. 227, 228
Schultz, M. 28, 63, 89, 92, 140, 141, 142, 149, 175
Schweizer, T.S. 5–6, 12, 91
secondary communications 218
Segal-Horn, S. 29
Semin, G.R. 257
service brands 6
service industry 39
    corporate brands and growth of 141–2, 154–5

Shakur, Tupac 16
Shandwick, W. 9
shareholder value 78–9
shareholders
    differences between stakeholders and 28–9, 48
    CEO letter to 294–5
    definition 28
Shell 9, 211–12, 241, 251
Shimp, T.A. 228
Siegel, D. 121
silence strategy, and issues management 306
Silver, D. 292
Simmons, J. 34, 140
Sinatra, Frank 16
Singapore Telecommunications (SingTel) 292, 293–4
situational crisis communication theory 310
six Cs of corporate marketing 139, *139*
Sky *10*
slogan 251
    rebranding and changes in 270–1
Smith, H.J. 29
Smith, S. 313
Smithkline Beecham 40
Smyth, J. 138
sociability 59, *60*, 61, 63, 72
social, impact of on corporate reputation *37*
solidarity 59, *60*, 61, 63, 72
Solomon, M. 195, 196
Sony 38, 274
Sora, K. 226
Sørensen, J.B. 239, 241
Southwest Airlines 66
sponsorship 278–82, 286
    and corporate entertainment 281–2
    dimensions of interaction 278, *279*
    and emotional intensity 281
    and naming rights 281
    network approach 280–1, *281*
    objectives of 279–81
Spotts, H.E. 229
Stadler, M.M. 250
stakeholder theory 126
stakeholders 28–9, *28*, 275
    and brands/branding 195, 201
    and corporate communication 214–15, 219
    crisis roles for 307–8, *308*
    definition 28
    differences between shareholders and 28–9, 48
    and issues management 306
Standard Chartered 79

Stango, V. 76
Starbucks 122, 123, 124
storytelling 66, 232, 254–5, 285, 294
    media relations as form of 304
Stuart, H. 249, 270, 271
Styles, C. 139
Sullivan, J. 68
Sunday Times '100 Best Companies to Work For' list 69, 96–7, *97*
Supa, D.W. 304
supermarkets 53
Sweden 70, 227
symbolic management 252
symbols/symbolism 251
    use of in developing corporate reputation 267–9, 286

tacit knowledge 63
Tamianau, Y. 295
Tata *245*
Taylor, M. 276, 312
technology, impact of on corporate reputation *37*
Tellis, G.J. 239
tertiary communications 218
Tesco 9, 10, 39, 66, 116, 184
    and CSR 124, 185–6
third sector
    and cause-related marketing 282
    definition 173
third sector corporate brands/branding 173–9, 180, 199
    and brand equity 175–6
    literature on 173, 175
    measuring 178–9, 181
    problems 176–7, 181
3M 255
Thwaites, D. 280
Tikoo, S. 68
TNS Knitwear 9
Toyota 312
training 64, 258

Transnet *245*
transparency 113, 268
    and corporate responsibility messages 259
triple bottom line (TBL) 125–7, *126*
Tripodi, J.A. 280
trust
    and corporate reputation 12, 22, 36, 42
    importance of to brands 113–16
Tsai, S.-P. 266
Turner, P. 62, 70, 84, 86
two-way asymmetric model of communication 247
two-way symmetric model of communication 247–8
Tyson, Mike 14

UK Investor Relations Society 291
UMIST 40–1
Unilever 9, 14, 135–6, 147, 197
universities 40–1
    logos of 271

Vallaster, C. 298
values 65–7
    and corporate brands 29, 66, 72, 110, 138, 175, 186, 198
van Bekkum, T. 226, 242
van Bruggen, G.H. 272
van den Bosch, A.L.M. 267
van Mesdag, M. 137
van Rekom, J. 257
van Riel, C.B.M. 31, 32, 36, 77, 80, 84, 118, 152, 213, 216, 250, 252, 254, 267, 272, 286, 313
van Ruler, B. 226, 243
van Woerkum, C. 222, 223
Varey, R.J. 211
vertical communication 228
Vick, E.H. 137
Victoria University of Manchester 40–1

Vioxx 311
Virgin 10, 137, *277*
visibility 267
Vodafone 46
Volvo 66

Wallach, E. 61
Wang, J. 83
Warburtons 205–6
Waterman, R.H. 9, 59
Watkins, M. 266
websites, and crisis communication 312
Weick, K.E. 222
Welch, J. 70
Welch, M. 299
Whetten, D.A. 32, 241, 246
White, J. 211
White, R. 272
Wijnberg, N.M. 5–6, 12, 91
Wikis 285
Williams, L.S. 244
Willis Group 281
Willmott, M. 113, 125
Wilson, A. 34
Wilson, R. 137
Wilts, A. 295
Winters, L.C. 250
Wolfson Microelectronics 259
Woodliffe, L. 176
Woods, Tiger 76, 98
Woolworths 9, 46–8
Wry, T. 211

Yamauchi, K. 211
Yell 282
Young & Rubicam's BrandAsset Valuator 168–70
YouTube 195

Zammuto, R.F. 61
Zhou, L. 295
Zoch, L.M. 304